THE DAMASCUS SEAT OF POWER

THE DAMASCUS SEAT OF POWER

Syria's Heads of State, 1918–1946

Sami Moubayed

I.B. TAURIS
LONDON • NEW YORK • OXFORD • NEW DELHI • SYDNEY

I.B. TAURIS
Bloomsbury Publishing Plc, 50 Bedford Square, London, WC1B 3DP, UK
Bloomsbury Publishing Inc, 1385 Broadway, New York, NY 10018, USA
Bloomsbury Publishing Ireland, 29 Earlsfort Terrace, Dublin 2, D02 AY28, Ireland

BLOOMSBURY, I.B. TAURIS and the I.B. Tauris logo
are trademarks of Bloomsbury Publishing Plc

First published in Great Britain 2023
This paperback edition published in 2025

Copyright © Sami Moubayed, 2023

Sami Moubayed has asserted his rights under the Copyright, Designs and
Patents Act, 1988, to be identified as Author of this work.

For legal purposes the Acknowledgements on p. ix constitute
an extension of this copyright page.

Series design by Adriana Brioso
Cover image: House of Governor of Damascus in Syria, February 1905
(GB/3/1/2/1/93), Bell (Gertrude) Archive, Newcastle University Library

All rights reserved. No part of this publication may be: i) reproduced or transmitted in any form, electronic or mechanical, including photocopying, recording or by means of any information storage or retrieval system without prior permission in writing from the publishers; or ii) used or reproduced in any way for the training, development or operation of artificial intelligence (AI) technologies, including generative AI technologies. The rights holders expressly reserve this publication from the text and data mining exception as per Article 4(3) of the Digital Single Market Directive (EU) 2019/790.

Bloomsbury Publishing Inc does not have any control over, or responsibility for, any third-party websites referred to or in this book. All internet addresses given in this book were correct at the time of going to press. The author and publisher regret any inconvenience caused if addresses have changed or sites have ceased to exist, but can accept no responsibility for any such changes.

A catalogue record for this book is available from the British Library.

Library of Congress Cataloguing-in-publication data:
Names: Moubayed, Sami M., author.
Title: The Damascus seat of power : Rue Nazem Pasha and Syria's heads of
state, 1918-1946 / Sami Moubayed.
Other titles: Rue Nazem Pasha and Syria's heads of state, 1918-1946
Description: London ; New York : I.B Tauris, 2023. | Includes
bibliographical references and index.
Identifiers: LCCN 2023012759 (print) | LCCN 2023012760 (ebook) | ISBN 9780755649198 (hb) | ISBN 9780755649174 (paperback) | ISBN 9780755649181 (epdf) | ISBN 9780755649211 (ebook) | ISBN 9780755649204
Subjects: LCSH: Heads of state–Syria–Biography. | Syria–Politics and government–20th century. | Syria–History–French occupation, 1918-1946.
Classification: LCC DS98 .M67 2023 (print) | LCC DS98 (ebook) |
DDC 956.9104–dc23/eng/20230419
LC record available at https://lccn.loc.gov/2023012759
LC ebook record available at https://lccn.loc.gov/2023012760

ISBN: HB: 978-0-7556-4919-8
PB: 978-0-7556-4917-4
ePDF: 978-0-7556-4918-1
eBook: 978-0-7556-4921-1

Typeset by Integra Software Services Pvt. Ltd.

For product safety related questions contact productsafety@bloomsbury.com.

To find out more about our authors and books visit www.bloomsbury.com
and sign up for our newsletters.

CONTENTS

List of figures	vii
Foreword	viii
Acknowledgements	ix

Chapter 1
THE PALACE   1

Part I
PRE-MANDATE RULERS OF SYRIA 1918–20

Chapter 2
EMIR SA'ID EL DJEZAIRI (26 SEPTEMBER–1 OCTOBER 1918)   11

Chapter 3
KING FAISAL I (1918–20)   29

Part II
HEADS OF STATE UNDER THE FRENCH MANDATE 1920–46

Chapter 4
SUBHI BARAKAT (1922–5)   47

Chapter 5
AHMAD NAMI (1926–8)   65

Chapter 6
MOHAMMAD 'ALI AL-'ABED (1932–6)   75

Chapter 7
HASHEM AL-ATASI (1936–9)   93

Chapter 8
BAHIJ AL-KHATIB (1939–41)   113

Chapter 9
KHALED AL-'AZM (APRIL–SEPTEMBER 1941)   133

Chapter 10
TAJ AL-DIN AL-HASANI (1941–3)   151

Chapter 11
ʿATA AL-AYYUBI (MARCH–AUGUST 1943)   171

Chapter 12
SHUKRI AL-QUWATLI (1943–9)   177

Notes   209
Bibliography   237
Index   250

LIST OF FIGURES

1	The palace of Nazem Pasha in al-Muhajireen in the 1940s	7
2	Emir Sa'id El Djezairi	28
3	King Faisal	43
4	Subhi Barakat	63
5	Ahmad Nami	74
6	President Mohammad 'Ali al-'Abed (center) surrounded by his prime minister Taj al-Din al-Hasani (second from left wearing turban) and Interior Minister 'Ata al-Ayyubi	92
7	Hashem al-Atasi	111
8	Bahij al-Khatib	131
9	Khaled al-Azm	150
10	Taj al-Din al-Hasani	169
11	Ata al-Ayyubi	175
12	Shukri al-Quwatli	208

FOREWORD

Scholarship on Syria during the French Mandate has concentrated for more than two decades on a variety of topics, in particular urban and industrial growth, new cultural expression, changing gender relations and great power intrigue.

Sami Moubayed's new book by contrast returns to a topic that historians have forgotten: the political behaviour of Syrian leaders. He is the first to examine in a single study the careers of the eleven Syrian heads of state who were either appointed or elected between 1918 and 1946.

These leaders practised what Albert Hourani labelled the 'politics of notables'. Their positions of wealth and social position derived from their landholdings, access to the Ottoman government and ability to maintain a 'delicate balance between central authority and provincial influence'. They were often educated in the leading Ottoman institutions in Istanbul and some were married into the Turkish elite. They belonged to an aristocracy of service.

Dr Moubayed makes clear that few Syrians today can recall who most of their first eleven heads of state were. He rightly points out that four generations have grown up knowing only two Syrian presidents, the Assads, father and son, whereas the eleven heads of state collectively were in office not much more than two generations. He reminds us that their disappearance is directly connected to the dramatic reduction of their wealth, and especially their landholdings, during the aborted Syrian-Egyptian union (1958–61) under Gamal Abdul Nasser. The Baathist rise to power in 1963 sealed their erasure from Syria's collective memory.

Dr Moubayed also reminds us that there was a 'vibrant political culture in Syria' that not only contested French imperial rule but also social and cultural norms prior to the rise of the Baath Party and its consolidation of state authority. His chapters on the eleven heads of state trace Syria's experiment with different forms of government from monarchism to federalism to republicanism. He also points to the immediate post-independence period in the late 1940s when coups coupled with autocracy became the norm, the harbingers of Syria's political future.

Sami Moubayed's close reading of important political memoirs in Arabic and his interviews with observers from the period he studies have permitted him to enrich our understanding of an important but neglected chapter in the political history of modern Syria.

Philip S. Khoury
Ford International Professor of History
Massachusetts Institute of Technology

ACKNOWLEDGEMENTS

This book was the product of hard work and research, made possible only through the support of friends and colleagues. I would like to start with my family: my mother, wife and two daughters, Sophia and Layla, who all had to bear with my repeated absences from home while working on this book. I thank Fadi Esber for reading through the manuscript and offering his meticulous comments and suggestions for improvement, and Sahban Abd Rabbo for serving as my sounding board – a task he has done diligently and quietly for the past quarter century.

And there is much gratitude overdue to Philip S. Khoury, who generously agreed to read the manuscript. When I was studying at the American University of Beirut (AUB) Philip's seminal book *Syria and the French Mandate* was less than ten years old, causing a sensation among students of Syria and the wider Middle East. We admiringly called it the 'Bible of Syrian Historians'. I communicated with him for the first time in 1998, after sending a copy of my first book *The Politics of Damascus*. He replied with a cordial message, wishing me the best in my future career as a historian.

That was almost thirty years ago. Today, I am proud that he has authored the foreword of this book – my tenth since 1998.

Chapter 1

THE PALACE

Unlike countries like the United States, where there is one White House, or France, where there is just one Elysée Palace, Syria has had six presidential palaces in the course of the past century.[1] This book is dedicated to the life and politics in the first and second palaces, both located in the neighbourhood of al-Muhajireen on the western slopes of Mount Qassioun, overlooking the ancient city of Damascus. One remains standing, while the second was demolished in 1974. Most historians, however, fail to differentiate between them, simply referring to the seat of power in Damascus as the 'Presidential Palace'. Neither of them has received a proper history chronicling their origins, occupants and the political events that unfolded with their walls. It was the history of ambitious men with big dreams, who tried – with limited degrees of success – to create a better future for their country, before they were dethroned, toppled and exiled. A deeper look shows that it was also a history of architecture and shifting social trends in Syria and the broader Levant; a history of power, households, patronage and women. It's also about the ordinary life within the chambers of the palace, whether of presidents and their families or of those who worked in their daily orbit. Three of these senior staffers lived long enough to tell their story and were vital in documenting the history of the Syrian presidency. They are Munir al-ʿAjlani, director of the presidential palace during the Second World War (who died at the age of ninety in 2004), Suhayl al-ʿAshi, military escort to President Shukri al-Quwatli (who died at eighty-eight in 2006), and ʿAbdullah al-Khani, secretary-general of the palace in the 1950s (who died at the ripe age of ninety-six in 2020).

Despite their advanced age, these men tried to diligently piece together a comprehensive oral history of the place in which they worked during their younger days, relying on mental notes, old photographs and their private papers. There were visible gaps in their memory, both collectively and as individuals, leaving behind plenty of questions that remain unanswered. There is absolutely nothing on the human history of the presidential palace, neither at the British or French national archives. There is also nothing at the Museum of Historical Documents in Damascus, which houses the archives of the Syrian state from the late Ottoman era up to 1958. We know plenty about the palaces of King Farouk of Egypt, and those of Saddam Hussein in Iraq, but very little about the ones in Damascus.

For thirty-two years, and until it was refurbished in 2010, the standing palace in al-Muhajireen stood right there on the slopes of Mount Qassioun – ignored, neglected and forgotten.

The palace of Nazem Pasha

Throughout the years of Ottoman rule in Syria, *valis* (governors) usually stayed in the spacious homes of the Old City, with their large courtyards, brimming lemon trees and gushing water fountains. Some had up to thirty rooms on their second floor, put entirely at the disposal of rotating governors by wealthy notables wanting to win favours with Ottoman officialdom. Some governors decided to establish palaces of their own, like As'ad Pasha al-'Azm, who ruled Damascus in the mid-eighteenth century, ordering construction of the famous 'Azm Palace in the heart of the ancient al-Bzurieh Market. It took 800 workers to build over a groundbreaking period of three years, and remained property of the 'Azm family until 1920, when it was sold to the French government.[2] Other Ottoman governors like Midhat Pasha (1878–80) decided to lodge at government headquarters in Dar al-Mushiriyya facing the Hamidieh Market (which has since been demolished and replaced with the current Damascus Palace of Justice).[3] It was always safer for governors to sleep next to their troops, after a rebellion had killed one pasha in 1831, and a bloody uprising led to the toppling and execution of another in 1860.[4]

In July 1897, a celebrated Ottoman statesman named Hussein Nazem Pasha was appointed governor of Damascus by Sultan 'Abdulhamid II. Abiding by tradition, he first stayed at the home of Damascus notable Mahmud al-Barudi in al-Qanawat, outside the Old City, but declined to make it his permanent residence, looking for open space upon which he could build a new palace for himself, just like As'ad Pasha al-'Azm had done in the mid-1700s.[5] At forty-five, Nazem Pasha was a worldly figure, having worked as a journalist, then as an instructor at the prestigious Galata Seray in Istanbul, before serving as cabinet minister in the Imperial Capital.[6] When arriving in Damascus, he asked to be taken on a tour of the city to decide on a suitable spot to build a palace for him and his family. He was shown the narrow streets behind the Umayyad Mosque, and the vast green territory of al-Rabweh, but none seemed to satisfy his taste. His escorts then took him to al-Muhajireen, where he stood among the rocky hills, facing Yazid, one of the water paths that stemmed from the fabled Barada River, named after the second caliph of the Umayyads. Behind it stood the orchards of al-Ghouta, the agricultural belt of fruit-laden trees engulfing the city of Damascus. At the time, al-Muhajireen was no-man's land; virgin territory waiting to be developed. It had been established in the early 1890s to accommodate Muslim emigrants coming from the Balkans (*muhajireen* means emigrants in Arabic).[7] An additional cluster of Muslim refugees would soon arrive from the island of Crete, fleeing sectarian violence in September 1898.[8]

Most of the empty land in al-Muhajireen was owned by members of the illustrious 'Azm family, relatives of As'ad Pasha.[9] Nazem Pasha admired the gentle breeze, asking in bewilderment: 'What is it wrong with the Damascenes? Why don't you build here what can potentially become an unparalleled resort?'[10] Apart from a few mud houses scattered behind him, there was no construction in sight, making the spot exceptionally attractive for the pasha. One of his escorts replied: 'But Your Excellency, who would agree to live in this exile? It would take him at least an hour to reach the market, or pray at the Umayyad (Mosque).'[11] Nazem Pasha decided to be the first gambler, ordering that a palace is constructed for him in al-Muhajireen. When buildings got numbers in Syria under the mandate, the address of the palace became 21, Rue Nazem Pasha.

Khorshid al-Masri

Hoping to win favours with the new governor, Shafiq Mou'ayyad al-'Azm offered to give him the land for free, but Nazem Pasha insisted on paying fifty gold coins.[12] A talented Egyptian architect named Khorshid Wehbe al-Masri was hired to build the palace, inspired by the magnificent imperial buildings of Berlin and Vienna.[13] Khorshid Bey had studied modern irrigation and architecture in Germany, on a state scholarship provided by Tawfiq Pasha, the khedive of Egypt.[14] Upon graduation he established a reputation for himself both as a great builder and as a sportsman, excelling in construction, weightlifting and wrestling.[15] He would carry heavy blocks with his workers from the hills of Mount Qassioun to al-Muhajireen, taking great pride in his strength.[16] An avant-gardist, Khorshid Bey abhorred smoking and urged his labourers to quit tobacco, offering extra pay to those who complied.[17]

The Egyptian architect built a two-floor villa for Nazem Pasha on 10,000 square metres, created entirely from white stone, with wooden doors and arched windows frames. The first floor housed the pasha's dining room and study, while living quarters were established on the second floor. Separating the two floors was a wide marble staircase, draped with a large red carpet, later used for official functions of the Syrian presidency. A three-level garden surrounded the palace, stretching south towards its back door, filled with apricot trees, white jasmines and a large water fountain feeding off the Barada River.[18]

It remains unclear when exactly Nazem Pasha's palace was completed, yet according to 'Abdullah al-Khani, a long-time employee at the future presidential palace, 'Life came to the palace in 1905, when Nazem Pasha finally settled into his new house.'[19] This means that he resided briefly at the palace, before being recalled to Istanbul in March 1906. He was eventually to return as governor for one year in 1909, and then for an additional six months in 1912.[20] Khani would enter the palace as a young employee in 1947, recalling conversations with octogenarian neighbours who could still remember the three eras of Nazem Pasha. When the pasha was summoned to Istanbul for the very first time, he had still not settled the bills of Khorshid al-Masri.[21] It was only logical for him to sell the palace, now that he was leaving Syria for good (or so he thought), and two Damascenes offered to buy it. One was a wealthy Christian notable named

Beshara al-Asfar, and the second was Mustapha Pasha al-'Abed, whose brother, Ahmad 'Izzat Pasha, was the influential second secretary to Sultan 'Abdulhamid II.[22] 'Mustapha Pasha al-'Abed offered to buy the palace for 7,000 Ottoman coins. Asfar almost doubled the bid, offering 12,000.[23] Khorshid eventually bought it for 5,000, writing off the 1,000 coins that Nazem Pasha still owed him for having constructed the palace.[24] Up until then, the al-Muhajireen Palace had been lit by kerosene lamps and scented candles to ward off malaria-carrying mosquitoes, before electricity came to Damascus in February 1907. The Umayyad Mosque was lit first, followed by the Damascus School of Medicine, and then, the home of 'Abdul Rahman Pasha al-Yusuf in Souq Sarouja, whose residence was the first private home to receive twenty-four hours of daily electricity.[25] The al-Muhajireen Palace was second, during the occupancy of Khorshid al-Masri.[26]

Khorshid Bey had decided not to return to Egypt, settling permanently in Damascus after marrying a Syrian widow and offering to raise her only son, Hamdi al-Idilbi. He moved into the palace with his new family, and soon, Damascenes began referring to the adjacent neighbourhood by his name, 'Khorshid', a name that has stood the test of time and remains in use as of 2023. Khorshid treated Hamdi al-Idilbi as a son, with paternal care and attention, sending him to study medicine, first at the American University of Beirut (AUB) and then in Germany.[27] Hamdi returned to Damascus and set up a successful clinic on Salhieh Street not far from the Syrian Parliament and married Ulfat Omar Pasha in 1929. Their wedding was held at the al-Muhajireen Palace and she was to eventually establish herself as one of Syria's foremost female novelists, taking on the pen name Ulfat al-Idilbi. Some of her popular novels were inspired by her youthful days at al-Muhajireen Palace.

The two Djemals

Khorshid took his adopted son to the Houran province in southern Syria, where he planned to establish an agricultural plantation with modern irrigation and machinery.[28] He fell short on cash, however, which forced him to rent his palace to the Ottoman government, shortly before outbreak of the First World War. The al-Muhajireen Palace was put under the disposal of Djemal Pasha, commander of the Fourth Army and one of the principal officers of the Committee of Union and Progress (CUP).[29] He had led successfully co-led a coup against Sultan 'Abdulhamid II, toppling him in April 1909.[30] A ruthless officer, Djemal ruled Syria with an iron fist throughout the Great War, famously executing twenty-one Arab nationalists at Marjeh Square on 6 May 1916. One of them – ironically – was Shafiq Mou'ayyad al-'Azm – owner of the very same property on which the al-Muhajireen Palace had been built.[31] Under Djemal Pasha, the al-Muhajireen Palace became a symbol of tyranny and persecution of Arab nationalists like Mou'ayyad al-'Azm and his creed. Ordinary Damascenes avoided walking past its high walls, and when they did, looked straight down at their feet, without daring to take a glance at one of its windows, so as not to be accused of spying on Djemal Pasha or plotting for his assassination.[32]

In November 1917, Djemal Pasha was recalled to Istanbul and replaced by his namesake Djemal Pasha 'al-Mersini' (also known as Djemal Pasha al-Saghir), a far less capable and much less feared Turkish officer. Djemal al-Mersini decided to move out of the al-Muhajireen Palace, working from the Victoria Hotel near Marjeh Square, another edifice inspired by German architecture, built in 1879.[33] The Victoria Hotel was better guarded and safer for the Ottoman officer, who by September 1918 had been reduced to commander by name only, besieged behind the stone walls of his hotel. Four centuries of Ottoman rule were coming to an end, and there was nothing he could do to end – let alone slow down – the rapid collapse of law and order. In mid-summer 1918, Nazem Pasha's palace was transformed into a military hospital at Djemal al-Mersini's orders, catering to wounded soldiers and those diagnosed with cholera, typhoid and syphilis. Its electric power was turned off and the hospital had to once again rely on scented candles after Ottoman authorities switched off all electricity in Damascus, no longer able to pay its bills.[34] Djemal al-Saghir was the last Ottoman occupant of the Nazem Pasha Palace.

The Royal Palace 1918–1920

Four months later, Ottoman rule collapsed and King Faisal I took over Syria. As he settled in al-Muhajireen, life returned to the palace, almost overnight. All the hospital beds and medical equipment were shipped out to the Hamidian Hospital in al-Baramkeh, and brand-new furniture was bought for what now officially came to be known as *al-Qasr al-Malaki* (the Royal Palace). Faisal set up a professional court with scheduled appointments, minute-takers and detailed agendas, although not a single foreign head of state visited him during his brief rule in Syria. His court was very unlike the casual tent gatherings that he had employed in the Arabian desert during his father's revolt against the Ottomans, staged from Mecca in 1916–1918. Gone were the Arabian mattresses on which Faisal would sit cross-legged with his supporters, and so were the giant coal trays used to warm up tents.

The beginning of French rule

In the summer of 1920, Faisal was dethroned and the French Mandate was imposed on Damascus. It was signed off by the Allies at the San Remo Conference on 25 April 1920. Syria was occupied, and so was the palace, by France's new high commissioner Henri Gouraud. The French general had lost an arm during the Great War, and was bent on bringing the Syrians into total submission. He entered the now well-used mansion in August 1920, making it his official premises (although his formal headquarters would remain in Beirut). Early into the mandate, he hosted a dinner for the Damascus gentry at the al-Muhajireen Palace. Gouraud spoke of the beauty of Damascus, and then looking around the hall in which he and his guests were seated, he mischievously asked: 'This was the palace of King Faisal, right?' Gouraud knew that it was. So did every Syrian in the room. Offended by the question, Finance Minister Fares al-Khoury retorted, 'Yes Your Excellency, King Faisal resided here. This palace was originally built by an Ottoman governor named Nazem Pasha. Djemal Pasha used it during the war, and now it has fallen under your command. We had dinner, right over here, with every one of them. All of them are now gone.' He then winked at Gouraud and added, 'But we have remained ... and so has the palace!'[35]

Mandate authorities continued to use the Nazem Pasha palace until August 1922, when it was restored to its rightful owners. Briefly in 1920-2, it was occupied by Haqqi al-'Azm, governor of the mini-state of Damascus, an appointee of General Gouraud. Hamdi al-Idlibi then rented the premises to the Iraqi consulate in Damascus until outbreak of the Second World War in 1939. Throughout the 1920s, Syria's two presidents, Subhi Barakat and Ahmad Nami, worked from government headquarters in Marjeh Square, never setting foot in the al-Muhajireen Palace. In 1932, President Mohammad 'Ali al-'Abed moved into the nearby palace of his uncle, Mustapha Pasha, making it the official presidential premises. When Mustapha Pasha's bid to buy the palace from Nazem Pasha failed, he built a copy right next to it, on exactly 10,000 square metres.[36] The 'Abed Palace continued to house every president until Taj al-Din al-Hasani died in one of its rooms in January 1943. When Shukri al-Quwatli succeeded him in August, he moved the presidential premises from the 'Abed palace back to the original one built by Nazem Pasha, saying that it was a bad omen to begin his term from the office of a deceased predecessor. Quwatli officially made 21 Rue Nazem Pasha the seat of the Syrian Presidency, and it remained as such, non-stop, until 1978.

The presidency after 1958

Briefly during the Syrian-Egyptian union of 1958-61, the presidential premises were moved from al-Muhajireen to Qasr al-Diyafa, a small two-floor guesthouse built by former president Adib al-Shishakli in 1953. Gamal 'Abdul Nasser preferred Qasr al-Diyafa to the al-Muhajireen Palace, because of the spacious street that lay before its perfectly suited balcony, from where he could address the Syrian masses. The old al-Muhajireen Palace was closed at Nasser's orders, without being returned to the family of Hamdi al-Idilbi. It was eventually reopened in December 1961, two months after a coup toppled the union republic, and was occupied then by Syria's newly elected president, Nazem al-Qudsi. When the Ba'ath Party staged its coup on 8 March 1963, Syria's new strongman Amin al-Hafez moved into the palace, and was followed by his two successors, Nur al-Din al-Atasi in 1966 and Hafez al-Assad in 1971. Assad ran Syrian affairs from al-Muhajireen throughout the 1970s, famously welcoming US Secretary of State Henry Kissinger after the October War with Israel, and in June 1974, hosting US president Richard Nixon. In the autumn of 1978, he abandoned the palace in favour of a new building in al-Rawda, next to Abu Alaa al-Maari Square, right behind the popular al-Rawda Mosque.

Assad's decision to move into a new palace came at the height of his confrontation with the Muslim Brotherhood, when security became a major concern for the Syrian leader. By then, the al-Muhajireen neighbourhood had become overcrowded, which made it impossible to secure the palace balconies or its vast gardens. Unlike the Nazem Pasha Palace, the one in al-Rawda was shabby, dull and un-impressive, with no gardens and courtyards. But it was easy to quarantine from the rest of the neighbourhood, in fear of a Muslim Brotherhood attack. Assad stayed at this premises until 1991, when he moved into a far better palace called Qasr al-Shaab (People's Palace), a large building of Carrara marble stretched across 31,500 square metres high atop a southern part of Mount Qassioun called Jabal 'Antar. The hilltop had been carved out of the original mountain by the waters of River Barada. The new palace had been under construction since 1979, and its beautiful brass gates were created by the world-famous Syrian Jewish metalworker Maurice Nseiri. The entire plateau of the mountain was added to the palace premises, making it the largest in Syria, with a presidential office view perpendicular to the main minaret of the Umayyad Mosque, designed by world-famous Japanese architect Kenzo Tange, winner of the 1987 Pritzker Prize for Architecture whose international works include the Supreme Court of Pakistan and the Tokyo Olympic Arena. Assad welcomed US President Bill Clinton at this palace in 1994, and it was at its main hall that world leaders assembled to pay their respects upon Assad's death in June 2000, ranging from Madelene Albright and Jacques Chirac to Vladimir Putin. The al-Muhajireen Palace was used to lodge Syrian officers, treated as old and demode. In 2010 it was refurbished by Syria's new first lady Asma al-Assad.

Figure 1 The palace of Nazem Pasha in al-Muhajireen in the 1940s.

Part I

PRE-MANDATE RULERS OF SYRIA 1918–20

Chapter 2

EMIR SA'ID EL DJEZAIRI
(26 SEPTEMBER–1 OCTOBER 1918)

In March 2015, I walked up to the home of Emir Fateh El Djezairi, the ageing son of Emir Sa'id El Djezairi, the first post-Ottoman ruler of Syria. It was a small and humble house, situated in the middle-class neighbourhood of Dummar on land formerly part of the Djezairi family's vast plantations, before they were nationalized during the short-lived Syrian-Egyptian union in 1958. Not far stood the Djezairi summer residence, a beautiful white villa which had been confiscated by the Syrian government and renovated by the European Union in 2001. The sound of sporadic gunfire could be heard in the distance, along with mortars landing from the Damascus countryside. The Syrian war was in its fourth year, with no end in sight. At the gates of the farm house stood Emir Fateh's son, Emir Sa'id Junior, named after his grandfather.

Emir Fateh lay stretched before a television set, unable to walk due to his advanced age, watching a beauty pageant on the Saudi satellite channel, MBC. This old man, the son of a former self-appointed 'president', had once been a walking, talking celebrity in Damascus. He drove brand-new convertibles in the 1950s, racing down the palm-tree-lined Abu Rummaneh Street with beautiful women wearing miniskirts seated next to him. When Syrian military strongman Salim Hatum tried to seduce one of his girlfriends in the mid-1960s, Emir Fateh bundled him into a chair at a candle-lit Damascus restaurant, and gave him a good beating.[1] Hatum was commander of a military unit stationed at the gates of Syrian Television. His name was enough to send shivers down the spine of any Syrian. He was also one of the leaders of the ruling Ba'ath Party. Hatum screamed, 'You dog! I am Salim Hatum!'[2] The young emir knew exactly who he was, but he did not care.

I took out my notebook, preparing myself to talk about his father, and how he had taken history into his own hands, three years short of a century ago, assuming control of Damascus in the immediate aftermath of the Ottoman evacuation back in 1918. The final two weeks of September 1918 were crucial for the modern history of Syria and the Arab World, marking the end of 400 years of Ottoman

Parts of this chapter were originally published in *Arab Studies Quarterly*, Vol. 37, No. 4 (Fall 2015), 'Two September Weeks that Saved Damascus', 367–85.

rule and the installation of an Allied-back Arab government in Damascus. Never has scholarly attention been given to events that took place inside the city during the days that preceded the triumphant Allied entry on 1 October 1918, and very little has been said about the locals who teamed up to protect Damascus from uncontrollable chaos that threatened to tear their city apart.

Most contemporary works dismiss our protagonist, Emir Sa'id El Djezairi, as a 'governor by accident'. Or they tend to portray him as an ambitious man with limited means and no charisma who does not merit serious academic study. Most don't even recognize him as a former head of state, omitting him from the list of presidents and rulers. Much of his demonization is due to the fact that he was abhorred by his adversary, the legendary British colonel T.E. Lawrence, whose seminal work *Seven Pillars of Wisdom* depicts Emir Sa'id as a charlatan and usurper.[3] Lawrence describes him as a 'low-browed degenerate with a bad mouth'.[4] A similar impression was sketched by Stephen Pichon, the foreign minister of France, who labelled the emir as 'unbalanced and unintelligent'.[5]

'The fate of Damascus would have been very different had it not been for my father', said Emir Fateh confidently in 2015.[6] 'He reflected a strong sense of purpose and a grand political ambition, inspired by the history of our family. Had he stayed in power, then we might have avoided much of what happened to Syria since then.'[7] He pointed to the loud thuds caused by the mortars landing nearby, shaking his head in disbelief about what had become of his beautiful Syria.

The city will fall, any minute now

The once-mighty Ottoman Army began its gradual evacuation from Damascus on 13 September 1918, marred by defeat at the hands of Great Britain and France. There was mayhem on the streets: violence, disorder and chaos. The last Ottoman troops left the city minutes after midnight on 26 September 1918, shortly before the empire as we knew it began to disintegrate and disappear into the pages of history books. It was a painful moment for the Ottoman Turks, parting ways with a city that they had occupied and admired since 1516, affectionately calling it, *Sham Sherif*. In English, that roughly translates into 'Damascus the Noble'. As the Ottomans withdrew, the people of Damascus reacted with mixed feelings. Some danced on the streets, happy to finally get rid of the Turks. Others, like Nasuh Babil, the future dean of Syrian journalists, watched the scene tearfully: 'I was saddened to see the demise of a grand Islamic Empire, brought down by conspiracy.'[8]

On 19 September, British, Indian and Australian units broke through Turkish defences in Palestine and pushed northwards towards Damascus. Air patrols were reporting no enemy in sight for the next twenty-four kilometres till the gates of the ancient capital of the Umayyads. 'People are just waiting for the city to fall', wrote Emir Sa'id in his memoirs, watching the dramatic collapse unfold from behind the high walls of his home in the Old City. Lawrence penned the following remark: 'When Damascus fell, the Eastern War – probably the whole war – drew to an end.'[9] Djemal al-Saghir was still in Damascus, arranging a safe exodus of his troops. For thirteen days, he ran what remained of Ottoman affairs from the Victoria Hotel, which was better guarded than government headquarters in al-Marjeh Square, and safer.

Abdelkader the Great

Born in 1883, Emir Sa'id was the grandson of Emir ʿAbdelkader El Djezairi, a titan of the nineteenth century who led a seventeen-year insurgency against French occupation of his country, Algeria, from 1830 until 1847.[10] At the age of thirty-nine, Emir ʿAbdelkader was arrested and exiled to various chateaus in Toulon, Pau and Amboise.[11] He and his family members were tortured, and those who died were buried in their damp prison cells. Shifting political currents in Paris eventually led to his pardon and exile to Ottoman Damascus in 1855, where he spent the next twenty-eight years with an enormous entourage and plenty of gold given to him by the now guilt-ridden government of Napoleon III. Some estimates put his annual stipend at 300,000 francs. Emir ʿAbdelkader's opulence enabled him to bankroll the entire city of Damascus from his dazzling home in al-ʿAmara, behind the Grand Umayyad Mosque. The Djezairi mansion was a colourful mix of North African and Levantine art, with stone and marble floors, water fountains and pistachio-painted ceilings.

Hundreds of Damascenes were employed in the service of the Djezairi family, as farmers, clerks, accountants, bodyguards, soldiers and scribes. In desperate need of a Muslim war hero, the people rallied around Emir ʿAbdelkader, proclaiming him uncrowned king of their city. They viewed him as champion of anti-colonialism and saviour of the city's poor and helpless. He purchased five homes along the banks of the Barada River, near Bab al-Faradis, one of the seven gates of Damascus. Being a descendant of the Prophet Mohammad, Emir ʿAbdelkader had religious legitimacy, power, money and intellect, and was also considered as the undisputed Sufi scholar of his generation. His charm was legendary, prompting the wife of a British diplomat to commend, 'His mind is as beautiful as his face. He is every inch a sultan!'[12] Henry Jessup, an American missionary educator who frequented Damascus in the 1860s, added, 'No visit to Damascus was complete without a call on the noble emir.'[13]

The Djezairi family's pinnacle of fame came in July 1860, when Emir ʿAbdelkader made history as the city collapsed into violence resulting from Maronite peasants in Mount Lebanon revolting against their Druze overlords. The sectarian battles led to a savage war that resulted in massive murder, rape, theft and wanton destruction of property. The killing spree soon reached the mainly Christian towns of Hasbayya, Rashayya and Zahle in what is today modern Lebanon. As their villages were sacked and burned to the ground, thousands of terrified Christians left their homes in darkness, pouring into the Christian quarters of Old Damascus. Some stayed with friends and relatives, while others would sleep on the pavements until being invited to stay at one of the neighbourhood's many churches. Tension was already high in the city itself. Rumours had spread that these Christian refugees were advance forces for European Powers planning to invade, occupy and dismember the Ottoman Empire.

On 9 July 1860, an angry and fanatic mob broke into the Bab Touma neighbourhood within the Old City, triggering an orgy of manslaughter that lasted for six entire days.[14] Five thousand Christians perished in less than one week, while the homes of Bab Touma, and all of its churches, were torched to the ground. Headed by Emir 'Abdelkader, Damascus notables intervened to protect what remained of the city's Christians, sheltering thousands at their homes. The bulk was taken into the Djezairi mansion, where men and women crowded in its arched corridors, weeping hysterically at the fate of their beloved. When the mob reached his house, the Emir ordered his horse saddled, put on his cuirass and mounted drawing his sword. He shouted at the murderous crowd: 'Wretches! Is this the way to please your Prophet? Shame on you! Not a Christian will I give up! They are my brothers!'[15]

'Abdelkader El Djezairi's valour put him in good favour both with Ottoman authorities and world leaders. Gifts poured into Damascus and were taken by festive entourage to the Djezairi mansion. They included a pair of gold-mounted revolvers from US President Abraham Lincoln, a sword from Queen Victoria, a medal from Pope Pius IX and the Légion d'honneur from none other than Napoleon III.[16] Fifty-eight years later, 'Abdelkader's grandson dreamt of playing a similar role to that of his grandfather, sheltering Damascus, yet again, from chaos and sectarian strife. In the figment of his own imagination, Emir Sa'id saw himself a natural extension of his great grandfather: a second 'Abdelkader.

The Great War in Damascus

With so much history looking over his shoulders, Emir Sa'id decided to regain his grandfather's status as uncrowned king of Damascus. He had grown up under his towering influence, although Sa'id was only an infant when 'Abdelkader died on 26 May 1888. It was his grandfather who named him Mohammad Sa'id, and well into old age, he could still be seen in a 1960s television interview referring to 'Abdelkader as '*Sayyidi al-Jidd*' (My Master Grandfather). As Emir Sa'id watched foreign consuls frantically evacuating the city in mid-September 1918, he knew that Ottoman rule would soon collapse, never to return, plunging Damascus into a new round of chaos, by far worse than that of 1860.

The First World War had humbled the mighty in Damascus, leaving the city, and its inhabitants, in very bad shape. The streets were paved with corpses, the gutters running in blood and so was the now-fetid Barada River, its fresh water turned crimson red as it poured into aqueducts of the city's homes.[17] The hospitals were packed, either with dead Syrians or those dying from dysentery, typhoid and cholera. Shrouded dead bodies were placed side by side at the Hamidiean Hospital in al-Baramkeh, awaiting identification by their families for a speedy burial. Some were still in military uniform, others in their underclothing and many stark naked. The hospitals crept with rats that gnawed at the dead Damascenes.[18]

The Ottomans had switched off the electricity grid of Damascus in early 1918; their coffers were empty and they could no longer operate the city's power plant. The streets were unsafe after dark, run by thieves, pickpockets and other petty criminals.[19] Despite having enjoyed electricity for an entire decade, the Damascenes had to go through their 1918 winter in cold and darkness. Thieves were plundering through the old markets, which were gripped by wild rumours. One said that units from the German Imperial Army based in Damascus were planning to blow up the entire city before the Ottoman withdrawal.[20] Another went that Bedouin troops were preparing to invade Damascus and rape its women. People were terrified. As if death and psychological trauma were not enough, a famine broke out in Beirut during the Great War and soon reached Damascus. Beiruti notables either escaped on European liners before the Port of Beirut was shut down or came to Damascus for sanctuary. As the population of Damascus quadrupled, that of Beirut dropped from 180,000 in 1914 to 75,000 in 1916.[21] A Christian pastor from Minneapolis who visited Syria noted that people were dying in the streets of Damascus every single day. 'Starvation and famine are everywhere', he wrote, adding that 'the men of Damascus are either in military service or hiding. The women and children are reduced to beggary'.[22] The Damascus Police collected no less than seventy unidentified dead bodies daily.[23]

Economically, Damascus was bankrupt. The Ottomans had paid advance wages up to December 1918, using paper currency worth only 12 per cent of its value in gold.[24] Police stations had shut their doors in mid-September, while evacuating German troops had destroyed the city's fire brigade. Fires broke out, demolishing private homes and government offices, waiting for Mother Nature to put them out. The city's prisons were smashed open, and 4,000 prisoners were released, some being convicted criminals.[25] They broke loose on the streets of Damascus, looting shops and entire households. Men aged eighteen and above had either been hauled off to battle in the dreaded *Safarbarlik* or were in hiding to escape almost certain death on the Ottoman battlefronts. Some returned to tell tales of agony, while thousands perished in faraway lands. Of the 2.8 million soldiers sent to fight, 325,000 died in combat between 1914 and 1918.[26] Another 240,000 died of disease, while no less than 250,000 were listed as 'missing' or 'prisoners of war'.[27] In addition, an estimated 1.5 million deserted the Ottoman Army, 50 per cent being Arab soldiers.[28]

The Djezairi Brothers

Djemal al-Saghir decided to talk directly to the city notables, pleading with them to protect his men from revenge killings. Most of the notables were either in jail, exile or on the outskirts of Damascus, having joined the rebel army of Sharif Hussein, the emir of Mecca who, with British assistance, was waging an armed insurgency against the Ottoman Empire, known as the Great Arab Revolt.[29] Two notables whom Djemal al-Saghir could trust, 'Abdul Rahman Pasha al-Yusuf and Mohammad Fawzi Pasha al-'Azm, were both in Istanbul.[30] They were senior Arabs at the Imperial Court who might have helped protect his troops had they been in Damascus during those fatal weeks. Unable to reach any of his old friends, Djemal al-Saghir summoned Emir Sa'id and asked him to use his Algerian troops to protect the evacuating Ottoman Army.[31] In total, there were anywhere between 12,000 to 15,000 Algerians under the command of the Djezairi brothers, Sa'id and 'Abdelkader Jr, armed with rifles, guns and swords.[32]

'The city is in absolute chaos and the army is retreating. Our enemies are nearing toward Damascus. Rumour has it that they have reached al-Ghouta and will enter the city any minute now', said Djemal al-Saghir.[33] His voice was trembling as he suggested arming the population and creating a national guard to man the streets, just like Parisians did during the French Revolution. Emir S'aid explained, 'Like my grandfather, 'Abdelkader the Great, I too want to save lives. I want protect women and children, and stop all the looting.'[34] Djemal al-Saghir smiled half-heartedly: 'I want you to protect me as well.'[35] Emir Sa'id nodded, chin-up, stressing that the pasha was safe 'in the hands of the Djezairi family'. He had one condition, however: 'I want your troops to withdraw completely, along with the Germans. They must leave with all of their arms and ammunition to prevent any clash with the locals. Only that will save Damascus from destruction and collapse.'[36]

The Algerian prince then ordered armed Algerians headed by his brother to hold guard at the seven gates of Damascus, with strict instructions to protect retreating Turkish soldiers. As far as he was concerned, this could be another 1860 and he had the moral responsibility of living up to his grandfather's legacy. One militia was stationed at al-Shaghour, south of the Old City, and another at al-Midan, a conservative neighbourhood nested outside the city wall. Al-Shaghour was vital because parts of it encompassed the Shi'ite and Jewish alleys of Old Damascus. A third contingent was despatched to the Christian neighbourhoods of Bab Sharqi, Bab Touma and al-Qass'a, while a fourth was sent to the Kurdish Hay al-Akrad on the slopes of Mount Qassioun.[37] Protecting religious and ethnic minorities, after all, was what the Djezairis were made for, thought Emir Sa'id, seeing growing similarities between 1860 and 1918. A fifth militia headed to the residential Salhieh district, and al-Muhajreen, home of the Ottoman governor to Damascus, while a sixth was despatched to guard the city central, from the ancient Bab al-Jabieh quarter and the arcaded Midhat Pasha and Hamidieh markets, running through Marjeh Square until reaching 'Arnous in the modern part of the city.[38] In 2015, Emir Fateh recalled, 'All it took was one hundred men. The city was small. Nobody in Damascus had arms but us, the Djezairis.'[39]

A self-appointed ruler

Emir Sa'id then walked up to government headquarters in Marjeh Square, accompanied by three of his cousins, all armed with guns. The two-floor building was empty; all officials had abandoned their offices, taking their papers, files and seals, and so had the sentry guards. The Grand Serail had been constructed on the southern bank of the Barada River in 1900, right behind the Damascus

Municipality. Emir Sa'id entered the desolate building, walked straight up to the governor's office and sat on his vacant chair, looking firmly at his cousins while proclaiming himself as the new ruler of Damascus. This is the same seat once occupied by powerful Ottoman men like Midhat Pasha, the reformer and Djemal Pasha, commander of the Fourth Army during the Second World War. 'My duty is to save Damascus', murmured Emir Sa'id, almost in a trance, as his cousins patted his shoulder and congratulated him on what seemed to have been an easy job. It had been carried out smoothly, with no blood and no political consequences – or, so it seemed.[40] At the young age of thirty-five, Emir Sa'id was now the first Arab ruler of Damascus in four entire centuries. The confusion of those early hours of independence manifested in how Emir Sa'id referred to his new job. Clearly uncertain of how to position himself without coming across as politically incorrect, he sometimes signed communiques as 'interim governor of Syria' and others as 'Deputy Sultan'.[41] Twice, he wrote 'Head of State'. Clearly, there was no agreement as to what exactly Emir Sa'id would rule and through what capacity. All he knew was that he seemed to have successfully inherited Damascus from the Ottomans, with none of their debts or enemies.

The emir then sent troops to seize the government printing press from which the Ottomans had cranked out their daily, *al-Sharq*. Until the previous week, the newspaper had been filled with rosy praise for the Ottoman sultan and his Great Army. At Emir Sa'id's orders, the sultan's portrait was taken down and the newspaper was renamed *al-Istiqlal al-'Arabi* (Arab Independence). Under the new name, it came out with one single issue, filled with praise for the Djezairi brothers.[42] In his memoirs, Emir Sa'id recalls how city elders met at the Grand Serail to swear allegiance to him as the new governor of Syria. Yusuf al-Hakim, a prominent Christian judge, confirms that the meeting did take place, but at the Damascus Town Hall not the Grand Serail.[43] Ahmad Qadri, a young physician in Sharif Hussein's army, argues that Emir Sa'id was never tasked with governing Damascus, saying that he 'stole' the job from Rida Pasha al-Rikabi and Shukri Pasha al-Ayyubi, two senior Arab officers in the Ottoman Army who had been mandated to run the city by Sharif Hussein.[44] He also accuses Emir Sa'id of being pro-Ottoman, unfit to rule a city just liberated from four centuries of Ottoman rule.[45] The Djezairi family, of course, had worked closely with the Ottomans at different junctures in their history: always as allies, never as agents or collaborators. Not all of them were on favourable terms with the Turks. Emir Sa'id's uncle, Omar El Djezairi, had been hanged for treason in May 1916, accused of conspiring with the French government against the Ottoman sultan.[46]

Challenging the officers

Rida Pasha al-Rikabi, at fifty-two, was a trained officer from a solid Damascene family who had reached the rank of general in 1912. Unlike Emir Sa'id, he was experienced in both politics and military affairs, having served as commander of Jerusalem, governor of Medina, deputy governor of Basra and mayor of

Damascus. Syrian officers held him in high esteem, and his family connections in Damascus secured the support of the city merchants. He had refused to join the Great War on the side of Germany, which led to his discharge from the Ottoman Army in 1914.[47]

Shukri Pasha al-Ayyubi was older, at sixty-seven. He had once served as commander of the Ottoman Military Academy in Damascus at the start of the Great War.[48] He joined the Arab underground in 1916, which led to his arrest at the Khan Pasha Prison in the Old City. The Ottomans had him flogged and forced to walk around in heavy chains, beating him with clubs to reveal the name of his comrades in al-Fatat, a secret society of Arab nationalists set up in 1911 to bring down the Ottoman Empire.[49] He was released during the jailbreak of September 1918. Sharif Hussein had specifically mentioned his name and that of Rida al-Rikabi to administer the city in the aftermath of the Ottomans, an order that either never reached Emir Sa'id or which he decided to ignore.[50]

The flag-raising ceremony

Emir Sa'id took his new job very seriously, fully investing in the power vacuum left behind by the Ottomans. He called on his friend the journalist Ma'arouf Arna'out, asking him to fetch the Arab Flag from his home, a symbol of the Great Arab Revolt. It had been given to him by Sharif Hussein, or so he claimed, with orders to raise it on the very same day that the Ottomans left Damascus.[51] There is plenty of controversy about who designed the Arab Flag. The British said it was the brainchild of their skilled diplomat Mark Sykes, while Ja'afar al-'Askari, a senior Iraqi officer in the Arab Army, says that it was designed by Sharif Hussein. Others claim it was created by nationalists in al-Fatat from its twin bases in Paris and Damascus.[52] The flag contained three horizontal stripes of green, white and black, representing the Rashidun, Umayyad and Abbasid caliphates of Islam.[53] The history of those dynasties was something that Emir Sa'id knew by heart. Under the first three caliphs, the capital of Islam was Medina, which housed the prophet's gravesite at the Masjid al-Nabawi (Prophet's Mosque). Medina was also the place where the final chronological verses of the Quran were revealed to Mohammad, the prophet of Islam. During the short tenure of the prophet's cousin, 'Ali, the Muslim capital was moved to al-Kufa in present-day Iraq, before reaching Damascus under 'Ali's successor, Muawiya Ibn Abi Sufyan, founder of the Umayyad state. The Umayyads were Islam's first dynasty, creating an empire that grew rapidly in territory, incorporating the Caucasus, Sindh, the Maghreb and the Iberian Peninsula, known as al-Andalus. At its peak, the Umayyad Caliphate covered 13.4 million square kilometres. Emir Sa'id saw himself as an extension of the Umayyads, ruling from none other than their ancient capital, Damascus.

Arna'aout returned to the Grand Serail carrying the Arab Flag, hoisted on Emir Sa'id's automobile. By the time he reached Marjeh Square, the crowd was already in the thousands, cheering the names of Sharif Hussein and Emir Sa'id. People were seemingly convinced, up to that moment, that the Djezairis were acting on behalf of Sharif Hussein and the Arab Revolt, rather than independently. Emir Sa'id grabbed the flag and handed it to Sa'id al-Hafi, a community leader from al-Midan, ordering him to raise it over the roof of the Grand Serail.[54] As he did, shots were fired into the skies of Damascus, a sign of joy in Arab societies. He then declared the city officially liberated from 400 years of Ottoman rule. Sadly, there is not a single photograph of the historic scene, and its events have been orally handed down from one generation to the next. That might explain why there are three different dates of when exactly the hoisting ceremony took place. Emir Sa'id says it was on Thursday, 26 September. Lawrence puts it as Monday, 30 September. The Damascus daily *al-Muqtabas* mentions Friday, 27 September. According to *al-Muqtabas*, the flag was hoisted on the same day that the last Ottoman troops left the city. Emir Sa'id's date means that he ruled Damascus for five days; Lawrence's date would mean he remained in power for no more than twenty-four hours. The *al-Muqtabas* editorial reads, 'Today is a big day for those who speak the Arabic language, and those who live the civility of Damascus. The Arab Flag with its four colors is now hoisted above everybody's head. The impossible has now been achieved.'[55]

During the flag-hoisting ceremony, Emir Sa'id asked his friend Fares al-Khoury to address the jubilant crowd from the Grand Serail balcony. Khoury was a former lecturer at the American University of Beirut, who had served as Christian MP in the Ottoman Parliament. That polished his oratory skills, far beyond those of the Algerian Prince.[56] Emir Sa'id's brother spoke next, asking people to go home and rest, assuring them that they were now safe in the hands of the Djezairi family. He reminded residents to obey the orders of the Algerian guards protecting their city, commanding, 'Cherish those who liberated you from darkness.'[57] He put the safety of women and children as a top priority, saying that they shouldn't venture outside their homes after sunset. At the Umayyad Mosque, prayers were conducted on Friday 27 September in the name of Sharif Hussein, 'king of the Arabs'.

Pulling the city back together

Emir Sa'id's short rule was marked with trouble from Day One. On 26 September, a Druze uprising broke out in the countryside of Damascus. Lawrence claims that the rebels 'cared nothing for Islam, the Caliph, Turks, or (Emir) 'Abdelkader' but saw it as an opportunity to rise against Christians, just as they had done in 1860. 'They ran to arms and began to burst open shops.'[58] Still stationed at the city outskirts, Lawrence refused to intervene because of the darkness, saying that nightfall makes 'a fool and a man equal'.[59] Emir Sa'id ordered that the Druze be shot as they approached the city centre.[60] Five of them were killed, and ten were wounded. He left their corpses to rot on the city pavements, and others to gruesomely float in the Barada River, in order to spread fear among the locals – fear that, he believed, would automatically trigger submissiveness. The Druze were subsequently expelled from the city, and only their elders were allowed to stay behind, with a valiant warrior named Sultan Pasha al-Atrash serving as adviser to

Emir Sa'id, then to Emir Faisal.[61] In 1925, he would become a household name in Syria for leading an armed uprising against the French Mandate.

No sooner had that been solved than another battle broke out, right in front of the gates of the Grand Serail, where Ottoman troops were attacked while making their way to the Dummar-Beirut highway. They fired back, causing havoc on the streets. Emir Sa'id descended from his office, carrying a pistol in hand, shouting, 'Halt! Do not fire at a retreating and defeated army'.[62] This, after all, was *Sham Sherif*, Damascus the Noble, and Emir Sa'id wanted to live up to the Ottoman name of his city. One of his men was badly wounded while climbing the column facing the Grand Serail, where from atop, he signalled Ottoman troops to march in safety.[63] Erected in 1900, the column was ironically marked with the Ottoman emblem and personalized signature of the former sultan, 'Abdulhamid II.[64]

When nightfall came, heavy looting rocked the Damascus countryside, mainly in the village of Mezzeh, southwest of the capital. Armed Bedouins tried breaking into the city at night, via the al-Rabweh Road, only to be confronted by the commander of the Damascus Police, 'Abdulhamid al-Sheikh.[65] At Emir Sa'id's orders, a machine gun was placed near the Victoria Hotel and it opened fire on the 100 horsemen approaching central Damascus, carrying guns and swords. Nearly half were killed, while others were caught and executed.[66] A final incident took place when a civilian train was ransacked in al-Ghouta by bandits who mistakenly believed that it was carrying Ottoman gold being smuggled out of Damascus.[67]

The next morning, Emir Sa'id was behind his office desk at 5.00 am. It was still dark outside, but he had a long list of political appointments to make, rewarding those who had supported him during the past forty-eight hours. He had to sign his decrees quickly, before the British and Arab armies reached Damascus next morning, on 1 October 1918. His friend Ma'arouf Arna'out was given control of the Department of Posts & Telegraphs and was asked to send out telegrams proclaiming his new state in Damascus. 'An Arab Hashemite Government founded on the pillars of honor has been established in Damascus', wrote Arna'out, 'in the name of His Majesty, Hussein Ibn Ali, King of the Arabs. Assure the people and calm them in the name of the Arab Government'.[68] The telegram was signed simply, 'Emir Sa'id'. He was already famous and felt no need to write his full name. Everybody knew who Sa'id El Djezairi was. The emir then confiscated what remained of Ottoman gold and put it under the supervision of his friend, Shukri al-Taji. The money was registered in government records, and signed off by the Algerian prince who appointed an officer named Mamduh al-'Abed, to guard its chests.[69] Sa'adi Kahaleh was made commander of the Damascus Gendarmerie, and Amin al-Tamimi, a Palestinian, was named commander of Public Security. Omar al-Da'ouk became governor of Beirut, and Ahmad Mukhtar Bayhum, director of public security in Beirut.

The next morning, life returned to normal in Damascus. Shops opened, selling spices, brocade and all kinds of sweets for which the Damascus markets were famed. Street sweepers returned to work, and so did staffers at government offices.

Schools and the Ottoman academies of medicine and law, however, remained closed. Tailors were already stitching together small Hejazi flags to sell to the children of Damascus, in anticipation of the arrival of Emir Faisal, tentatively scheduled for 1 October 1918. He arrived two days late, on 3 October.

The interim Djezairi government

Emir Sa'id then set up a five-man interim government to run the city's day-to-day affairs. It included Fares al-Khoury, 'Ata al-Ayyubi, Shaker al-Hanbali, Jamil al-Ulshi and Badi Mou'ayyad al-'Azm. Born in 1877 in the town of Hasbayya of what is now modern Lebanon, Khoury was eldest among the group, having begun his career by teaching elementary schools in the Golan Heights before joining the AUB Faculty. Ayyubi, aged forty-one, was Emir Sa'id's brother-in-law. He had studied public administration in Istanbul and worked in the Ottoman civil service, becoming *mutasarrif* of Latakia in 1908, and MP in the Ottoman Parliament in 1912.[70] Hanbali, aged forty-two, was an Istanbul-educated Damascene lawyer who served as *mutasarrif* of Hama during the final years of the Ottoman Empire.[71] Jamil al-Ulshi was a defected officer from the Ottoman Army who had served in Jerusalem during the Great War. Mou'ayyad al-'Azm had studied law in Istanbul and worked at the public debts department in Mosul before joining the Customs Department of Istanbul. Like Khoury and Ayyoubi, he was also an ex-MP in the Ottoman Parliament.[72] In future years, Khoury, Ulshi and Ayyubi went on to become prime ministers of Syria. There were no portfolios in the Djezairi camarilla of ministers, and all of its members were treated as political equals, answering directly to Emir Sa'id. A Damascene officer named Zaki al-'Azma was summoned to the Grand Serail and asked to escort British troops entering the city on 1 October, on the behalf of his boss. Two letters were penned to Allied officers accompanying Lawrence, asking them not to enter Damascus before the Djezairi government receives an official blessing from Sharif Hussein. That blessing, of course, never came.

Come up, this is Emir Sa'id

At approximately 6.00 am on 1 October, 10,000 troops entered Damascus, commanded by the Australian Major Arthur Olden, three hours before Colonel Lawrence made his grand entry into the city at 9.00 am.[73] Hundreds turned out to welcome them, but Emir Sa'id was not among the crowd. He watched the procession from his office balcony overlooking Marjeh Square, waiting for Lawrence to formally request an audience with the new ruler of Syria. Outside the Grand Serail, women threw rice and rosewater and young men danced on sidewalks. Children waved flags of the Arab Revolt, mispronouncing Lawrence's name as 'Aurence'. Lawrence's boss, General Edmund Allenby, made a far more dramatic entrance, driving into the city in a convertible white Rolls Royce. The Damascenes watched in bewilderment and awe, having never seen such a fancy automobile. Lawrence describes the scene in *Seven Pillars of Wisdom*, saying: 'Every man, woman, and child in this city of a quarter-million souls seemed on the streets, wanting only the spark of our appearance to ignite their spirits. Damascus went mad with joy!' He made particular mention of the Turks and Germans who had destroyed their weapons while retreating and set their ammunition stockpile ablaze:

> They fired the dumps and ammunition stores, so that every few minutes, we were jangled by explosions, whose first shock set the sky white with flames. I turned to (Colonel) Stirling and muttered, 'Damascus is burning,' sick to think of the great town in ashes for the price of freedom.[74]

Major Olden marched confidently to the Victoria Hotel, with orders to raise the British Flag over its rooftop. He looked up, only to find the Arab Flag already on its mast. He had orders to take Djemal al-Saghir alive, seemingly unaware that the Ottoman officer had left the city the previous night. Such misinformation was strange, of course, and it speaks of how chaotic the Allied front was in the hours preceding their entry into Damascus. Standing at the staircase, Olden shouted: 'If the commander is here let him come forward'. His eyes were trained on the hotel's balcony, fingers firmly placed on the trigger, ready to shoot. Instead of Djemal al-Saghir, Emir Sa'id came out of the governor's balcony. He spoke to him in English, saying, 'Come up, this is Emir Sa'id.'[75]

Olden stood there in full military uniform, facing Sa'id wearing his Ottoman fez, seated on gold-inlaid furniture with Oriental fittings. Pride was oozing out of the room, Olden the Orientalist coming to free Arabs from Turkish tyranny, Emir Sa'id the grandson of 'Abdelkader the Great, coming face-to-face with a European general whom he regarded as no different from the Frenchmen who had imprisoned and tortured his grandfather, more than half a century ago. With a stern rictus, he harangued the Australian general: 'You have entered a sovereign city with your arms, infringing on its laws and traditions.'[76] This time he was speaking in Arabic, wanting to make a point with the Major Olden. One of his cousins handled translation into English.

'I entered on the orders of General Allenby', said the Major, '... a Turkish city in order to occupy it militarily'. Emir Sa'id interrupted him calmly: 'It *was* a Turkish a city but not anymore. It is now free and independent. Had you not been with the Allies, I would have had you arrested!'[77] Olden tried to explain: 'Your Highness, I did not come here to insult anybody. We are here to place our troops at your disposal, so you can restore security to Damascus.' Emir Sa'id snarled: 'The security of Damascus was handled by our men even under Turkish rule. When you came here, did you find anything but peace and tranquility? We have many troops and volunteers. Should you need assistance, we are ready to help you!'[78] He then sent Algerian troops with Major Olden to Bab Sharqi to see for himself the orderly retreat of Ottoman troops from the Christian quarter of the Old City.[79] The dramatic conversation is recounted only in Emir Sa'id's memoirs, and none of his contemporaries say anything about it, and nor does Colonel Lawrence.

Lawrence versus the Algerian emirs

Emir Sa'id then received a visit from Sharif Nasser, acting as special envoy for Emir Faisal. Sharif Nasser was Faisal's nephew who headed Arab guerrillas against the Ottomans in Medina. He asked Emir Sa'id if he had a mandate to rule the city, to which the Algerian prince nodded affirmatively. He sincerely believed that he had the support both of the Hashemites and of the Syrian people. 'If it were not for us, the Germans would have burnt Damascus.'[80] Emir Sa'id claims that Sharif Nasser seconded the decision to name him governor of Damascus, although this is strongly contested by Lawrence. He was invited for dinner at the Djezairi mansion that evening, hosted by Emir Sa'id and Emir ʿAbdelkader Jr. As large trays of lamb shops and rice were being served in the spacious courtyard, a British soldier showed up, inviting the Djezairis – or ordering them – to the Victoria Hotel. Colonel Lawrence wanted to have a word with them, he said.[81]

Lawrence was upset with how things had played out in Damascus, and he was determined to bring an end to the Djezairi family coup. Sa'id El Djezairi needed to be toppled before Emir Faisal entered the city on 3 October. If he resisted, then he would be either clamped in chains or shot. Emir Sa'id abruptly declined Lawrence's 'invitation', saying that he and his guests were busy, asking the British messenger to leave and come the next morning. He was unhappy with Lawrence's tone, along with the fact that he had completely ignored him since entering the city earlier that morning. The envoy left, only to return in an hour, this time with stricter orders, saying that he would have Emir Sa'id and his guests arrested if they failed to show up at Lawrence's makeshift office 'immediately'.[82] Emir ʿAbdelkader Jr. was furious; both he and his brother considered Lawrence a spy, and the British Colonel had nothing but ill-feelings for the Algerian brothers.[83] The animosity between ʿAbdelkader and Lawrence dated back to their work together during the Great Revolt, when he had refused obeying British orders to blow up sections of the Hejaz Railway running through Wadi Khaled, northern the present Syrian-Lebanese borders.[84]

The Djezairis abruptly ended their dinner and went to the Victoria Hotel. When they entered its lobby, Shukri al-Ayyubi and Rida al-Rikabi were already there, also waiting for Lawrence, along with the al-Fatat leader Ahmad Qadri. Lawrence came down the large staircase, still wearing his military fatigues. He walked slowly, looking Emir Sa'id straight in the eyes. Emir ʿAbdelkader Jr. was first to snap: 'Lawrence! Are you threatening the sons of ʿAbdelkader the Great? We fear neither jail nor death. In fact, we fear nobody but God!'[85] Lawrence tried controlling his temper; he was itching to shoot, claiming that the Algerian brothers 'had murder in their eyes'.[86] Emir Sa'id did not say a word, letting his brother do all the talking.

ʿAbdelkader pointed to the Arab Flag now fluttering above the Victoria Hotel, saying: 'We pledge loyalty to this flag only, which was raised in Mecca and prayed upon by 40,000 Muslims! When this conflict is over, we will thrust this chair—the seat of power in Damascus—with our two feet. We don't want it.'[87] He quickly added, 'Unlike many, we are not agents in the hands of foreigners. British coins cannot seduce us and no honor is higher for us than that of the Prophet.'[88] Ahmad Qadri interjected, saying that there seemed to be a grave misunderstanding between the Algerian brothers and 'our brother Lawrence'.[89] Shaking with fury, 'Abdelkader exploded: 'Silence. Nobody in this room can interrupt me!'[90] He haughtily walked up to Shukri al-Ayyubi, placing his hand on the pasha's white head. 'Do you Shukri, pledge loyalty to this flag?'[91] Shukri Pasha nodded, shaken by the emir's physical gesture, along with the fact that he had addressed him rudely without the title of 'pasha', which had been bestowed upon him by the Ottoman sultan. 'Then take it; we do not want it anymore', snapped 'Abdelkader.[92]

Adding spice to the high drama, Emir Sa'id stood up and embraced his younger brother, kissing him paternally on the forehead: 'God bless you 'Abdelkader. You are indeed worthy of being grandson of 'Abdelkader the Great.'[93] Marking their family role in history seemed more sacrosanct for the two brothers than saving the position that they had assumed for themselves in Damascus. Realizing that resistance would have been equal to political suicide, Emir Sa'id officially relinquished his post, not to Shukri al-Ayyubi but to Sharif Nasser, him as the official representative of the Hashemite family in Syria. 'I occupied the seat of power out of necessity and now leave it at will', he said calmly.[94]

That evening, he presented Sharif Nasser with the keys to the Grand Serail, ending one of the shortest governments in the modern history of Syria. Depending on what version of history one wants to read, it lasted anywhere between twenty-four hours to four days.

Emir Sa'id, post 1918

Lawrence stayed in Damascus for three nights and departed on 4 October, only after firmly installing Emir Faisal as the new ruler of Syria. A formal cabinet of ministers was established, led by Rida al-Rikabi, and on 8 March 1920, Faisal was crowned king. He was to be dethroned and exiled by the invading French Army, four months later. Faisal was banished with orders never to return, and after a brief stopover in Europe, headed to Baghdad, where he was installed as king of Iraq until his death in September 1933. Lawrence never returned to Syria and died in an accident while driving his Brough Superior SS100 motorcycle, in May 1935. He was killed not far from his cottage in Dorset, near the English Channel coast, thousands of miles away from the Arabian Desert and from Damascus.

One of Rikabi's first orders was to have Emir Sa'id arrested.[95] He was released with no trial and banished, first to Beirut and then to Paris – a belated punishment for having proclaimed himself ruler of Syria, with no mandate from the Hashemites. He had just rented a home in a new neighbourhood outside the Old City, which was confiscated by Rikabi, along with the emir's private automobile.[96] In 1919, he met with the King-Crane Commission that

US President Woodrow Wilson had sent to Syria, advising: 'Faisal should have nothing to do with Syria. He is a stranger.'[97] 'Abdelkader Jr was killed shortly after the debacle with Lawrence, on 17 November 1918, gunned down at Rikabi's orders while trying to flee an arrest warrant.[98]

The emir would return to Syria shortly after the French Mandate was imposed in 1920, occasionally making a public appearance to remind locals of his ancestry: that he was the grandson of 'Abdelkader the Great, and heir to his glorious legacy. In October 1925, the French mercilessly bombed Damascus during the Great Syrian Revolt. Emir Sa'id rushed to save the Christians of Bab Touma, seeing panic in their eyes. Three thousands of them were herded into his home in al-'Amara, the very same mansion that had sheltered Damascus Christians in 1860.[99] Echoing a line similar to that of his grandfather, Emir Sa'id assured them that they were now safe under protection of the Djezairi family. He then headed a delegation of Syrian notables to Beirut, where they demanded a ceasefire from the French high commissioner Maurice Sarrail.[100]

The Syrian throne question

In mid-1924, Emir Sa'id set up a Caliphate Society in Damascus, modelled after the Khilafat Movement in India.[101] Its aim was to find a suitable replacement to the last Ottoman caliph, 'Abdulmejid II, whose position in Istanbul had just been terminated by President Mustafa Atatürk that March. Emir Sa'id gathered a number of Syrian notables around his project, saying that the world's fifteen million Muslims needed a single authority to follow, proposing – to nobody's surprise – that he assumes the job himself. He fulfilled all the requirements of being caliph; he was a Sunni Muslim from *Ahl al-Bayt*, tracing his lineage directly back to the prophet, and a Qurashi from Mohammad's tribe. If he couldn't secure the governorship of Damascus then perhaps he might aim higher for leadership of the entire Muslim world. Many supported the Caliphate Society, if not necessary Emir Sa'id's ambitions, including the mufti of Damascus, Sheikh 'Atallah al-Kasm and Badi Mou'ayyad al-'Azm, a former member of the emir's interim government.[102] The Caliphate Society didn't succeed, however, and no serious caliph hunting took place. By 1928, the project had fallen apart.

In the early 1930s, French commissioner Henri Ponsot toyed with the idea of restoring a crown to Syria.[103] He set about finding a king who would be affiliated to colonial France, rather than to Great Britain, as Faisal had been. Ponsot wrote a letter to French foreign minister Aristide Briand saying that the vast majority of Syrians still favoured a throne, claiming that it 'assured stability, protected national traditions, and safeguarded prestige of the country'.[104] Since there was no royal blood in Syria, Ponsot drew up a list of potential candidates, whom he considered suitable for the job of king. Prime on the list was Sa'id El Djezairi, followed by Ahmad Nami, a fifty-year-old Circassian aristocrat and former head of state who happened to be the ex-son-in-law of Sultan 'Abdulhamid II.[105] A third candidate was 'Abbas Hilmi II, the Switzerland-based ex-khedive of Egypt, who had never visited Syria and was more interested in a political comeback to his throne in Cairo, from where he had been evicted by the British in December 1914.[106] Like the Caliphate Society, the project never picked up steam and died out by 1932 – yet another setback to Emir Sa'id's seemingly never-ending ambition.[107]

Failed assassination

In 1936, Emir Sa'id suffered an assassination attempt, carried out, very surprisingly, by his first wife, Husniyya, who also happened to be his cousin.[108] She tried to kill him after he announced plans to re-marry, choosing a twenty-three-year-old Turkish woman whom he had met at the Grand Serail. Blonde, beautiful and unveiled, she was thirty years his junior and they had met at the office of his old friend and in-law, 'Ata al-Ayyubi. Although polygamy is perfectly legitimate and accepted in Islam, Husniyya El Djezairi vowed that the marriage would never pass. She had one of her sons plant a bomb in the burning furnace around which Emir Sa'id and 'Ata al-Ayyubi were seated on a cold evening.[109] They emerged from the assassination attempt, unscratched.[110] Emir Sa'id did marry the woman, and was to re-marry a third time into the Tirijman family of Damascus. His third and last wife, Bahiyya al-Tirijman, died in 2008.[111]

In 1927, Emir Sa'id was one of the co-founders of the National Bloc, the leading anti-French movement that led the nation until France's evacuation in April 1946.[112] He witnessed twenty-six years of French occupation and all the coups and counter-coups that rocked Syria from 1949 onwards. In September 1958, the Djezairi family suffered a major blow when the socialist state of Gamal 'Abdul Nasser confiscated vast tracts of land bequeathed to them by Emir 'Abdelkader, almost a century ago. Forty thousand dunums were seized in one day, from the Houran valley and the Kawkab village onto Hosh Blas and Ashrafiyat Sehnaya in the Damascus countryside.[113] The Djezairis were left with just 800 dunums of irrigated lands, from which they had to live off for the rest of their lives.[114]

The final years

In the 1960s, Emir Sa'id managed to re-invent himself as special adviser to Algerian president Houari Boumédiène, who invited him to return to Algeria, restoring many of the Djezairi family's fertile plantations.[115] He was treated lavishly as a guest of honour in Algiers, as grandson of Emir 'Abdelkader the Great. In 1965, Boumédiène worked with Emir Sa'id at returning Emir 'Abdelkader's remains to Algeria, for official burial at the El 'Alia Cemetery in the commune of Qued Smar.[116] Upon his death in 1883, Emir ʿAbdelkader had been laid to rest at a beautiful shrine on the slopes of Mount Qassioun, next to the thirteenth-century Sufi mystic, Ibn ʿArabi. A grand procession unearthed the emir's remains and placed them in a coffin wrapped neatly with the Syrian and Algerian flags. It was then paraded through the streets of Damascus by the Syrian Guard of Honour, carried on a shining cannon wagon before boarding a plane to Algiers. Emir Saʾid, now in his eighties, could be seen in the front row standing next to President Nur al-Din al-Atasi and Baʾath Party strongman Salah Jadid. The socialists had long abandoned the Ottoman dress code in favour of Maoist jackets and olive military fatigues, but Emir Saʾid stuck to his sartorial habits and was still dressed with the same attire of 1918 Damascus: a double-vest morning suit with gold cufflinks, and an Ottoman *tarboosh*. That is the Damascus he knew and the image in which he wanted to be remembered by history. He was then invited for a courtesy visit to the office of Defense Minister Hafez al-Assad, who acknowledged him as a former head of state and welcomed him at the Grand Serail.[117] It was to be his last public appearance in Syria. Emir Saʾid died at the age of eighty-seven, on 16 July 1970. He was buried at the Sidi Qada cemetery, north of Algeria.

The story of the Algerian prince's role in Damascus has often been treated as a non-event. Emir Saʾid eventually sat down to write his own memoir in 1968, but the 334-page book, pretty much like its author, received no more than passing attention in the Arabic press. Published shortly after the Six-Day War, it went by largely unnoticed. People were too busy lamenting the occupation of east Jerusalem, the Sinai Peninsula and the Syrian Golan to pay much attention to an Ottoman-bred politician from a bygone era. The memoirs were republished in Damascus in 2015 by his great-grandnephew Emir Jaʾafar El Djezairi, founder of the Emir ʿAbdelkader El Djezairi Foundation. This time, people were too busy with the war in Syria to pay any attention.

Figure 2 Emir Sa'id El Djezairi.

Chapter 3

KING FAISAL I (1918-20)

In early 1920, members of the royal diwan searched frantically the homes of Damascus, looking for a chair that could be used as a throne for their king-in-waiting, Emir Faisal.[1] He was due to be crowned on 8 March and needed a throne that would match up to the occasion. The country was unprepared for royalty, certainly not for any of the pomp and grandeur that came with it. Faisal wanted a fancy cathedra, similar to the throne of King George V. They searched all the mansions of the Old City, but were unable to find something suitable. He finally had to settle for a mother-of-pear inlaid armchair, borrowed from a member of the Farra family.[2] The 'throne' was polished exclusively for the event, with its thick, green upholstery changed into rich crimson. It was eventually returned to its owner, when the king was through with his coronation.[3] What Faisal got was a humble ceremony, especially when compared to the throning of the Windsors of Great Britain or the Romanovs of Imperial Russia. His family, the Hashemites, were noblemen by birth, tracing their lineage back to the Prophet Mohammad through his favourite daughter, Fatima al-Zahraa. That gave them the honorific title of *ashraf* (noblemen) and Faisal was registered at birth in Ottoman records as 'al-Sharif' Faisal. The title entitled him to respect in society and obedience on the battlefield, but that pretty much is where royalty ended. The king of Syria had no palaces, no estates – and no crown. He was also not Syrian.

The British had installed him as ruler of Syria in October 1918, immediately after toppling Emir Sa'id El Djezairi. Upon making his triumphant entry into Damascus, the 35-year-old emir headed first to the Umayyad Mosque, accompanied by the city's mufti, Abu al-Kheir 'Abidin. Just a few months back, the mufti had called for Faisal's assassination for defying the Ottoman sultan.[4] Now with the Ottomans gone and seemingly never to return, he put himself at the disposal of the Hashemites royals, rubbing shoulders with Faisal as they entered the splendid mosque. Faisal would soon have him dismissed and replaced with Sheikh 'Atallah al-Kasm, another prelate who nevertheless had been more sympathetic to Hashemite ambitions during the First World War. Damascus was a city of conservatives, and if Faisal wanted to secure a hereditary throne for himself in Syria, then he had to earn the support of its clergy. Faisal started his rule by distributing favours to the *ulema* (the unelected body of Islamic scholars), like evacuating the Tanqiz Mosque, which had been used as a military barrack during the Great War, and making the Islamic judge Sheikh Taj al-Din al-Hasani secretary-general of the newly established Royal Palace.[5] He also appointed Muhib al-Din al-Khatib, a Salafi cleric, as editor-in-chief of the government mouthpiece, al-'Asima newspaper.[6] A third cleric, Sheikh Rashid Rida, was subsequently installed speaker of the Syrian parliament in May 1920.

Faisal promised his subjects to abide by the rules of Islam, making the Quran his constitution and the behavior of the Prophet his benchmark. Mohammad's actions are considered the ultimate benchmark for all good Muslims, referred to in Arabic as *Sunnat Rasoul Allah*. That applied to everything from prayer and dress code to decision-making in times of war and peace. In honour of his family lineage and proclaimed piousness, Syrian clerics did not hesitate to offer Faisal the *ba'yah*, an oath of allegiance by Muslims to their sovereign. They put themselves, their families and their wealth at Faisal's disposal, even before knowing exactly what kind of government he was planning to establish in Damascus. Was he going to proclaim himself sultan, as the Ottomans had been for four solid decades, or caliph, as mandatory in Islam? The notion of a president, let alone a republic, did not cross his mind nor that of his subjects. Republicanism was alien to the entire Arab World and never had Muslims experienced it throughout their long history (with exception of the Tripolitarian Republic of Libya that emerged after the First World War).

The Great Arab Revolt 1916–18

Emir Faisal was born in the city of Taif, southeast of Mecca, on 20 May 1883. His father, Sharif Hussein, was a Meccan notable who in 1892 was summoned to the Imperial Capital and appointed to an advisory board at the palace of Sultan 'Abdulhamid II. At the age of nine, Faisal moved to Istanbul, where he lived with his father and elder brothers, Emir 'Ali and Emir 'Abdullah. It is during that tender period of his life that Faisal first came into contact with Syrians, who in future years were to become his subjects and foremost enthusiasts. The first Syrian he got to know was a lecturer at the Istanbul Military Academy named Safwat al-'Awwa, who taught him Ottoman grammar, geography and Islamic history.[7] Another Syrian, Sheikh Mohammad Qahib Alban, tutored him in Arabic, while his father handled his Quranic studies.

At twenty-one, Faisal married his cousin, Huzaima Bint Nasser, whose sister Misbah was married to his brother Emir 'Abdullah.[8] In 1912, Faisal and 'Abdullah were elected MPs in the Ottoman Parliament. Four years later, they switched careers at the command of their father, taking up arms in the Great Arab Revolt. Sharif Hussein had been appointed emir of Mecca in 1908, but came to blows with the Committee of Union and Progress (CUP) in Istanbul. He was singled out by the British as early as 1914 to assist them in bringing down the Ottoman Empire. The Arab Revolt was the product of ten letters exchanged between Sharif Hussein and Sir Henry McMahon, the British high commissioner to Egypt. The first was dated July 1915; the last, March 1916. The agreement stipulated that in exchange for launching a military revolt against the Ottomans, Sharif Hussein and his male children would be given a hereditary throne in all Arab territory liberated from the Ottoman Empire. Hussein interpreted that this would mean him becoming king of the Hejaz, while his sons, Faisal and ʿAbdullah, would be enthroned in Syria and Iraq.[9] Part of that agreement was fulfilled with Hussein's crowning as king of Mecca in 1916 and the subsequent enthronement of Faisal in Syria two years later. Since the future of Iraq was still uncertain due to a brewing Shiite rebellion against the British, its fate was postponed until an unspecified date, leaving its sovereign-in-waiting, Emir ʿAbdullah, with the job of foreign minister in the kingdom of the Hejaz.

The Great Arab Revolt lasted from 10 June 1916 until Sharif Hussein's troops entered Damascus with the Allied forces on 1 October 1918. Shortly before its final wrap-up, while Faisal was camped near Maʾan (present-day Jordan) in late August, he received two haggard Damascenes who had fled their city to take up arms with the Hashemites. One was Tahseen Qadri, a 26-year-old defector from the Ottoman Army, along with his younger brother Ahmad. They were to become his closest advisers in future years, with Tahseen serving as military escort to the king and Ahmad as adviser and doctor. Other Syrians were already enlisted in Faisal's army, like the Bakri brothers, Nasib and Fawzi, and the tribal leader, Fayez al-Ghusayn. With these men by his side, Faisal marched into Damascus on 3 October 1918, establishing a government in the name of his father, Sharif Hussein.

Faisal was an impassioned young man with plenty of war medals pinned to his uniform, both by his father and Colonel Lawrence. Many Syrians looked up to him as a liberator and war hero. He also enjoyed full religious legitimacy, a must for becoming king in any Muslim country. Family lineage was no simple matter in Muslim society. It could make or break any person's bid for power, and in Faisal's case, it was a cornerstone on which he based his entire claim to the throne of Syria. Sunni Muslims were desperately looking for a caliph, now that the Ottoman sultan, who claimed to be the legitimate successor of the prophet, was officially no longer their sovereign. Some continued to see him as an imported king who knew very little about the country. Others were worried by his connections to the British, and it was an open secret that Faisal admired European ways of life. He was rumoured to lead a westernized lifestyle within his own home, teaching his children, for example, how to sing and play the piano. Faisal was a newcomer to the city, having only visited twice during the Great War. Apart from the handful of Syrians who had fought with him, he didn't know the people of Damascus or their ways of life. He also spoke with a heavy Bedouin accent, very different from that of his new subjects.

Hashemite rule in Syria

Faisal's first action in Damascus was to stop at Marjeh Square, where Djemal Pasha had executed twenty-one Arab nationalists back in May 1916. Standing solemnly before its tall column and miniature mosque, he read verses from the Quran, praying for the souls of those who had perished under the Ottomans. He then headed to the Umayyad Mosque along with Sheikh Hussein Faqfaq, a Meccan scholar who had accompanied him the Hejaz, and who was now appointed as the emir's *imam* (guide) in Syria.[10] Faisal wanted to come across as a pious Muslim, praying five times a day and not serving alcohol at his dinner table.[11]

His wife was kept away from all official functions, including his coronation, and when appearing in public in Damascus, she always wore a conservative headscarf.[12] She only took it off and assumed the title of queen of Iraq in the mid-1920s although her sister was recognized as queen of Jordan from 1921 until her death in 1961. One could easily spot the difference when comparing his tenure to that of his Egyptian counterpart, King Fouad I, whose wife, Nazli Sabri, had taken on the title of 'sultana' before she became Queen of Egypt. She was to eventually interfere in matters of state and send tongues wagging in Cairo over a love affair with the king's head of diwan. There was no queen in Syria and Faisal had no intention of antagonizing conservative Muslims for the sake of his wife.

From all over the Arab world, forward-looking men flocked to Damascus to get their share of the new government. High-ranking military posts went to Iraqis, while cabinet offices were occupied by Syrian, Lebanese and Palestinians. Rida Pasha al-Rikabi was appointed military governor and Yusuf al-'Azma, a former commander of Ottoman troops in Bulgaria, became minister of war.[13] At thirty-six, he was the youngest of Faisal's ministers. To give his government a pan-Arab character, he appointed Sa'id al-Husseini, a Palestinian notable from Jerusalem, as his first foreign minister and Yassin Pasha al-Hashemi, a decorated Iraqi general, as his army chief-of-staff.

Paris, 1919

Having barely settled in Damascus, Faisal travelled to France for the international post-war conference, deputizing on the behalf of his father who said that he was too busy finishing off the revolt in Arabia to attend the convention. Faisal had no experience to date in international affairs. His career in politics was restricted to his brief 1912 tenure as MP in the Ottoman Parliament. He had begged Sharif Hussein not to go to Paris and to send Emir 'Abdullah instead.[14] Faisal had never travelled beyond Arab territory and, although fluent in French, felt that he was not ready to face powerful world leaders like France's George Clemenceau and Britain's Lloyd George. When he arrived at the port of Marseilles on board the British ship, *Gloucester*, nobody in the French government knew what to do with the Arab prince. His name was not on the list of invitees, and he claimed to represent a nation that nobody in the international community recognized as independent. The young emir panicked. Lord Derby, the British ambassador to Paris, swiftly contacted the Foreign Office, asking them to grant him an on-the-spot entry permission. The French said that they could not welcome him as head of state. He would be treated as a royal guest, a son of Sharif Hussein and a friend of Great Britain. He would also be allowed to address the Paris Conference, which was due to open in six weeks, but would have no say over any of its decisions.[15]

A progressive leader

At home, Faisal proved a very progressive leader. He never differentiated between sects and religions, treating his subjects as Syrian citizens with equal rights and duties. When staffers tried to introduce a guest through his religious background, Faisal would cut them off saying: 'I want to hear that he is Syrian. Anything further than that does not concern me.'[16] He ordered that the mention of religion is omitted from Syrian IDs, and in the first government established under his role, Christians were given important posts. Fares al-Khoury became minister of finance, while the Latakia judge, Yusuf al-Hakim, became minister of commerce. A Christian from Deir al-Qamar in present-day Lebanon, Iskandar ʿAmmoun, was made head of municipality, while another from Choueifat, Saʾid Shuqayr, became director of finance. A Palestinian Christian named ʿIssa ʿIssa was made scribe at the royal palace.[17] When Faisal visited the Maronite lawyer Yusuf Nammour at his home in Zahle in the Beqqa Valley, Christian residents said that he looked like Jesus Christ, pointing to his black beard and frail body. The parallel did not annoy Faisal – a direct descendant of the Prophet Mohammad. On the contrary he seemed to enjoy it, especially after hearing it again from President Woodrow Wilson in Paris.[18]

Faisal also reached out to Muslim Shiites through his Shiite adviser Rustom Haydar, a native of Baalbak, making their sacred occasions an official event, attended by government officials. He gave asylum to Sayyid Mohammad al-Sadr, an Iraqi Shiite prelate and, after assuming the throne of Baghdad, appointed him to the Council of Elders. He also appointed the Druze warrior Sultan al-Atrash as one of his advisers, and another Druze statesman, Emir ʿAdel Arslan, as deputy to the military governor of Syria.

The Faisalilian era set the foundations of the modern Syrian state, and all future leaders built upon what it established during its brief rule in Damascus. The civil service was expanded to 13,000 employees.[19] Faisal created ministries from scratch, with special attention to the portfolios of finance, interior, foreign affairs and war. His main achievements include Arabizing the civil service, reopening the faculties of medicine and law, and establishing an Arab Language Assembly to promote and protect the Arab language. It was the first of its kind in the Arab World, inaugurated at *al-Maktaba al-ʿAdiliyya*, a thirteenth-century school behind the Umayyad Mosque. A namesake with similar functions was only founded in Egypt in 1932. Under Faisal, a Jewish newspaper emerged in Damascus, with half its editorials published in Hebrew.[20] Faisal personally had it licensed, fighting off pressure from conservative Muslims. He made routine visits to the Greek Orthodox Church in Old Damascus and to *Haret al-Yahud*, the Jewish quarter, frequently meeting Chief Rabbi Yaacoub al-Dannoun. He also made sure to give the newly elected chamber of deputies a bigger role in decision-making, transforming politics from talk of the elite into a topic debated at the cafes, public baths and within the homes of Damascus.

Three blocs emerged in Faisal's parliament, not entirely loyal to him. One was headed by conservatives and religious clerics, and it included his bureau chief Sheikh Taj al-Din al-Hasani, the Salafi cleric Sheikh Rashid Rida and Sheikh 'Abdul Qader al-Khatib, preacher at the Umayyad Mosque. A second bloc was led by young impassioned nationalists from al-Fatat, the secret underground society founded by Arab students in Paris in 1911. This group included Sa'adallah al-Jabiri of Aleppo and Riad al-Solh of Sidon, who were to become future prime ministers of Syria and Lebanon. In 1919, Jabiri was twenty-six, and Solh was twenty-four. The third bloc was made up of an elder generation of notables who had held high posts under the Ottoman Empire, like Mirii Pasha al-Mallah and 'Abdul Rahman Pasha al-Yusuf, who saw Faisal as amateur and too populist for their aristocratic taste.

The coronation

On 8 March 1920, the Syrian Congress crowned Faisal as king, declaring the day as Syria's official Independence Day.[21] Two ceremonies were prepared for the event: one public, to take place at the Damascus Municipality, and the second private at the al-Muhajireen Palace, attended by Faisal, his family and royal entourage. Neither event was too fancy or dramatized beyond the collective cognitive understanding of Damascene society, but they were kept rather simple. Ahead of the coronation, a talented Damascene calligrapher, Abu Suleiman al-Khayyat, was commissioned to decorate a special section of the second floor of the palace with Islamic inscriptions.[22] It was separated from the rest of the living quarters, and furnished with brocade-covered sofas inlaid with mother of pearl and ornate walls. Faisal's staff called it the Throne Room – although there was no throne in Faisal's kingdom, and no crown.[23] One wall carried the inscription 'Justice is the Basis of all Rule', a famous quote from the fourteenth-century Arab philosopher Ibn Khaldun.'[24] The Throne Room lived far longer than Faisal in Damascus, and remains standing as of 2023.

All over Damascus, posters were plastered on walls with the detailed schedule of the coronation, which was due to begin at exactly 2.00 pm on 8 March 1920. Notables were required to show up in dark morning suits decorated with Ottoman medals and sashes, and they were seated in the front rows facing Faisal, who reached the City Hall in Marjeh Square in a coach driven by two white Arabian horses. Preceding him were members of the Syrian Congress, also in horse-driven coaches. As their entourage moved slowly through the heavy enthusiastic crowd, people chanted: '*Aash al-Malik*' (Long Live the King). Faisal was perched on a small platform with a draped canopy, wearing his military fatigues from the Great Arab Revolt, covered with a white scarf and black robe.[25] Standing next to him was his eight-year-old son Emir Ghazi (technically the future king of Syria), along with the Mufti Sheikh Atallah al-Kasm, the Greek Orthodox Patriarch Gregarious IV Ḥaddad and the Chief Rabbi Yaacoub al-Dannoun.

The rituals were performed by speaker of the Syrian Congress Hashem al-Atasi and its secretary, ʿIzzat Darwaza, who addressed the crowds from a balcony overlooking Marjeh Square.[26] The speaker and his secretary pledged allegiance to their new king, who, in return, made them an oath of his own: to obey God, respect all religions and uphold equality of all his subjects.[27] The markets of Damascus remained open for three festive nights, and evening parades were staged throughout major Syrian cities.

The highlight of the ceremony was when an official stamp was sent to the royal guests in a sealed envelope, issued by the Department of Posts & Telegraphs. It carried the proclamation of Faisal as king of Syria with the words: 'In Commemoration of United Syria's Independence.' Some claim that up to 750 stamps were issued on that day, equal to the number of guests, although the actual number has never been confirmed. It was pasted onto an official letter signed by Hasan al-Hakim, director of Posts & Telegraphs.

As the coronation ceremony was taking place in Marjeh Square, 101 celebratory shots were fired into the skies of Damascus from Mount Qassioun. As the cannon fire boomed, marking the beginning of Faisal's rule as sovereign, employees at the Department of Posts & Telegraphs were stamping the document carrying Hasan al-Hakim's signature. When the last cannon ended, they all rose in choreographed order and broke their stamps in two, signalling that the ceremony was over.[28] This was strange ceremony for Syria, unheard of before and never practised after. It was loosely based on the Lord Chamberlain of Buckingham Palace breaking his wand to mark the end of his service to the British monarch. Faisal had never attended a monarch's coronation in his life but may have heard of its rituals from his British friends, Colonel Lawrence and Gertrude Bell. The 'wand breaking ceremony' had last been practised at King Edward VII's funeral in London in 1910, exactly ten years before Faisal's crowning in Damascus. Syrian protocol seems to have copied the ceremony, although in reverse, using it to mark the beginning of Faisal's reign.

Women's rights

The city of Damascus got a total of eleven MPs in the Syrian Congress of 1919–20. Two of them were Christians and one was a Jew. The Syrian Parliament held its first session at the Arab Club in a modern upscale part of Damascus, before it moved to ʿAbed Building in Marjeh Square. Several progressive discussions were held at ʿAbed Building after Faisal's coronation. Although they did not lead to laws, the mere raising of such ideas shows how avant-gardist the Faisalian era really was. One was related to the *hijab* and another to women's rights, raised after a number of Syrian ladies petitioned the king asking for the right to vote and run for public office.[29] Many countries, far more advanced than Syria, had not yet granted women's suffrage. In the United States, women voting was allowed in some states but had not yet become federal law. It only became such after amendment of the US Constitution in August 1920, four months after the topic was raised in Syria. During the First World War, Germany had given its women the right to vote, and so did Austria and Sweden. In the UK, voting was restricted to women above the age of thirty. In Belgium, women could vote in municipality elections but not for parliament. The topic raised eyebrows in Syria and was vetoed by the conservative bloc of Islamic MPs. The chamber's speaker Hashem al-Atasi asked that the subject be postponed until a future session, which never happened due to the French invasion in July 1920.[30]

The French ultimatum

On 14 July 1920, King Faisal sent a cable to the French high commissioner Henri Gouraud, congratulating him on the anniversary of the French Revolution, the Bastille Day. Gouraud replied with a cordial message, followed by a strong-worded ultimatum, asking Faisal to dismantle the Arab government in preparation for establishing the French Mandate in Syria.[31] This was based on the Sykes-Picot Agreement of 1916, which gave Syria and Lebanon to France as mandates – a wartime deal between Paris and London that was to eventually cost Faisal his throne. Gouraud's ultimatum required Faisal to hand over a major railway to the French Army, confiscate arms from the locals and arrest those who were perceived as anti-French.[32] But most importantly it demanded that Faisal disband the small army that he had just created, headed by war minister, Yusuf al-ʿAzma. He was given a deadline to meet those demands, until midnight on 19 July, or suffer the wrath of the French Army.[33] In perhaps what was to be one of the king's most controversial decisions, he said yes to all of Gouraud's dictates, hoping that this might help save his throne.

Cabinet ministers and army generals pleaded him to reconsider, saying that they could hold off the French Army until the British intervened to stop the attack. Faisal knew better. By then he had come to the realization that Great Britain was not going to lift a finger for his sake, or that of Syria. If forced to choose between him and France, it would go for the French. With that in mind, the king accepted all of Gouraud's demands in writing, and gave orders for the Syrian Army to disband.[34] Soldiers were ordered to surrender their arms to the nearest army office, and those who refused were fined and arrested. Furious, the war minister resigned in protest. On 19 July, Atasi announced a royal decree suspending the Syrian National Congress for two months.[35]

Gouraud was not ready to accommodate Faisal, however. He sent word to the king saying that his letter of acceptance had arrived past the given deadline and its extension, ordering his troops to continue their march towards Damascus from the Beqqa Valley.[36] The king was left with no option but to fight back. His acceptance of Gouraud's ultimatum, and the abrupt dissolve of the armed forces, had triggered a mini-revolt in Syria. Young men took to the streets, calling him a traitor. These were the same Syrians who had shouted his long life and good health less than two years aback. Some stormed police stations to steal weapons, saying that if the king would not defend Syria, then they would take up the duty themselves. Faisal wrote to his father in Mecca saying: 'The revolt has reached the gates of Damascus.'[37]

A suggested coup in 1920?

Some even touted his half-brother Emir Zayd as a possible replacement to Faisal. Zayd was a young man, at twenty-one, who had served with Sharif Hussein in the Great Arab Revolt.[38] Pro-Zayd demonstrations were staged in Damascus, which were suppressed by the king.[39] One of Faisal's staunchest supporters, the Lebanese intellectual As'ad Dagher, wrote in his memoirs: 'I think that Emir Zayd, had he been older, could have been the savior due to the great support that he enjoyed throughout the country.'[40] Dagher adds that angry Syrians went as far as trying to talk War Minister Yusuf al-'Azma into staging a military coup against Faisal. Dagher secretly met Emir Zayd, saying: 'The situation requires a strong hand. We *need* a dictator.'[41] He was implying of course that 'Azma dethrones Faisal and replaces him with Zayd. Had the two men been lured into such an adventurous project, then it might have saved the country from the Battle of Maysaloun and, perhaps, from twenty years of French occupation. Had they staged a coup in 1920, they would have preceded that of Husni al-Za'im, which only came in 1949 and was considered the first of its kind in Syria.

The Higher National Committee

After being chastened by Gouraud, the king ordered 'Azma to retract his resignation and re-mobilize the armed forces. It was already too late. Many soldiers had returned to their towns and villages, while others had already joined the underground. The only people who could pull the country back together, he reasoned, were the clerics – the *ulema* – whom he had turned to when first entering Syria. The king then created the Higher National Committee, a gathering of mosque preachers, Islamic teachers and scholars, charged with recruiting, training and arming volunteers, and raising funds for the war effort.[42] It was headed by a Damascus cleric named Kamel al-Qassab, who, at fifty-nine, was one of the most respected names in Syria.[43] He owned and ran a religious school in the Bzurieh Market, named after him, *al-Kamiliyya*, and his disciples held important posts throughout the country. Dressed in Islamic garb, with white turban and a navy-blue *abaya* (cloak), Qassab showed up at Faisal's palace, promising 10,000 fighters and 300 gold coins for arms procurement.[44] Given repeated delays in cash payments from Mecca, Faisal couldn't hide his smile, nor turn down such a generous offer. Since arriving in Syria, he had relied heavily on regular stipends from his father, which, when delayed, led to chronic shortages in the Syrian treasury. During that summer, the Syrian kingdom hadn't paid the salaries of soldiers and civil servants for three months. Faisal was broke and couldn't even settle the bill for his palace furniture, a measly 733 dirhams.[45] He needed the money badly, and the fighters, to save his throne. None of the young politicians who surrounded Faisal could meet Qassab's offer, nor could his old friends in al-Fatat.

Qassab suggested passing a law for forced military conscription, applicable to all able-bodied men aged fifteen to fifty.[46] He also wanted Faisal to allocate the entire state revenue for what remained of the year 1920 for the purchase of arms.[47] The king signed off both requests, without hesitation. The Higher National Committee quickly became a shadow parliament, calling for elections to choose members for its general assembly. They divided Damascus into eighty-four neighbourhoods, electing four members for each, mainly from big religious families like the Hamzawis, Ustwanis and Tabbas.[48] It had only two Christians on its steering committee, Tawfiq Shamiyya and Father Mikhail Shehadeh, and one secular Muslim, a Damascus notable named Sami Pasha Mardam Bey.[49]

Faisal ordered Qassab to 'militarize the nation and transform its streets into one big military barrack'.[50] Qassab then penned bylaws for his organization, saying that all Syrians were bound by birth, both legally and patriotically, to the Higher National Committee. Defying its orders would be a capital offence, punishable by jail.[51] And finally, Faisal imposed a tax, at Qassab's urging, 2 per cent on the net income of rich Syrians, to bankroll the Higher Committee.[52] It would apply to the large landowning families like the Yusufs, Mardam Beys and 'Azms of Damascus, the Barazis and Shishaklis of Hama, and the Mallahs and Jabiris of Aleppo.

Heading the chamber of deputies by then was Sheikh Rashid Rida, who had succeeded Hashem al-Atasi in May 1920.[53] A Salafi cleric, Rida was a household name among Islamists, well known as publisher of the Cairo-based *al-Manar* periodical, a flagship for Salafi literature. As parliament speaker, he was tasked with debating and adopting Syria's new constitution, which had just been penned by Hashem al-Atasi. To Faisal's dismay, the royal charter had greatly limited his powers, transforming him into a constitutional monarch. Although the Syrian throne was guaranteed for him and his male lineage, the constitution had empowered the chamber of deputies at his expense, giving lawmakers the right to declare war and peace, and to dethrone the king if he failed to meet Syria's national aspirations. He did not appreciate the trappings of democracy that came with the new charter, rejecting a clause that forced him to obtain parliamentary approval for all his decrees. 'Who are you?' he aggressively asked Rashid Rida, adding 'I am the one who created Syria'.[54] That of course is what Faisal believed.

The Maysaloun fiasco

In a last-ditch effort to save his kingdom, Faisal sent his trusted Education Minister Sati al-Husri to Aley for talks with General Gouraud.[55] The minister returned to Damascus, empty-handed. On Saturday, 24 July, Faisal's tiny army clashed with the French at the Khan Maysaloun pass on the Damascus-Beirut road, twenty-five kilometres west of the Syrian capital. The Syrian Army was composed of 850 soldiers, commanded by General Tahseen Pasha al-Faqir. It included sixty-four foot soldiers, sixty Royal Guards, twenty cannon soldiers and sixty horsemen. The rest of the troops were 300 volunteer civilians.[56] On the opposite side of the battle stood the formidable French Army, with 9,000 soldiers, 48 cannons, 100 transport trucks, 15 tanks and 5 aeroplanes.[57] More than 1,000 Syrians had volunteered to fight, but failed to show up on the day of Maysaloun. The 10,000 fighters that Kamel Qassab had promised Faisal did not show up for battle. Only a handful of prelates answered his call, like Sheikh ʿAbdul Qader Kiwan, who had just returned from jihad in Libya, having fought the Italians with Libyan resistance leader ʿOmar al-Mukhtar.[58]

The Maysaloun battle left behind 1,100–1,200 Syrians dead, including 120 volunteers and War Minister Yusuf al-ʿAzma.[59] He was the only officer killed from the Syrian side. It was King Faisal's first, and last, defeat in battle. Its outcome, and the massacre of Syrian troops, sealed the king's fate in Syria. It also created a permanent scar in the psyche of the Syrian nation that continued to haunt him for years. Less than twenty-four hours after the guns went silent, French soldiers marched into Damascus, playing their national anthem, *Les Marseillais*. Syrian officials were waiting for them at the gates of al-Mezzeh, a small village near the capital (now a major neighbourhood). Only this time, they weren't carrying arms but white flags. Two members of the king's inner circle, Nuri al-Saʾid and Jamil al-Ulshi, presented the French commanding officer with the keys of Damascus, saying that the city was open to him and his troops, and they could enter whenever they pleased, in peace.[60] Both were to become future prime ministers, Ulshi in Syria that November and Nuri Pasha in Iraq starting in 1930. One of Faisal's field officers, Subhi al-ʿOmari, who had fought with him first in the Arab Revolt and then at Maysaloun, bitterly recalled the defeat, saying: 'How painful it was when we left Damascus, which we had entered two years ago with the joy of conquest and liberation, to leave it now, overwhelmed with disappointment.'[61] Fires had broken out at the Hamidieh Market, threatening to devour the city's old bazaars, identical to the ones triggered by the Ottomans before they had withdrawn from Damascus in September 1918.

Upon hearing the terrible news from Maysaloun, Faisal fled to the nearby village of al-Kisweh, south of Damascus, with a small handful of officials including Prime Minister Atasi, the Qadri brothers and head of the Royal Diwan, Ihsan al-Jabiri. They spent the night sleeping on the wooden benches of a train, dinning on crusty bread with their king. Young men took turns at guarding him, fearing a commando operation by the French to take his life. From al-Kisweh, Faisal moved to the Houran province, where he stayed in the city of Daraa. Until then, he still believed that all was not lost and he could still reach a compromise that would return him to the throne. He had taken none of his personal belongings, under the assumption that this was nothing but a short exile. On 26 July, French warplanes flew over Daraa, dropping leaflets warning residents from the consequences of hosting Faisal. They were asked to evict him immediately or suffer an attack by the French Army.

Before departing, the forlorn monarch signed his final decree as king of Syria, naming ʿAlaa al-Din al-Droubi as prime minister. At fifty, Droubi was an experienced civil servant from the midland city of Homs who had served as Ottoman ambassador to the Balkans. Faisal hoped that in his new capacity as prime minister, he could reach a settlement with the French. Droubi was the first to backstab him, however, instructing the king that he ought to leave Syria for good, and never to return. He held a banquet in Gouraud's honour at the Grand Serail, dropping the title of 'King' when referring to Faisal, addressing him simply as 'al-Sharif'.[62] When the royal car tried to fill up at a military gas station, they were denied entry by soldiers.[63] Faisal sent an envoy to reclaim his gas reserves, but he was cut off with the words, 'We don't recognize him as king anymore'.[64]

On 1 August 1920, the ex-king headed to British-controlled Haifa in Palestine.[65] Before crossing the border, he took a long hard look at the country that he now considered home, and which he was never to visit again for the remainder of his life.

Post-Syria

The first hint that the British were thinking of how to compensate Faisal for his loss came as early as 31 July 1920, one day before he left Syria. It was mentioned in a despatch to London from the British civilian administrator of Iraq, Andrew Wilson.[66] In Haifa, Faisal was hosted at the home of a certain British lady, Miss Newton, while his entourage was lodged at Nassar Hotel. He wrote to his father explaining what had just happened in Syria: 'We were forced to show lenience, given that their troops were superior to ours. My life was in danger. People walked towards the frontline with no arms, and we couldn't stop them. The people of Syria preferred death to surrender.' Sharif Hussein wrote five letters to world capitals objecting to the humiliating manner in which his son had been ejected from Syria, saying that it 'wasted my dignity and compromised my honor'.[67]

Faisal immediately set out on contacting his old British friends. They all said that His Majesty's Government was still committed to its wartime promises and that it considered Faisal a friend of London. Clearly from the cables of General Edmond Allenby, who had orchestrated the Great Arab Revolt with Sharif Hussein and accompanied Faisal to Damascus in 1918, their private views were completely different. He wrote to London saying that he has no advice to give his former friend, warning that any official contact with Faisal might harm British-French relations. He even suggested putting him on the next train back to the Hejaz, and severing all correspondences.[68]

At this low point, Faisal learned that Prime Minister Lloyd George was travelling to Switzerland to attend a meeting at the League of Nations that November. Faisal decided to meet him in person, travelling to Egypt, from where he would sail to Napoli, then Switzerland. King Fouad of Egypt no longer recognized him as king of Syria and, thus, sent no royal guard to welcome him at Port Said. Faisal was seen at the Egyptian port, leaning on his luggage, like any ordinary passenger.[69] He needed official documents to cross into Europe, since the French had just cancelled his Syrian passport, so his father sent him a diplomatic passport from the Hejaz Kingdom.

On 25 August, the king docked at the port of Napoli. From there he headed first to Rome, then to Milan, only to receive word from the British that Lloyd George would be unable to receive him in Geneva.[70] He was asked to stay in Italy and wait for an invitation to visit London. Faisal did just that, taking up residence at a villa near Como Lake, close to the Swiss borders. This is where he stayed for the next three months. He was so frustrated with the endless wait that he threatened to reach out to the USSR if the British continued to treat him with such disrespect.[71] Sharif Hussein sent him a letter saying that he should just pack up and return to the Hejaz. Faisal said no, claiming that he would rather die than return to the Arabian Desert as an ordinary citizen.[72] On 21 November, he sent a letter to Lord George Curzon, Britain's foreign minister, saying that if Lloyd George would not receive him, then he would like to meet King George V. Nuri al-Sa'id carried the letter to London, and its response came exactly two weeks later, on 1 November 1920. It said that the king of England was ready to receive the former king of Syria.

Many had lobbied on Faisal's behalf in London, including Lord Curzon and Colonel Lawrence, who was writing favourable articles about him in the British press, namely *The Observer* and *The Times*. Lawrence wrote saying that Faisal was a loyal friend of the British and they shouldn't abandon him at any cost. The Director of Protocol at Buckingham Palace gave Faisal strict instructions on how to address King George V, along with a list of topics that ought to be avoided. Prime on the list was what had just happened to him in Syria. Faisal decided to put on a Western suit, abandoning his Arab cloak and headgear. Lord Curzon asked: 'Where is your splendid *abaya*?' Faisal answered that he took it off the minute he lost his throne in Damascus. The British minister replied: 'Don't worry, you will wear a new one.'[73] On 9 December 1920, the British formally approached him with the idea of becoming king of Iraq.

He took up the offer, gladly, and was crowned sovereign of Baghdad on 23 August 1921, exactly 388 days after leaving his throne in Syria. A handful of Syrians crossed the border to Iraq to work with him. The ever-loyal Sati al-Husri took charge of writing Iraq's curriculum and establishing the Faculty of Law at Baghdad University. Subhi al-Omari was tasked with establishing the Iraqi armed forces, while Ahmad Qadri was made Iraqi consul to France. His brother, Tahseen, continued to serve as military escort to Faisal until his death. All of them were given Iraqi passports. In her memoirs, Faisal's niece, Princess Badi'a Bint 'Ali, wrote of Faisal's Syria obsession saying: 'My uncle continued to think fondly of Syria until the end. Within the family, we used to say that he continued to covet the throne in Damascus, perhaps because its people showed greater obedience to his rule, far more than the Iraqis.'[74]

In Baghdad, he ordered the construction of the two-floor Qasr al-Zuhoor palace, which was similar in size to the one he left behind in Damascus, but far less impressive in terms of architecture. It was subsequently destroyed by the US invasion of 2003. In 1937, his son and successor King Ghazi built the al-Rihab

Palace in Baghdad, where members of the royal family were massacred during the 14 July Revolution of 1958. In its gardens, Faisal's grandson, King Faisal II, was shot to death.

The comeback that never happened

Even as king of Iraq, Faisal never forgot Syria. Nor did any of his brothers and nephews, who considered themselves as the legitimate and only royal family in Damascus. When talk of restoring the Syrian monarchy surfaced in the early 1930s, they each sent letters to the French, marketing themselves as kings-in-waiting, ready to reassume the throne of Damascus. In September 1931, Faisal travelled to Paris for talks with the director-general of the Quai d'Orsay, Philippe Berthelot.[75] He had already raised the subject with Berthelot at least once before in November 1925.[76] By now, Faisal was no longer the Bedouin prince that Syrians had known in 1918. Urbanization had been good to him. He wore custom-made suits designed exclusively by the best tailors of London, and dabbled in English, speaking with the wisdom of a sovereign who had been in power for almost fifteen years.

Faisal told the French official: 'I know the people of Syria well. They love me and would accept nobody else as king.'[77] Faisal suggested merging Syria and Iraq under his crown, and that he alternate between Damascus and Baghdad, spending six months in each capital. The premiership would go to a Syrian, he said, while army command would be held by an Iraqi officer. The prime minister would get two Iraqi deputies, and the speaker of parliament would be an Iraqi with two Syrian deputies. Remaining government posts would be neatly divided between Syria and Iraq, while the two armies would merge into one.[78] Backing him were members of the Damascus ulema, who claimed that Islam knew no other form of government than a king, sultan or caliph. So did retired officers who looked next door at the Iraqi Army under Faisal. They saw that their Iraqi counterparts were well fed, well paid and well trained, all thanks to Faisal. They hoped that if he returned to Syria, they would earn similar perks and bonuses.[79] Syrian republicans lobbied aggressively against the idea, however, with Shukri al-Quwatli saying: 'Hasn't the Faisal interlude proven its faults? An imported king will not do! Syria needs to be ruled by a native of Syria, a president who is made in Syria, and not one created by the French or the British.'[80]

The idea never materialized, and the French eventually settled for a republic in Syria. King Faisal died in Switzerland at the age of fifty-three, on 8 September 1933. The medical report mentioned a ruptured artery caused by advanced arteriosclerosis. One year before Faisal's death, Iraq had been formally admitted to the League of Nations on 3 October 1932. Until the very last days of his life, he had continued to receive Syrian visitors at his private quarters at the Bellevue Palace Hotel in Berne, treating them affectionately as his loyal subjects. His first question would be: 'Tell me, how are things in Syria?' Former associates like Emir 'Adel Arslan and Ihsan al-Jabiri were the last Syrians Faisal saw before his death. Two of his former officers, 'Aref Pasha al-Idlibi and Rida Pasha al-Rikabi, went as far as to create a monarchical party in Damascus called *Hizb al-Ummah al-Malaki*, whose only programme was to restore the Hashemite crown to Syria. News of his death caused both men to collapse, both physically and politically. Black banners were raised on the balconies of government buildings in Damascus, while flags were flown at half-mast on the Grand Serail. A moment of silence was observed in the Syrian Chamber of Deputies, called for by Speaker Subhi Barakat.[81] President Mohammad ʿAli al-ʿAbed eulogized the late king as the founder of Syria's independence.

Today, nearly a century after Faisal's death, there is one street carrying his name in central Damascus, bestriding the city's chamber of commerce. The date of his coronation was officially proclaimed a national holiday in 1920, also considered as benchmark of Syrian independence from the Ottoman Empire. The French made it an ordinary day, but many Syrians continued to celebrate it in private until 1946, when Syria got its formal independence from the French Mandate. In 1963, the date of Faisal's crowning was replaced with the coup of the Ba'ath Party. Since then, 8 March has been officially observed as 'anniversary of the Ba'ath Revolution'. No mention is made of King Faisal I.

Figure 3 King Faisal.

Part II

HEADS OF STATE UNDER THE FRENCH MANDATE 1920-46

Chapter 4

SUBHI BARAKAT (1922–5)

On Sunday 18 October 1925, 400 armed horsemen marched into Damascus, heading for the ʿAzm Palace in the heart of the Old City. This was just months into the Great Syrian Revolt, staged against the mandate regime by Druze leader Sultan Pasha al-Atrash. The rebels had fallen prey to a rumour that the French commissioner Maurice Sarrail would be spending the day at the palace for talks with Syrian president Subhi Barakat. They had orders to arrest him and trade him off for hundreds of Syrian prisoners in French jails.

Sarrail, however, did not show up in Damascus on that day. No sooner had the rebels landed in the Bzurieh market than French forces sealed off the Old City and bombs began falling on the palace and its environs. The shelling continued non-stop for two days, whipping up a death toll of anywhere between 500 and 1,000 Syrians.[1] The Midhat Pasha and Bzurieh markets were the worst hit. The iron roof of the Hamidieh market was completely blown off, and nearly 100 yards collapsed onto the small shops. The streets of the Old City, usually busy with commercial activity, were showered with broken glass, destroyed merchandise and remains of the dead. In the neighbourhoods of Bab al-Jabieh, al-Kharab and al-Shaghour, 150 homes were destroyed.[2] The intense shelling led to the displacement of 336 Syrians.[3]

Ten days later Maurice Sarrail was recalled to France in disgrace. The French press accused him of 'liquidating Syria'. When he arrived in Paris, demonstrators marched outside his home shouting, 'Assassin!' Back in Damascus, President Subhi Barakat was subjected to similar character slaughter. Many claimed, rightfully or not, that he had shown great indifference to the bombing of the Syrian capital.

On 21 December 1925, Barakat resigned from the Syrian presidency. He was the first head of state to submit a resignation letter, setting a precedent that would be copied by six of his successors: three under the mandate and three during the independence era.

The aristocrat from Antioch

Subhi Barakat was born to an aristocratic Turkish family in 1882. Originally from Hama, his ancestors had emigrated to Antioch in 1600, eighty-four years after the Ottoman occupation of Syria. Antioch was the main city in the Sanjak of

Alexandretta, a narrow coastal plain backed by a chain of mountains on the lower valley of the Orontes River.[4] The Barakats traced their lineage back to Khaled Ibn al-Walid, the legendary Muslim warrior and companion of the Prophet Mohammad, who won over 100 battles while conquering Persian Mesopotamia and Roman Syria. Barakat made it customary to sign his official communiques as 'Subhi Barakat al-Khalidi'. His father, Rifaat Agha, had served as an MP for Aleppo in the Ottoman Parliament in 1908. He was close to Sultan ʿAbdulhamid II, and when he died, was buried next to Sultan Mahmud, at the graveyard of the sultans.

Subhi Barakat was the third of six children, growing up in wealth and comfort. He studied at Mektebi-Sultani in Istanbul, a famous school for the moneyed elite, and spent his early years managing his father's estates. For obvious reasons, he had little respect for the Hashemite family that rose in revolt against the Ottomans in 1916, insisting that despite its faults, the sultanate ought to be strengthened and maintained, at all costs. When nationwide elections were first held under King Faisal in 1919, Barakat nominated himself as a representative for Antioch, winning a seat on the Syrian National Congress. It was chaired by Hashem al-Atasi, who would soon become his archrival in French Mandate Syria.

Barakat took up arms with his colleague Ibrahim Hananu, leading an armed insurgency against the French, who had landed on the Syrian coast since November 1918.[5] Fighting in the Belan Pass (now in southcentral Turkey), Barakat's men were supported and armed by Mustapha Kemal (Ataturk), who dreaded the thought of a French colony on Turkey's borders. When the Hananu revolt was crushed Barakat returned to his native Antioch, making his peace with High Commissioner Henri Gouraud.

Divide and rule

Gouraud had just divided Syria into four border-free states, linked by roads, commerce and economic interdependence. They were the states of Damascus, Aleppo, the Alawite territories and, last, the Druze Mountain, which came into existence in March 1921.[6] French Prime Minister Alexander Millerand wanted eight, not just four, states for Syria, ruled by republican institutions, but Gouraud argued that eight were too difficult to control, both militarily and politically.[7] He marked the frontiers between Syria and British Palestine on one front, and with the newly created state of Greater Lebanon. Another border was drawn up with the newly created Emirate of Transjordan in April 1921, which was ruled by King Faisal's brother, Emir ʿAbdullah. The Lebanese enclave was carved out of the Syrian motherland and given independent status in the summer of 1920, while four of Syria's *cazas* (*qada'* in Arabic) – the Beqqa Valley, Hasbayya, Rashayya and Baalbak – were annexed to Greater Lebanon, with Beirut as its new capital.[8] Fares al-Khoury warned the French Commissioner's secretary-general, Robert De Caix, saying: 'I advise that you shrink Greater Lebanon and restore its Muslim territories to Syria, while keeping a Smaller Lebanon with Beirut as its capital.'[9] Faisal's last prime minister, ʿAlaa al-Din Droubi, registered an official complaint over the annexation of the four *cazas* to Lebanon.[10] Syrian officials had been dreaming of an expanded state encompassing present-day Palestine, Jordan, Lebanon and stretching up to Mosul in Iraq. They were unhappy with the mitigated borders of French Mandate Syria, unable to grasp how they would now need visas to travel to Beirut or Jerusalem, let alone accept a completely new entity created in their south called the Emirate of Transjordan. Henri Gouraud did not seem to care. He took all of these decisions unilaterally, carving up Syria without consulting any of its residents, community leaders and elders. No plebiscite was held, no referendum and no vote.

The mini-states of Syria

Damascus: On 3 September 1920 an independent state was created in Damascus (*État de Damas*).[11] With its capital being the ancient city of Damascus, this state encompassed the cities of Homs and Hama in central Syria, and the Orontes River Valley. *État de Damas* was headed by Haqqi al-'Azm, an Istanbul-trained politician born in 1864. 'Azm had been raised in Ottoman splendour, yet when he failed to win a seat in the Ottoman Parliament of 1912, moved to Cairo to establish an opposition party with his cousins.[12] With the 1920 occupation of Syria, he returned to Damascus, made friends with mandate authorities and positioned himself as a friend of colonial France. Like Subhi Barakat he was never too fond of King Faisal or of his kingdom, considering it too populist for his taste. He once described the Hashemite victory over the Ottomans as akin to that of 'barbarianism over civilization'.[13]

According to an early French census, 75 per cent of the inhabitants of the State of Damascus were Sunni Muslims (447,000 people), 11.3 per cent Christian (67,000), followed by 0.8 per cent Alawite (5,000), 0.7 per cent Druze (4,000) and a small but affluent Jewish minority. Additionally, 49,000 of the city's residents were foreigners (8.2 per cent), bringing the state's total population to just below 600,000 inhabitants in 1920.[14] The new state got its own blue flag, with a white circle in the middle and small French Flag on its upper left corner. The Damascus State, by French design, had no foreign or defence ministries. 'Azm governed with no constitution, no system of checks and balances, and no real authority. Henri Gouraud was retainer of the State of Damascus, controlling everyone and everything, including the governor. In June 1921, while accompanying Gouraud on a visit to the Golan Heights, 'Azm was wounded by a failed attempt on the general's life, carried out by a rebel named Adham Khanjar. At the gates of al-Quneitra, four horsemen disguised as gendarmerie opened fire on the French high commissioner. Gouraud ducked, but his interpreter, Lieutenant Branet, was killed. 'Azm's wounds would stand proof of his unwavering loyalty to Gouraud and the French.

Aleppo: The State of Aleppo was also created in September 1920.[15] The jewel of the crown in this large and prosperous state was the ancient city of Aleppo, located forty-five kilometres east from the Syrian-Turkish border. Dating back to the sixth millennium BC, it was a hub for regional industry under the Ottomans, and grew to become the empire's third largest city after Istanbul and Cairo. Aleppo was a magnet for traders and merchants, positioned at the western tip of the Silk Road that connected China and India to the rest of the world. This unique position made Aleppo a wealthy city until the Suez Canal was inaugurated in 1869, prompting the world to rely on sea routes for international commerce, while abandoning overland trade that went through Aleppo. The Aleppo State's borders reached east to the Euphrates River to include the city of Deir ez-Zour and its environs.

Unlike Damascus, where the city's elite accepted, and in most cases welcomed Haqqi al-'Azm's authority, Aleppo was far more resistant to its governor, Kamel Pasha al-Qudsi. A 75-year-old retired officer, he had served as Ottoman envoy to Cyprus and *mutasarrif* of Tripoli (Libya), before becoming military escort to Sultan 'Abdulhamid II, then governor of Aleppo under King Faisal.[16] Aleppo residents petitioned their king asking for Qudsi's removal, accusing him of gross nepotism and packing the bureaucracy with sixty of his relatives.[17] The French renewed his tenure just weeks after the occupation of Aleppo in July 1920.[18]

Qudsi had pursued a pacifist policy towards the mandate, urging Aleppines to accept French rule with no resistance.[19] When Qudsi was made governor, the State of Damascus objected, refusing to accept Aleppo's autonomy. Haqqi al-'Azm claimed that Kamel al-Qudsi did not have the legal authority to fire and hire officials, nullifying all decrees carrying his signature. 'Azm recognized nobody but himself as the leader of Syria, insisting on paying the salaries of Aleppo from the Damascus treasury.[20] Qudsi retaliated by firing Damascenes from the Aleppo bureaucracy and replacing them with native Aleppines.[21]

The population of the Aleppo State was mostly Arab, but it also included Kurds in its eastern region and a substantial number of Christians belonging to different congregations. The State of Aleppo was slightly more populated than Damascus, with 604,000 inhabitants in 1920. Eighty-three per cent of them were Sunni Muslims (502,000), 8.6 per cent Christians (52,000), five per cent were Alawites (30,000), 1.2 per cent Jews (7,000) and 0.5 per cent foreigners (3,000).[22] The flag of the new state was fixed in white with five yellow stars in the middle, and a small French Flag in the upper left-hand corner.[23] It was raised at a festive procession attended by Kamel al-Qudsi on 15 January 1921.[24] The five stars referred to the cities or areas that made up the State of Aleppo: Aleppo, Deir ez-Zour, the largely autonomous Sanjak of Alexandretta, Urfa and Marash (the last three now officially part of Turkey). Two of the stars were subsequently cancelled in October 1921 after signing of the Treaty of Ankara in 1921 (also known as the Franklin-Bouillon Agreement), which ceded those areas to Turkey.[25]

The Alawite State: A close-knit esoteric community dating back to the tenth century, the Alawites lived in the rugged mountains east of Syria's Mediterranean coastline. An additional cluster was based in the towns surrounding Homs and Hama, and within the Sanjak of Alexandretta.[26] Much of what outsiders knew about them was based on imagination, myth and gossip. The earliest mention of the Alawites dated back to Crusader chronicles, traveller tales and the diplomatic dispatches of European consuls stationed in the Levant. Foreigners often depicted them as a closed community that lived in fear, superstition and repression. During the fourteenth century, a controversial Damascus-based Muslim scholar named Ibn Taymiya issued a religious *fatwa* accusing them of being 'greater infidels than Jews and Christians'.[27] This controversial verdict influenced Ottoman policy towards the Alawites following their conquest of Syria. As Canadian historian Stefan Winter notes in his seminal work *A History of the 'Alawis*, a more complex relationship was to emerge in the succeeding centuries, between city-based authorities (namely the tax collectors) and the mountain-dwelling community, in which Alawite clan chiefs positioned themselves as mediators between the state and their community.[28] The Ottoman predecessors, the Mamluks, had considered the Alawites non-Muslims, trying to convert them to Sunni Islam with mass arrests and flogging. Terrible stories of brutality and injustice were passed down from one generation to the next, and continued to live in the minds and hearts of the Alawite community elders well into the 1920s, when they finally got their own state.

With the passing of time, an Alawite enclave emerged within Ottoman Syria: a place that was dramatically backward, void of any officialdom. Neither government clerks nor schoolteachers or policemen wanted to serve in the Alawite villages. Electricity came to Damascus in 1907 but did not reach the Alawite villages until the 1960s.[29] By the First World War, the Alawites were still living on agriculture, namely as landless serfs.[30] Alawite labour was cheap, and they produced cotton, silk and tobacco, an export that sold well in Europe. Most of that produce was sold by the Alawites farmers to the absentee Sunni landlords, who in turn sold it to Europe through Christian intermediaries. They made fortunes from the tobacco trade, compensating the Alawite villagers with mediocre daily salaries, often way beyond minimum wage.

Henri Gouraud created the Alawite State, first named *Territoire des Alaouites* (Territory of the Alawites), in September 1920.[31] The new state's authority would cover the coastal cities of Latakia and Tartous, and their surrounding mountain villages adjacent to Syria's Mediterranean coast. The Alawite State was divided into eight *cazaz*, each with its own prefix (*qa'im maqam*), and each *caza* was divided into *nahyas* (districts), each with its own *mudir* (director). It was the first time in history that the term 'Alawite' was coined, in parallel with 'Mohammadian', which was used by the Europeans to describe Sunni Muslims. Before that, the community had been referred to as 'Nusayris'.[32] According to a 1923 French census, population of the Alawite State stood at 101,000 Alawites, 94,000 Sunnis, 34,000 Christians and 5,000 Ismailis.[33] Sunni Muslims and Greek Orthodox Christians, who lived in mixed and overlapping villages along the Syrian coast, composed two-thirds of the Alawite State's population. They got the upper hand in the new state, given that they surpassed the Alawites in numbers, wealth and education.[34] Even with autonomy, the Alawites only made up 4 per cent of the work force in the new state now bearing their name.[35] The Alawite State, nevertheless, had all the trappings of statehood: a local government, police force, land registry and a municipality. Its inhabitants even got their own ID cards and their own flag: a yellow sun on a white ground with all corners coloured red, except for the top-left corner, which was occupied by a French Flag.[36]

Unlike Damascus and Aleppo, which both got their own local governor, the Alawite State was put under the direct command of two officers who had excelled in enforcing French rule in Morocco: Colonel Emile Niéger and General Gaston Billotte.[37] French bureaucrats were brought in to assist them, presiding over the postal service, public works, finance and customs.[38] The departments of education and justice were handled by Syrian Christian appointees of the mandate regime, not by Alawites.[39] Three French officers were given control of the local military contingent, intelligence service and the gendarmerie. A twelve-man Administrative Committee was created to help the French governor run day-to-day affairs of the Alawite State. Seven of its members were Alawites, two were Christians, one Ismaili and two were Sunni Muslims. They were handpicked by Gouraud's secretary-general Robert De Caix and their tenure would last for one year and could be renewed only by the high commissioner. Given that the Alawite territories lacked everything, from schools and clinics onto aqueducts and bridges, the cost of developing these lands was staggering: a whopping 1.2 million French Francs in 1921. Since the Alawite State treasury was empty, their first provisional budget was deducted from the coffers of Damascus, Aleppo and Beirut.

Syria's brief federal experiment

In June 1922, Gouraud decided to institutionalize the partition of Syria, on the mandate's second anniversary. This was just one month before the League of Nations formally approved the mandates of Syria and Lebanon. The name Gouraud chose was alien to the Syrian political lexicon, *Itihad al-Duwwal al-Souriyya* (Union of Syrian States), often abbreviated as *Dawlet al-Itihad* (State of the Union). Officially inaugurated on 28 June 1922, it created a federal union between the states of Damascus, Aleppo and the Alawites, based loosely on the Switzerland model.[40] Gouraud travelled from his headquarters at Qasr al-Sonobar in Beirut to attend the birth of his new project in Syria, delivering a long speech outlining objectives and structures of federal government. Most Syrians were shocked to learn that the capital of the new state would be Aleppo rather than Damascus. To please the Aleppine notability, Gouraud devised a rotating capital for *Itahad al-Duwwal al-Souriyya*, with Aleppo serving as capital first. Fares al-Khoury objected, saying: 'If you don't please the Damascenes, the situation will never stabilize in Syria. You will never rest if the heart of Damascus remains broken.'[41]

The Syrian Union federalized important sectors of government, like finance, justice, public works, land registry, religious endowments (*awqaf*), posts and telegraphs services, education and the gendarmerie.[42] Each state would get to keep its own school curriculum, flag, stamps, land ownership papers and birth certificates. On French maps, each had its distinct borders and was required to contribute 50 per cent of its annual income to other members of the union, shouldering both profit and loss.[43] The new state observed the main Muslim and Christian holidays in all three states, including Christmas, Easter and New Year's, in addition to Bastille Day (14 July), the anniversary of the French Revolution.[44]

Gouraud chose fifteen delegates for the Syrian Union's first council (five for each), who in turn were required to elect a federal president while keeping Kamel al-Qudsi and Haqqi al-'Azm at their respective posts in Aleppo and Damascus.[45] Each of the three states got one single vote on any matter of federal concern, which needed a simple majority to pass. Delegates had to meet twice a year, and their decisions were binding to all the three member states.[46]

The Syrian Union's first – and last – president

Colourful flags of the three states decorated the huge stone-arched entrance of the Aleppo Grand Serail, leading to its magnificent staircase, covered with a shining red carpet. On 11 December 1922 the fifteen delegates elected Subhi Barakat as their first president.[47] On the very same day, a demonstration was staged in the city's old bazaars, demanding admittance to the League of Nations, release of political prisoners and abolishing of the Syrian Union. Barakat tried to calm the street, twice using the word 'independence' in his opening speech. The Damascenes knew very little about him, and apart from brief visits during his tenure as member of parliament in 1919, he barely knew anything about Damascus as well. The French regarded him as an ally rather than a subordinate, always addressing him with great respect. His family wealth gave him plenty of leverage to treat the French as political equals, rather than patrons.

From Day One, Subhi Barakat proved to be a brave man. One of his close friends, 'Adel al-Solh, described him saying: 'He liked being described as chivalrous and patriarchal. If one wanted to win his favor all he had to do was to arouse these feelings within him.'[48] During the early weeks of his presidency, Damascus nationalists dared him to set foot in their city, threatening to kill him if he does, accusing him of being a French puppet. Barakat responded by saying that he will be in Damascus on a specific date and time, walking alone and unarmed.[49] He promenaded through the city in broad daylight, daring his opponents to shoot. He was then confronted at the lobby of a hotel in Beirut by a young man from Homs, carrying a pistol. His name was 'Abdul Basit al-Bunni and he was studying engineering at AUB.[50] Accomplice to the crime was a young university student named Akram al-Hawrani, who would become one of the leaders of the Ba'ath Party in future years. Barakat pushed his bodyguards aside, grabbed the gun and wrestled the young man to the ground. During the push and shove that followed, the Syrian president killed his attacker.[51] Hawrani says: 'I don't know for sure if he committed suicide or was killed.'[52]

Damascus notables were furious with an Antiochian president ruling over their city, although Barakat had tried pleasing them by appointing one of their notables, Sami Pasha Mardam Bey, as vice-president of the Syrian Union. That was still not enough to win their blessing, or silence their opposition, given that they were also upset by the fact that they had been put on equal footing with the Alawites and the Aleppines. 'They strove to humiliate Damascus', wrote Fares al-Khoury angrily in his memoirs.[53] Barakat identified himself as more Ottoman than Arab, making it more difficult for the Damascenes to accept him, given that they took great pride in their Arab history, considering themselves guardians of Arab nationalism. Additionally, Barakat's Arabic was cranky and he was more comfortable with Ottoman Turkish, making it the language of all his cabinet meetings.[54] The Damascus press ridiculed him by publishing his inauguration speech verbatim, which was riddled with grammatical mistakes, without correcting a single word.[55]

Aleppines did not think too highly of the federal system as well, despite the fact that their city had been declared its first capital. They too had little affection for the Alawites, or the Damascenes.[56] Many did not want to share their wealth with fellow Syrians, fully aware of the fact that Aleppo was far more prosperous than the other two states, considering it the milch cow of the Syrian Union.[57] They suddenly found Aleppo taxes being channelled to the Damascus-based Arab Faculties of Law and Medicine, or to agricultural projects in the Alawite State. The Aleppines demanded that Aleppo's wealth remain in the coffers of Aleppo, and used for its development only – a demand that Subhi Barakat did not mind and secretly supported.[58] They also complained that because of the higher cost of living, salaries were higher in Damascus than in Aleppo.[59]

As if these grievances were not enough, reduced rainfall that year meant a poorer harvest of fruits, wheat and barley from the plains of Aleppo. Turkey was no longer importing anything from Aleppo due to the French-imposed border tariffs, hence worsening the city's plight. Aleppo was already suffering from major economic challenges, with 40,000 Armenian refugees arriving in the city to permanently settle from 1915 onwards, fleeing persecution and death at the hands of the Ottomans. Sharing their city's income with Damascus and the Alawites was simply too much for the Aleppines to handle.

Alawite notables were also suspicious of the new federal government, as it gave the Damascenes and Aleppines an upper hand in the new Syria, taking away the privileges they had briefly enjoyed with the autonomous Alawite State of 1920–2. Those privileges included local schools, improved infrastructure, expansion of cultivated lands and, above all, Alawite Sharia Courts. For the first time in their history, the Alawites had been taking their legal matters to their own courts, without prejudice by non-Alawite judges. Twice in 1924, the Alawites threatened to withdraw from the Syrian Union.[60]

The cabinet of Subhi Barakat

President Subhi Barakat created a small cabinet of four directors (ministers): two from Damascus and two from Aleppo. No minister was chosen from the Alawite State. From Aleppo, he chose the lawyer Nasri Bakhash as director of interior and Hasan 'Izzat Pasha, a former army general, as director of public works. Damascene millionaire Mohammad 'Ali al-'Abed was chosen for the directory of finance. He was soon to become Barakat's father-in-law as well, albeit briefly, after his daughter Layla married the president in 1924.[61] 'Ata al-Ayyubi, an acclaimed civil servant who had served as minister of interior in 1920, was chosen director of justice. He had also been part of Emir Sa'id El Djezairi's interim government in 1918. The nationalist leader Fakhri al-Barudi, although at daggers end with Barakat, could not but praise the man saying that he and his ministers 'were exceptionally clean, financially'.[62] Ayyubi and 'Abed were also among the five MPs chosen by the French to represent the State of Damascus. The other three were Fares al-Khoury representing Christians, Rashed al-Barazi representing Hama and Mufti Taher al-Atasi, representing the city of Homs. The MPs of the State of Aleppo were Ghaleb Ibrahim Pasha, Rashid al-Mudarres, Hussein Orfali and Iskandar Salem. The Alawite State representatives were Ismail Junaid, Jaber al-'Abbas (head of the Khayyatin clan) and Ismail Hawwash (head of the Matawra clan), in addition to 'Abdul Wahab Haroun (Sunni) and Ishak Nasri (Christian).

French insults

When nationalists complained that the new government was an appointed one, rather than elected, Gouraud replied that the Syrian nation was young and not ready for democracy. That condescending attitude was mirrored through the actions of the mandate's secretary-general Robert De Caix, who treated Barakat's ministers as subordinates, rather than political equals. De Caix once received them at an office with one seat only – which he occupied – keeping them standing throughout a long meeting.[63] French president Raymond Poincaré was equally impolite, welcoming the Barakat government with a derogatory saying that France maintains the 'sentiments of guardianship towards Syria'.[64] The word 'guardianship' was ill-advised, noted Fares al-Khoury in his memoirs, since it implied that the people of Syria were underdeveloped and needed chaperoning. When the Syrian ministers asked to send an official delegation to the Lausanne Conference that had commenced in November 1922, they were given a cold shoulder by Gouraud. When they asked for a political amnesty allowing those exiled by the French to return home, they were ignored. Last among the insults was drawing up a new flag for the Syrian Union without consulting any of its ministers or MPs. It was composed of green and white banners of the Arab Revolt, in reference to the Rashidoun and Umayyad caliphates, omitting the colour black that represented the Abbasid dynasty. Drawn in the middle was the tri-colour of the French Flag. 'I don't see any reason to insert a French flag', argued Fares al-Khoury. 'The mandate is temporary, after all, while the Syrian Flag is permanent.'[65] He then added: 'We knew nothing about this flag, and who chose it on our behalf.'[66]

The 1923 elections

Gouraud's successor, Maxime Weygand, was more nuanced and open-minded towards Syrian aspiration. Weygand was a national hero in France, having served as chief of staff for the legendary General Ferdinand Foch, commander-in-chief of the Allied Forces during the final months of the First World War. In 1919, he attended the Paris Peace Conference as assistant to Fosch, who was attached to the official French delegation headed by Prime Minister George Clemenceau. He had met Faisal and been briefed on Syrian aspirations.[67] In June 1923, Weygand called for general elections in all three Syrian states. They would be the first in Syria since 1919, and were packaged as a major concession by the mandate regime, given financial constraints that were gripping the French treasury. The budget of the High Commission for Syria and Lebanon had been slashed from 181 million francs in 1921 to a mere 8.2 million by the time of Weygand's arrival to Syria.[68] Weygand promised to move ahead with political reforms and to allow Syrians to elect their representatives to three respective parliaments, which would form a central chamber for the Syrian Union. It would be a two-tier electoral system open to adult males only, aged twenty-five and above. Women were excluded from voting, and candidates had to meet a six-month residency requirement in their respective state before their nominations were accepted.[69]

Rural dwellers were purposely given a disproportionate number of electors in the primaries, given that they were less politicized, and therefore less likely to vote for candidates with an anti-French agenda. Weygand reasoned that the smaller group of electors to emerge from the primaries could be more easily divided and manipulated than the whole electoral population in the three states. There was little politics in the Syrian countryside or along the coast, only overwhelming poverty and illiteracy. Although seven publications had emerged in the Alawite State, including the Alawite flagship paper *Al-Sada al-'Alawi*, residents had no access to the political dailies that came out in Damascus, which were filled with anti-French editorials. Political pamphlets from Damascus and Aleppo rarely reached the hands of the Alawites. 'Party programmes', in the narrow sense of the word, were of no interest to the residents of the Alawite mountains. Weygand seemed confident that because of their history of neglect, the Alawites were not going to vote for political campaigns or appealing candidates, but only for those who were bound to uphold their independence.

Despite everybody's reservations about the Syrian Union, Syrians took the parliamentary elections very seriously. Three powerful parties competed for political office that autumn. The first was headed by President Barakat, campaigning against governor of the State of Damascus, Haqqi al-'Azm. Barakat put his full weight in the elections, wanting to become an elected president, rather than an appointed one. Another presidential hopeful was Rida al-Rikabi, Faisal's former prime minister who had moved to Amman, serving as prime minister of Transjordan between March 1922 and February 1923.[70] He was the same Rikabi who had sidelined Emir Sa'id, and who was blamed for the murder of his brother, Emir 'Abdelkader Jr. When he returned from Amman to nominate himself for the Syrian Union elections, Emir Sa'id threatened to take his life in revenge for his slain brother.[71] Unlike Barakat and 'Azm, who posed no threat to the French in Syria, Rikabi was considered dangerous. He was a nationalist at heart and the French didn't trust him. Challenging the ambitions of all three men was Fawzi al-Ghazzi, a brilliant 33-year-old attorney from Damascus. He was an acclaimed man of letters and a respected professor at the Arab Faculty of Law. His 1923 campaign focused on unity of Syrian lands, an amnesty, admittance to the League of Nations and the toppling of Subhi Barakat. He came one step short of demanding an immediate end to the mandate, but never said it, so as not to get disqualified from the election.

The Shahbandar opposition

Working to disrupt the elections, however, was Ghazzi's friend and colleague 'Abdul Rahman Shahbandar, an AUB-trained medical doctor who had served as Faisal's last foreign minister in 1920. Shahbandar was a fiery orator, an essayist and a self-made man. He was also well connected, both regionally and internationally, having met with US President Woodrow Wilson at the Paris Peace Conference and corresponded with his second successor Calvin Coolidge. Shahbandar considered the 1923 elections as the mother of all evils, aimed at sugar-coating the mandate. He called for a nationwide boycott, demanding nothing less than immediate, complete and unconditional independence.[72] He too wanted to take down Subhi Barakat. Shahbandar's monumental influence succeeded in an effective boycott throughout his native Damascus. In the primaries, only 25 per cent of registered Damascene voters (49,000) cast their ballot.[73] A British report claimed that voters were marshalled into the polling stations by the police, who had received orders to ensure a 'decent turnout'. Most votes, the report noted, were registered in 'ignorance and apathy'.[74] In Aleppo, Homs and Hama, where Shahbandar's influence was no match to that of Barakat, 49 per cent of citizens cast their ballot. As the French had correctly predicted, voter turnout was highest in Aleppo and the Alawite State. In the countryside of Aleppo, it stood at 99 per cent, whereas in the Alawite villages, at 77 per cent.

The elections were scheduled for 26 October 1923, but were called off by the French to deprive Shahbandar from a successful boycott. They were then resumed with no prior warning on 29 October. Caught off guard, Shahbandar was unable to mobilize his followers or save his friends from defeat. Fawzi al-Ghazzi was crushed by Haqqi al-'Azm, who won most of Damascus' eleven seats. Rida al-Rikabi was also defeated and he accused the French of rigging the elections. In Aleppo, Subhi Barakat won sixteen out of the nineteen seats, and his allies in the Alawite State took ten out of twelve seats.[75] In total, Barakat's bloc reached an impressive twenty-eight MPs, becoming the largest in Parliament. Subhi Barakat was satisfied; nobody could accuse him now of being an appointed head of state. He had won a fair election and seemed very proud about that.

Death threats

Shahbandar was not one to accept defeat, however, pressuring the newly elected deputies to resign before the Syrian Union Parliament held its first session. He resorted to thuggery and violence, nudging masked men to break into the home of Damascus MP Sheikh 'Abdulhamid al-'Attar, giving him a hard beating.[76] Attar was preacher of the Umayyad Mosque, and when he showed up for Friday prayer two days later, visibly bruised, Shahbandar made sure that worshippers walked out on 'Attar's sermon.[77] Another Damascus MP, Rushdi al-Sukkari, an influential merchant at the Bzurieh Market, suffered a citywide boycott of his goods. Shahbandar said that he would only call it off if Sukkari stepped down from the Union Parliament and severed all ties to Subhi Barakat.[78] Other MPs received letters containing death threats, adorned with the image of a bullet and dagger.[79]

Renewing Barakat's term

All of Shahbandar's efforts were still not enough to disrupt Syria's new parliament. Barakat nominated himself for a second term at the presidency, challenging Haqqi al-'Azm. He advised 'Azm to withdraw from the race, offering to keep him as governor of the State of Damascus if he abandoned his claim to the presidency. 'Azm played along, pretending to accept Barakat's offer. On Election Day, however, he nominated his cousin, Badih Mou'ayyad al-'Azm, to challenge Barakat. Aleppo MPs made sure to drown the ambition of both 'Azms, dealing them a heavy defeat. The president then had 'Azm dismissed from the governorship of Damascus, saying that he had failed to live up to his promise. His cousin Badih was compensated, however, with the post of speaker at the Damascus Parliament.[80] Haqqi al-'Azm threw a childish tantrum, unfit for a statesman of his calibre. He staged a sit-in at government headquarters, refusing to hand over his office.[81] He was eventually ordered to evacuate the building by Barakat, but the French decided to compensate him as well with presidency of the Shura Council, a post that he had held during the first weeks of the mandate.[82]

End of the union

Realizing that the mandate had gone too far in courting Aleppo at the expense of practically everybody else in Syria, the union parliament took a decision to restore the capital permanently to Damascus, on 30 October 1923. But by the time, it was almost too late for the union itself and for President Barakat. Maxime Weygand was starting to lose faith with the entire project due to never-ending complaints from the three states and their inhabitants. Federalism was clearly not working. Everywhere he went, people were complaining. The Damascenes wanted to return their city to its previous status as capital of all of Syria, and Aleppines were saying that their treasury had been devastated by faraway development projects, also pleading for a way out from the federal system. In Latakia, Weygand heard a chorus of complaints from Alawites notables, who pushed for the restoration of their state's autonomy, arguing that they were the weaker link within the union's three components. The Damascenes and Aleppines were still treating them as an underclass, they said. Clearly something had gone horribly wrong and Weygand did not want to pay the price for a political experiment that he had neither invented nor devised, which bore the name of his predecessor, Henri Gouraud.

When unity of Syrian lands was discussed within the union parliament, delegates from Damascus and Aleppo voted in favour.[83] One Alawite State parliamentarian also voted in favour, being the Sunni MP 'Abdul Wahab Haroun. Two Alawites and one Christian MPs walked out, while Jaber 'Abbas skipped the entire session.[84] On 5 December 1924, Weygand issued a decree abolishing the Syrian Union, in accordance with a majority vote at its Chamber of Deputies. That also happened to be his last day in Syria. Before returning to France, he signed two decrees: one establishing *Etat de Syrie* (State of Syria) instead of *Itihad al-Duwwal al-Souriyya*, and the second restored autonomy of the Alawite State.[85] To justify his second decree, Robert De Caix said that it was inspired by the 'wishes of the local populations' as expressed by their elected representatives. By the time, he too had left Damascus and was serving as permanent French ambassador to the League of Nations, handling Syria and Lebanon.

Weygand's second successor, Henri De Jouvenel, came to Syria with a reformist agenda in 1925. He promised parliamentary elections in all areas where there was no martial law and no revolt, thereby excluding Damascus, the Druze Mountain and the Houran province. To emphasize the restored autonomy of the Alawite Mountain, he said that special elections would be conducted on its territory, to be decided at a later date. Subhi Barakat used that as a pretext to resign from office, on 21 December 1925.[86] His resignation letter was carefully crafted to sound appealing to the nationalist movement, and more importantly, to the Syrian street. That was just two months after Barakat had been scrutinized for failing to stop the bombing of Damascus, and six months after start of the Great Syrian Revolt. He wrote to Henri De Jouvenel:

There are problems that we have been unable to solve, which oblige me to present you with my resignation. As a nationalist who shares with this nation its aspirations and suffers with its hardships, I cannot but turn your attention, during my last hour in office, to the fact that this country will not achieve true stability unless its rightful demands are accommodated.

Barakat then specified those demands saying that Syria needs a constitution, a democratic government, admittance to the League of Nations and a political amnesty 'with no exceptions'. The French were unhappy with his resignation. They didn't except Barakat to turn his back on them, certainly not in the middle of a nationwide uprising. No other head of state had stepped down since start of the mandate. He set a precedent that was to be repeated by three of his successors: Ahmad Nami in 1928, Mohammad 'Ali al-'Abed in 1936 and Hashem al-Atasi in 1939.

Forgotten achievements

Although it ruled for no more than two years in total, from December 1922 to December 1924, the Barakat government boasted of some memorable feats, and was far more progressive than any of its predecessors had been under the mandate. Its top achievement was merging the faculties of law and medicine in Damascus into one institution of higher education, named the Syrian University in 1923. Months before the union dissolve, work began on drawing fresh drinking water from the ʿAyn al-Fijeh Spring to the aqueducts and homes of Damascus, a vital project initiated by the nationalist leader Lutfi al-Haffar, which took another nine years to complete.[87] The Syrian Union oversaw creation of the modern Syrian Police, and cancellation of all special court privileges granted to European citizens since Ottoman times. On 1 August 1924, President Barakat signed an agreement with the newly formed Lebanese government, establishing the Bank of Syria and Lebanon. Based in Paris, it was charged with issuing Syria's currency and served as the state's official bank until creation of the Central Bank of Syria in 1956. Barakat also allocated funds for accommodating and feeding thousands of Armenian refugees still arriving from Turkey, who had reached 100,000 in 1922.[88] In 1923, he penned Syria's first pension law for government employees, fixing retirement at the age of sixty.

Barakat took a keen interest in safety, forcing all three states to prepare schools, government buildings and hospitals, with fire extinguishers. He tried raising health awareness by printing books and distributing them to schoolchildren, with instructions on what to do in case of fires or earthquakes in Damascus, cyclones and mud slides in Latakia, and drought in the countryside of Idlib. Prisoners with less than a three-year sentence were allowed to work while in jail. It was a paid job, considered part of their community service. The highest wages went to those who taught fellow inmates how to read and write, while other jobs included sweeping cells, washing clothes for elderly prisoners, attending to the ill and sewing. A quarter of their wage was paid in cash while still in jail; the rest was paid accumulatively after release.[89]

Politically, Barakat's era witnessed the birth of Syria's first political party: an opposition one founded by ʿAbdul Rahman Shahbandar in June 1925, weeks before outbreak of the Great Revolt. Known as the People's Party, it called for end of the mandate, unity of Syrian lands and restoration of the Hashemite crown in Syria. Barakat had an axe to grind with Shahbandar for trying to foil the Syrian Union elections, but he allowed his party to pass, with minimal interference from the state. He did forbid members of his government from joining the party, and banned civil servants from engaging in any political activity. Shortly before the party's formation, Shahbandar's loyalists had staged a citywide demonstration in Damascus, objecting the visit of Lord James Balfour, author of the infamous Balfour Declaration. Balfour came to Syria on 8 April 1925 and was scheduled to have lunch with President Barakat. The Shahbandarists made sure that he spend no more than three hours in the Syrian capital. The People's Party took credit for the expulsion of Balfour, and it was eventually disbanded a few weeks later for expressing support for the Great Syrian Revolt. The decree that put an end to the party's short-life was signed by the French high commissioner, however, and not President Barakat.

Barakat returns as parliament speaker

In January 1926, barely two weeks after his resignation, Barkaat was elected MP in the Aleppo Parliament. This brief post-presidency tenure is generally overlooked by historians of the mandate, and it signalled the first break in Barakat's relations with the French. At the chamber's first meeting, he demanded not only unity of Syrian lands but re-incorporation of Lebanon into the Syrian motherland. Unimpressed, the French suspended the Aleppo parliament, with the hope of silencing Subhi Barakat. Fearing arrest, he kept a low profile for the next five years, watching politics unfold from the comfort of his Antioch mansion. In December 1931, he nominated himself for parliament once again and established a political party to support him, called the Syrian Union Party. He also set up a newspaper called *al-Zaman,* which he bankrolled. Barakat won an impressive 28-man bloc in 1932, equal to the one he had commanded back in 1923. It was the largest in the 1932 parliament, outdoing even that of the National Bloc, whose members won only seventeen seats. Barakat was so popular that he even defeated the nationalist leader Ibrahim Hananu in Aleppo, leading the National Bloc to claim that the elections had been rigged. At fifty, Barakat was elected speaker of the Syrian Chamber, and on 11 June 1932, he presented his candidacy for the Syrian presidency. His rivals included his former minister and ex-father-in-law Mohammad 'Ali al-'Abed, his historic archrival Haqqi al-'Azm and Hashem al-Atasi of the National Bloc. Atasi decided to withdraw his candidacy and put his full weight behind the election of Mohammad 'Ali al-'Abed. As a result, 'Abed was elected president and Barakat kept his post as speaker. The two men had not spoken since Barakat had divorced 'Abed's daughter in 1924. They were forced to reconcile, unwillingly, in order to manage state affairs.

Barakat's tenure in parliament was far less eventful than his earlier stint as president. Clearly by now he had outgrown French patronage and in November 1933 took mandate authorities by surprise by voting against a proposed Franco-Syrian Friendship Treaty. During a trip to Paris, Barakat hosted a dinner at the luxury George V Hotel, off the Champs-Elysée. Present at his table were former high commissioner Maxime Weygand and French MP and future president, Vincent Auriol. Barakat went to great lengths to talk to his French guests about how ill-advised it was to impose a treaty on Syria that didn't mention termination of the mandate. He took a piece of bread from the dinner table and kissed it, as customarily done in Muslim societies, making his vow: 'I swear by God's bread that I will not accept a treaty that doesn't achieve independence of Syria, an independence that is correct and final.'[90] One of his guests, 'Adel al-Solh, remarked in his memoirs: 'Barakat forgot that he was in Paris not standing with voters in Aleppo. His French guests laughed at the gesture, unable to grasp its meaning.'[91] But when it reached his powerbase back home, the gesture took him far in nationalist circles, to an extent that National Bloc leader Jamil Mardam Bey even suggested inviting him to join the National Bloc, arguing that Barakat had mended his ways.[92]

At one point, Bloc leaders held a convention at his residence, based on his invitation.[93] Many still had doubts that he would help them bring down the

Friendship Treaty, seeing that he was still bitter about the Bloc supporting 'Abed for president in 1932. Barakat surprised them all when the proposed treaty was debated in parliament, and debunked on 21 November 1933. As he walked into the building, crowds had gathered demanding that the treaty is aborted. One pregnant woman threw herself at his feet as he walked into the chamber, screaming: 'Subhi Barakat. If you want to sign the treaty then you will have to do it over my dead body.'[94] He smiled and said: 'Get up sister. There will be treaty.'[95] Once in the chamber, he voted against the proposed treaty.[96]

Upset by the drowning of the Friendship Treaty, the French suspended Barakat's chamber for an unidentified period, bringing the career of its speaker to an abrupt end. Three years later, Barakat still considered himself the legitimate head of Syria's legislative branch, when he issued a declaration in support of a sixty-day strike staged by the National Bloc, against both the mandate and President Mohammad 'Ali al-'Abed. Barakat addressed his strong-worded statement to French high commissioner Henri De Martel, sending copies to the League of Nations. By referring to himself as speaker of parliament, he was also saying that he did not recognize France's suspension of Syria's chamber. Barakat wrote: 'I object, in the strongest terms, the arrest of MP Fakhri al-Barudi with no trial, the aggressive use of force, and bloodshed on the streets', adding that the closure of the Bloc offices in al-Qanwat was 'unjustified'.[97]

Returning to Antioch

That, however, was the end of his career in politics. Barakat spent his final years farming at his family estate in Antioch, now the Liwan Boutique Hotel, a historic building surrounded with restaurants and shops selling silk and soap to tourists.[98] After divorcing Layla al-'Abed, he re-married Khalida, the beautiful daughter of a powerful Turkish pasha, in August 1925. Technically Khalida Hanim was the first lady of Syria from August to December 1925. Two of their children were born in Damascus: Salah al-Din, who became a successful engineer, and Seniyeh, born in 1934. His eldest son Rifaat, named after Barakat's father, also worked in engineering, while Khaled Barakat handled the family's lands and business. One of his daughters, Suhayla, married Oguz Koraltan, the son of the Refik Koraltan, president of the Turkish Parliament in 1950–60, while Zahra Barakat married the son of Vahit Melih Halefoglu, Turkey's foreign minister in 1983–7. Barakat would warn his children: 'Never, under any circumstances, should you work in politics.'[99]

After settling in Antioch, Barakat watched the political standoff between Syria and Turkey over the Sanjak of Alexandretta. Throughout the step-by-step annexation, which led to the entire region becoming a part of Turkey in 1939, he chose to remain in Antioch, thus legitimizing Turkish claims to Syrian territory. He didn't openly support the annexation, but nor did he oppose it. Towards the end of his life, Subhi Barakat suffered from leukaemia, which led to his death, at the age of sixty-seven, on 28 July 1949. That was just four months after Syria's first coup, carried out by Army Commander Husni al-Za'im in March. Barkaat was buried at the family cemetery in Antioch. There is one single picture commemorating his career in Damascus today, a black-and-white photo framed at the old hall of the Syrian Parliament, along with over twenty predecessors and successors. He stands smiling with a toothbrush moustache, wearing a tuxedo decorated with Ottoman and Syrian medals. It remains standing as of 2023. All other mention of the man has been erased from Syrian history books and monuments, bridges and streets established during his era, including the landmark premises of Damascus University, which he inaugurated in 1923.

Figure 4 Subhi Barakat.

Chapter 5

AHMAD NAMI (1926-8)

Ahmad Nami was France's choice to head the newly created State of Syria in mid-1926. Like his predecessor Subhi Barakat, he was an appointed head of state, this time to rule over a united Syria, minus the Alawite and Druze Mountains. He came to power with no parliament, no constitution and no referendum or election. In addition to assuming the presidency, he was also named prime minister, holding the country's top two posts in the midst of the Great Syrian Revolt. History books often refer to him erroneously only as premier, forgetting that for nearly two years he was also president of Syria. Merging the presidency and the premiership was not new, having been practised before under Subhi Barakat. It was copied from the United States, where the president is also the chief of cabinet.[1] The French had recently bombed the capital Damascus on 18 October 1925, triggering massive opposition to Subhi Barakat, who was helpless at stopping the onslaught. They had tried, with no luck, to make the Damascene cleric Sheikh Taj al-Din al-Hasani premier, but he set forth a series of conditions that were impossible to meet, among which was issuing a political amnesty and admitting Syria to the League of Nations. Ahmad Nami had no conditions.

He was, nevertheless, a strange choice for the presidency, having never lived in Syria before occupying its top job in 1926. In fact, he didn't even hold a Syrian passport and, like Barakat, was more at ease with French and Ottoman Turkish than Arabic. King Faisal had been a non-Syrian, however, while Barakat was an ethnic Turk, making Nami's nationality less problematic than one would have expected. Unlike both men, however, Ahmad Nami had no war credentials, having never fought a battle in his life. A tall and handsome Circassian aristocrat, he was born in the Musaitbeh neighbourhood of Beirut in 1878. He studied at the military academy of Istanbul but dropped to join the Ottoman Public Debt Administration (Düyun-u Umumiye-i Osmaniye). On 11 August 1911, he married Princess 'Aisha, the daughter of Sultan 'Abdulhamid II, two years after her father's dethronement. They had been engaged since 'Abdulhamid's final days on the throne, but were forced to postpone their marriage because of the coup that toppled her father in 1909. The sultan's tenth child and sixth daughter, she was nine years younger than her husband, who was automatically given the princely title of Damad (a Persian word that means son-in-law of the sultan). He would retain it after divorce in 1919, as father of the sultan's grandchildren.

Under the Ottomans, Nami had served as secretary of the vilayet of Beirut, then of Izmir on the Aegean coast, before travelling to Switzerland, where he stayed throughout the First World War. His first son Emir ʿOmar was born in Istanbul in 1911 followed by Emir ʿOsman, born in Geneva in 1918. The Damad's ex-wife died in Istanbul on 11 August 1960, aged 73.

The Damad's family legacy in Beirut

Nami's grandfather, Emir Mahmud, had fled the Caucasus after the Russian invasion in the early 1800s, settling in Cairo to join the court of its viceroy, Mohammad ʿAli Pasha. Himself an Albanian and not a native Egyptian, Mohammad ʿAli relied on many non-Arabs to run his state, like Emir Mahmud and the Armenian statesman Nubar Pasha, who became prime minister of Egypt under Mohammad ʿAli's grandson ʿAbbas Hilmi I. In 1828 Emir Mahmud was sent on a state mission to Paris, where he stayed for nine years, studying military strategy of the French Navy. When he returned to Egypt, he was appointed governor of the port city of Damietta, then aid-de-camp to the viceroy's son, Ibrahim Pasha. According to one account, Emir Mahmud's wife (Ahmad Nami's mother) was one of the ex-wives of Mohammad ʿAli Pasha.[2] When Egyptian troops marched into Syria in 1831, temporarily dislodging it from the Ottoman Empire, Emir Mahmud joined the military expedition, both as an expert in navy warfare and as an assistant to Ibrahim Pasha.[3] During Egyptian rule in Syria, Emir Mahmud was appointed the governor of Beirut from 1833 to 1841.[4] He created the Beirut police, named streets and established guilds for traders. He took great care of the city's *khans* (resting place for travelling caravan), renovating those near the port to increase storage capacities. Emir Mahmud effectively transformed Beirut into the modern city that it is now.

When Ibrahim Pasha's forces came under attack by the Europeans, he retreated to Beirut and eventually to Egypt, ending nine years of Egyptian rule in Syria. Emir Mahmud chose to remain in the Levant, however, where his son Ibrahim Fakhri Bey was born in 1839. He was named after Ibrahim Pasha of Egypt, and in 1878 he went on to succeed his father as president of the Beirut Municipality, where he created gardens, planted trees and was accredited with both the Burj Square (later Martyr's Square) and Khan Fakhri Bey in Souq al-Tawileh (now part of the Beirut Souks).[5] He also improved Beirut's sanitation system, introducing wastewater treatment and public lighting to illuminate the city and organize its markets.

Few in Syria had heard of Ahmad Nami's name prior to 1926, although the achievements of his father were well known to many Syrians, especially Damascene merchants who travelled frequently to Beirut. He spent the Great War at the Berne opera, thriving on European culture while leading a completely Westernized lifestyle. Ahmad Nami indulged himself with smoking cigars and playing chess, two habits that were relatively new to Damascus society, even its upper-crust. France's new high commissioner Henri De Jouvenel thought that he was someone with whom the French could do business. He too was also new to Syria, having just replaced Maurice Sarrail in December 1925. A former editor of the Paris daily, *Le Matin*, De Jouvenel had served as minister of public instruction under Raymond Poincare, then as member of the French Assembly and finally as France's representative to the League of Nations. He was the first civilian to become high commissioner, after Gouraud, Weygand and Serail, who were all officers. De Jouvenel's main task was to end the military uprising, disarm the rebels and pull Syria back together, three monumental tasks that, he believed, Ahmad Nami was well-suited for and could help achieve. Upon arriving in Beirut to take on the job of high commissioner, De Jouvenel announced his intentions with the words: 'Peace to those who wish peace, and war to those who wish war.'[6]

A compromise head of state

Syrian nationalists had no reservations about Nami, although he was named president on the very same day that the French had laid siege to al-Suwayda, capital of the Druze Mountain and headquarters of the Great Revolt. He made sure to surround himself with nationalists, consulting them throughout the cabinet formation process. His early entourage included respected men like Sa'adallah al-Jabiri of Aleppo and Fawzi al-Ghazzi of Damascus, who in future years were to make a name for themselves as leaders of the National Bloc.[7] Nami wanted to know why the Syrian union had failed and why Subhi Barakat had lost support of the Syrian street. Given his family relation with Sultan 'Abdulhamid, they addressed him respectfully as 'Your Highness' and managed to convince their nationalist colleagues to support his government, which was formed on 5 May 1926.

One of their friends who was talked into working with the Damad was Lutfi al-Haffar, deputy president of the Damascus Chamber of Commerce, who was made minister of public works and commerce, seconded by the Hama notable Husni al-Barazi, a former co-founder of al-Fatat, who became minister of interior. Last was Fares al-Khoury, the famous Christian lawyer who had been MP first in the Ottoman Parliament then under Subhi Barakat, in addition to serving as minister during Emir Sa'id's interim government back in 1918. Ahmad Nami named him minister of education, banking on his teaching experience at the Greek Orthodox School of Damascus and at the American University of Beirut. Other prominent Syrians who served under Nami were the judge Yusuf al-Hakim, a former Faisal protégé, who became minister of justice, and Wathiq Mou'ayyad al-'Azm, a former Ottoman ambassador to Spain, who was appointed minister of agriculture. All of them were respected men of high social standing, stemming from large and powerful families.

Running the Damad's bureau were Lebanese nationals like himself who were summoned from Beirut to support the new Syrian administration, like Bahij al-Daouk and the poet Fouad al-Khatib (brother of future premier Bahij al-Khatib). Their first public appearance with the president was at the funeral of Mehmed VI, the thirty-sixth and last Ottoman sultan, who died at his San Remo exile on 16 May

1926 and was transferred to Damascus for burial at the Tekiyya Suleimaniyya Mosque. The Damad refused to tap into the Syrian treasury to fund the expenses of transferring his body from Italy, covering everything from his own purse.[8]

The Damad's programme

Nami and his ministers were invited to a meeting at Qasr al-Sonobar in Beirut – premise of the French high commissioner. After five long hours they came up with an ambitious programme, which included the following objectives:

One: Holding elections for a constitutional assembly that would draft a new charter for Syria, replacing the monarchial one of King Faisal that had been aborted by the French invasion of 1920.
Two: Replacing the mandate with a Franco-Syrian treaty that would last for thirty years, outlining the rights and duties of each country, along with a clear timetable for its termination.
Three: Unity of Syrian lands, thus re-incorporating the Druze and Alawite mountains with the rest of Syria, along with the autonomous Sanjak of Alexandretta.
Four: Syria's admittance to the League of Nations.
Five: A general amnesty for all those arrested in connection to the Great Syrian Revolt.
Six: Cancelling all war tax imposed on major cities that had risen in revolt.
Seven: Compensation for families whose homes had been destroyed by the fighting.

De Jouvenel approved each of the points, one after another, hoping that this would satisfy the angry street and end battles of the Druze Mountain and Damascus countryside. Lebanon had just gotten its first constitution on 24 May, and the French commissioner hoped that he could do the same for Syria. Nami asked for his approval in writing, to which De Jouvenel replied: 'Isn't my word good enough? You can announce your programme, with my blessing.' The president insisted on something written, so De Jouvenel signed the document with his initials, adding a phrase conditioning that Ahmad Nami stays at his post to implement the government programme, and not resign before any of the abovementioned points are achieved.[9] Nami then came out with a statement that was distributed to the press, outlining his vision. It read poorly in Arabic, having obviously been originally written in French, perhaps by De Jouvenel. 'We cannot reach our objective with force, but through negotiations and justice', he said. 'We will succeed by helping the mandate state, rather than fighting it and each other.'[10]

Nami then began a series of confidence-building measures to build trust with the Syrian people. He had the director of internal security fired, a Frenchman by the name of Colonel Bejean, who was blamed for arbitrary arrests and torture. All those jailed by him with no legal warrant were released on Ahmad Nami's orders. All military courts that had sprung across the country during the revolt were cancelled and their cases transferred to ordinary courts at the Palace of Justice. He then had the high commissioner renew the passport of ʿAbdul Rahman Shahbandar, one of the revolt commanders, inviting him for a face-to-face meeting in Egypt.[11] Nami also came out with two appeals to the rebels of the Druze Mountain, asking that they lay down their arms so that he can talk the French into issuing a general amnesty. Both were turned down by Sultan Pasha al-Atrash, who agreed to the principle of confidence building but said that it was the French who ought to start. Sultan Pasha wanted an amnesty first, followed by a ceasefire. The French responded by shelling the Damascus neighbourhood of al-Midan shortly after the Damad's inauguration, as if to say that they too were not interested in a truce.

A surge in violence

In early June 1926, the French Military Command declared al-Ghouta a 'war zone', intensifying its assault on rebel strongholds. The number of French troops in Syria had risen from 14,000 in 1925 to over 50,000 by mid-1926. French generals were unhappy with a civilian like De Jouvenel handling the High Commission, inspired by recent battlefield victories against the rebel forces of ʿAbdul Karim al-Khattabi in Morocco. If they could win in Morocco with no vouchsafing, then they could do the same in Syria, reasoned the officers. On 13 June 1926, they ordered that three of the Damad's top ministers are forced to resign, and then arrested on charges of communicating with the al-Ghouta rebels. The arrested officials were Interior Minister Husni al-Barazi, Public Works Minister Lutfi al-Haffar and Education Minister Fares al-Khoury. In his memoirs, Haffar claims that they resigned from their posts before being arrested, not after. He cites their collective resignation as the real reason for their arrest, along with a stormy meeting with French generals when he banged his fist on the table, causing an ink jar to spill on the white suit of one officer.[12]

All three were sent to a desert jail near the Syrian-Iraqi border and then put under house arrest in al-Hassakeh in the Syrian northeast before being exiled to Lebanon. The president's two nationalist friends and advisers, Saʿadallah al-Jabiri and Fawzi al-Ghazzi, who had helped form his first cabinet, were also arrested on similar charges. The relief committee that Ahmad Nami had created to compensate victims of the French bombing was disbanded, despite having been signed off personally by De Jouvenel.[13] Fuming, the Damad called on Pierre Alype, the French administrator of Syria who deputized on behalf of the high commissioner during his absence in Beirut. Alype was an autocrat who had imposed martial law on the capital, pushing for maximal confrontation with the rebels. He had also served as interim governor of Syria from February to April 1926. He was a good hater and he hated Ahmad Nami.

Trying to mince his words, the president said: 'You are a stranger here, and you will return to France, one day. I am a native of this land and its well-being concerns me, so does the trust of its people. I demand to know why you have arrested my ministers?' Alype replied that the Damad will receive an official explanation from the High Commissioner's Office. If no logical explanation was forthcoming, threatened the president, then he would have to come out with a harsh statement condemning the arrests. He did not threaten to resign, only to 'condemn' the abduction of his ministers. When he was officially briefed of the charges brought against Haffar, Barazi and Khoury, Nami released a mild statement that was published in the Damascus daily *al-Rai al-Yawm*, claiming that he had not been informed of the arrests, nor did he approve them. The French shut down the newspaper for running the president's statement without consulting the High Commission in Beirut. *Al-Rai al-Yawm* was actually a Lebanese newspaper, founded by the Damad's Lebanese friend, Taha Madwar. He had invited its publisher to relocate from Beirut to Damascus in 1926, giving him an office at 'Abed Building in Marjeh Square. It is not to be confused with another daily with the same name that operated out of Damascus in the 1950s, owned by the journalist Ahmad 'Usseh.

On 18 July 1926, the French launched the biggest – and last – offensive in al-Ghouta, sending four columns of 5,000 troops, along with armoured cars, tanks and aeroplanes, to wipe out the rebels. They ordered carpet bombing of the Damascus countryside, and in just three days 1,500 people were killed. Only 400 of them were rebels. The rest were Syrian civilians. They then blocked water channels that irrigated the orchards of al-Ghouta, inflicting collective punishment on its residents.[14] The brutality of the offensive, topped with the arrest of the ministers, made Ahmad Nami look weak and ineffective in the eyes of his people. The French generals did not care. Their objective was to force the people of al-Ghouta to kneel, and either to expel the rebels or have them come out carrying white flags, announcing unconditional surrender.

An internal coup

Left powerless and toothless, the Damad embarked on a nationwide tour to calm the Syrian street, starting 1 August 1926. He visited the Sanjak of Alexandretta, staying in Antioch for two nights and then went to Aleppo for a week, followed by Homs and Hama. Meanwhile, two of his ministers were sent to Latakia to meet with Alawite leaders. It was brave of Nami to leave the capital, with the revolt still raging in its countryside. He spoke to merchants, the ulema and farmers, promising a better future for Syria. They clapped and showered him with praise, calling for his long life and good health. Few believed him, however. Upon returning to Damascus, the Damad received reports that his new Interior Minister Wathiq Mou'ayyad al-'Azm was meeting secretly with cabinet ministers, trying to rally them against their boss. His aim was to unseat the president.[15]

Mou'ayyad al-'Azm had just replaced Husni al-Barazi at the Ministry of Interior. People had great respect for him and his father Shafiq Mou'ayyad al-'Azm, a nationalist who had been hanged by Djemal Pasha back in 1916.[16]

The Damad sent Justice Minister Yusuf al-Hakim to talk to Mou'ayyad al-'Azm. Hakim was one of Ahmad Nami's few friends in Damascus and he had genuine respect for the president. He accused his colleague of treason for backstabbing the Damad, to which Mou'ayyad al-Azm replied: 'This is not treason but legitimate political aspirations. Let the Damad return to where he belongs in Beirut and let us solve our own problems with the French. Ahmad Nami is a noble man, but I am the son of this country and more worthy of the presidency than him.'[17] Hakim tried explaining: 'But the presidency is not guaranteed', to which Mou'ayyad al-'Azm snapped: 'Yes it is, and you will be one of my ministers'.

'I will not betray my boss', said Hakim firmly. 'But I will be your boss', insisted Mou'ayyad al-'Azm. 'Who promised you that?' asked Hakim. Mou'ayyad al-'Azm answered, 'The High Commissioner's representative, Pierre Alype.' When Mou'ayyad al-'Azm lost hope of talking Hakim into defecting, he reached out to the director of public security Khalil Rifaat, asking him to arrest frontline nationalists, hoping that this would tarnish Ahmad Nami's image on the Syrian street. Rifaat said that he had no legal pretext to put them in jail, so Mou'ayyad al-'Azm called on police chief Nicolas Chahine, who also turned him down.[18]

Nami could have fired Mou'ayyad al-'Azm. But he decided to keep with him while scarring him into submission. During cabinet meetings, staffers would call from another office at the Serail, saying that the high commissioner wanted to speak to the Damad urgently, multiple times in less than two hours. Mou'ayyad al-'Azm would watch in bewilderment as the president laughed and joked with the high commissioner, implying that they were good friends. Nobody was on the other line, but Nami felt that by simply pretending to be so close to the high commissioner, this would get Mou'ayyad al-'Azm to reconsider his attempted coup.

On 26 December 1926, the Damad finally reshuffled his cabinet, firing Wathiq Mou'ayyad al-'Azm. He was replaced with Raouf al-Ayyubi, a former governor of Tiberius, Nazareth and Jaffa under the Ottomans. The troublesome minister was left with no cabinet post, and certainly, no presidency. Pierre Alype did not lift a finger to protect him.

With that out of his way, Nami tried to mend broken fences with the nationalists, who were still scornful about his indifference to the arrest of Khoury, Haffar and Barazi. In December 1926, he invited their leader Hashem al-Atasi to serve as prime minister. An official letter was sent to Atasi through his son Sirri, and when he declined, Nami reached out to 'Ata al-Ayyubi with the same offer. Neither of them wanted to associate themselves with a controversial president, forcing Nami to assume the premiership himself, as he had done since April. It was to prove his third and final cabinet.

With the exception of Justice Minister Yusuf al-Hakim and Education Minister Shaker al-Hanbali, who were both kept at their post, all other ministers were newcomers. A retired officer from the Ottoman Army, Nasuhi al-Boukhari, was made the minister of agriculture, while Mou'ayyad al-'Azm's cousin 'Abdul Qader, dean of the Damascus University Law Faculty, was appointed minister of finance. Pierre Alype, still at daggers-end with the Damad, tried talking him into abandoning the two ministers, Hakim and Hanbali. He even said: 'You chose Shaker al-Hanbali, who conspired against you with Wathiq Mou'ayyad al-'Azm?' Nami smiled and said, 'Yes I am aware of that. I wanted to reward him for returning to his senses.'[19]

Wathiq Mou'ayyad al-'Azm was still determined to bring down the Damad, teaming up with other presidential hopefuls like Haqqi al-'Azm and Taj al-Din al-Hasani.[20] Together, they staged a twofold lobby, one with French authorities, aimed at convincing them to drop Ahmad Nami, and another within the Syrian street, aimed at discrediting him. They played on the fact that he was not Syrian and silent about the arrest of his ministers and the raid on al-Ghouta. The French High Commission contributed to the character slaughter by delaying all decrees carrying the Damad's signature, sometimes for months, forcing citizens whose interests were jeopardized by the delay to by-pass the Syrian government and appeal directly to the High Commission.

By early 1928, it was clear that Nami's fortunes were drying up. He had failed to achieve any of the big promises made in 1926, not because of any change on his part but due to lack of cooperation from De Jouvenel's successor, Henri Ponsot. Not wanting to sink with the Damad, all six of his ministers decided to step down collectively, claiming that he ought to look for new talent and men who could better serve the country's interests. This was a coup, not much softer than the one that Wathiq Mou'ayyad al-'Azm had tried to pull off. The president was informed of their decision through a letter sent to him via Public Works Minister Rashid al-Mudarres. The Damad was in Lebanon for his mother's funeral, while the minister was travelling to Beirut to attend his son's graduation from AUB. When visiting him at the condolence service, Ahmad Nami thought that Rashid al-Mudarres was coming to pay his respects, only to realize that he was carrying collective resignation letter from all the ministers. He was shocked, feeling both backstabbed and abandoned. The despondent Damad took the letter to the High Commissioner's Office, along with his own resignation, on 8 February 1928. Ponsot replied: 'I did not know that you and your ministers have such little faith in France.' He did not try to talk him into re-considering, signing off both resignations on 14 February. After Subhi Barakat, Ahmad Nami was the second Syrian president to resign.

The Damad, post-1928

Ahmad Nami was immediately replaced by the Damascus cleric Sheikh Taj al-Din al-Hasani. The Damad returned to Beirut, saying that he would have nothing further to do with Syria. Briefly in November 1931, he visited Damascus to serve on a committee of former heads of state, which included him, Subhi Barakat and Sheikh Taj, advising on the country's upcoming parliamentary elections.

The committee of presidents was short-lived, however, and it dissolved after one meeting.²¹ His name appeared in French correspondences later that year, as a possible king for Syria. The French had toyed with the idea of restoring the monarchy, either through him or Emir Sa'id El Djezairi. The idea never materialized, however, despite Nami's eagerness to assume the throne, based on his blood line and relation to Sultan 'Abdulhamid II. This was not a new ambition for the Damad – it actually dated back to 1928 – and many believed that it was the real reason why the French didn't ask him to re-consider his resignation from the presidency. He was accused of wanting to transform the republic into a monarchy, albeit independent of French influence. In 1932, he supported the election of Mohammad 'Ali al-'Abed, a close associate of his ex-father-in-law, Sultan 'Abdulhamid, as president of Syria.²²

The Damad came close to full comeback in April 1941, when he was officially approached by the French High Commissioner Henri Dentz to return to the Syrian presidency.²³ That was in the midst of the Second World War, after the German occupation of Paris. Ahmad Nami took up the offer, calling on the respected industrialist and ex-foreign minister, Khaled al-'Azm, to become his prime minister.²⁴ He was the son of the powerful 'Azm family and his father, Mohammad Fawzi Pasha, was a good friend of the Damad's father. 'Azm accepted the job, setting forth a series of conditions that included taking over the department of police and full control of bread distribution, which was vital for all Syrians during the Second World War. The Damad took 'Azm to Dentz's office's office in Beirut, confidently introducing him with the words: 'I present you with my prime minister.' The presidency, he thought, was a done deal. He seemed very excited about a comeback.

Nami and Dentz then went into serious talks, discussing candidates for Khaled al-'Azm's cabinet. The Damad suggested a five-man government, with two Shahbandarists and two members of the National Bloc. He even put forth the following names: Nasuh Babil, editor of the Damascus daily *al-Ayyam*, 'Abdul Qader Zahra, one of the founders of the Damascus University Faculty of Medicine, and Fouad al-Qodmani, dean of the Lawyer's Syndicate. All expressed no reservations about working with the Damad, and nor did Nasib Bakri, a former co-founder of the National Bloc who had defected from its ranks in the mid-1930s. The Bloc's president Hashem al-Atasi refused any cooperation with Ahmad Nami, saying that he was unacceptable, regardless of who his prime minister would be.

That painfully hurt the Damad, who had tried previously to work with Atasi, with no luck. It was under the Damad's era that the National Bloc had been founded in October 1927, and he considered Atasi's rebuttal as unappreciative. Given the Bloc's veto, Khaled al-'Azm reported to Dentz that forming a cabinet with Ahmad Nami as president was going to be difficult, if not impossible. 'The Damad is apparently no longer the man of the hour', he said. Vichy France eventually decided to abandon Ahmad Nami and appoint Khaled al-'Azm as premier, to rule Syria for the next five months, with no president or parliament.

Early retirement

At this point, Ahmad Nami announced that he would be retiring from politics, forever. He lived a long life, but never returned to Syria. President Shukri al-Quwatli didn't invite him to the country's first Independence Day celebrations on 17 April 1946. He watched Syria slip into political chaos, starting with the Husni al-Za'im coup of 1949. Four other coups took place, and in 1958, Syria and Egypt merged to form the United Arab Republic. Lebanon's political elite crossed the borders to congratulate Gamal 'Abdul Nasser, but the Damad refused to join. He considered Nasser as too populist for his taste – too humble for statesmanship, and too anti-Ottoman. He also felt that Nasser's socialism would greatly harm the Syrian economy – a prophecy that proved entirely correct. Nami divided the remainder of his years between Beirut and Paris, where he served as a visiting lecturer on Middle East history at the Sorbonne University. He would speak passionately about history of the Ottoman Empire and his family's contributions to Syria and Lebanon. He was happy to see the short-lived union republic collapse in September 1961. Digging into the letters of congratulations that poured into Damascus that autumn, one can find a cable sent by the Damad, in his capacity as former head of state, addressed to the secession coup leader, 'Abdul Karim al-Nehlawi. Fourteen months later, Ahmad Nami died in Beirut at the ripe-old age of eighty-four on 13 December 1962. There is not a single monument commemorating his era in Syria, nor have any of his administration's documents survived to this day.

Figure 5 President Ahmad Nami (seated) with members of his cabinet in 1926. Ahmad Nami.

Chapter 6

MOHAMMAD ʿALI AL-ʿABED (1932–6)

On 11 June 1932, Mohammad ʿAli al-ʿAbed rose to the podium of Syria's parliament to be sworn in as the country's first republican president. The republic had just been established, replacing the State of Syria that had existed between 1925 and 1932. At sixty-two, he was the eldest president to date in the history of the nation (Subhi Barakat was forty in 1923, and Ahmad Nami was forty-eight in 1926). ʿAbed's white hair and goatee made him look both experienced and dignified. His voice trembled as he pledged to serve the nation 'in the name of the people'. A standing ovation ensued from within the chamber, and a twenty-one-gun salute was fired in the skies of Damascus.[1] Syria's new flag was unfurled before the new president, a white, green and black tri-colour, with three red stars in the middle. Green stood for the four righteous caliphs who had succeeded the prophet.[2] White was for the Umayyad caliphs, black for the Abbasids of Islam. The three red stars in the middle represented the three national revolts against the French. ʿAbed stood firm saluting the flag.

One immediate concern was from where the new president would rule the nation. His predecessors Subhi Barakat and Ahmad Nami had both lived in rented homes, given that neither were natives of Damascus. He was the first Damascene head of state, and his home was at his father's estate in Souq Saruja, a Mamluk-era neighbourhood outside the Old City, occupied by the city's upper-crust. The ʿAbed home was one of the splendours of nineteenth-century Ottoman Damascus, spread across three alleys, with three huge courtyards – but unfit for presidential office, tucked deep within the crooked overlapping alleys of Old Damascus. Foreign dignitaries would have had a hard time reaching it, as no car or motorcade could enter the narrow neighbourhood.[3] No military parade could stand at its doors to play *Humat al-Diyar*, Syria's new national anthem, and ʿAbed would have found it difficult to manage its security, given its proximity to other homes in the neighbourhood.

With that in mind, President ʿAbed decided to move into his uncle's old palace in al-Muhajireen, making it the official premises of the Syrian Presidency. His

---

Parts of this chapter were originally published in the *British Journal of Middle Eastern Studies*, volume 41, #4 (2014), 'Syria's Forgotten President Mohammad ʿAli al-ʿAbed,' 419–41.

uncle had died just three years before his election as president, and ownership of the palace had gone to his son Hawlu, a Cambridge University-educated agronomist who decided to offer it to him on the day of 'Abed's swearing-in ceremony.[4] Contrary to popular lore, the palace was not given to 'Abed for free. He was required to pay a monthly rent, which was provided by the Ministry of Finance. In 1935, the Damascus newspaper *al-Shaab* ran a legal notice saying that the heirs of Mustapha Pasha al-'Abed were demanding a 300-gold coin increase in rent from the Syrian government.[5] The paper does not specify what the original rent for the palace was, but it only said that the current contract between them and the state expires on 13 July 1935, three years into the 'Abed presidency.

The new president gave orders that the Damascus Tram railway should be extended to reach the gates of the 'Abed palace in al-Muhajireen, in order to facilitate the travel of citizens seeking his audience and favours.[6] 'Abed ruled Syria longer than any of his predecessors under the mandate, from June 1932 until December 1936. With relative longevity came new norms and culture at the presidency. He hired Najib al-Armanazi, a prominent lawyer who, like him, had studied at the Sorbonne University in Paris, and made him secretary-general of the Presidential Palace.[7] Armanazi had been secretary of the Syrian National Congress back in 1919. The French-trained civil servant Emir Kazem El Djezairi, a cousin of Emir Sa'id, was commissioned as bureau chief to the new president.[8] Khalil al-Sa'adawi, a public servant of Libyan origins, was employed as assistant head of the presidential office.[9] He would continue to work at the palace for the next four decades, serving under every president from Mohammad 'Ali al-'Abed to Hafez al-Assad.

Eight policemen were delegated to guard the new presidential palace, rotating in shifts at its front gate. A staff sergeant from the Damascus Police, Amin al-Kurdi, was hired as the president's driver.[10] 'Abed's old tutor, an Italian named Pablo, was given an office on the second floor, next to that of the president, serving in unofficial capacity as adviser on protocol (his salary was paid for by 'Abed, not the Syrian government).[11] In total, 'Abed employed sixteen people at his palace, who continued to work by his side until his resignation in 1939.[12] Little did he know that he would be ejected from that same palace just four years later with none of the fawning he had seen in 1932. He didn't realize that this position, which was largely ceremonial back in French Mandate Syria, would dominate national politics for the next ninety years, as nineteen successors came to power in Damascus, some through the ballot box, others through violence, coups and revolutions. Few were given the luxury of resignation and a dignified exit, like President 'Abed. Most were either killed, jailed or exiled.

Four generations of service to the empire

The story of Mohammad 'Ali al-'Abed would not be complete, nor would his personality be fully understood, without delving into the career of his multi-dimensional father, the luminary Ahmad 'Izzat Pasha al-'Abed, a senior adviser to Sultan ʿAbdulhamid II. Ahmad ʿIzzat Pasha was a tough, sober and self-made tycoon who dominated public life in Ottoman Syria from the 1880s until 1908. Mohammad ʿAli not only lived in his shadow but owed him almost everything in life: his wealth, his political connections, his social standing and, even perhaps, his presidential office, although it came eight years after his father's death. The Damascus press considered them, both father and son, as the richest men in all of Syria.[13]

Born and raised in Ottoman Damascus, Ahmad ʿIzzat came from a family that worked in the grain and livestock trade. His grandfather, ʿOmar Agha, had used his social influence to protect Christians of his native al-Midan from being slaughtered by the mob, while their co-religionaries were being butchered in the old alleys of Bab Touma, within the Old City.[14] He worked closely with Emir ʿAbdelkader El Djezairi during the bloody events that swept through Mount Lebanon and Syria in May–July 1860.[15] ʿOmar Agha was a second-tier merchant at the time, with no power, no links to government and no political ambitions. He nevertheless had a reputation for fairness and honesty, which put him in good favour with the locals. He used that reputation to save Christian lives, helping transfer hundreds of families to the home of Emir ʿAbdelkader.[16] When the violence ended, he was charged with relocating them to homes of Muslim notables in the al-Qaymariya neighbourhood.[17]

The Ottomans realized how imperative it was for them to cultivate new allies – powerful men whom they could rely on – within the old city of Damascus. The clerical community, backbone of Syrian society for centuries, had disappointed the Ottoman sultan greatly during the summer of 1860. A handful of former notables were arrested and exiled to Famagusta, or executed on charges either for instigating the violence, fanning it or refusing to stop it. Replacing them were the Damascene families that had contributed to the protection of Christians, namely the ʿAbeds, Djezairis and Mardam Beys. This is when the ʿAbed family began adapting the honorific title of *agha*, although it is unclear whether this title was bestowed upon them because of their command of the business community in al-Midan, or because of their protection of Christians, or both.

Unlike other *aghas* of the 1860s, the ʿAbeds did not control a militia, nor did they have an infantry at their disposal. Their only assets were wealth and an honourable reputation, which took them far in society. ʿOmar Agha's first son Hawlu (1824–95), admiring the prestige that came with community service, joined the Ottoman bureaucracy in the late 1860s.[18] He was appointed *mutasarrif* of Homs and Nablus in the 1870s, earning the princely title of *pasha*, which was granted by the Sublime Port. In 1890, Hawlu Pasha was made president of the Administrative Council of Damascus – the highest government job ever reached to date by an ʿAbed. He also served as president of the Chamber of Agriculture and president of the Court of Appeals.

Hawlu Pasha's brother, Mohammad, was awarded a seat on the District Council of the city, while his second brother Mahmud became president of the Municipality of Damascus. Much of their social elevation came in reward for their father's services to the empire. Hawlu's political clout, along with his successful business, made him a rich man. He purchased shares in the Suez Canal Company, using their profit to buy vast tracts of fruit farms in al-Ghouta.[19] Hawlu al-'Abed was the only Syrian shareholder in the Universal Suez Ship Canal Company, which landed him an invitation to attend its opening in 1869, where he was given an audience with Ismail Pasha, the khedive of Egypt.[20] In 1904, his son acquired shares in the Panama Canal linking the Atlantic and Pacific Oceans, elevating the 'Abeds to international standing.[21]

The illustrious career of Ahmad 'Izzat al-'Abed

Hawlu Pasha mastered the patron-client system in Damascus, buying allegiance in exchange for protection of the locals while serving as a liaison between them and Ottoman authorities in Istanbul. Ahmad 'Izzat grew up under the strong influence of his father, studying at Catholic schools in Beirut.[22] Born in 1851, he joined the Ottoman civil service as a scribe.[23] Ahmad 'Izzat was married twice. His first wife, Bahiyya al-Muradi, was a direct descendant of Rumi, the thirteenth-century Muslim poet and scholar, while the second, Nibras Hanim, was a Circassian from the Caucasus. Her son, Mohammad 'Ali, was born in Damascus in 1867.

By the late 1870s, Ahmad 'Izzat al-'Abed had risen to become senior scribe in Damascus, which gave him access to the newly appointed governor Ahmad Jawdat Pasha.[24] A distinguished historian and man of letters, the governor saw 'Abed as a valuable asset to the Ottoman civil service. Briefly in 1873–5, he was commissioned to edit the state-run periodical *Souriyya*, which was printed in both Arabic and Ottoman Turkish. When the Ottoman reformer Midhat Pasha was appointed governor of Syria in 1878, Ahmad 'Izzat applied for a licence to found his own periodical, *Dimashq*.[25] It was the first private bi-lingual newspaper in Syria, with four pages in Arabic and Turkish, and it continued to print until 1887. *Dimashq* advocated reforms in the Ottoman Empire and yet pledged full allegiance to Sultan 'Abdulhamid II. Its readership was limited, however, because of high illiteracy in Damascus.[26]

After suspending *Dimashq*, Ahmad 'Izzat Pasha served as senior inspection officer at the justice department in Syria, before moving to Istanbul in 1886.[27] He was appointed judge at the Mixed Commercial Court, attracting the attention of 'Abdulhamid, and joining his court in 1895, first as director of the budget committee, then as senior adviser to the sultan, and finally as second secretary at the Imperial Palace. He used his new post to develop infrastructure in his native city, lobbying for the Hejaz Railway Station connecting to Medina, and for the telegraph system linking Izmir to Benghazi and Medina to Damascus.[28] 'Abed also introduced electricity to Damascus in 1907, at a time when leading European cities like Lyon were still lurking in darkness. With electricity came the first form of public transport, the Damascus Tram, which would eventually grow into six lines, all embarking from Marjeh Square. It would remain operational until being dismantled in stages in the early 1960s.[29]

In 1879, ʿAbed built a lavish three-floor hotel in the heart of Damascus, called the Victoria Hotel, on the banks of the Barada River. His choice of architecture seemed peculiar to the Damascenes, who were used to Islamic-style domes and calligraphy, rather than white stone. ʿAbed's hotel, however, looked like the old buildings of Europe and it boasted of an impressive clientele, among whom was the German emperor Wilhelm II during his 1898 visit to Damascus. Ahmad ʿIzzat also built the ʿAbed Building in the southern section of Marjeh Square, originally as another hotel designed by the Spanish architect Fernando De Aranda. It was completed in 1901, and Syria's first parliament met at its main hall in 1919.[30] By the time Mohammad ʿAli al-ʿAbed came to office in 1932, the building had been transformed into compartmental government offices, housing the departments of interrogations, persecution and medications.[31] Only two of Ahmad ʿIzzat Pasha's achievements remain standing as of 2023; the ʿAbed Building and the Hejaz Station. While the station is well-kept, the ʿAbed Building is now a shadow of its former self: dirty, battered and neglected.

A princely childhood and youth

Ahmad ʿIzzat Pasha spent his politically active years divided between Damascus and Istanbul, running his home in the very same manner that he managed his office at the Imperial Palace, on discipline, loyalty and good manners. While growing up, Mohammad ʿAli rarely spent quality time with his father and enjoyed none of the indulgencies of ordinary Syrian children. He was constantly attended to by a wide array of chamberlains and servants, hired from Ukraine, Bulgaria, Egypt and the Sudan.[32] He was prohibited from playing outdoors or mingling with neighbourhood children. In Ottoman Damascus, the ʿAbeds were the closest thing to royalty, and their children had to act and look like Ottoman princes. The young boy spoke softly and excelled in topics that were usually boring for children of his age, like French literature and Ottoman history. As a result, he was a miserable child, who grew accustomed to loneliness and carried this misery with him well into adulthood, even into the corridors of the Presidential Palace. Throughout his life, he had very few friends.[33]

Mohammad ʿAli studied with religious sheikhs, memorizing the Quran at an early age, and was given private lessons in Arabic grammar and composition. An Italian instructor taught him Latin and Western literature, and remained by his side, as an old man, well into his presidency.[34] During his childhood, Mohammad ʿAli also learned to ride horses and memorize complex pre-Islamic poetry, in addition to mastering Arabic, English, French, Italian and Ottoman Turkish. In 1885, Ahmad ʿIzzat sent his son to Beirut to study Islamic jurisprudence at the hands of the famous Egyptian cleric Mohammad ʿAbdo, a great reformist of his era.[35] After his father joined the Imperial Court, Mohammad ʿAli moved to Istanbul to complete his education at the elite sultanate school Galata.[36] He then went to Paris to study law and civil engineering at the Sorbonne University, graduating with a double major in 1905. One of his few friends at university was Ahmad Shawqi, the world-famous Egyptian poet, who was on scholarship in France, sent by Khedive ʿAbbas Hilmi II.[37] Burhan al-ʿAbed, a relative who later became a ranking physician in Syria, recalled how President ʿAbed would visit the family home in the 1930s and drill him with geography questions and quizzes in French grammar.[38] During his spare time, the president kept his mind alert by reading Voltaire and Victor Hugo.

Political marriage

Upon completing his studies in France, Mohammad ʿAli was hired as a legal consultant at the Ottoman Ministry of Foreign Affairs. He married Zahra al-Yusuf, the sister of ʿAbdul Rahman Pasha al-Yusuf, another ranking Damascene in the Ottoman court who held the important post of Emir al-Hajj since the 1890s. The Yusufs and ʿAbeds were lifetime neighbours in Souq Sarouja, but had their own share of differences. When ʿAbdul Rahman Pasha was nominated for the job of Emir of Hajj, Mohammad ʿAli's father objected to the Ottoman Sultan, saying that he was too young for such a senior position.[39] He probably wanted it either for his son or for his brother, whom he had helped appoint as governor of Mosul. That objection led to a prolonged period of tension between the two families, which was only solved after Mohammad ʿAli married Zahra, while his younger brother married her sister. It was a classic case of political marriage, serving the interests of the two powerful Damascene families. The wealth of the Yusufs and the respect that they enjoyed, both at home and in Istanbul, made them perfect in-laws for the ʿAbeds. When his family wealth failed him – although it rarely did – ʿAbed could always rely on that of his wife.

Ottoman ambassador to Washington

To reward his father's countless services to the sultanate, Sultan ʿAbdulhamid appointed Mohammad ʿAli as Ottoman ambassador to Washington, DC. He would reach the United States in 1908, during the presidency of Theodore Roosevelt.[40] Ottoman ambassadors were usually appointed on a temporary and limited tenure, as opposed to resident ambassadors that the sultan received from Europe and the United States, who stayed in Istanbul for much longer periods. Sultan ʿAbdulhamid feared that if an Ottoman diplomat stayed abroad for too long, he might be bribed in to serving the host country's interests, rather than those of the Empire. In other words, his diplomats might become spies, working to topple him with the help of foreign powers. He sincerely believed that everyone and everything could be bought off for a handsome amount of money, and conducted his diplomacy accordingly, never fully trusting his own diplomats, or those accredited to his capital by other states. This also applied to ʿAbed, regardless of how trusted his father was in Istanbul.

As Imperial ambassador, Mohammad ʿAli al-ʿAbed was received at the White House by President Roosevelt, where he presented his credentials after meeting with Secretary of State Elihu Root. Aged only fifty in 1908, Teddy Roosevelt was the youngest president in US history, with an abundance of energy, wit and a variety of interests that included boxing, horseback riding, tennis, hiking, travel and writing. ʿAbed was enchanted by Roosevelt's buccaneering spirit and his love of knowledge, two traits that remained imprinted in his mind until his coming to the presidency in 1932. Roosevelt and ʿAbed exchanged notes on literature, but had very little in common when it came to sports and hunting. ʿAbed developed a genuine admiration for the Roosevelts, and through them, learned to understand American politics.[41] When serving as president, he sent off a congratulatory telegram to America's new president Franklin D. Roosevelt, Teddy's fifth cousin, in 1933.[42]

ʿAbed's first exile

Barely six weeks after arriving in Washington, Ambassador ʿAbed got a cable from home saying that a coup had rocked the Imperial Palace in Istanbul on 23 July 1908. The young diplomat had barely settled, having not yet fully furnished his apartment on Dupont Circle. The coup leaders allowed Sultan ʿAbdulhamid to remain at his post but stripped him of his vast and uncontested powers, forcing him to re-adopt the constitution, which he had personally dissolved three decades ago. He was also obliged to call for nationwide elections and to re-instate the Ottoman Parliament that he had also dissolved, which automatically transformed him from a caliph with absolute powers into a constitutional monarch with very limited ones – a shadow of his former self.

One of the first victims of the 1908 revolt, who actually fell from grace before ʿAbdulhamid himself, was Ahmad ʿIzzat al-ʿAbed. Considered as the main force behind ʿAbdulhamid's rule, and keeper of the sultan's secrets, he was forced out of office and banished from Istanbul, with orders never to return.[43] CUP informers spread all kinds of slander against the pasha, ranging from corruption and bribery to autocracy and nepotism. Young revolutionaries roamed the streets of Istanbul, carrying signs that read: 'Death to the Traitor Ahmad ʿIzzat.'[44] Defeated and insulted, he boarded a British ship to the United States, hoping to join his son in exile, carrying a diplomatic passport given to him by the sultan, ostensibly for an official mission to Egypt.[45] While preparing to cross the Atlantic, he received news that Mohammad ʿAli had also been fired from his job as ambassador, and consequently, banned as well from returning to Istanbul. They decided to meet in Europe, dividing their time between Switzerland and France for what seemed to be a permanent exile.

Through secret proxies, Ahmad ʿIzzat continued to communicate with the sultan before he was fully dethroned in April 1909 and replaced by his brother Sultan Mehmed V Reşâd. ʿAbdulhamid was conveyed to dignified captivity at Salonica and, when it fell to the Greeks in 1912, was restored to one of his former palaces in Istanbul. He spent his last days in custody, studying, carpentering and writing his memoirs at Beylerbeyi Palace, where he died on 10 February 1918, seven months before collapse of Ottoman rule in Syria. The ʿAbeds continued to show complete loyalty to the family of Sultan ʿAbdulhamid II, providing his eldest son, Emir Mehmed Salim, who settled in Damascus in March 1924, with a monthly stipend of fifty gold coins. Emir 'Adel Arslan, a Lebanese Druze politician of the 1920s, describes how Mohammad 'Ali al-'Abed would continue to bow in Mehmed Selim's presence, 'just like he did when they were living in Istanbul during the era of Selim's father'.[46] The respect, it must be noted, was mutual. 'Abdulhamid named his youngest son 'Abed (born in 1905), in honour of his friend and confident Ahmad 'Izzat al-'Abed.[47] He once said: 'I have found in him a loyal friend.'[48]

Tension with the Hashemite royals

Seeing the terrible fate of the sultan, the 'Abeds were discouraged from any further political activity, watching in dismay as the Arab revolt broke out against the empire in 1916, which they refused to support.[49] They also declined to back Emir Faisal or his kingdom, considering it a populist monarchy run by a wide permutation of Arab nationalists who were all vehemently anti-Ottoman. Radicalized Arabs in Faisal's court demanded that he strip members of the Syrian aristocracy of all titles and ranks bestowed upon them by the Ottoman sultan. Anybody who had refused to support the Arab Revolt was considered an outcast, an enemy of Arabism and the Hashemite family. Ahmad 'Izzat did not like Faisal, but he nevertheless agreed to meet with him at the Paris Conference of 1919 and was even considered for the post of speaker of the Syrian National Congress, an office that he declined for ideological reasons.[50] The pasha found it painfully difficult to shed off his entire past and part ways with the Ottomans, with whom his family had worked for three generations. Other Syrian notables did not seem to mind, however – like Mohammad Fawzi Pasha al-'Azm, a former minister under the CUP who took on the job of speaker under Faisal, while Mohammad 'Ali's brother-in-law, 'Abdul Rahman Pasha al-Yusuf, became first deputy to the Syrian Congress president. The 'Abeds felt that they were morally incapable of making such a shift, although they generously put the 'Abed Building in Marjeh Square at the disposal of Syria's new king, where parliament held its opening session in 1919.

They shed no tears, however, when Faisal's kingdom was toppled in July 1920. Henri Gouraud was an old friend of Mohammad 'Ali al-'Abed; they were the exact same age and had met frequently during the 'Abed family exile in Paris. 'Abed was a valuable primary source for Gouraud, given his excellent command of French and deep knowledge of Arab and Islamic affairs. Once firmly in control of Syria, Gouraud invited his old friend back to Damascus, reasoning that if Ahmad 'Izzat returned home, then this would add credibility to French rule in Syria. If treated with the respect that they had been denied since 1908, the 'Abeds might even be convinced to invest part of their huge capital in Syria.

Their mansion in Souq Sarouja had been closed since the family departure in 1908, shuttered and guarded first by Ottoman, then Faisalian and now Senegal soldiers conscripted from France's African colonies. Damascus, however, had not changed much since they had last visited; there was very little urbanization in sight – testimony as to how little Faisal had contributed to the city during his brief tenure as monarch. The dusty streets were empty; the only sound was that of marching men patrolling the capital, carrying guns.

The Damascene notability welcomed the ʿAbeds with open arms. Red carpets were thrust at the gates of the Grand Serail when Ahmad ʿIzzat visited Syria's new premier, ʿAlaa al-Din Droubi. He was an old man now, fully retired but still extremely wealthy and well connected. Ambitious notables stood in line for an audience, hoping that he would put a good word in their favour with either mandate authorities in Beirut or state officials in Paris. The local press, however, was less welcoming, criticizing ʿAbed for keeping much of his wealth in Swiss and American banks, reported at no less than £1 million, at a time when Syrian coffers were empty and in much need of foreign investment.[51] During his brief 1920 visit to Syria, Ahmad ʿIzzat bankrolled a handful of projects, including an orphanage and a hospital in his native al-Midan, but decided to return to Egypt, which had become his new home. His son, however, stayed in Syria.

Family problems

In June 1922, Gouraud handpicked Mohammad ʿAli al-ʿAbed for the post of director of finance in the cabinet of Subhi Barakat. ʿAbed helped negotiate Syria's first currency with the Paris-based Banque Liban et Syrie, in addition to deciding on fiscal policies and the state budget. He took leave to Egypt in order to spend time with his ailing father, who died in Cairo on 15 October 1924. The mass circulation Egyptian daily *al-Ahram* wrote in his obituary: 'He was one of the greatest men of the East in brilliance of reputation, and one of the most experienced in political affairs. He was everything (in the Empire). Nothing passed without his approval.'[52] It was a devastating blow to ʿAbed. Ahmad ʿIzzat Pasha had become his son's adviser and sounding board, and it would be very difficult to navigate the political landscape without his good advice.

Back home, his relations had soured with Subhi Barakat after his failed marriage to ʿAbed's daughter Layla. She was an open-minded and liberal woman educated at the Jesuit School in Beirut, dedicated to combating syphilis in the countryside of Cairo, through her connections to the Egyptian Red Cross. The divorce left Mohammad ʿAli al-ʿAbed very angry. He vowed never to speak to Subhi Barakat for the rest of his life, but had to renege on his pledge after Barakat became speaker of parliament during his presidency, forcing the two men to meet weekly to discuss state affairs.[53] Layla moved to France with her family in 1936, where she worked with the French Red Cross and befriended Eugenie Petain, wife of Marshal Philip Petain, a decorated First World War officer who went on to rule Vichy France during the Second World War. During the war years, Petain appointed Layla director of foreign correspondences in Paris, a post she held until 1944, six years after her father's death.[54]

Running for president

Shaken by his father's demise, Mohammad 'Ali temporarily withdrew from politics for almost eight years, concentrating on running his family estates in Syria and Europe.[55] He staged a comeback in late 1931, running for parliament as an independent. Elections were scheduled for 20 December 1931, right after the holy month of Ramadan. Contesting the Chamber of Deputies was ex-president Barakat, former premier Taj al-Din al-Hasani and Hashem al-Atasi of the National Bloc.[56] During the primaries, and due to what was generally believed as gross meddling in the polls, the National Bloc suffered a major blow in the city of Aleppo. To compensate, it put its full weight behind elections in Damascus, which took place on 30 March 1932, when 'Abed was running in his native al-Midan.

The elections played out nicely in favour of the mandate regime, bringing forty-eight moderates into the chamber, twenty-nine of whom were considered either allies or creations of colonial France. They rallied around Subhi Barakat, electing him as speaker of parliament, much to 'Abed's dismay. 'Abed had won his parliamentary seat with ease and began planning for the next step of his awakening political ambition: presidency of the young republic. He conferred with an old friend, the judge Yusuf al-Hakim, saying that he would run for president only after making absolutely sure that former head of state Ahmad Nami was not interested in the job.[57] Although Nami had long divorced the sultan's daughter, he remained father of 'Abdulhamid's grandchildren, and in no way did 'Abed want to be seen as defying or challenging the family of his former patron.

On 30 May 1932, he wrote a confidential letter to the French high commissioner Henri Ponsot, announcing his intention to run for the presidency. 'I consider that the authority of France must remain entire and unquestionable in Syria, and in order for it to fulfill its tasks every Syrian government must acknowledge to itself that it is subordinate to that authority. As for my program, it can be resumed in one phrase: economy in every domain, and justice for all.'[58] Reaching out to the French high commissioner seemed like the only logical thing to do, given that 'Abed had no political party to back him and no powerbase in Damascus. He had always been close to the French and never joined any of the anti-French parties that emerged in the 1920s, not even the National Bloc, despite his personal friendship with its leaders. 'Abed had even agreed to join a handful of the Bloc's projects, without ever becoming an official member. He owned shares in its economic enterprise, the National Cement Company, and had donated 5,000 Syrian pounds to the Bloc newspaper, *al-Ayyam*.[59]

In French archives, there is no formal reply to 'Abed's letter but one can assume, from the turn of events, that Ponsot decided to support him. When the new chamber met for an open one-week session to elect a new president, 'Abed presented his candidacy on 7 June 1932. In the meantime, he had distributed generous stipends to the heads of all sects in Damascus and met with investors with the promise of establishing a new Syrian bank (which never saw the light).[60] He was running against Subhi Barakat, Haqqi al-'Azm, ex-prime minister Rida al-Rikabi and Hashem al-Atasi. With no MPs to support him in Aleppo, Atasi withdrew his candidacy in favour of ʿAbed. Four National Bloc MPs seconded ʿAbed's nomination: Jamil Mardam Bey, Fakhri al-Barudi, Nasib al-Bakri and ʿAfif al-Solh.[61] The National Bloc controlled a total of seventeen seats in the Chamber of Deputies, who all voted for ʿAbed. He won the election with thirty-six votes, defeating Barakat, who came in second with thirty-two. It was a double victory, taking sweet revenge from Barakat while securing the presidency for himself. He watched with joy as a humiliated Barakat had to read out the votes, announcing his own defeat and the victory of ʿAbed.

Different views

Addressing the chamber with a brief, solemn speech, ʿAbed promised to remain 'a friend to all' and restore the 'glorious history' of Syria.[62] Rather than pledge to terminate the mandate, ʿAbed promised to work with it, thanking 'the noble French nation' for its services to Syria.[63] That resounded negatively on the Syrian street and within the National Bloc that had supported him. They had expected a more patriotic speech, prompting the Bloc leader ʿAbdul Rahman al-Kayyali to comment: 'He (ʿAbed) thought that the nation had elected him; that he earned people's confidence through merit. He believed he would uphold his oath and promises. In reality, however, what made him president was Mr. Solomiac (Henri Ponsot's delegate in Damascus).' Kayyali added: 'His background had nothing to do with public service, nor does it show that the fate of Syria and its independence mattered to him. He has no virtues to speak of, or white (charitable) hands.'[64] Others thought more favourably of ʿAbed, like the scholar Mohammad Kurdi ʿAli, founding president of the prestigious Arab Language Academy, who described him as 'the greatest politician in Syria', claiming that his company was 'soul enriching'.[65] Kurd ʿAli added that ʿAbed was a philanthropist who would hold large banquets for the needy during Ramadan, accommodating 1,000 poor Syrians every night. He would 'feed the poor (with food) and the rich (with bribes)', said Kurd ʿAli, noting that during his presidency, ʿAbed would collect his government salary and donate it to the poor and needy.[66] In 1933, he used his personal wealth to subsidize 20 per cent of students studying at private Syrian schools, who were unable to pay their tuitions due to inflation.[67]

Getting domestic house in order

ʿAbed's first act as president was appointing Haqqi al-ʿAzm, the all-time French favourite, as his first prime minister on 15 June 1932. The French wanted ʿAzm compensated for having failed to secure either the speakership of parliament or the presidency. ʿAzm looked and behaved like the old school statesmen of the Ottoman Empire. He dabbled in Turkish, excelling at pomp and ceremony copied from the Imperial Palace in Istanbul. Among other things, ʿAzm insisted that his ministers appear at official receptions wearing brocade and silk, with different uniforms and gold laces for different titles and ranks.[68] Thirty ranks of bureaucracy emerged under his government, all copied from the Ottoman order. He was also a rich man, both from estates of the ʿAzm family and from the fertile cotton plantations that he owned in Egypt – no less than 700 acres, which generated a handsome annual revenue of 6,000 Egyptian pounds.[69]

Seeing that ʿAzm was too pro-French, President ʿAbed called on two members of the National Bloc to become ministers in the new government, hoping that this would strike a balance and please the Syrian street. Jamil Mardam Bey, a Paris-educated statesman, was given the ministries of finance and agriculture, while Mazhar Raslan, a pasha from Homs who had briefly served as prime minister of Jordan in the early 1920s, became minister of education and justice. The president's bureau chief Najib al-Armanazi was married to Jamil Mardam Bey's sister and on the night before his swearing-in ceremony, ʿAbed had spent his evening in their company at the Mardam Bey residence, practising his inauguration speech.[70] The Bloc's leadership was furious with their appointment, claiming that ʿAbed was using Mardam Bey and Raslan to sugar-coat his pro-French administration, and that the two ministers had accepted office without consulting their colleagues. Ibrahim Hananu and Hashem al-Atasi insisted that with ʿAzm at the Grand Serail and Barakat at parliament, the ʿAbed administration would never fulfil nationalist aspirations. Early into the new era, they promised to bring it down.

Land sale in Palestine

Hananu found easy targets to use against Syria's new president. One was the issue of land sale in Palestine, conducted by Syrian landowners related to the ʿAbed family. They were reportedly selling vast tracts of lands to Jewish businessmen coming from Europe, acting as front-men for the Jewish National Fund. The trend began in the late 1920s, but most of what had been sold was uncultivated land that attracted little public attention. Civil society began lobbying against land sale in Palestine in 1934, petitioning President ʿAbed to issue a law prohibiting Syrians from selling land sale to non-Arabs. In March 1934, a rumour spread in Damascus that relatives of the president's wife had sold land on the Syrian shore of Lake Tiberias to the Jewish National Fund. ʿAbed's brother-in-law, Saʿid al-Yusuf, was in financial trouble, about to be foreclosed by Asfar & Sara Bank for a debt of 3,892 Turkish gold coins.[71] He had borrowed heavily, using land as collateral, failing to predict the collapse of world food prices and the exceptionally harsh winter that damaged crops in 1934. Among the lands mortgaged by the Yusufs were the fertile plains of al-Btayha on the shore of Lake Tiberias in Palestine, a staggering 300,000 dunums of agricultural land (approximately 75,000 acres).[72] In total, debt of the Yusuf family stood at a staggering 12,000 gold coins.[73]

In 1934, the Yusufs received a most unusual visitor, that is, Chaim Weizmann, president of the Zionist Commission, who showed up at their mansion in Souq Sarouja, unclear whether unexpected or by invitation.[74] Weizmann offered to buy the lands of al-Btayha for an astronomical price, which prompted relatives to try and settle the problem before it snowballed into a national controversy. Hussein Ibish, a wealthy landlord married to the niece of the First Lady, settled part of the loan on behalf of the Yusuf family. ʿAbed used his personal influence with Asfar & Sara Bank to reschedule what remained of the Yusuf family debt. He then took two measures to distance himself from the controversial deal, first creating a Society for Exploitation of the Village of al-Btayha. A shareholding company, it was supposed to raise the amount demanded by Asfar & Sara and buy the land from the Yusufs, capitalized at exactly 150,000 Turkish gold.[75] When that failed to raise the needed amount, he issued decree #2813, creating the Syrian Agricultural Company for the same purpose, capitalized at the same amount and divided into 50,000 shares. Neither project succeeded, however, and the Yusufs had to borrow more money to settle the Asfar & Sara Bank loan. Weizmann's dramatic appearance in Damascus, however, gave ʿAbed's enemies plenty of ammunition to be used against him, despite his efforts to obstruct the land sale.

While trying to shake off the bad publicity caused by the al-Btayha ordeal, the president's opponents were busy touring the Arab world, rallying regional leaders against ʿAbed. In July 1934, Hashem al-Atasi went to Alexandria to meet with ex-prime minister Mustapha Nahhas Pasha, the influential chief of the popular Wafd Party.[76] In March 1935, Fakhri al-Barudi went to Riyadh for talks with King ʿAbdul-ʿAziz Al Saud. When ʿAbed failed to show up at the fourteenth anniversary of the Battle of Maysaloun, the National Bloc's Damascus leader Shukri al-Quwatli took to the podium, using the occasion to call for the president's resignation.

The treaty of friendship

The French, meanwhile, were focused on getting the Syrian president to sign a treaty of friendship that would regulate future relations between the two countries. It was proposed by Henri De Martel, who had replaced Ponsot as high commissioner in October 1933. ʿAbed agreed, in principle, to sign the Friendship Treaty, but on condition that Syria is first admitted to the League of Nations.[77] The treaty was penned in French, with no Arabic translation, and it gave France the right to manage Syria's foreign relations, schools, police, minority rights and future army.[78] It would last for five years, renewable by consensus, without specifying whether the mandate would end with its termination.[79]

Objecting to the friendship treaty, the National Bloc got its two ministers to resign from the ʿAbed administration, on 20 April 1933. Two weeks later, Haqqi al-ʿAzm created a new cabinet, appointing the respected judge Suleiman Joukhadar as minister of justice. Joukhadar was not a member of the National Bloc but the nationalists held him in high esteem. Under Sultan ʿAbdulhamid II, he had served as judge of Mecca and Medina, before becoming mufti of Damascus. When the Friendship Treaty was put up for voting, all pro-French ministers and MP voted in favour, except for Joukhadar. He abstained, seemingly at the president's orders, in order to drown the treaty without ʿAbed having to obstruct it in person. Surprisingly, so did Subhi Barakat and Public Works Minister Saleem

Jambart, a prosperous Catholic politician from Aleppo, who resigned from the 'Azm cabinet in protest of the Treaty of Friendship.[80] Of the sixty-eight MPs present, fifty-two voted against the treaty.

The French responded by dismissing parliament for three days, hoping that this would pressure Syrian nationalists into re-considering their position. On 2 November 1934, another suspension was signed by De Martel, this time indefinitely. The Syrian Chamber of Deputies was never to reconvene for what remained of the 'Abed presidency. The Syrian constitution was then suspended by the French, an act that played out nicely in the president's favour. By constitution, his term ought to have ended in June 1935, yet with no charter and no parliament, he hung on to office for an additional year and a half, until December 1936, without having to be formally re-elected.

The 60-Day Strike

Failing to secure the Friendship Treaty, Haqqi al-'Azm was forced to resign from the premiership on 17 May 1934. Replacing him was Sheikh Taj al-Din al-Hasani, the anti-National Bloc statesmen who had served as premier in 1928–30. He created a six-man cabinet of independents, choosing a National Bloc defector for the Ministry of Education. 'Abed had no say in naming Sheikh Taj premier. Although friends, the two men did not get along politically, and yet, the president was forced to accept him because his name had been dictated by the high commissioner's office in Beirut.[81] Sheikh Taj's reputation worried the president, fearing that it would give his administration a bad name. He confessed to his bureau chief Najib al-Armanazi saying: 'I fear that the cabinet crisis will soon develop into a presidential one.'[82] Protesting the appointment of Sheikh Taj as premier, the National Bloc staged a citywide strike in the old bazaars of Damascus, bringing commercial life to a halt.

On 21 November 1935, Ibrahim Hananu died after a prolonged illness, possibly tuberculosis.[83] The National Bloc invested in his death to drum up anti-French sentiment on the streets, calling for the resignation of both Sheikh Taj and 'Abed.[84] This was the same year in which 'Abed's term ought to have ended, making it easy for the Bloc to call for his resignation, considering the extension of his term a constitutional violation. Hananu received a hero's funeral in Aleppo, where loud anti-French slogans were raised and clashes ensued between young Syrians and the police. A total of 150 people were arrested, including Hananu's protégé Sa'adallah al-Jabiri. The Hananu funeral triggered a series of anti-French demonstrations throughout the country, which accumulated with a sixty-day strike that began in January 1936. It was led by the National Bloc in response to the arrest of their Damascus MP Fakhri al-Barudi, who had just been deported to the city of al-Hassakeh. Damascus closed down its markets, with 20,000 people marching through the Old City. 'Abed called for calm but the French ignored his appeal, opening fire at the demonstrators and killing two civilians. Hundreds of young men were hauled off to the dungeons of the Damascus Citadel. ʿAbed lobbied for their release, to no avail. The French then pushed for a more aggressive approach in Damascus, placing the Bloc leaders Shukri al-Quwatli, Lutfi al-Haffar and Nasib al-Bakri under house arrest while banishing Jamil Mardam Bey to a remote town on the Syrian-Turkish border.[85] They then had Fares al-Khoury fired from his post as dean of the Faculty of Law at Damascus University.

The National Bloc pledged to continue the strike until all its demands were met, which included the release of Fakhri al-Barudi, the lifting of martial law, a general amnesty and a timetable for termination of the mandate. They came short of including the resignation of President ʿAbed on their list of conditions. He realized, however, right there and then that his days in office were numbered. During the last eight months of his presidency, ʿAbed became increasingly sensitive to criticism, more so than any point in his career. He was visibly upset by what the papers were saying about him, and felt insulted by a French speech at the League of Nations, which described him as a 'creation of the mandate'.[86] A French ally he was indeed, but for someone with his excessive hubris, being coloured a 'creation' was simply too much to handle. When ʿAbed and Sheikh Taj showed up in Aleppo to attend prayer at the Great Mosque, National Bloc supporters occupied the special section that had been reserved for them, forcing them out with loud insults.[87] Young people threw rotten tomatoes at the president and premier, which led to the arrest of 188 demonstrators.[88]

Beginning of the end

With time, however, the French adduced that sheer force would not solve the crisis in Syria. Henri de Martel decided to sit down for talks with Hashem al-Atasi, agreeing to dismiss Sheikh Taj and replace him with an independent who enjoyed backing of the National Bloc. Sheikh Taj was sacked in favour of his Interior Minister ʿAta al-Ayyubi, who drove to Beirut for marathon talks with the French.[89] He convinced Atasi to call off the strike in exchange for a political amnesty and for sending a delegation from the National Bloc to Paris to negotiate Syria's future. When Fakhri al-Barudi and his colleagues were released from prison, Atasi walked down to the old Hamidieh market of Damascus, where a green cord was strung at its entrance. Atasi symbolically cut the cord, to massive applause from the Damascus business community. He was sending a clear message to President ʿAbed: only the Bloc had the power to close down Damascus and only the Bloc was capable of re-opening the city.

A senior Bloc delegation travelled to France on 21 March 1936, headed by Hashem al-Atasi. ʿAbed appointed two cabinet ministers to join the delegation, namely Edmond Homsi and Emir Mustapha al-Shihabi. They were seen off by a jubilant crowd, which delayed them for twenty minutes at the train station, chanting for the long life of Atasi and the National Bloc.[90] Nobody dared call out the president's name, to avoid being hissed or cussed by the crowd. As the talks opened in Paris, the ʿAbed administration began its long march into history, which came to a rapid and rather colourless end. The Bloc delegation stayed in France for six months, meeting with Foreign Minister Pierre Etienne Flandin and his successor, Yvon Delbos, two meetings that, technically, ought to have occurred with the Syrian head of state, not with a delegation representing the opposition to his rule.

The Bloc leaders returned to Syria six months later, after signing an agreement with Prime Minister Leon Blum, securing gradual independence over a twenty-five-year period. Atasi had managed to include a clause for re-incorporation of the Alawite and Druze Mountains to Syria, thus obtaining unity of Syrian lands, which 'Abed had failed to achieve. The treaty also expanded powers of the Syrian government, allowing for the establishment of a Ministry of Foreign Affairs and a Ministry of Defense, two institutions that had been absent under 'Abed. Fares al-Khoury described the treaty as 'miracle of the twentieth century'.[91]

When the Bloc declared the signing of the Franco-Syrian Treaty on 9 September 1936, 'Abed reasoned that it was now time to leave. Watching massive celebrations on the streets of Damascus, he waited for parliamentary elections to conclude in November before presenting his resignation. Citing health concerns as the main reason for his retirement, he said:

> Now that the country has entered a new era, and a new team is about to take over the reins of government, a team in which the nation has placed its trust and entrusted its aspirations, I have come to believe that my mission has ended. It is time to make way for this new team to carry the burden of governance bestowed upon them.[92]

Atasi ran for office unopposed and was sworn in as Syria's second republican president on 21 December 1936. 'Abed congratulated his friend-turned-opponent and successor, before going on an open-ended vacation in the serenity of the French Riviera. He never returned to Syria. Very little is known about the president's final years in his self-imposed exile. He spent his days with his old-friend 'Abdulmejid II, the last caliph of the Ottoman Empire, who was also serving a lifelong exile in France. Together they spent weekends in Nice, where they would be seen drinking afternoon tea at the Negresco Hotel. Mohammad 'Ali al-'Abed died in exile at the age of seventy-two, on 17 November 1939. The former president's body was flown back to Syria, according to his will, to be buried in Damascus. He was given a state funeral, and his coffin was draped with the Syrian Flag and then put on display on a marble floor at the main entrance of the Syrian Parliament. Ordinary Syrians stopped to pay their respects, before two Circassian officers snapped their heels and escorted a horse-driven cannon to the al-Midan cemetery, where President 'Abed was carried shoulder-high to his final resting place. Prime Minister Bahij al-Khatib led the cortege and ordered that a main street, facing the Syrian Parliament in central Damascus, is named in 'Abed's honour.

'Abed's name was dropped from Syria's first Independence Day celebrations on 17 April 1946. He left behind no written memoir, no family member in politics to defend his name and no archive of his presidency. The minutes of the 1934 talks over the Treaty of Friendship were destroyed during a French assault on the Syrian Parliament in May 1945.[93] Another reason for ʿAbed's name being omitted from public discourse was the series of coups and counter-coups that rocked Syria starting in 1949, leading to the Syrian-Egyptian Union. During that decade, history books glorified the anti-French resistance, treating men like Mohammad ʿAli al-ʿAbed with little respect. Then came the Ba'ath Party, which systematically obliterated entire sections of modern Syrian history. Anything that came before the socialist revolution, they claimed, was capitalistic, imperialistic, elitist, backward and ultimately wrong. Any longing for ʿAbed or his social class became a criminal offence, often resulting in harassment or jail.

When Gamal ʿAbdul Nasser passed his Agricultural Reform Law in September 1958, what remained of ʿAbed's assets, and those of his wife, were seized by the socialist state. Up until then, his widow Zahra al-Yusuf had been quite active in Damascene society, hosting an intellectual salon at her home in Damascus well into the 1950s, while serving on a handful of charitable NGOs. When she was nationalized by Nasser, Zahra went into retirement, and passed away at the age of seventy-six in 1971. The subsequent political, economic and social disappearance of the ʿAbed and Yusuf families made it easier for consecutive regimes to overlook Mohammad ʿAli al-ʿAbed.

The abandoned mansion of the ʿAbed family

The biggest manifestation of his demise was the fate of his family mansion in Souq Sarouja. In 1948, nine years after his death, ʿAbed's sons sold the home to Saleem Yazagi, who turned its courtyards into a secondary school, while living on its second floor with his family.[94] It was a respected school with distinguished graduates, and its honorary president was Asma Eid, wife of Prime Minister Fares al-Khoury.

After the Six Day War with Israel in 1967, President Nur al-Din al-Atasi ordered confiscation of the ʿAbed residence and transformed it into a state-run school for refugees from the occupied Golan Heights.[95] The mansion required plenty of maintenance, however, which the Ministry of Education failed to provide for lack of funds. By the late 1970s, its walls and ceilings began collapsing, making it unsafe for students. The school was closed, and its premises were then rented to shoe-maker workshops until a fire destroyed large parts of it on New Year's Eve in 1993. The Yazagi family filed a court case to regain property of the mansion, which it finally won in 1995. It remains standing as of 2023, but in miserable condition. The shoe-makers are back, and so are other craftsmen who work at the premises of what used to be the seat of power in Damascus. There is no sign mentioning his name at its entrance, nor that of his father, Ahmad ʿIzzat Pasha al-ʿAbed.

Figure 6 President Mohammad ʿAli al-ʿAbed (center) surrounded by his prime minister Taj al-Din al-Hasani (second from left wearing turban) and Interior Minister ʿAta al-Ayyubi.

Chapter 7

HASHEM AL-ATASI (1936–9)

Hashem al-Atasi woke up at daybreak just in time for morning prayer. At eighty-seven, he was still in good shape, and continued to enjoy a meticulously sharp memory, remembering names, dates and events dating back more than half a century. Preparing for prayer required washing the hands, arms, face, head and feet. The ex-president tripped and fell while performing the *wudou'*, slipped into coma and died on 6 December 1960. Syria at the time was part of the United Arab Republic (UAR), known as *Al-Iqlim al-Shamali* (The Northern Province). President Gamal 'Abdul Nasser expressed a desire to take part in Atasi's funeral, but the Atasi family insisted on a speedy burial, as mandated in Islam.

The ex-president was nevertheless given a state funeral, carried on a cannon through the silent streets of Homs, draped with the flag of the union republic. It had two stars in its middle white bar: one for Syria and one for Egypt. Nasser's Syrian deputy Nur al-Din Kahaleh walked behind the coffin, next to Interior Minister 'Abdul Hamid Sarraj and Gamal Faisal, commander of the First Army. Forty days later, a crew from the newly established Syrian Television arrived at the Atasi residence to film a documentary about the former president's life. They unlocked his bedroom, which had been left untouched since his passing. Hanging above his bed was the Hashimiyya calendar, which could be found in every Syrian home. It was fixed at 6 December 1960. Behind every page was a quote and word of wisdom, which made the Hashimiyya calendar so popular in Syria. The last quote that Hashem al-Atasi had read before death was: 'Never regret.'[1]

Hashem al-Atasi had no regrets. A national paragon and state-builder, he had led a tumultuous life, assuming the most senior posts in post-Ottoman Syria. On three occasions he had served as president, in 1936, 1949 and 1954. Twice, he was prime minister, in 1920 and 1949. In 1919 he had chaired Syria's first democratically elected parliament under King Faisal I. Atasi had also presided over the drafting of Syria's first, second and third constitutions, a monarchial one in 1920 and two republican charters in 1928 and 1949. Syrians affectionately called him '*Al-Ra'is al-Jaleel*' (The Venerable President). Others labelled him 'Father of the Nation'. He was a man of the people, someone who championed good citizenship, high morals and democracy.

A senior bureaucrat

Born in the city of Homs on 11 January 1873, Atasi grew up in a family of Islamic judges and religious scholars of Qadiriya Sufism.[2] Since 1535, his ancestors had served as muftis of Homs. His father, Sheikh Khaled, had also been deputy for Homs in the Ottoman Parliament in the 1870s.[3] Atasi studied at state-run schools then at the Islamic College in Beirut, before joining the Mulkiyye School in Istanbul, where he was trained in public administration by the Ottoman Empire's finest instructors. Upon graduation, he married his cousin Ward-Shan al-Atasi in 1894, before receiving his first appointment. He was named assistant to the governor of Beirut and then transferred to the *caza* of Al-Marqab (Banias today) on the Syrian coast, serving as *qa'im maqam* for one year.[4] He later became *qa'im maqam* of Sahiyoun (al-Haffa, east of Latakia) until 1902, when he was moved to the city of Safad in Palestine and then to Jabal Amil in southern Lebanon. In 1904, he became *qa'im maqam* of al-Salt and *wakil mutasarrif* of al-Kark (both in present-day Jordan), until 1907. He was then named *qa'im maqam* of Jableh on the Syrian coast.[5] During that tenure, a coup took place in Istanbul, and many Arab bureaucrats were fired, especially those loyal to Sultan 'Abdulhamid II. Atasi was a professional civil servant, with no political affiliations. The new rulers kept him at his post, making him *qa'im maqam* of Jaffa, Palestine, in 1912.[6]

Atasi under King Faisal

One year later, Atasi was promoted to the rank of *mutasarrif* and named governor first of Homs and Hama, then of Acre in Palestine. When the First World War broke out in 1914, he was transferred to western Anatolia, where he worked until collapse of Ottoman rule in Syria in 1918. Atasi resigned from the Ottoman government and returned to Damascus, pledging loyalty to Emir Faisal, who re-appointed him *mutasarrif* of Homs from November 1918 to March 1919. Atasi then nominated himself for Syria's first elections, running for a seat on the Syrian National Congress. When the congress' first president Mohammad Fawzi Pasha al-'Azm died that winter, Atasi succeeded him as speaker on 3 June 1919.

Atasi chaired all the congress meetings and personally organized the throning of Faisal as king on 8 March 1920.[7] Although friends both with Faisal and his father, Sharif Hussein, Atasi was never pro-Hashemite.[8] He was also both anti-British and anti-French. Faisal mandated him, however, to chair a constitutional committee, penning Syria's first (and last) royal constitution. It included Aleppo MPs Sa'adallah al-Jabiri and Theodore Antaki, law professor 'Ali Sultan and Sheikh 'Abdul Qader Kaylani from Hama.[9] They completed the job in a matter of weeks, right before the July 1920 confrontation with the French. The new charter, with 148 articles, called for a parliamentary democracy, making the cabinet responsible to the chamber of deputies, rather than the king.[10] It guaranteed Faisal's right to the throne, followed by his eldest mail heir, but stripped him from the authority to declare war and peace or to appoint members of the royal family to the executive branch. Despite

Atasi's religious upbringing, there was no mention of Islam in the constitution, except for Article 3, which said that the king of Syria must be a Muslim.[11] Article 13 guaranteed the right of religious practice and belief.

Atasi's first cabinet (May–July 1920)

As French troops began advancing from the Beqqa Valley towards Damascus, King Faisal created a war cabinet, headed by Hashem al-Atasi, on 5 May 1920. Atasi had no military experience but was a tough and uncompressing statesman. The Sidon notable Rida al-Solh, a former MP in the Ottoman Parliament, was made minister of interior, while General Yusuf al-'Azma took over as minister of defense. 'Abdul Rahman Shahbandar was brought onboard as minister of foreign affairs. Atasi presided over state affairs during the final two months of King Faisal's kingdom. He was at the seat of power when the Battle of Maysaloun took place on 24 July 1920. The next morning Faisal replaced Atasi with 'Alaa al-Din Droubi as premier, hoping that he could negotiate a return of the Syrian monarchy. Atasi retired to his home in Homs, steering clear from any political activism during the first five years of the French Mandate. His successor was gunned down in the Houran province less than one month after assuming office, on 21 August 1920.

Birth of the National Bloc

Atasi didn't join the Great Revolt of 1925 but nudged his brother into supporting the rebels of Sultan al-Atrash. The French had the ex-premier arrested and sent to the Arwad Island Prison, with no warrant and no right to an attorney. He was soon released for having neither taken up arms nor helped finance or the organize the uprising. His only crime was 'sympathizing' with Sultan al-Atrash. Although brief, this was the first and last time that Hashem al-Atasi served time in prison, and his name remains inscribed on a marble plaque at Arwad Island.

In October 1927, Atasi called for a meeting in Beirut, attended by a handful of Syrian notables, which lasted for six days. Its final communique gave birth to the National Bloc, which was to lead the nation until independence was achieved in 1946. Atasi and his colleagues issued a ten-clause declaration demanding abolition of martial law, a general amnesty, halt of arbitrary arrests and a roadmap for when and how the mandate would end.[12] The Beirut conference signed off with a carefully worded statement: 'We are certain that France supports our national cause and shares in a mutual desire to re-establish confidence with the people of Syria. We believe in the need to collaborate, based on reciprocity and mutual obligations.'[13]

Atasi and his friends were open to talks with Paris. Military confrontation had been suicidal for Syria, they believed, clearly from the wide-spread destruction left by the Great Revolt. They would work towards independence through public diplomacy and the powerful tools of information and propaganda, rather than bullets. The mandate, Atasi would say, ought to be dismantled politically rather militarily.[14] This was a far cry from what ʿAbdul Rahman Shahbandar and Sultan Pasha al-Atrash had demanded since 1925: unconditional and immediate independence, with nothing less than a military defeat for France. The French government reasoned that it ought to invest in this change of rhetoric, to help restore calm to Syria.

For the next twenty years, Bloc leaders would meet in the old mansions of Damascus and Aleppo, debating politics in spacious courtyards filled with jasmine and snow-white rose blossoms. Here they would discuss what Syria should look like following the departure of the French, how to reach that point in time, how to run the country and through what form of government. In November 1932, at a general congress in his native Homs, Atasi was elected lifetime president of the National Bloc.[15] With a mastery of the Arabic language, he spoke softly but affirmatively, although seldom. When he did, everybody listened. He had a reputation for being financially honest and politically reliable.[16] Coming from a wealthy family, he cared little for money or personal grandeur. He had seen plenty of it during his teens and early manhood. A serious statesman by all accounts, he rarely joked with friends, refused to follow delicious gossip, and did not allow light talk to prevail in any of his meetings.[17] His blue eyes glimmered as he spoke of what an independent Syria should look like, but he was never worked into a frenzy, and never raised his voice beyond conversational tone.[18] Short with narrow shoulders, he always dressed to designer perfection with a crimson Ottoman fez neatly fixed on his head. His trimmed white beard gave him a striking resemblance to old school politicians of nineteenth-century Europe.

He always emphasized that the National Bloc was a coalition of like-minded men with good intentions, and not a political party. When it was transformed into one after 1946, Atasi quickly distanced himself, refusing to join its successor, the National Party.[19] The Bloc members were all prominent and wealthy landowners united by the goal of a free and independent Syria. They advocated 'honorable cooperation' with France, pledging a secular programme that didn't differentiate between sects and religions, while raising the slogan: 'Religion is for God and obedience to the National Bloc!'[20] It was devised by the Sorbonne-educated attorney Munir al-ʿAjlani.

Following the Beirut conference, the National Bloc did not meet again until March 1928. During those five months the French issued a general amnesty, allowing the National Bloc to expand its ranks and recruit new members. In the upcoming years, many familiar names joined the Bloc like Shukri al-Quwatli, Nasib al-Bakri, Fakhri al-Barudi, Fares al-Khoury, Jamil Mardam Bey and Lutfi al-Haffar. Each brought with him influence, character and a new entourage of followers from a particular sector of Syrian society. Jamil Mardam Bey, for example, had considerable following within the old bazaars of Damascus, where his family's mansion was located. Nasib al-Bakri was popular among local quarter bosses (*qabadayat*), while Lutfi al-Haffar was influential in the Damascus Chamber of Commerce, on which he served as vice-president. As dean of the Faculty of Law at Damascus University Fares al-Khoury commanded university students, while Fakhri al-Barudi enjoyed unparalleled popularity among secondary and high school students. It was due to these men that the National Bloc became a household name in Syria.

The founding fathers of the Bloc came from two different generations. Hashem al-Atasi, Fares al-Khoury and Ibrahim Hananu were born between 1870–90, while Shukri al-Quwatli, Sa'adallah al-Jabiri and Fakhri al-Barudi were all born in the 1890s. They shared common values, however, forming the political orthodoxy of the interwar years. Almost all had lived similar careers in the Ottoman, Faisalian and early French eras. Many were Ottoman educated, having studied either at the Ottoman Military Academy or like Atasi at the Mulkiyye School in Istanbul. Many were former members of al-Fatat, with parallel experiences of agony in Turkish jails.

The Bloc leadership was 90 per cent Sunni Muslim, and 8 per cent Christian. Fifty per cent of its top command came from Damascus and 40 per cent from Aleppo. The remaining 10 per cent were from Homs, Hama, Latakia, Tripoli, Sidon and Beirut.[21] Around 90 per cent of Bloc members had obtained a secular education, while only 8 per cent had received religious schooling.[22] Almost 20 per cent were educated in Western schools, either in Europe or at the American University of Beirut. Fifty-six per cent of its members had studied in Istanbul.[23] Fifty per cent had undergone professional training, either in the Ottoman civil service or the Ottoman Army. Forty per cent were full-time politicians, while 28 per cent were lawyers.[24] Medical doctors accounted for 12 per cent of the National Bloc's membership base, while 8 per cent were merchants, another 8 were Ottoman civil servants and 4 per cent were retired officers from the Ottoman or Arab armies.[25] Social class was fundamental in determining the identity of the National Bloc. All Bloc founding fathers came from the same social milieu and were often related by marriage.

Hashem al-Atasi's son Riad married into the Rikabi family of Damascus, whose dean Rida Pasha had been premier under Faisal back in 1920. Lutfi al-Haffar's daughter Salma, who was to become a prominent novelist in the 1950s, married the brother of the Tripoli leader 'Abdul Hamid Karami (a future prime minister of Lebanon), while 'Abdullah al-Yafi of Beirut married into the 'Azm family. The Bakri brothers were maternal uncles of Quwatli's wife Bahira al-Dalati, and Fakhri al-Barudi was her second cousin. Riad al-Solh married the niece of his Syrian counterpart Sa'adallah al-Jabiri, while his daughters 'Alia al-Solh and Mona were roommates with Jamil Mardam Bey's daughter Salma at the English School of Alexandria Dormitories.[26] Saeb Salam, scion of a leading Beiruti family, was married to Tamima Mardam Bey, a cousin of Jamil Mardam Bey, while Fares al-Khoury's only son Suhayl married the sister of Habib Kahaleh, publisher of the influential political periodical *al-Mudhik al-Mubki*.

The 1928 constitution

Atasi's first feat as National Bloc president was contesting the constitutional assembly elections of April 1928. It was only logical for him to pen the constitution, having written Syria's royalist charter back in 1920. He tried to work with Prime Minister Taj al-Din al-Hasani through submitting joint lists, but their election alliance collapsed when the premier's men were caught tampering with the ballots in Damascus.[27] The Bloc won twenty-two out of seventy seats in the Constitutional

Assembly, a little less than one third. Hashem al-Atasi was elected president of the assembly, while the Bloc's legal mind, Fawzi al-Ghazzi was tasked with writing the constitution. They completed the job in fifteen days.

The republican charter of 1928 was modelled on European democracy and inspired by the French Revolution. It called for a single chamber that was to be elected for four years by universal suffrage exercised in two stages. One article mentioned Islam as the religion of the president, while another guaranteed freedom of worship and the right to establish schools for different sects and congregations. The president of the republic was limited to one five-year term only.[28] Atasi believed that it was improper for a head of state to spend his last year in office campaigning for a new term.[29] This would distract him from running state affairs, he once said to 'Abdul Wahab Homad, a justice minister in the 1950s.[30] He could, however, run for office indefinitely after spending four years as a private citizen. The 1928 constitution guaranteed freedom of property and speech, free trials, an independent judiciary and obligatory primary education.[31] It also set a quota for minorities in the Syrian parliament.

Six of the charter articles, however, were vetoed by the French, as they made no mention of the mandate. Article 2, for example, referred to all lands liberated from the Ottomans as one geographic entity. This implied that as far as Syrian lawmakers were concerned, Palestine, Jordan and Lebanon were still consisted parts of Syria. Article 110 gave Syria the authority to re-establish its own army, which had been crushed and then dissolved after the battle of Maysaloun. Article 74 gave the president of the republic, rather than the French high commissioner, the right to formulate international treaties, issue pardons and declare martial law. Henri Ponsot added his own article numbered 116, which specifically mentioned the mandate regime as the supreme authority in Syria.

Atasi refused the amendment, arguing that in neither the Egyptian constitution of 1922 nor the Iraqi one of 1925 was such a clause mentioned. A session was set for 9 August to debate the controversial articles within the Constitutional Assembly.[32] It lasted for two days and on 11 August, Syrian lawmakers ratified Atasi's constitution. Ponsot struck back by adjourning the chamber for three months, then headed to Paris to discuss the constitutional crisis with his superiors at the Quai d'Orsay.[33] Neither the Bloc nor the French were willing to budge, it seemed.[34] He returned with clear orders to dissolve the Constitutional Assembly on 5 February 1929 and to postpone any future talks with the National Bloc. In May 1930 he decreed the constitution with the six articles in modified form, including Article 116 which effectively legalized the mandate. Hashem al-Atasi was not consulted, nor were any members of the Constitutional Assembly.[35]

The Treaty of 1936

In 1932, Atasi ran for the country's first presidential elections, but withdrew his candidacy after realizing that he could not win, since the Bloc had lost all its seats in Aleppo. He supported Mohammad 'Ali al-'Abed's bid for president before moving into the opposition and working to bring him down. In 1936, Atasi led the 60-Day Strike with other members of the National Bloc, and on 21 March 1936, sailed to France with his colleagues to discuss the future of Franco-Syrian relations.

Headed by Atasi, the National Bloc delegation included Jamil Mardam Bey, Fares al-Khoury and Sa'adallah al-Jabiri. Attached to it were two ministers from the Ayyubi cabinet, and three secretaries, namely Edmond Rabbat, Na'im Antaki and Khaled Bakdash, president of the nascent Syrian Communist Party. Before departing, Atasi appointed Shukri al-Quwatli as vice-president of the National Bloc. Atasi had tried to bring Shahbandar onboard the Syrian delegation, but his name was vetoed both by the French and the Damascus Office of the National Bloc.[36] On 2 April, the negotiations commenced at the Quai d'Orsay in Paris. The Bloc team wore tuxedos and fedora hats, blending-in with French aristocracy. General elections in France toppled the government of Edouard Daladier, and it was replaced by a left-wing coalition headed by Leon Blum, a socialist. The new government was much less committed than its predecessors towards the French Empire. Constitutionally, however, the Blum government could not assume office until the beginning of June, which led to the suspension of talks during the month of May. The Syrian delegation went sightseeing in the French capital, visiting the Eiffel Tower, the Arc de Triomphe and the Louvre Museum. This introduced Atasi and his friends to a very different France than the one they had fought since 1920. Here in Paris, there were no military barracks, no tanks and no Senegalese soldiers. Pierre Vienot, the new undersecretary for State Affairs responsible for the Levant, took over negotiations with the Syrian team in June 1936. A realist, he saw France's role in the Levant as that of a 'tutor', assuring Atasi that it was 'transitory' and ought to respect the legitimate rights of the Syrian nation.

An agreement was finally reached and signed at the Salon de l'Horloge at the Quai d'Orsay on 9 September 1936. Based on 'Peace, Friendship, and Alliance', it outlined the obligations and duties of both Syria and France, mainly through the following points:

1. The treaty would lead to Syria joining the League of Nations, and it would last for a period of twenty-five years, expiring in 1961. After that, Syria would become fully independent.
2. Syria would be allowed to establish its own army of at least one infantry division and a cavalry brigade. This army would be trained and armed by the French.
3. France would be given two military air bases in mutually agreed locations, no less than twenty-five miles from any of the four interior towns, along with harbour and transit facilities. These facilities would help France fight any upcoming war in Europe.
4. French garrisons would be stationed in the Alawite and Druze Mountains for five years but the territories would be reincorporated formally into the Syrian state.
5. A limited measure of financial and administrative autonomy would apply to the Druze and Alawite territories, but judges, policemen and teachers would be affiliated to the central government in Damascus.

6. The two countries would come to each other's assistance in case either was attacked by a third party.

The Franco-Syrian Treaty of 1936 pledged to 'define, on the basis of complete freedom, sovereignty, and independence, the relations which would subsist between the two states after the end of the mandate'.[37] Government offices in Damascus closed in celebration when news reached them that the treaty had been signed, and for the first time since 1920, Syrian and French Flags were hoisted willingly on balconies, side-by-side.[38] Electrical lights were placed at the gates of the old markets of Damascus, where young men danced and chanted for the long life of the National Bloc leaders. The Bloc delegation arrived in Aleppo and travelled in procession through Hama and Homs, finally reaching Damascus on 29 September. Triumphal arches had been erected from the Hejaz Station to the Marjeh Square, and thousands gathered in the streets to escort Atasi to the Grand Serail.[39] The celebrations lasted for four days solid.[40]

Parliament reconvened after a twenty-five-month suspension, but the seat of the French delegate, once situated at the centre of the front row, was pushed to the far left at the request of Hashem al-Atasi.[41] Receiving seventy-four out of eightyfive votes in the Chamber of Deputies, Atasi was elected president on 21 December 1936. He ran unopposed, replacing Mohammad 'Ali al-'Abed. Fares al-Khoury was elected speaker and Jamil Mardam Bey was tasked with forming the first National Bloc government.[42]

The first Atasi presidency (1936–9)

Under Atasi, all posts in both the government and civil service went to members of the Bloc or their affiliates. Mardam Bey kept the economic portfolio for himself, making Sa'adallah al-Jabiri minister of foreign affairs and interior, 'Abdul Rahman al-Kayyali minister of justice and education and Shukri al-Quwatli minister of national defence and finance. On 22 December, Pierre Vienot landed in Damascus to congratulate Atasi and his team on their well-earned victory.[43] Four days later, the Syrian parliament voted unanimously for the treaty, but the French Chamber was seemingly nowhere as enthusiastic and it failed to get the necessary votes to pass in Paris. Leon Blum fell from power in June 1937, and the colonialist press, namely *Republique* and *Paris-Soir*, launched a massive propaganda campaign against him and the 1936 Treaty.[44] He was accused of being too soft with the Syrians.[45] A similar campaign was staged against Blum's Interior Minister Roger Salengro, who was accused of deserting the French Army during the First World War. In disgrace, he ended up committing suicide in November 1936, further embarrassing Blum and rendering him an essentially helpless political creature. As he fell in France, so did the 1936 Treaty.

The arguments put forth by the colonialists for keeping the mandate were plentiful. One was 'if we leave Syria, Great Britain will snatch it'. Another warned against encouraging the Arabs so as not to inspire nationalist sentiment in North

Africa. Critics of the treaty argued that France had an obligation to protect Lebanon from Syrian hegemony, and to shelter Syria's minorities from the 'tyranny' of the Sunni Muslim majority.[46] More importantly, the rise of Adolf Hitler in Germany and the probability of a new war in Europe added to French fears that its territories in the Middle East needed to be protected rather than relinquished to the Syrians. France's naval and air bases along the Syrian coast – namely in the Alawite State – required complete political security in the Syrian heartland.[47] No less than sixty French commercial and industrial establishments based in Lyon and Marseilles lobbied against the 1936 Treaty within the two cities with the strongest ties to the Levant. As far as those establishments were concerned, giving up Syria was equal to business suicide. The country was providing them with not only high revenue, but cheap labour as well. Among the companies that lobbied against 1936 Treaty were Société du Chemin de Fer Nord-Syrie, Regie Générale des Chemins du Fer et Travaux Publiques de Paris, Sociétiés des Tramways et d'Electricité and finally, the powerful Banque du Syrie.[48] Blum's successors, the Radical Socialists, pledged to 'defend France's menaced colonial empire, the security of French territory, and French communications along the Mediterranean'.[49]

Loss of the Sanjak

The greatest blow to the National Bloc and to Hashem al-Atasi, more so than France's refusal to ratify the 1936 Treaty, was the step-by-step annexation of the Sanjak of Alexandretta, which occurred between 1934 and 1939. No defeat could have been more humiliating for the president and his team, who helplessly watched the Sanjak slip away from their hands. Despite all their bravado, none of them were able to postpone, let alone prevent, the annexation. The Sanjak's population stood at 220,000 inhabitants: 39 per cent Turks, 28 per cent Alawites, 11 per cent Armenians, 10 per cent Sunni Arabs, 9 per cent Christian Arabs and a 4 per cent minority of Kurds, Circassians and Jews.[50]

Turkey refused to recognize Syria's sovereignty over Alexandretta, claiming that its real population stood at three hundred thousand of which 150,000–200,000 were native Turks.[51] Ankara's rejection of the Treaty of Sevres led to a 1921 adjustment that moved the border delineation further south, raising eyebrows in Damascus and Aleppo. The business community of Aleppo, after all, relied greatly on the port of Alexandretta for its commerce.[52] The Turkish government called for a special autonomous administration in the Sanjak, the right to use the Turkish language, operate Turkish schools and promote Turkish culture. It also demanded a special flag for the Sanjak, and leasing its port to Turkey for goods in transit to Ankara. The new borders were officially confirmed by Article 3 of the Lausanne Treaty of 1923.

Under the mandate, the French had brought electricity to the Sanjak, along with a modern sewage system, roads, bridges, telephones and a postal service.[53] The Turkish press was constantly filled with editorials about the Sanjak, often arguing that Ankara should control both sides of the Gulf of Alexandretta, along with the entire railway from Adana to Nisbin.⁵⁴ In March, Turkish residents of the Sanjak staged loud demonstrations demanding independence from the central government in Damascus, highlighting their ethnic loyalties and identity. Ankara presented an official request to France for the independence of the Sanjak on 10 October 1936, eleven days after Hashem al-Atasi's return from Paris. The statement made no mention of annexation, just autonomy.⁵⁵

When returning to Syria, via Ankara, Atasi had spoken to Turkish journalists saying that the Sanjak will forever remain Syrian.⁵⁶ In November 1936, President Ataturk twice made reference to the Sanjak, once before the National Assembly, where he described it as 'the burning issue of today'.⁵⁷ In an outburst of support, Turkish MPs threatened to take it by force if Hashem al-Atasi refused to abide by Ataturk's bid. The Turkish president suggested taking the matter to the League of Nations, where Syria was not a member.

When Syrian parliamentary elections took place in late 1936 voter turnout in the Sanjak stood at a measly 8 per cent. Pro-Turkey residents boycotted the elections, and attacked the homes of three freshly elected MPs, all on a National Bloc ticket.⁵⁸ The French intervened, killing three people and wounding seventeen.⁵⁹ A referendum was held which the National Bloc dismissed as a sham, and its results allowed the League of Nations to establish a special administrative system for the district, where the Turkish language would be officially recognized and Turkish culture would be preserved. In January 1937, the League of Nations called for a Syrian-Turkish treaty to determine the fate of the Sanjak. The territory would be renamed Hatay in September 1938, and placed under a completely independent administration only linked to Damascus by monetary and economic affairs.⁶⁰

President Atasi argued vehemently against such a move, claiming that it would prove 'disastrous' for the residents of Aleppo, and fatal for the Syrian republic as a whole. He sent a strongly worded letter to the French high commissioner, saying that he would 'never consent' to the independence of the Sanjak.⁶¹ The French responded by shutting down the National Bloc offices in Antioch. They then despatched 1,000 troops to the Sanjak and ordered the arrest of Arab activists leading public awareness campaigns against the annexation. They then allowed Turkish troops to march into Alexandretta under the nose of President Atasi and the entire National Bloc command. A forty-seat assembly was then established for the Sanjak. Twenty-two seats went to pro-Turkish politicians, while the speaker was automatically voted into the Ankara-based Turkish Parliament.⁶² On 29 November 1938, Hatay was declared an autonomous entity from Syria, with both Arabic and Turkish as its official languages.

The annexation of the Sanjak led to the displacement of 50,000 terrified refugees, who drifted into Damascus and Aleppo. Of them 20,000 were Armenians, 10,000 were Alawites, 10,000 Sunnis and 5,000 Christian Arabs.⁶³ The chaotic mass movement constituted a major embarrassment for the National Bloc. Atasi was furious, but equally powerless to change the course of events. As if territorial loss were not enough, two of the Bloc's leaders, Lutfi al-Haffar and Nasib al-Bakri, resigned from its Executive Council. Prominent figures like the poet Shafiq Jabri also walked out on the Bloc, and so did young members in Aleppo, including Nazem al-Qudsi and Rushdi al-Kikhiya, who were to eventually form an opposition party in 1948. Others like Zaki al-Khatib and Munir al-ʿAjlani defected to the Shahbandar-led opposition.[64]

Shahbandar returns

Loss of the Sanjak had widened fissures within the National Bloc and made its leaders the laughing stock of opponents like Shahbandar, who had returned to Syria from his Egyptian exile in March 1937. He was amnestied by the 1936 Treaty, only to find that there was no room for him in an altered political landscape, one that was very different from the Syria he left in 1927. The National Bloc leaders were now in full control of Damascus and unwilling to share the city with Shahbandar. They had built their careers as moderates willing to sit down and talk with French officials, while Shahbandar was the self-described 'father' of armed resistance. From the very start, there was very little room for cooperation between Shahbandar and the Bloc.

Shahbandar despised the Franco-Syrian Treaty, claiming that it had given too much to France, in return for nothing.[65] Although the Bloc was lukewarm to his comeback, ordinary Syrians showered him with homage and respect. Shahbandar gave them his full attention, promising that the 'era of negligence' would soon come to an end. Interior Minister Saʿadallah al-Jabiri instructed the press to stop referring to him as 'great leader'.[66] He also denied him permission to re-launch his People's Party, which had been disbanded in 1925, forcing Shahbandar to use his clinic for political meetings.[67] Jabiri considered Shahbandar demode: a relic of the past who did not deserve all the homage he was receiving. 'Where was Shahbandar when we created the Bloc, fought for the constitution, or engineered the 60-Day Strike?' asked Jabiri.[68] President Atasi liked Shahbandar, however, having appointed him minister in his cabinet of 1920. He asked Jabiri and Mardam Bey to stop harassing him but both ignored his orders.[69] When his criticism of the Bloc became too loud, Shahbandar was placed under house arrest in Bloudan, with Syrian police stationed at his doorstep.[70] Atasi was quick to apologize, sending a car to bring him to the Presidential Palace, where he was received with red carpets.[71]

A bomb then exploded in Mardam Bey's car as he was driving to Beirut to attend the opening of its port.[72] He escaped unharmed but shaken. Rather than blame it on the French, he accused ʿAbdul Rahman Shahbandar of trying to kill him. Even before investigations had started, Mardam Bey ordered the arrest of Shahbandar's brother-in-law Nazih Mouʾayyad al-ʿAzm, and his close associate Zaki al-Khatib.[73] The failed assassination gave the National Bloc all the reason it needed to strike forcefully against Shahbandar. The pro-Shahbandar daily *al-Ayyam* was shut down and its publisher Nasuh Babil was jailed. Babil was handcuffed and sent to the Sheikh Hasan Police Station in al-Midan, and then deported to the Citadel of Damascus.[74]

Atasi sent Mardam Bey to Paris in November 1937 to sign off amendments that might convince the French Assembly to reconsider its veto of the 1936 Treaty. He pledged to protect minorities and approved more French technical assistance for public services. In August 1938, Mardam Bey returned to France for more give-ins, this time renewing banking concessions, permitting oil exportation, giving the French language predominance in the Syrian education system and changing the treaty's date to 30 September 1939. This meant that the mandate would expire in 1964 rather than in 1961.[75] None of that worked and in November 1938, France took the final decision not to ratify the 1936 Treaty. Four months later, Jamil Mardam Bey stepped down as premier in defeat on 18 February 1939. He had bitten off more than he could chew, fighting the French for the 1936 Treaty, the Turks for Alexandretta and Shahbandar at home. Mardam Bey's resignation and the annexation of the Sanjak prompted the journalist Najib al-Rayyes to resign from the Bloc in April 1939.[76]

Struggling to save his administration, President Atasi called on Lutfi al-Haffar to form a cabinet, which lasted for no more than forty days, before it too was forced to resign for lack of progress on the 1936 Treaty. Haffar was replaced by an independent, Nasuh al-Boukhari, who also failed to resolve the crises. By then, the French were already re-affirming their iron grip over Syria, seeing that it was just a matter of time before Atasi himself is forced to step down. They staged a crackdown on National Bloc members, arresting Nabih al-'Azma and forcing Mardam Bey to go into hiding.[77] Sa'adallah al-Jabiri, now out of office, called for a new strike in northern Syria. This time, it was nowhere as orderly as in 1936. Many shopkeepers, fed up with the National Bloc, refused to obey.[78] Their windows were smashed and tramcars were set on fire, passers-by were beaten with clubs, and a bomb was detonated at the Aleppo branch of the Banque du Syrie.[79] In July, the French suspended the constitution and dissolved parliament, arguing that the National Bloc was unfit to rule Syria. Hashem al-Atasi, as expected, resigned on 7 July 1939.

The National Bloc leaders suddenly found themselves back at Square One, out of power, with no treaty, no money, a shrinking power base and far from seeing Syria independent. Their record was scarred by crippling divisions and defeat. British journalist Patrick Seale sums up the first Atasi era saying: 'The treaty they (the National Bloc) had worked so hard to negotiate had been tossed into the dustbin of history.'[80]

Returning to power (1949–51)

Atasi returned to his native Homs, officially retiring from politics. Two months following his resignation, the Second World War broke out in Europe. After liberating Syria from Vichy forces, General Charles de Gaulle came to Damascus on 7 July 1941. A former undersecretary of state for national defence, De Gaulle, had created and led the French resistance, with help from Great Britain. He declared a war of liberation from BBC on 18 June 1940, whose first rewards were reaped in Syria. Politicians from all stripes and colours showed up at his residence in the al-'Afif neighbourhood of Damascus, trying to score points with the commander of the Free French Forces. Hashem al-Atasi was not among the crowd, however, quietly crossing the border into Lebanon, ostensibly for a quiet summer vacation with his family. He didn't want any connection to any of the French rivalries, and had no desire to return to office so long as French troops remained in Syria.[81]

De Gaulle noticed his absence, and while heading to Beirut, called upon the ex-president in Chtaura, near the Syrian-Lebanese border. Atasi's son ʿAdnan, an accomplished lawyer and diplomat who spoke flawless French, handled the translation. De Gaulle formally asked him to return to the presidency, promising to revive the 1936 Treaty.[82] Atasi had little reason to believe him, still upset with how the French had reneged on their promises. He gently asked De Gaulle: 'What sort of powers will the president have?' The French general replied: 'Terms of the 1936 Treaty can, in principle, be the basis on which relations are restored between Syria and France.'[83] Atasi raised his right hand, mimicking a veto: 'Years have passed since that treaty, and circumstances have changed. Today, we demand something much broader than what we had been offered in 1936.'[84] After a two-hour meeting, De Gaulle headed on to Beirut, empty-handed.

When the French left Syria in April 1946, Atasi was invited to Damascus to sit next to President Shukri al-Quwatli on Independence Day, hailed as one of the founding fathers of the Syrian Republic. A main street was named in his honour in every Syrian city, along with schools in Damascus and his native Homs. He remained on the margins of political life, however, until December 1948, when seven months into the Palestine War, President Quwatli invited him to form a government, replacing that of Jamil Mardam Bey. Atasi had been in retirement for an entire decade, despite having endorsed the election of Quwatli as president in 1943. He accepted the challenge, and after negotiations with various parties in Damascus, declined the post and returned to Homs, saying that the country was not ready for a cabinet of national unity.[85]

Atasi's comeback had to wait another eight months, until August 1949. Colonel Sami al-Hinnawi had just staged a coup, toppling and killing Syrian military dictator Husni al-Zaʾim.[86] He convened a meeting at army headquarters, attended by veteran politicians from all the major political parties. They called upon Atasi to return to office, begging him to lead the nation towards a civilian, republican government. Hinnawi made it known that he had no intention of assuming the presidency, as Husni al-Zaʾim had done, or establishing a military dictatorship. The army would return to the barracks and Atasi would be free to run Syria as he sees fit, promised Hinnawi. Based on these assurances – and supplications of the political elite – Atasi came out of retirement and formed his government on 14 August 1949. It was Atasi's second cabinet, coming twenty-nine years after his first in May 1920.

The second Atasi cabinet was the most comprehensive government to date in the history of Syria. By then, several political parties had emerged, and the National Bloc had formally disbanded and re-emerged as the National Party, headed by Damascus statesman Sabri al-ʿAsali. Another party had been formed in Aleppo, called the People's Party, and it was headed by Rushdi al-Kikhiya and Nazem al-Qudsi, two Bloc defectors. It was formed in mid-August 1948 to stand up to the National Party. Its main goal was unity with Hashemite Iraq. The president's son ʿAdnan had joined the People's Party, and so had his nephew, Faydi al-Atasi. Kikhiya and Qudsi were brought onboard the new Atasi government, as ministers of interior and foreign affairs respectively, representing the People's Party. The founder of the Ba'ath Party Michel 'Aflaq was made minister of education, while Akram al-Hawrani was appointed minister of agriculture (before establishing his Arab Socialist Party). The Atasi cabinet supervised elections for a constitutional assembly to draft a new charter for Syria. The People's Party won thirty out of 142 seats, making their leader, Rushdi al-Kikhiya, president of the Assembly. On 14 December, the chamber elected Atasi as head of state and the People's Party co-chair, Nazem al-Qudsi, replaced him at the premiership.

Atasi was sympathetic to the People's Party programme, which was also supported by Sami al-Hinnawi and the Hashemite royals in Baghdad. In late 1949, the party found itself fully in charge of Syria, controlling the presidency, the premiership and parliament. Atasi and Hinnawi entered into talks with the Iraqi government, led by Atasi's old friend Nuri al-Sa'id. The two men had worked together under King Faisal, where Nuri Pasha had served as adviser to the monarch, and Atasi as parliament speaker, then premier. They now agreed on a federal union where the monarchy would go to the Hashemites, the premiership to a Syrian, and the speakership of parliament, to an Iraqi.[87] For the first time since King Faisal's humiliating exodus from Damascus thirty years ago, the Hashemites felt that a return to Syria was now within reach. Syria would definitely benefit from Iraqi oil revenue, but would inevitably be drawn into the pro-Western orbit, then at its apogee due to the Cold War.

The union project, utopian as it was, never got past the drawing board. Just days before Nazem al-Qudsi was due in Baghdad to sign the union charter, another coup was staged in Damascus on 19 December 1949, led by Colonel Adib al-Shishakli.[88] He was a staunch republican who wanted to prevent the union – and return to monarchial rule – at any cost, considering the Hashemite family as agents of British imperialism in the Arab World. 'The republic will fall over my dead body', he fumed.[89] His coup was limited, targeting Sami al-Hinnawi, who was relieved of his duties at army command and sent to jail. Shishakli announced that he had no intention to go further, keeping Atasi at the presidency but conditioning that any future government appoints his right-hand man, Fawzi Selu, as minister of defence. That was a must, he said, to make sure that union with Iraq is never raised again in the cabinet of ministers.

Leading of the opposition

Atasi unwillingly accepted those dictates, and so did his two prime ministers, Nazem al-Qudsi and Khaled al-'Azm. The truce with Shishakli allowed them to pass the 1950 constitution, which was a landmark charter in the history of Syria, empowering the office of prime minister at the expense of the presidency. Atasi never liked Shishakli, considering him a brute and adventurer threatening the very foundations of Syrian democracy.[90] On 28 November 1951, Atasi appointed People's Party leader Ma'arouf al-Dawalibi as premier, who refused to abide by Shishakli's orders, assuming the portfolio of defence himself. In his memoirs, Dawalibi claims that he was talked into taking such a hardline position by his colleagues in the People's Party.[91] Shishakli commanded him to re-consider, threatening action if he did not. When Dawalibi stood by his decision, a third coup was staged on 29 November 1951.[92] Dawalibi was arrested, along with his entire government, and so were all members of the People's Party. President Atasi summoned Shishakli for a dress-down, but realizing that there was no room for compromise with the officers, presented his resignation to parliament on 3 December 1951.[93] Shishakli by then had already disbanded the Chamber of Deputies. Glad to see Atasi gone, he appointed Fawzi Selu as both head of state and prime minister.

Atasi returned to Homs, just as he had done in 1939. Only this time he didn't retire from politics but remained very active, despite his old age. From his family residence, he led the opposition to Shishakli's rule, inviting politicians to a congress on 20 January 1953 that denounced Shishakli's ambitions and accused him of imposing a dictatorship on Syria.[94] Shishakli had penned his own constitution, staged his own parliamentary elections and, in July 1953, ran unopposed for the Syrian presidency. Atasi said that his presidential term was un-constitutional, calling on Syrians to rise in revolt. Due to his age and reputation, Shishakli found it difficult to arrest him. But he did arrest his son ʿAdnan, along with Mansour al-Atrash of the Baʿath Party, the son of Sultan Pasha al-Atrash, who was allied with Atasi in the anti-Shishakli movement.[95]

A military uprising was staged to bring down the Shishakli regime in December 1953. One of its leaders was Faisal al-Atasi, a nephew of President Atasi. It began in the Druze Mountain and Homs and then spread to Aleppo and Latakia. Only two cities remained pro-Shishakli until curtain fall, being Damascus – his capital – and his native Hama. On 25 February 1954, Shishakli resigned and fled, first to Lebanon, then to Saudi Arabia, before settling permanently in Brazil. Four days later, Army Commander Shawkat Shuqayr headed to Homs to escort Hashem al-Atasi back to Damascus, recognizing him as the constitutional president of Syria. At eighty, Atasi returned to the Presidential Palace for one last time. Now a widower (his wife died in 1946), he decided to both live and work at the palace on Rue Nazem Pasha. Atasi resumed his term by acting as if the Shishakli era had never passed. The constitution of 1950 was restored, along with the 1949 Parliament. He then called for new elections in September 1954.

Atasi's final comeback

His last tenure was, technically, a continuation of the term that began in 1950. It was marked with heavy Cold War politics, as the United States and Eastern bloc struggled for control of Syria. By then, Gamal ʿAbdul Nasser had emerged as president of Egypt after toppling his predecessor, Mohammad Neguib, two years into the Egyptian Revolution. Atasi never liked Nasser and the rebellious officers who surrounded him, since they looked, spoke and acted like the officer class in Syria, whom he also detested and blamed for the country's woes.[96] With the exception of Naguib, who had briefly assumed the presidency between 1952 and 1954, the Egyptian Free Officers were all erratic, and inexperienced. They were also too young for Atasi, all born after 1918 when he was already an established name in Syria. They were as old as his children, speaking a rough and aggressive political language that he did not accept and which sounded very unfamiliar to the Ottoman-trained Syrian leader. Anybody who opposed them was written off as imperialistic, Zionist and pro-American. As far as Atasi was concerned, they were no different from Husni al-Za'im and Adib al-Shishakli.[97]

There was also no love between Atasi and the United States, but he was also never sympathetic with communism and Marxism.[98] Atasi found himself caught in the crosshairs of the Baghdad Pact, which the Americans had proposed to stand up to international communism and the USSR. Iraq and Jordan tried talking him into joining the Baghdad Pact, and so did Iran, Turkey, Pakistan and Great Britain. Nasser had begun to aggressively spread anti-Iraq and anti-Baghdad Pact propaganda through the Cairo-based Voice of the Arabs Radio. It had been set up in January 1954 and reached every home inside Syria with a one-hour daily broadcast. By July 1954, the broadcast had been expanded to four hours, launching a loud war of words against Baghdad, much to the displeasure of President Atasi and his People's Party allies who were suddenly being scrutinized for their relationship with Iraq.[99] For hardline Arab nationalists, supporting the Baghdad Pact became akin to supporting Zionism. That didn't daunt Atasi and his new prime minister Sabri al-'Asali was quoted in *The New York Times* saying that Syria offered 'open endorsement' of the Baghdad Pact. Backing it openly as well was the president's nephew Faydi al-Atasi, who was serving as foreign minister in the 'Asali government.[100]

The Eisenhower administration saw promise in Atasi's position, sending General Arthur Trudeau, the Deputy Chief-of-Staff of the US Army, for talks with the ageing president.[101] Trudeau hinted that Syria might be eligible for US aid if it continued to side with Iraq against Gamal 'Abdul Nasser. Similar assurances were given by Turkish president 'Adnan Menderes, who visited Atasi in January 1955.[102] By then Atasi had recently replaced Prime Minister 'Asali with his old-friend Fares al-Khoury, who was also open to joining the Baghdad Pact. Atasi and Khoury went a long way back, having worked together first under Faisal and then during the first national era in 1936. When Khoury showed no objection to the Baghdad Pact, leftist parties led by the Ba'ath accused him of being an agent of the United States. He was toppled by angry demonstrations at the gates of the Syrian Parliament, on 13 February 1955.[103] Atasi took note. If someone with Khoury's age and reputation was so provocative to the hardboiled Arab nationalists, then something major had changed in Syria. If they found it difficult to accept a moderate like Fares al-Khoury, then there was no room for compromise with the Syrian leftists. Gamal 'Abdul Nasser was beginning to win minds and hearts throughout the Arab World, even before the 1956 nationalization of the Suez Canal. Bringing him down would be Atasi's final battle. It would also be the only battle that Hashem al-Atasi failed to win.

The battle with Nasser

The Syrian president decided to confront Nasser, openly and fully, first by giving asylum to members of the Egyptian Muslim Brotherhood, who had tried and failed to assassinate the Egyptian leader in Alexandria in October 1954. In rage,

Nasser withdrew his ambassador from Damascus on 13 November 1954. Atasi then welcomed Egyptian journalist Mahmud Abu al-Fateh, publisher of *al-Misri* newspaper, mouthpiece of the Wafd Party, who fled Cairo after Nasser sentenced him to fifteen years in jail and confiscated all of his property. He was treated as a guest of honour by both President Atasi and Prime Minister Khoury. Abu al-Fateh eventually moved to Iraq, with Syrian help, and was given both asylum and Iraqi citizenship by Nuri al-Sa'id.[104] On 4 December 1954, Nasser hanged six Brotherhood members in Egypt, arousing massive demonstrations in different parts of Syria, which held up traffic, and nearly brought schools and university to a grinding halt.

Atasi's anti-Nasser campaign came against a brick wall when in April 1955, a pro-Nasser officer in the Syrian Army named Colonel 'Adnan al-Malki was gunned down at the Al-Baladi Football Stadium in central Damascus. Malki was an Arab nationalist and his brother Riad was a ranking member of the Ba'ath Party. Army officers – lying low since Shishakli's ouster – promised revenge for their slain colleague. They used the murder to stage a political comeback, one which Atasi could not obstruct due to Malki's popularity with the officer class. As they mourned the death of Malki, Atasi had no choice but to accommodate them but only after realizing that many were Nasserist to the bone. The president was forced to appoint a young 29-year-old colonel named 'Abdul Hamid al-Sarraj as director of the Deuxième Bureau (military intelligence), charged with investigating the Malki murder. Sarraj unleashed bitter rancour against all Syrians, using his dungeons to persecute anybody accused of being pro-West and anti-Egypt. His main target was the Syrian Social Nationalist Party (SSNP), after three of its members were caught red-handed in Malki's assassination. The SSNP was both anti-Nasser and pro-union with Iraq. Atasi had no choice but to sign a decree banning the party, and it would remain outlawed until 2005. But that was the furthest he would go, refusing a request from the officers to impose martial law on Syria.[105]

In September 1954, Atasi attended the opening of the Damascus International Fair, a major economic function attended by representatives from both the United States and USSR. The event was used to promote Syrian industry and trade, hosting famous Arab singers on its stage like Um Kalthoum and Fairuz. It was also Hashem al-Atasi's last major achievement before his term ended one year later, in September 1955.

Atasi post-1955

Shukri al-Quwatli was elected to succeed him and Atasi became the first Syrian president to hand over power in a democratic process. All other presidents had either died while in office, or been toppled or killed. The two former Bloc leaders entered a convertible and were driven to parliament on 'Abed Street. Atasi sat to the right, with Quwatli at his side. The speaker, Nazem al-Qudsi, awaited them at the gates of parliament, where a musical band greeted them with *Humat al-Diyar*, Syria's national anthem. Atasi delivered his farewell speech, ending sixty years of government service, and the two presidents then exchanged documents outlining the transfer of power. The president of the Supreme Court of Syria served as witness to the ceremony. Atasi and Quwatli signed two copies of the documents. One was stored at the Presidential Palace, and the other in Parliament. They were then driven to the Presidential Palace, this time with Quwatli seated to the right and Atasi to the left. A grand luncheon was held in Atasi's honour, attended by deputies, ministers, army officers and foreign ambassadors. A presidential entourage then escorted Hashem al-Atasi to the outskirts of Damascus, to the village of al-Qaboon, north of Jobar. Soldiers took a final salute as the musical band played military music. At the gates of his native Homs, another band welcomed him, along with the governor of Homs and its army commander. The third and final procession took place at Atasi's residence, from where he had led the opposition to Adib al-Shishakli's rule. Director of Protocol 'Abdullah al-Khani accompanied President Atasi until the very end, and then headed back to Damascus to assume his duties with his former boss, Shukri al-Quwatli.[106]

Atasi spent his final years taking long walks in his garden, reading Syrian newspapers and lamenting the sharp slump in Syrian democracy. His son 'Adnan was arrested in 1956 on charges of conspiring against Gamal 'Abdul Nasser and his allies in the Syrian Army. He was jailed by none other than 'Abdul Hamid al-Sarraj, who Atasi had appointed to head military intelligence after the Malki murder. 'Adnan al-Atasi was charged with masterminding 'an Iraqi plot' to bring down the republic. A military court added that he was helping arm and train insurgents to assassinate Ba'ath leader Akram al-Hawrani and Communist Party President Khaled Bakdash.[107] The court that assembled at the main stadium of Damascus University was headed by General 'Afif al-Bizri, a declared communist who sentenced 'Adnan al-Atasi to death. The former president refused to attend any of its hearings, describing it as a mock trial.[108] Many reasoned that if his son was executed, no one in Syria could be considered safe anymore (the younger Atasi's sentence was eventually commuted to life imprisonment). It was a sad end game for somebody who had led the nation at critical junctures in its modern history to see his son being sent to the gallows without being able to save him. President Quwatli lobbied to change 'Adnan al-Atasi's verdict to life imprisonment.[109] 'Adnan had originally held office during Quwatli's first tenure as president, serving as Syria's ambassador to France. Atasi also refused to seek clemency for his son and forbade any member of the family from making such a request in his name or on his behalf. He never once visited his son at Mezzeh Prison.[110]

Last seen in public

Despite his reservations about Gamal 'Abdul Nasser, Atasi travelled to Damascus to congratulate the Egyptian president on the Syrian-Egyptian Union in February 1958. It was a glorious day for the Arabs and he did not want history to say that he had skipped the celebrations for his son's sake. Atasi was welcomed with full honours at the presidential palace on Abu Rummaneh Street. Nasser received him at the palace gates, and behind him stood Sarraj – the man to have arrested his son – and Anwar al-Sadat, the future president of Egypt. The last photo ever taken of Hashem al-Atasi shows him standing before a radiant Nasser, with Shukri al-Quwatli in the background. Atasi looked old, weak and heartbroken. When he died two years later, Nasser refused to give ʿAdnan al-Atasi permission to attend his father's funeral.

Figure 7 Hashem al-Atasi.

Chapter 8

BAHIJ AL-KHATIB (1939–41)

When Hashem al-Atasi first resigned from the presidency in July 1939, a stern administrator named Bahij al-Khatib was summoned to replace him. His era lasted from 10 July 1939 until 1 April 1941. Unlike Mohammad ʿAli al-ʿAbed and Sheikh Taj, he had no influential father to lean on and no family history in politics. Unlike Hashem al-Atasi, he had no party affiliation and was not a member of the National Bloc. For ten solid years, however, Bahij al-Khatib had been the source of gravity in Syria, a tough leader who nobody dared cross or defy. Most history books only make passing mention of him, mainly as a French collaborator and *intidabi*, or creation of the mandate. A closer look, however, shows a far more complex character – someone with sharp political acumen and a formidable survival instinct.

From Mount Lebanon to Syria

Bahij al-Khatib was born in Chehime, the largest Sunni village in the Chouf region of Mount Lebanon, located forty-two kilometres southeast of Beirut. He came from a well-to-do family and was educated at private schools in Souq al-Gharb, then at the American University of Beirut. With the collapse of Ottoman rule, he moved to Damascus to join the civil service under Emir Faisal, marrying into a Damascene family. His first job was a junior bureaucrat at the Ministry of Interior, headed by another Lebanese named Rida al-Solh of Sidon. Khatib remained at his post after the toppling of Faisal in July 1920. He had expressed no sympathy with the ex-king and in December 1920 was appointed bureau chief to Haqqi al-ʿAzm, governor of the State of Damascus. Under the state of Syria starting January 1925, Khatib returned to his job at the Ministry of Interior, technically abiding by the rules of the mandate, which forbade civil servants from engaging in political life.

In February 1928, Khatib was handpicked for the post of police director, chosen from a long list of bureaucrats by High Commissioner Henri Ponsot.[1] He applied for Syrian citizenship, based on a 1924 law that entitled any Ottoman subject living in post-First World War Syria to obtain a Syrian passport and ID.[2] The Directorate of Police was France's iron fist in the Levant, used to crush demonstrations and arrest 'troublemakers', a term used to loop any Syrian with anti-French views. One of its branches was a political intelligence department, a predecessor for the modern *mukhabarat*.³ In the absence of a Syrian army, which had been disbanded with the French occupation in 1920, policemen were the only locally armed forces in the country, rivalled only by the French-created Army of the Levant, which included a high number of troops from France's faraway colonies in North Africa.

Khatib had a reputation for being a stern and serious official. He was rarely seen in public, had few friends and boasted of an exceptionally unblemished financial record. He revamped the Police Directorate, creating sub-departments for crime, traffic and night security. He also introduced a modern archiving system, creating dossiers for former criminals and 'troublemakers'.⁴ Before taking charge of the department, he had watched how one of his predecessors, the cunning administrator Hamdi al-Jallad, had been fired from his job on accusations of embezzlement in 1925.⁵ Accused of pocketing public funds allocated for the construction of Baghdad Street, Jallad had landed in jail, only to be released by President Ahmad Nami in 1926. Making sure to avoid such a fate, Khatib focused strictly on security-related matters and stood at arm's length from any financial dealings. He hired a team of lawyers to advise on public spending, and rarely signed off budgets that would have caused him a headache, either with the press or with the high commissioner. When becoming premier eleven years later, he fought to raise the police department's budget to 67,000 SP, making it one of the best-paying employers in Syria. He used the money to buy new uniforms for his troops and to shower them with perks, bonuses and rewards, creating a cult personality among policemen and officers.⁶ Syrian policemen swore by his name and offered him full allegiance.

The 1928 elections

Khatib also cuddled up to Syria's new prime minister, Taj al-Din al-Hasani, who had come to office in February 1928. Sheikh Taj issued a general amnesty, setting hundreds of political prisoners free. Many had been in jail since 1925–7, charged with supporting the Great Syrian Revolt. Khatib was tasked with opening the doors of Syrian prisons and lifting press censorship, along with martial law that had been in place for nearly three years. Such bold gestures were seemingly not enough to shelter both Bahij al-Khatin and Sheikh Taj from accusations of corruption, levied by the National Bloc. Its leadership accused the police chief and his boss of using four million francs from the state treasury to bribe journalists into writing their praise.⁷

During the 1928 elections, policemen were caught red-handed intimidating voters to cast their ballot for government-backed lists in Shaghour, Bab Sharqi and al-Qanawat.⁸ Fawzi al-Ghazzi lead a demonstration against Sheikh Taj on 12 April 1928. Bahij al-Khatib ordered him handcuffed and sent to jail at the Damascus Citadel.⁹ The National Bloc then claimed said Khatib had tried buying votes in al-Ghouta, sending police-escorted automobiles to distribute 600 Turkish pounds to every village, ostensibly as relief money for damage inflicted during the Great Syrian Revolt.[10] Shukri al-Quwatli conducted a house-to-house campaign in the name of the National Bloc, calling on village elders to refrain from taking Khatib's money. The cars returned to Damascus with the money untouched.[11]

Hashem al-Atasi called for another demonstration, this time at the gates of the Grand Serail in Marjeh Square. Five people were killed, and Bahij al-Khatib was said to have personally opened fire against the demonstrators.[12] He scoffed at the Bloc, saying that he could overrun the party and the entire city of Damascus, with just forty policemen.[13] This was no longer gentleman politics but rather survival of the fittest regardless of talent, merit or character. Never had corruption and thuggery been so flagrant, and these were games that the nationalists were bad at playing. The Damascus daily *al-Qabas* ran a front-page editorial accusing Bahij al-Khatib of being 'a coward who couldn't even reload the gun he was using, asking a policeman to do the job for him'.[14]

Despite the disturbances, voter turnout in Damascus was recorded at an impressive 60 per cent.[15] Out of the nine MPs elected in the Syrian capital, seven were members of the National Bloc. Thanks to Khatib, Sheikh Taj personally polled 539 of 690 maximal electoral votes in Damascus but two of his allies were defeated: Interior Minister Sa'id Mahasin and Public Works Minister Tawfiq Shamiyya. When *al-Qabas* accused him of rigging the elections, he sent policemen to its office and had it closed for five months.[16] Upon returning to print, the newspaper editor Najib al-Rayyes penned a lengthy editorial against Khatib, saying: 'Manhood is a trait that doesn't suit you. You wore a tiger's outfit during the elections yet for ten years, you were hidden in the clothes of a fox. The truth is that you are nothing but a murderer.'[17] Rayyes added: 'If justice mattered, then you would be no more than a fourth-degree prefix in Chehime, or selling oil on the back of a donkey in the alleys of Damascus.'[18]

The murder of Fawzi al-Ghazzi

The constitution of 1928 never passed, despite ratification from the chamber of deputies. The constitutional crisis left the country in political paralysis. Four months later, Syria collapsed into turmoil with the death of the constitution's author, Fawzi al-Ghazzi of the National Bloc. He was found dead at his home in the Damascus countryside. Tongues waged that the French had killed him through Bahij al-Khatib. Ghazzi had led the 1928 demonstrations against Khatib and Sheikh Taj. They didn't like him but had no reason to want him dead.

The prime minister and his police chief took part in Fawzi al-Ghazzi's funeral, standing side-by-side with their main opponent, Hashem al-Atasi. Mourners cussed at both men, shouting: 'The father of the constitution is dead; long live the constitution.' Khatib personally supervised the investigations into Ghazzi's death, which led to a stunning revelation that shocked the conservative society of Damascus. All evidence traced directly to Ghazzi's wife, who seems to have poisoned her husband in order to marry his young nephew Rida, with whom she was having an affair. The two lovers had bought a flask of mice poison from a pharmacy in al-'Amara, which she then gave to her husband to drink, guised as medicine to cure him from diarrhoea. Khatib was tipped by Ghazzi's sister, saying that his young daughter had seen her mother sneak into a desolate home in the Sha'lan neighbourhood, along with her cousin. Khatib had her arrested and interrogated, along with her lover and the pharmacist who sold them the poison.[19] He then dug up Ghazzi's grave and ordered an autopsy, which proved that he had been killed by poison. They stood trial in Damascus and were both sentenced to death, but their verdict was commuted to life imprisonment, at the advice of Khatib and the French High Commission, who felt that hanging the two lovers would create unnecessary tension in the Syrian capital, given that they both hailed from two important families.

Khatib would remain at his post until November 1934 – a total of six years – outliving the era of Sheikh Taj and well into the presidency of Mohammad 'Ali al-'Abed. In 1934 he was decorated with the Order of Merit of the French Republic for arresting five Lebanese communists distributing pamphlets calling for civil disobedience against the mandate regime. They were caught in the middle of a crowd commemorating the fourteenth anniversary of War Minister Yusuf al-'Azma's death at the Battle of Maysaloun.[20] The French were extremely happy with him, until Khatib made the grave mistake of arresting eleven women who had staged an anti-government demonstration at the gates of the Syrian Parliament. One of them belonged to the large Mahasin family, whose relatives held important positions among the city's clergy. Another hailed from the large Tarabishi family of Damascene merchants.[21] They were handcuffed by Khatib's police, taken into custody and then brought before a military court, at his orders. Damascus men were boiling with rage, threatening to storm the palace of justice if Khatib didn't order their immediate release. Jailing women was a redline in Damascene society, an act that not even the French dared commit during the 1925 revolt.

Fearing that Khatib had gone too far with his crackdown, the high commissioner had him dismissed and replaced with a more nuanced police director named Safouh Mou'yyad al-'Azm. Like Khatib, he too was a civilian and graduate of the American University of Beirut. Unlike him, however, Mou'ayyad al-'Azm was a native of Damascus, hailing from one of the powerful landowning families that were deeply rooted in society. People welcomed the change, glad to see the end of Khatib.

Governor of Damascus (6 February–2 March 1936)

But those who rejoiced were forced to re-consider when briefly on 6 February 1936, President 'Abed signed a decree naming Bahij al-Khatib governor of Damascus. This was during the midst of the 60-Day Strike, when France was looking for reliable figures to silence dissent on the Syrian street. The National Bloc had initiated the strike in response to the January 1936 arrest of its Damascus MP Fakhri al-Barudi. Scores of National Bloc leaders were exiled or jailed for demanding the downfall of 'Abed, his prime minister Sheikh Taj – and now, the Damascus governor Bahij al-Khatib. Khatib's appointment had added insult to injury in Damascus, not only because of his Lebanese origins but also due to him being extremely unpopular with practically everybody, from the merchant class to young people and leaders of the National Bloc. When Hashem al-Atasi negotiated an end of the strike in return for the dismissal of Sheikh Taj, Khatib was automatically relieved of his duties on 2 March, less than one month after being named governor.

A brief stint in with the Druze

Six months later, the National Bloc signed its famed treaty in Paris, which led to the election of Hashem al-Atasi as president, and re-incorporation of the Alawite and Druze Mountains into Syria. Not all their residents were pleased with the re-unification, fearing hegemony by the central government in Damascus. President Atasi gave them plenty of incentives, promising to build schools and clinics, and to carry out much needed roadbuilding and water conservation projects. He also pledged that they would be equal to other Syrians in terms of rights and obligations. The Druze Mountain had suffered from French carpet bombing during the Great Revolt, which had destroyed its crops, homes and most of its infrastructure. Hundreds of its best men had been killed on the battlefield, exiled or were still in French jails. The Druze had every reason to doubt French assurances, and those of the National Bloc. Their relationship with the Bloc was strained from Day One, ever since its leaders had called on Sultan al-Atrash to surrender his arms and settle for compromise with the mandate regime.

Once the Druze Mountain was formally re-attached to Syria, President Atasi selected a Damascus notable named Nasib al-Bakri to serve as its governor. He was a member of the National Bloc Executive Council and one of the commanders of the Great Revolt. Despite his history of friendship with the Druze, many of them frowned upon his appointment, because he was a Muslim Sunni, and not a Druze. The Bloc then pushed for a broader amnesty, allowing Sultan al-Atrash to return to Syria in May 1937, after a decade in exile. He too objected to Bakri's appointment and so did his relatives, Emir Hasan al-Atrash and 'Abdul Ghaffar Pasha al-Atrash. To appease the Druze, President Atasi had Bakri dismissed in June 1937 and replaced briefly by a Druze notable named Tawfiq al-Atrash. That also failed to solve the problem and heightened internal Druze rivalry for governorship of the Druze Mountain. Neither a National Bloc member with close ties to the community had worked nor had a native Druze from the Atrash family.

At this point, Atasi took the most unusual decision of selecting Bahij al-Khatib to serve as governor, although in an acting capacity, as of 1 August 1937.[22] The appointment took the political class by storm, given the bad blood between Khatib and the National Bloc leadership. They were still bitter, remembering only too well how he had clamped them in chains during the 1928 elections. Khatib was chosen for his toughness, hoping that he would frighten the Druze into submission – which he did. He served as acting governor of the

Druze Mountain for three months, supervising municipality elections in their towns and villages, and was eventually replaced by Emir Hasan al-Atrash in November 1937.[23]

The cabinet of technocrats

The National Bloc government collapsed in the summer of 1939, after the French People's Assembly refused to ratify the 1936 Treaty. Following President Atasi's resignation on 9 July, the French re-imposed imposed martial law and suspended the Bloc-led Chamber of Deputies that had been elected in December 1936. They then put the constitution on hold and called on Bahij al-Khatib to serve as an interim prime minister, after cancelling the positions of president and speaker of parliament. He was named head of a government of directors (*hukumat al-mudireen*), or what in today's world is called a cabinet of technocrats. Government posts would go to managing directors of their respective ministries; men who had worked at their departments for years, some as far back as the Faisal era. They were chosen for their professional merit, rather than political affiliation. Their mission was surmised a transitionary one, intended to last until new parliamentary elections were held that winter. That never happened, however, due to the outbreak of the Second World War in September 1939.

Khatib's five-man cabinet included the judge Khalil Rifaat, who was appointed director of justice. He had served as Khatib's deputy at the police department back in the early 1930s. A long-time veteran of the Finance Ministry named Husni al-Bitar was made director of finance, hailing from an illustrious family of Damascene merchants, while Yusuf ʿAtallah, a French-trained agronomist, was appointed director of agriculture.[24] ʿAbdul Latif al-Chatti, coming from a family of religious scholars, was made director of education, and Nuri al-Mudarres, a notable from Aleppo, became director of public works.[25] The departments of defense and foreign affairs were cancelled, as the mandate regime re-took charge of both portfolios, which it had unwillingly granted to the National Bloc in 1936–9.[26]

In his memoirs, publisher of *al-Ayyam* newspaper Nasuh Babil recalled: 'Bahij al-Khatib was accorded all the trappings of a head of state, with a Syrian flag hoisted neatly on his car and military salutes made to his honor as he walked in and out of government headquarters.'[27] Meanwhile, the British consul in Damascus said that the Khatib cabinet 'was welcomed by the general public with relief, after the constant turmoil of the past two years'. He added: 'Bahij Bey al-Khatib enjoys the unusual reputation of being a conscientious, able, and honest administrator.'[28] The consul's report from Damascus concluded: 'The present indications are that Syria should now be able to look forward to a period of calm and economic reconstruction.'[29] A similar view was shared by the journalist Amin Saʾid, who wrote in his memoirs: 'Bahij al-Khatib was one of the finest, if not the finest administrator in Syria. His abilities and intellect earned him the trust of French officials, which he used to strike a balance between colonial interests and national aspirations.'[30]

Khatib's first task as premier was to welcome the four-year-old boy king of Iraq, Faisal II, grandson of Syria's ex-monarch Faisal I, who was passing through Damascus while travelling to Lebanon on 12 July 1939. Khatib received him at an old Damascene mansion in the al-Qanawat neighbourhood, owned by the late sheikh Mahmud Abu al-Chamat. It was the first time that Khatib had stood in the front row of any reception, shaking hands with head of state, who addressed him as 'Your Excellency, Mr. President'. Previously his job had been to handle security matters for visiting dignitaries, never to dine with them or be treated as a political equal.

Economic challenges

Once through with his Iraqi guest, Khatib drove to government headquarters for a meeting with Syrian journalists who were summoned for a brief about his cabinet's policy. Lacking oratory skills, he asked Yusuf 'Atallah, the director of agriculture, to address the press on his behalf. The Khatib government had two main objectives, said 'Atallah. One was to balance the budget and second was to develop Syria's economic resources. Wheat production, which accounted for half of Syria's cultivated land, had fallen by 16 per cent.[31] In al-Ghouta orchards surrounding the Syrian capital, severe frost accompanied by violent winds had damaged 60 per cent of apricot trees, destroying the spring harvest.[32] The cessation of imports, topped with merchants unable to settle their bank loans, had led to bankruptcies across the business communities of Aleppo and Damascus. Syrian exports to Europe had fallen by one half, while the value of imports fell by 38 per cent. Wool fell by 86 per cent, silk by 81 per cent and textiles by 56 per cent. Seventy-seven thousand people had been registered as unemployed in Damascus alone, due to the collapse of traditional handicrafts. The number of trades in the Syrian capital dropped from 750 in 1932 to less than 100 by 1939. Agricultural exports fell by 47 per cent and imports rose by 19 per cent. These were no easy challenges for Bahij al-Khatib. 'Above all', added 'Atallah, 'we have no ambition beyond giving the country good administration instead of bad politics'.[33]

Khatib appointed a small team of highly trained civil servants to run his office, headed by Emir Kazem El Djezairi, a salient instructor of French literature at Damascus University who happened to be grandson of Emir 'Abdelkader El Djezairi, and a cousin of Emir Sa'id.[34] He hired a reputed legal consultant named Fouad Shabat, who made sure that all the prime minister's actions were in accordance with both French and Syrian laws. For political consul Khatib would rely on his brother Fouad, a Beirut-based eminent poet who had previously served as bureau chief to President Ahmad Nami in 1926–8.

The Nazi witch hunt

Taking his cue from the French, Khatib opened an investigation into the financial dealings of Jamil Mardam Bey during his stint at the premiership, between 1936 and 1939.[35] He had a historic vendetta with the nationalists and started hunting them down, one after another. The two remaining Bloc members in power, Latakia governor Mazhar Raslan and Secretary-General of the Interior Ministry 'Adel al-'Azma were both fired at his orders.[36] Fearing arrest, Mardam Bey fled to Beirut, where he stayed for the next two years.[37] Hashem al-Atasi retired to his native Homs, while Shukri al-Quwatli left for Iraq, accused by Khatib of being a Nazi collaborator. By then, many National Bloc leaders were starting to voice Nazi sympathies, assuming that if Hitler won the war in Europe, then he would put an end to the mandate in Syria.

Immediately after the German Army invaded Poland, Khatib came out with an official declaration, pledging to support France and Great Britain in their war against the Axis Powers.[38] 'Nazi sympathizer' was a deadly accusation that could easily be slapped on any opponent, very similar to the word 'terrorist' after 9/11. Fakhri al-Barudi attended a welcoming reception for a visiting German delegation headed by the Nazi youth leader Baldur von Schirach.[39] He then took the unwise decision of translating Hitler's memoir into Arabic through his home-based think-tank, the Barudi Bureau for Propaganda and News. The Barudi Bureau was shut down and Barudi's para-military arm, the National Youth, was disbanded.[40] Barudi himself was forced to flee to Amman when two rifles were discovered in the garden of his home, raising Khatib's suspicions that he was smuggling arms on behalf of the Nazis.[41] His National Bloc colleague Hajj Adib Kheir was also jailed, accused of being on Nazi payroll.[42] So was 'Izzat Darwaza, a Damascus-based Palestinian nationalist, who was sentenced to three years in jail and a fine of 1,000 gold coins. Khatib then arrested Fahmi Abu Saud, a Bloc-affiliated chemist said to have received instructions on bomb-making from Herr Walter Beck.[43] Beck had come to Syria ostensibly on an educational mission, distributing seventy scholarships to Syrian students wanting to study in German.[44] The Bloc leaders were also accused of distributing swastika armlets to Nazi sympathizers in Damascus.[45]

Khatib's failed assassination

Two weeks after coming to office, the Prime Minister's office announced that it had uncovered a plot against Bahij al-Khatib's life, organized by two natives of Hama; 'Uthman and Akram al-Hawrani.[46] The first was a schoolteacher and veteran of the Great Syrian Revolt while Akram was then a law student at Damascus University.[47] This was the second assassination attempt against a sitting head of state in less than two years, after Jamil Mardam Bey barely survived death when a bomb exploded near his car while travelling to Beirut in 1938.[48] On 27 July 1939, Khatib published a full report of the assassination attempt, ordering a manhunt throughout Syria. Those who had been spared the Nazi accusation now found themselves in jail on suspicion of being part of the Hawrani conspiracy against Prime Minister Khatib. Fifteen people were arrested and eleven were charged in *absentia*. Among those jailed were the journalists Munir and Najib al-Rayyes, and the merchant ʿUrfan al-Jallad.[49] All three had been on Khatib's blacklist since 1928. The Bloc leader ʿAdel al-ʿAzma, who had just been relieved of his duties at the Interior Ministry, was accused of financing the ring leaders, forcing him to flee to Baghdad.[50] Seven of the accused were sentenced to death, but their terms were commuted to life imprisonment, before they were eventually pardoned and released on 25 September 1940.[51] Najib al-Rayyes claimed in his newspaper that the entire assassination story was baseless, fabricated by Khatib and used as pretext to get rid of his enemies. The premier responded by having him arrested and sentenced to twenty years of hard labour, followed by another twenty of exile.[52]

Outbreak of the Second World War

With the outbreak of the Second World War, the French government began a major rehaul of its Levant-based army. Many of its officers had gotten accustomed to the easy life of the Mediterranean, having not engaged in active combat since the Great Syrian Revolt. The French government appointed ex-high commissioner Maxime Weygand to command French troops in Syria and Lebanon. A small, sharp-eyed man now at seventy-one, Weygand knew Syria and Lebanon well. He had an old score to settle with the Germans, having witnessed their surrender at the French Compiegne Forest back in November 1918. He declared martial law throughout the country, which Khatib was asked to put into force, digging trenches in public gardens and warning the people of Syria that they should expect the worse from Nazi Germany. Streetlights were shut off in Damascus, and automobiles were instructed to only use subdued headlamps at night.[53] Power cuts occurred daily and local newspapers were heavily censored for articles showing the slightest inclination towards the Nazis. In many cases, they were restricted to one sheet per day. Fakhri al-Barudi's Arabic translation of *Mein Kampf* was banned in Syrian bookstores.[54] German citizens living in Syria – businessmen, archaeologists and educators – were briefly detained at Khatib's orders. They were eventually flown out of the country and their residency permits cancelled.[55] Those connected to the Third Reich had their assets frozen, worth an estimated fifty million French Francs.[56]

Like the National Bloc, ordinary Syrians were naturally drawn to the German Führer, following an old Arabic proverb that said: 'the enemy of my enemy is my friend.' Listening to Hitler at coffeehouse gatherings was a favourite pastime for young Syrians. It became a capital offence under Bahij al-Khatib, with a penalty ranging from three months to three years in prison, and a fine anywhere between twenty and 200 Syrian Pounds.[57] Khatib's intelligence service then spread a rumour that Hitler ranked Arabs next to apes in human genealogy, hoping that this would help degrade the German leader in the eyes of local Syrians.[58] Foreigners were denied visas and those wanting to enter Syria had to obtain special permission from Bahij al-Khatib. Foreign diplomats were forbidden from using codes and cyphers while radios at cafes were confiscated and any person speaking German over the telephone was summoned to the nearest police station for interrogation.

Khatib promised that there would be no food shortages in Syria, and no profiteering at the people's expense.[59] That was easier said than done, however, as the price of one gallon of petrol rose to a whopping six Syrian pounds on the black market (it's official rate was 2.55 SP), while a can of kerosene rocketed from 1.74 SP to 4 SP.[60] The exchange rate under the Khatib era was 1804 Syrian piasters to one French gold coin.[61] Khatib ordered that all petrol and kerosene be confiscated by the government, to avoid hoarding or sale on the black market. He also ordered that mules, donkeys, buses and motorbikes are seized by the police, to curb smuggling of goods and cash money, compensating them from state coffers.[62] The influx of 20,000 Armenians from the Sanjak of Alexandretta, which had just been occupied by Turkey, added to Khatib's worries. These internally displaced Syrians drained the economy, forcing the government to establish shelters for them in Aleppo.[63] They were housed and fed by the Khatib government.

To keep Syrian storehouses full Khatib banned the export of foodstuff to the Arab World as of 31 August 1939, while exempting the wheat imports from any tariffs.[64] Nine months later, he signed an agreement with the Iraqi Petroleum Company (IPC), granting them a fifteen-year concession to drill for oil in Syria. Depending on its quality, IPC would pay the Syrian government 400,000 gold shillings per annum if the oil was over 35 degrees, or 100,000 if inferior to twenty degrees.[65] During the funeral of former president Mohammad 'Ali al-'Abed in November 1939, who had died at his self-imposed exile in the French Riviera, Khatib addressed mourners and journalists, warning that the upcoming days were not going to be easy for Syria.[66]

The Shahbandar murder

On 6 July 1940, 'Abdul Rahman Shahbandar was shot dead at his clinic in Damascus. Three men disguised as farmers had entered his clinic facing the Franciscan nun's school, disguised as farmers from al-Ghouta. As he put on his stethoscope to examine the first patient, one of the assassins took out a carefully concealed gun and fired a bullet through Shahbandar's head, at close range. It ripped through his head and hit the wall, breaking the frame of his AUB certificate. As Shahbandar collapsed in a pool of blood, they rushed out – now all very visibly waving their guns – threatening to shoot the old Kurdish nurse if he raised the alarm.[67]

The Shahbandar murder shook Syrian society at its core. No name was dearer to the hearts of young people growing up in French Mandate Syria. The National Bloc leaders were never too fond of him but they were nevertheless furious with his assassination. Hashem al-Atasi called for nationwide mourning. The British consul in Damascus wrote: 'Dr. Shahbandar has just been assassinated. Presumably, the murder was instigated by Jamil Mardam Bey's party, though there is no proof.'⁶⁸ Bahij al-Khatib was at his office that morning with his friend, Amin Sa'id, owner of *al-Kifah* newspaper. 'He got a phone call saying that Shahbandar had been shot', recalled Sa'id. 'His face changed colors. He nearly chocked on the news.'⁶⁹ Khatib rang his bureau chief, Kazem El Djezairi, asking him to call Justice Director Khalil Rifaat and make sure that Syria's borders are immediately closed, before the assassins could flee to Lebanon, Transjordan or Palestine.⁷⁰ Khatib saw the Shahbandar assassination as a blessing in disguise, hoping to blame it on Jamil Mardam Bey and his colleagues, who had every reason to want Shahbandar dead. It gave him the pretext he needed to get rid of them all, with one sweeping blow.

Khatib took part in Shahbandar's funeral procession, walking solemnly with 200,000 mourners who laid him to rest next to the tomb of Saladin, behind the Umayyad Mosque. Jamil Mardam Bey was in the front row and so was former president, Hashem al-Atasi. There was agony and blind grief in the air. Young girls passed by the premier, carrying 500 bouquets to the Shahbandar family.⁷¹ Little did Mardam Bey know that while the nation was grieving, Bahij al-Khatib was devising a scheme to blame him for Shahbandar's murder. 'Justice for Shahbandar and down with the National Bloc', screamed one bereaved Shahbandaist, while another tore a photo of Mardam Bey. A third started a chant: 'There is no God but Allah and Jamil Mardam Bey is his enemy!' Mardam Bey looked the other way, pretending to hear nothing.

That evening, Shahbandar's brother-in-law, the wealthy landowner Nazih Mou'ayyad al-'Azm received a visit from Joseph Gemayel of French Intelligence. He asked Mou'ayyad al-'Azm: 'Why don't you kill one member of the National Bloc in revenge for Shahbandar's blood?'⁷² Mou'ayyad al-'Azm was stunned by the proposal, but after thinking it over, clearly found it a very attractive idea. He too never liked the National Bloc. Mou'ayyad al-'Azm agreed to blame the murder on four Bloc leaders: Jamil Mardam Bey, Sa'adallah al-Jabiri, Lutfi al-Haffar and Shukri al-Quwatli. Jabiri was one of the co-signatories of the 1936 Treaty who had served as minister of interior and foreign affairs under Mardam Bey. Haffar was Mardam Bey's successor at the premiership while Quwatli was the first minister of defence and finance under the National Bloc. They were the ones who had persecuted Shahbandar after his 1937 return to Syria, denying him permission to re-establish his political party while arresting many of his friends and sympathizers. They looked guilty and were perfect scapegoats for Shahbandar's murder.

A committee was created to handle the case, headed by Attorney General 'Abdul Raouf Sultan and First Interrogator Vladimir Sabe, two Khatib appointees.⁷³ A bounty of 5,000 SP was put on the heads of the assassins, who were identified in appearance by Shahbandar's nurse. The reward was offered by Shahbandar's friend 'Uthman al-Sharabati, a wealthy industrialist, leading to the arrest of the ringleader, Ahmad 'Assasa. He had been hiding in the orchards of al-Midan, outside the gates of the Old City.⁷⁴ The remaining culprits were identified as a tailor, a vegetable seller, a grave-digger and a night watchman. All of them were deeply religious Damascus natives from impoverished families. Within a week, they were all round up and jailed.

He deserved to die

Bahij al-Khatib and Justice Director Khalil Rifaat then went to the Damascus Citadel (state prison) to have a word with Ahmad 'Assasa.[75] It was very un-presidential for Khatib to make such a visit but he needed to handle the case in person, banking on his previous experience as police director. 'Assassa was shuffled into the room barefoot, chained at the hands and feet. Khatib was seated behind an office desk flipping through a stack of papers. He didn't look up, pretending not to notice 'Assassa's heavy presence. Over the past twenty-four hours, the young man had been beaten with a bamboo stick on the soles of his feet, making it difficult for him to walk or stand straight. He took turns in lifting his bare feet for comfort, leaving blood stains on the floor. After wobbling and waiting for what seemed like an eternity, 'Assassa was asked a straightforward question: 'Did you kill 'Abdul Rahman Shahbandar?' Without hesitation, he replied: 'Yes I did. He was an atheist; an enemy of God and his Prophet. He deserved to die.'[76]

Khatib raised his eyebrows in bewilderment. He didn't expect such a swift and straightforward confession. It was the quickest he had ever extracted from a prisoner during his entire career. Suddenly pieces of the puzzle began falling into place. He knew, as did everybody in Damascus, that Shahbandar was a secular intellectual who had spent a lifetime challenging the role of Islam in Arab societies. Inspired by Western political thought since his student days at AUB, Shahbandar had called for separation of state from religion. When serving as foreign minister under Fasial, he had famously refused accompanying the king to the Umayyad Mosque, a protocol-must during Ramadan and the two Eids, saying that he had vowed never to enter a mosque or a church in his life. And he died without ever setting foot in either.[77]

Wild rumours had surrounded Shahbandar since his return from Egypt in 1937. He was once overheard saying: 'Arabs will never rise until they abandon this desert religion that a Bedouin had brought to them (in reference to the Prophet Mohammad).'[78] Another claimed that he had condescendingly addressed Syrian veiled women saying: 'Until when will you wear these headscarves? Isn't it time to start copying the women of Europe?'[79] None of these quotes were authenticated but that didn't really matter, their mere mention at the old bazaars, mosques and baths of Damascus was enough to discredit him with the masses. In his memoirs, Emir 'Adel Arslan goes further, saying that while studying at AUB, Shahbandar seriously considered converting to Christianity, but was prevented by his American teachers, who said that such a defection would get him killed.[80]

Since their idol's murder, members of the Shahbandar movement had gone out of their way to clean his name from the damming accusation of atheism. They re-published his 1906 valedictorian speech at AUB, where had said: 'We Muslims believe in one God, the source of good in whom perfection is manifested.'[81] They also reminded that when calling to arms in 1925, he had made his appeal 'In the name of God and the Nation.' None of that mattered for Bahij al-Khatib, who seemed convinced that religion was the main reason why 'Assasa and his friends decided to kill Shahbandar.

But how could he link that to the National Bloc, and specifically to Jamil Mardam Bey who was no less secular than Shahbandar? He ordered ʿAssassa to say that he had been paid by Mardam Bey to kill Shahbandar, both for his secular views and connections 'to the English'.[82] The young man said that he had never met Mardam Bey in his life. Khatib got up from behind his desk, grabbed ʿAssassa by the shoulders and shook him aggressively. He then slapped him across the face, threatening: 'Do you want to get out of here alive? Do you want to see your mother again? If so, you have to do what I tell you!'[83] ʿAssassa was promised a commuted sentence, if he complied with Khatib's 'wishes'.

Khatib had a similar encounter with the second assassin, Khalil Ghandour, this time in the presence of Shahbandar's in-law. They met him at the office of Damascus police director Safouh Mouaʾyyad al-ʿAzm. Ghandour was a Salafi student who wore his black beard long and trimmed. He made a living from night guarding the orchards around Damascus. He too was beaten, this time with a cane on his back, and ordered to blame the murder on Mardam Bey and his bureau chief, a young lawyer named ʿAsem al-Naʾili.[84] ʿAssasa and Ghandour eventually complied with Khatib's orders, and a lawsuit was filed by the Shahbandar family against the three Bloc leaders: Jamil Mardam Bey, Saʿadallah al-Jabiri and Lutfi al-Haffar.[85] Charges against Shukri al-Quwatli were dropped, given his strong connections with the House of Saud, who Khatib did not want to offend.[86]

Prime ministers can kill as well

On 5 August 1940, the three Bloc leaders were summoned to police headquarters for an official criminal interrogation.[87] Mardam Bey testified that he was at Hosh al-Matban, his family orchards in al-Ghouta, when the murder took place, claiming that he had not seen Shahbandar in three weeks. A French officer took out a stack of pro-Bloc dailies, some dating back to 1937. All contained editorials that were critical of Shahbandar, penned during Mardam Bey's tenure as premier, with phrases underlined by the French persecutor. 'These are proof, Monsieur Mardam Bey, that you wanted him dead!' He added that in June 1940 Mardam Bey had accused Shahbandar of treason in front of two Damascus merchants, Shukri Sukkar and Mohammad Hasan al-Khatib. 'Accusing somebody of treason is an open invitation for people to kill him', said the French officer.[88] Irritated Mardam Bey snapped, 'I refuse to hear this!' The French officer banged his fist on the table: 'Silence! Be seated Jamil Bey and if you don't, I am capable of keeping you in custody until I finish my work. You are not giving a speech in Parliament. You are being questioned in a crime case.'[89]

Lutfi al-Haffar tried to calm Mardam Bey, who was shaking with anger. He quietly addressed the interrogator: 'What you are saying is a great insult, not to us as individuals, but to the country as a whole and to the political office that we represent. Just listen to yourself. You are accusing two prime ministers and two ministers of murder.' The Frenchman smiled and said, 'Indeed I am; ministers and prime ministers can kill as well.'[90] The French officer reminded Mardam Bey of an incident that had occurred while he was driving through Damascus with his colleague 'Abdul Rahman al-Kayyali back in 1937. They had been approached by an angry mob of Shahbandarists in Souq al-Hal. When one spotted Mardam Bey, he shouted, 'It's him. Kill him!'[91] Mardam Bey's driver took out a gun, threatening to shoot. 'Remember that incident', asked the French interrogator with a wicked smile. 'They tried to kill you and now, you have killed their leader!'[92]

On 18 October 1940, a Lebanese national travelled to Damascus in the dead of night. He was an Arabic interpreter working at the French High Commissioner's office, and he was carrying bad news for the Bloc leaders. The French were planning to order their arrest the very next morning, he said. Within one hour, Mardam Bey escaped to Baghdad, driven by his chauffeur who had worked with the Iraqi Petroleum Company and knew the desert road by heart, thereby evading French checkpoints.[93] Seated next to him was Lufti al-Haffar. Jabiri fled from Aleppo via Deir ez-Zour at 4.00 am.[94] Quwatli stayed in Damascus to form a legal team for the defence of his comrades. The next day, at the orders of Bahij al-Khatib, Syrian dailies ran front-page mug shots of the Bloc leaders, side-by-side with Ahmad 'Assasa, Khalil Ghandour and their accomplices. The headline read: WANTED FOR MURDER. Khatib sent an official letter to the Iraqi government, demanding their extradition.[95]

The Shahbandar trial

A military court was convened for the Shahbandar murder. Ironically, it was the same court that had tried both him and Mardam Bey for their role in the Great Revolt back in 1925, sentencing them to death in *absentia*.[96] The court opened in the main hall of the Syrian Parliament on 9 December 1940, five months after Shahbandar's death, and lasted until 7 January 1941. A daily briefing of court proceedings was typed and sent to Khatib's office, which he read with great interest. When it was 'Assasa's turn to address the jury, he repeated exactly what Khatib had ordered him to say, that he had been visited at the Umayyad Mosque by Mardam Bey's bureau chief 'Asem al-Na'ili on 1 June 1940. Na'ili reportedly said to him that Shahbandar was 'an agent of the British and an enemy of Islam'. 'Assasa said that Na'ili offered him 400 Ottoman gold coins to kill Shahbandar, along with assurances of safe passage to Iraq.[97]

The Bloc lawyers called on Sheikh Mekki al-Kuttani as their primary witness. Kuttani was a Damascus-based Moroccan scholar and founding vice-president of the Ulema Association. Before killing Shahbandar, 'Assasa had called on him to ask: 'What is the punishment for treason?'[98] Kuttani replied, without hesitation: 'Death.' He did not know that 'Assasa was referring to 'Abdul Rahman Shahbandar, or that his religious verdict would be used as a pretext to kill him.[99] When Kuttani walked into the courtroom, accompanied by Lebanese lawyers Habib Bou Shahla and Emille Lahhoud, 'Assasa and his friends jumped to their feet, heads bowed in reverence. He looked sternly at the young men, addressing each by his first name. 'When you visited me and asked about the punishment for treason, I replied in general terms, not knowing that the question was in reference to Shahbandar.' He added that Shahbandar was a national figure who did not deserve to be killed, and that by eliminating him, the young men had done Syria a great injustice by killing him. Kuttani walked up to ʿAssasa and asked him to take a solemn oath on the Quran. From behind bars, ʿAssasa extended his trembling right harm and put it on the holy book. Kuttani looked him straight in the eyes and asked: 'My son Ahmad, did ʿAssem al-Naʾili order you to kill Dr. Shahbandar? Remember that you are under oath.' In a dramatic scene that sent shockwaves throughout the Syrian Chamber, ʿAssasa broke into a panic attack and began sobbing hysterically: 'I never met ʿAssem al-Naʾili in my life.' He then uttered his final confession:

> We killed Shahbandar because he was an atheist. We were also told that he was an agent of the British. We wanted to kill both him and Jamil Mardam Bey because both of them are traitors.[100] We then decided to kill one, and blame his murder on the other, after realizing that the French wanted us to incriminate the National Bloc. So did Bahij Bey (al-Khatib).[101]

After restoring calm and asking for a recess, the judge read out his verdicts, declaring all the National Bloc leaders 'not guilty'.[102] The assassins were sentenced to death and hanged in public at Marjeh Square in February 1941. It was a major blow for Bahij al-Khatib. He never imagined that this is how the Shahbandar trial would conclude. Two weeks later, Mardam Bey and his comrades returned to Syria in triumph, promising to take Bahij al-Khatib and Nazih Mouʾayyad al-ʿAzm to court.[103] His mishandling of the Shahbandar case was a major embarrassment for the French, who had no choice but to relieve him of his duties on 30 March 1941.

Before leaving office, Khatib inaugurated an old-age home in Damascus.[104] He also attended opening of the new Damascus Post Office, which he had constructed with 250,000 SP from the state budget.[105] He wanted to go down in history as a great builder, not for the Shahbandar case that was to be forever associated with his name and era.

Khatib's 1941 comeback

For the next two years, Khatib allowed himself to slip into obscurity. Nothing was heard of him nor was he seen at any official function. The National Bloc did not live up to its threats and filed no legal charges against him. His immediate successor was Khaled al-ʿAzm, an independent who ruled Syria briefly between April and September 1941, before he was replaced by Khatib's old friend, Taj al-Din al-Hasani. In his memoirs, ʿAzm says that when discussing his cabinet formation, the elephant in the room was Bahij al-Khatib, whom the French wanted compensated with a government portfolio. 'He is a loyal friend of France', said High Commissioner Henri Dentz, '… we simply cannot abandon him'.[106] ʿAzm tried to explain, saying that Khatib would give the government a bad name, because he was 'extremely unpopular' in Syria. At the end, they agreed to give him a break for three months, before deciding on when and how he would return to power.[107] By then, the Allies had invaded Syria and expelled the pro-Nazi regime of General Dentz, bringing the country under control of the British and the Free French. Sheikh Taj insisted on restoring Khatib to office, describing him as one of the most capable administrators in Syria.[108] Khatib needed little convincing, only this time; he was appointed interior minister in a government headed by Hasan al-Hakim, a respected nationalist who happened to be a former right-hand-man to ʿAbdul Rahman Shahbandar.

Politically, Bahij al-Khatib had been degraded from prime minister with presidential powers to cabinet minister in a government over which he had no control. The new prime minister was a prolific author who lived into the 1980s and authored important books on the modern history of Syria, including his two-volume memoir, published in 1965. He does not say why he chose to work with someone as controversial as Khatib, and whether he was imposed on the government by President Taj al-Din al-Hasani, or by the French. Did he actually manage to convince Hakim that he had nothing to do with Shahbandar's murder? Khatib probably took to the job in order to drop much of the heavy luggage hanging over his shoulder for the past fifteen years, of being a French pawn. Nothing would clean his name better than working with somebody as respected and honourable as Hasan al-Hakim. At cabinet meetings, he made sure to sit next to Hakim and then to joke with some of the very same nationalists whom he had persecuted in the past, like Hashem al-Atasi's nephew Faydi al-Atasi (now serving as minister of education) and Fares al-Khoury's brother Fayez, now the minister of foreign affairs.

During his seven-month tenure as interior minister, Khatib took part in the declaration of Syrian independence on 27 September 1941. Charles de Gaulle announced that he was officially abolishing the mandate but keeping French troops in Syria until combat operations in Europe came to an end. Celebrating the event, the Ministry of Interior issued a collection of postal stamps, carrying Sheikh Taj's picture next to the tricolor of the Syrian Flag. On 27 April 1942, Foreign Minister Fayez al-Khoury sent a cable to world capitals, announcing that in accordance with de Gaulle's pledge, Syria was now formally independent from the French Mandate. World leaders sent congratulatory messages to Damascus and King George II of Greece even paid a state visit to Sheikh Taj. Khatib handled all security and protocol, making sure that the king's visit went by smoothly, with no disturbances.

Abandoning the French

Khatib was a smart man. He worked with Hasan al-Hakim with the aim of re-inventing himself for a greater role in post-mandate Syria. To do that, he needed to come across as a nationalist, no longer an *intidabi*. When mandate officials asked him to confiscate private property in order to build a French school on the Damascus-Beirut highway, Khatib refused to comply.[109] 'Syria is now an independent state', he wrote back to the High Commission in Beirut, 'and any such confiscation of property requires approval of His Excellency the President of the Republic'. His relationship with Hasan al-Hakim would eventually sour, when the premier tried re-opening the Shahbandar case, saying that he was never convinced with the original 1941 verdicts. Sheikh Taj objected, arguing that this would create unnecessary friction with both the French and the National Bloc.[110] Khatib seconded that opinion, fearing that any new trial would reveal his murky dealings with Ahmad ʿAssasa and the rest of the assassins. On 17 April 1942, Hakim presented his resignation to Sheikh Taj. He was replaced by an old Hama notable named Husni al-Barazi.

Barazi was one of the co-founders of the National Bloc who had defected during the 1928 constitutional crisis. Briefly in 1926, he had served as minister of interior under Prime Minister Ahmad Nami, in the midst of the Great Revolt. That tenure was cut short with his arrest, on charges of supporting the rebels of al-Ghouta. Now back at the helm of power, he decided to re-assume the portfolio of interior, along with the premiership, transferring Khatib to the largely ceremonial post of director of the Ministry of Interior. Never had a former premier been downgraded in such a manner since the Ottoman evacuation in 1918: from premier to minister, then to ministry director. When leaving office, other premiers usually either retired from politics or waited for a comeback to the premiership. The Directory of the Ministry of Interior was the very same office from which Khatib had started his career as a young bureaucrat, back in 1919. It was a junior post when compared with the premiership, with a much lower salary. His appointment put Syrian protocol in crisis, given that Khatib retained the honorific title of *Dawlet al-Ra'is*, which applied to all former prime ministers and speakers of parliament. That's how people addressed him in public and how he was formally introduced at state functions, where due to his political seniority, he was seated on the right side of the president, like both his predecessor Jamil Mardam Bey and successor Hasan al-Hakim. How could he be addressed as *Dawlet al-Ra'is*, when serving only as director of the ministry? Against all odds, Khatib accepted the job, and remained at it until 1943. He didn't need the money, still relying on his family wealth in Chehime for a living. He also didn't need the positioning, having already served at Syria's top job.

A three-day governorship of Damascus

In January 1943, Sheikh Taj died, fourteen months into his term, creating a giant lacuna at the seat of power in Damascus. He was the first president to die in office; all others had either resigned or been toppled. The French called for national elections later that summer, first for parliament and then for the presidency. The National Bloc announced that it would contest all seats in the Chamber of Deputies, under a list headed by Shukri al-Quwatli, who would also be running for president. He and Khatib did not get along. In 1928, Quwatli had taken part in anti-Khatib demonstrations and they took gabs at each other during the Shahbandar trial when Khatib tried to incriminate Quwatli with his colleagues.

Two secret meetings were arranged between Quwatli and Khatib. The first was at the residence of Kurdish notable Omar Shamidn Agha in Hay al-Akrad, attended by Khatib's friend, the journalist Amin Sa'id.[111] The second was in the town of Shuqayf in Mount Lebanon, initiated by Quwatli's friend Hajj Adib Kheir, who Khatib had once arrested on Nazi charges.[112] Quwatli asked Khatib to forget the past, making him an offer for future cooperation. In exchange for a democratic election, with no intimidation from the Ministry of Interior, he promised Khatib a political comeback.[113] Khatib took up the offer, and handled the 1943 elections in a manner that was deemed satisfactory to the National Bloc. The Bloc won a majority, and on 17 August 1943, Quwatli was elected president. True to his word, Quwatli issued a presidential decree on 13 October 1943, naming Bahij al-Khatib governor of Damascus. The appointment shocked the old notables of the Syrian capital, who had lobbied against Khatib's first stint as governor in February–March 1936. How could somebody with Quwatli's national history work with someone as loathed as Khatib? Ever since the fall of the Ottomans, the post of Damascus governor had been held by a native Damascene, with the sole exception of Husni al-Barazi, who held the job for one month in 1942, and Khatib himself, who held it for less than a month in 1936. Not only was Khatib non-Damascene, he was also non-Syrian, although twenty years had passed since he obtained a Syrian passport. The Presidential Office was bombarded with complaints from city notables and nationalists, asking for Khatib's dismissal.[114] Not wanting to start his era on a sour note with the people of Damascus, who had welcomed his ascent with tremendous outpouring and support, Quwatli had Khatib dismissed just three days later. He also had him pensioned off to prevent Khatib from making any future comeback.[115] A new governor was installed in Damascus, 'Aref al-Hamzawi, who hailed from one of the oldest Damascene families that had traditionally held the honorific post of *naqib al-ashraf* (dean of the prophet's descendants).

Khatib was naturally very upset with Quwatli's aberration, feeling both betrayed and outsmarted. Quwatli denied responsibility for Khatib's dismissal, saying that the decision had been taken by his prime minister, Sa'adallah al-Jabiri.[116] And it sounded perfectly logical for Jabiri to dismiss Khatib in revenge for having wrongfully blamed him for the Shahbandar murder three years earlier. This time, however, Khatib did not put up a fight to stay in office. Quietly, he packed his belongings and retired to his home in the quiet Mazra'a neighbourhood of Damascus. Friends would visit him daily, including Amin Sa'id, who had arranged Khatib's secret pre-election meeting with Quwatli. When his visits became too frequent, Sa'id was approached by the president's bureau chief, Najib al-Armanazi, who advised him against getting too close to Khatib. Amin Sa'id refused abiding by Armanazi's 'advice', saying that he and Khatib have been friends for thirty years, and there was no reason for him to suspend relations. Authorities then ordered policemen stationed at the doors of Khatib's home, but that too failed to dissuade visitors. Quwatli finally sent him a private message: 'Go back to Lebanon. That would be better for you and for Syria.'[117] A few days later, Khatib silently crossed the border, first to Sidon then to his native Chehime, where he lived in solitude for the rest of his life. When Amin Sa'id visited Quwatli to complain, the president explained:

> I respect Bahij Bey and appreciate his talent. The current situation forced us to ask him to leave. We wanted to tell the people that the government can function without him. This will put an end to all talk that Bahij al-Khatib was the soul of the state and both its director and facilitator. We also want to show the people that the era of French hegemony is now over. Bahij al-Khatib is indispensable, and we wait for the day when we can once again work with him.[118]

That day never came ...

Figure 8 Bahij al-Khatib.

Chapter 9

KHALED AL-ʿAZM (APRIL–SEPTEMBER 1941)

In the midst of the First World War, two powerful Ottoman officers, Enver Pasha and Djemal Pasha, came to Damascus and lunched at the home of Mohammad Fawzi Pasha al-ʿAzm in Souq Sarouja, outside the Old City. Enver was minister of war in the Ottoman Empire, while Djemal was commander of the 4th Army in Syria. They were leaders of the Committee of Union and Progress, which had assumed control of the state since 1913. ʿAzm was an elderly Damascus gentleman who had served as minister of religious endowments in Istanbul. His thirteen-year-old son, Khaled, stood next to him, welcoming the two pashas. Enver patted the boy on the head, asking what he did in life. ʿAzm replied: 'I publish a newspaper.'[1] He was referring to a school journal that he edited with his friends, which was distributed to four subscribers only (one of whom was his father). Enver laughed at the boy's remark, asking: 'What paper is this that I haven't heard of?' Khaled al-ʿAzm took out a copy of the hand-written paper with amateurish political editorials and a fulsome article on its front page about Enver Pasha. Smiling the pasha said: 'Don't be in a hurry to get into politics. It's a hard job.'[2] Khaled al-ʿAzm smiled back, rather innocently, not fully comprehending the small piece of valuable advice that Enver Pasha had just offered him. When penning his memoirs from exile in Lebanon fifty years later, ʿAzm recalled the story in hindsight, regretting having not listened to the Ottoman pasha.

Khaled al-ʿAzm went on to become one of the pillars of Syrian politics: an enigma in the modern history of the Middle East. Between the years 1940 and 1962, he created five cabinets, also serving as minister of foreign affairs, finance and defence. Twice he nominated himself for the Syrian presidency, in 1955 and 1961. He was defeated the first time and withdrew on the second, both being democratic elections. Twice he was arrested, in 1949 and 1962, only to be exiled permanently by the Baʾathists after they seized power in March 1963. In September 1958, he suffered a major blow with the confiscation of his family's vast plantations by the socialist state of Gamal ʿAbdul Nasser. Throughout an illustrious career, ʿAzm had seen the two faces of life: the good and bad. People hailed him as one of the founding fathers of the Syrian nation in 1946, only to end up just three years later in a damp prison cell, wounded in his left arm, treated like an animal at the orders of Husni al-Zaʾim, architect of Syria's first coup. The words of Enver Pasha kept coming back to him, ringing in his years as he did the exact opposite of what the pasha had said to him.

The early years

Khaled al-ʿAzm was born at his father's mansion in Souq Sarouja on 6 November 1903. Two male brothers had died at infancy, greatly troubling his father, who longed for an heir to the family's wealth and political standing. ʿAzm's mother, Efakat al-Istanbuli, was a native Turk whose grandfather ʿOthman Pasha had been governor of Ottoman Damascus in the nineteenth century.[3] When pregnant with Khaled she visited the mosque of the Muslim warrior Khaled Ibn al-Walid in Homs to pray for a son, pledging to name him Khaled.[4]

ʿAzm was raised in extreme luxury at the hands of two nannies brought exclusively from Switzerland and France to look after him. One had tutored the children of the Romanov family in St Petersburg before their toppling at the hands of the Bolsheviks in 1917.[5] Private teachers were hired from Istanbul for early home schooling, before Khaled al-ʿAzm was sent to Galata, the elite school for the Ottoman aristocracy in Istanbul, after his father's election as an MP in the Ottoman Parliament in 1908.

Mohammad Fawzi Pasha al-ʿAzm was scion of a leading political family that had ruled Damascus throughout most of the eighteenth century. Born in 1860, he joined the Ottoman civil service, becoming scribe at the vilayet of Syria, then director of correspondences under the governor Hamdi Pasha. In 1900, he was named president of the Damascus Municipality, where he helped establish the Hamidian Hospital at al-Baramkeh, which later became the official hospital of Damascus University. He also played an important role in founding the Hejaz Station with his friend and neighbour, Ahmad ʿIzzat Pasha al-ʿAbed. Unlike ʿAbed, who was fired with the 1908 coup, Mohammad Fawzi Pasha managed to remain relevant, allying himself with the Committee of Union and Progress. In 1912, they appointed him minister in the cabinet of the Grand Vizier, Ahmad Mukhtar Pasha. Back in Damascus, he became good friends with Djemal Pasha, who would frequently visit him for long evenings of poker and gambling.[6] Djemal Pasha cherished those nights, where he would always win, returning home with pockets filled with gold. Khaled al-ʿAzm's mother was appointed chair of an NGO created by Djemal to care for the wounded in Damascus. At one of its events, a young Khaled al-ʿAzm had met Djemal Pasha for the first time, recalling in his memoirs: 'I stood next to my mother looking at Djemal Pasha's majestic face, with his dark black beard and eyes that radiated with intelligence and pride.'[7] When Djemal realized that he was her child, he extended his hand so that ʿAzm could kiss it, as customarily done in Ottoman society. He then said: 'I hope that one day, he becomes like his father.'

With the liberation of Syria from the Ottomans in 1918, Mohammad Fawzi Pasha was elected speaker of the Syrian National Congress but died before assuming office on 15 November 1919. He had just recently married his son to Seniyeh Mardam Bey, the daughter of respected judge named Rashed Pasha Mardam Bey. She had been engaged to her cousin Haydar, a scribe at Emir Faisal's office, but ʿAzm asked her father to call off the engagement so that she could marry his son.[8] Emir Faisal attended the marriage ceremony, where the proud father distributed gold coins to his guests, celebrating the festive occasion.[9]

Seniyeh died in labour while giving birth to her only daughter, 'Aliyya, on 24 July 1920. It was the very same day that the Syrian Army was defeated in the Battle of Maysaloun.

'Azm the industrialist

Khaled al-'Azm studied law at Damascus University, graduating in 1922. He briefly served on the municipality of Damascus before venturing into his first industrial project, the National Cement Company. Established in January 1930, it was a joint-stock company founded by the National Bloc and capitalized at 144,000 gold Ottoman coins distributed among 24,000 shareholders.[10] The region around Damascus was rich in limestone deposits and clay, providing for good cement that could be extracted and manufactured thanks to cheap labour. Cement was rapidly replacing stone in the construction business, and real estate was becoming the safest investment in Syria due to political disturbances that made all other sectors volatile. Additionally, tariff barriers were raised on Syrian goods headed for Europe, allowing Syrian cement to reach new markets and compete with foreign cement on the Syrian market.[11]

The factory produced 30,000 tonnes of cement in 1932, and by 1938 it was producing 63,500 tonnes, meeting 50 per cent of Syria's domestic needs. Foreign cement in 1932 cost four gold coins per ton, while local cement cost only two.[12] By 1936, the price of local cement had dropped to one gold/tonne.[13] This boom led to the implementation of similar projects around Syria. By 1934, there were sixty-three modern companies in Damascus and seventy-one in Aleppo, all inspired by 'Azm's Cement Company.[14] Sitting on the board of directors were seasoned statesmen who were to become 'Azm's colleagues in future years, like Jamil Mardam Bey and 'Ata al-Ayyubi. In 1934, 'Azm established the Damascus Chamber of Industry and was voted as its first president.[15]

'Azm's first cabinet post

In April 1939, while on a business trip to Germany, 'Azm read that a major cabinet crisis had erupted in Syria during the final months of Hashem al-Atasi's presidency. The National Bloc was struggling to stay in power after failing to ratify the Franco-Syrian Treaty of 1936. President Atasi called on Nasuhi al-Boukhari to serve as premier, hoping that as an independent, he could revive talks on the 1936 Treaty. Boukhari was married to 'Azm's cousin and knew him from family gatherings. On 4 April 1939, Khaled al-'Azm was named foreign minister in the Boukhari government; his very first public office, handling a ministry that has just been restored to Syria. The ministry was small, with only two ambassadors, being 'Adnan al-Atasi in Turkey and Asa'ad Haroun in Iraq. 'Azm devised a plan to upgrade and expand his ministry, but the Boukhari government collapsed just three months after it was formed, on 8 July 1939, having tried – and failed – at advancing talks with the French.

'Azm returned to his jobs at the Cement Company and the Damascus Chamber of Industry, indulging himself with a football team that he had just set up called Nadi Mu'awiyya, named after the founder of the Umayyad Dynasty in Islam.[16] In March 1941, he was approached by ex-president Ahmad Nami, the damad, who had been promised a return to power by High Commissioner Henri Dentz. Nami offered 'Azm the premiership, but that cabinet was never formed due to a National Bloc boycott. Dentz decided to abandon the Damad as president and keep Khaled al-'Azm as premier, formally inviting him to create a government on 1 April 1941. He was an independent, rich, well connected and fluent with languages.

Premier during the Second World War

'Azm's five-man cabinet was tasked with leading the nation for what remained of the Second World War. It was a technocrat government that would last for more than five months, composed of experts in their fields, mostly with no political affiliation. His friend, the Christian economist Jean Sehnawi, was made minister of finance, while the Montpellier University-trained attorney Muhsen al-Barazi was appointed minister of education. A former National Bloc member, Nasib al-Bakri, was appointed minister of economy and public works, while Safwat Qater Aghasi, the second president of the court of cassation, was made minister of justice. 'Azm himself took on the ministry of interior, in addition to the premiership. At thirty-eight, he was the youngest person in his cabinet. Technically, 'Azm was an appointed acting head of state, who, like his predecessors Ahmad Nami and Bahij al-Khatib, was to rule Syria with no constitution or parliament.

On 10 May 1940, Hitler had launched his *Blitzkrieg* against Belgium and France. Within one month, 70,000 French troops were killed, and on 14 June Paris fell to the Nazis. The city was literarily surrendered to the Germans at a solemn ceremony held at the Hotel de Crillon at the Place de la Concorde. Eight days later, France signed an armistice with Germany. Syrians suddenly found themselves under the command of Hitler's proxy in France, decorated First World War officer Marshal Philippe Petain. He became prime minister on 16 June, abolishing constitution of the Third Republic and creating a pro-German cabinet, first in Bordeaux then in Vichy. Though their country was allowed to keep its empire, fleet, merchant shipping and national flag, at the end of the day, France had effectively surrendered to Hitler, wounding the pride of every Frenchman. Thrilled at how swiftly France had fallen, Hitler expected Great Britain to come next.

The occupation of France spread panic among Arab tourists spending their summer in Syria and Lebanon. The two Mediterranean colonies suddenly found themselves immersed in the complex web of Second World War politics, coming under the direct rule of Nazi Germany. Fourteen thousand Arabs packed their bags and returned home, abandoning their Levantine summer resorts and villas, dealing a heavy blow to the Syrian tourism industry. 'Azm had hoped that this sector would generate good income for his government, but its collapse signalled a bumpy start.[17] Communication lines to Syria were temporarily cut off, and French troops were faced with the difficult choice of siding either with Marshal Petain, a national celebrity, or Charles de Gaulle, a relative newcomer. If they sided with Petain, however, they would be legitimizing an officer who had willingly agreed to play by Nazi rules. If they stood with de Gaulle and Germany won the war, they would be putting their careers – and lives – at stake. Syrians had a hard time hiding their smiles as they watched the mighty French get a dose of their own medicine. After twenty years of gruesome occupation, many viewed the fall of France as sweet revenge.

The battle for grain

The British had enforced a land and sea blockade of all French territory, causing the price of medicine, coal and wood to go through the roof in Syria. Basic commodities like sugar, rice and petrol disappeared from the market. Syrian resources were rationed for the French war effort, sending thousands of Syrians into hunger and financial ruin. On 28 February 1941, Damascus shopkeepers went on strike, protesting an increase in the price of bread.[18] Grain was scarce due to poor crop that winter, and heartless merchants were hoarding their stocks, causing prices to soar. By the time Khaled al-'Azm reached the Grand Serail, the strike had spread to Homs and Hama. In his memoirs, Dentz wrote: 'I must absolutely win the battle of wheat, and I have everybody against me; the people, the merchants, the English!'[19]

Khaled al-'Azm was a giant of a man, with a keen understanding of international affairs and plenty of indulgences in life. He loved music, was a gifted photographer and excelled in drawing sketches of his friends. He walked slowly with a difficult gait because of a chronic weight problem, and rarely wore an Ottoman fez, considering it démodé. When he did, it was also tipped at a stylish sharp angle. A worldly figure, he had spent his early adulthood travelling European capitals and drinking wine with aristocrats, politicians and artists. Back home in Damascus he led a lifestyle that was strikingly different from that of his countrymen, housing concerts and mixed-sex parties at his grand mansion in Souq Sarouja. Many saw him as too distant and too aristocratic, very different from populist leaders with a wide powerbase, like Hashem al-Atasi and Shukri al-Quwatli. His first real challenge was to prove that although rich and comfortable, he was not alien to the problems of the Syrian people.

Leading the bread strikes was Shukri al-Quwatli, the only National Bloc member whose reputation had not been affected by the back-to-back setbacks, starting with collapse of the 1936 Treaty, onto the loss of the Sanjak and Shahbandar's murder. He and 'Azm had known each other for years, and they never got along. 'Azm considered himself a friend of the National Bloc, but never an official member. Like Quwatli, he believed that military confrontation with the French was suicidal, insisting on diplomacy and statesmanship instead of bullets. Quwatli had lobbied against the appointment of 'Azm as premier, saying that a real head of state should be elected by the people, like Hashem al-Atasi had been, and not appointed by the French. 'Azm argued that if he didn't accept the job of premier, then the French would keep Bahij al-Khatib at his post. Quwatli replied that if 'Azm declined Dentz's offer, then the French would have no choice but go for parliamentary elections.[20] 'Running a country', he told a gathering at his home, 'is not like selling a bag of cement'. He then told 'Azm bluntly: 'We at the National Bloc cannot support you, nor can we stand neutral.'[21] Quwatli had managed to get former prime ministers Lutfi al-Haffar and Jamil Mardam Bey to veto 'Azm's appointment.[22] For the next five months, they spared no effort to discredit him and bring down his government, when it was formed in April.

The 1941 invasion of Syria

On 29 May 1941, British Foreign Secretary Anthony Eden walked into Mansion House, the official residence of the Lord Mayor of the City of London. He was expected to address the issue of Syria. Damascus was all ears, and so was its premier. Reflecting the thoughts Prime Minister Winston Churchill, Eden said: 'Many Arab thinkers desire for the Arab people a greater degree of unity than they now enjoy. His Majesty's Government would give full support for any scheme that commands general approval.'[23] A similar declaration followed, this time from Churchill to Charles de Gaulle:

> You know that we have sought no special advantage over the Free French and have no intention of exploiting the tragic position of France for our own good. I welcome therefore your decision to promise independence to Syria and Lebanon, and as you know, I think it is essential that we should lend to this promise the full weight of our guarantee.[24]

Deep inside 'Azm wished for an Axis defeat, having admired the liberalism and culture of European society prior to the Second World War.[25] He hated dictators, and Hitler was among the worst he had ever come across in his life, yet could not voice such feelings because he had come to power with the blessing of Vichy.[26] On 8 June 1941, a joint Anglo-French army arrived in Syria headed by General Henry Wilson. They had one objective: driving pro-Nazi Frenchmen out of Syria. The 5th Indian Brigade would enter Syria via Daraa in the south and al-Qunaytra in the Golan Heights. They would open the way for the Free French to march on Damascus. Meanwhile, the 7th Australian Division would march into Syria via Haifa, while the 10th Indian Brigade would come through Iraq up the Euphrates River towards Deir ez-Zour, al-Raqqa and Aleppo.[27] Their task would be to seize all of Northern Syria and cut off Vichy lines of communication. It was a French civil war on Syrian territory, with Great Britain taking sides against Vichy. De Gaulle commanded six thousand troops in Syria, along with twelve planes and ten tanks. Vichy France stood at 35,000 troops, including four battalions of the highly trained Foreign Legion and seven thousand recruits from North Africa. General Dentz also had fourteen battalions with ninety tanks, seventy armoured cars and 250 aeroplanes. He had enough petrol and munitions to last his men for six weeks.[28]

The first battle, that of the Litani River, began on 9 June, followed by al-Kisweh near Damascus. On 18 June, the Allies took Damascus. Vichy troops put up a fierce resistance in the ancient city of Palmyra on 1 July, and in Deir ez-Zour three days later. Prime Minister 'Azm stood by and watched, completely incapable of influencing the outcomes of the war. It was wiser to lie low, as the Syrian crisis had clearly been blown completely off track, and was no longer between his countrymen and France, but rather between European countries fighting on Syrian territory. The fall of Damascus was marked with remarkable ceremony that reminded 'Azm of the 1918 fall of the Ottomans. General de Gaulle's envoy George Catroux drove into the Syrian capital accompanied by Paul Legentilhomme, commander of the 1st Division of the Free French Army. They were escorted by Circassian cavalry with their feather decorated uniforms. Ordinary Syrians came out to watch the procession, but they neither showered the Free French with flowers and rice, nor sung praise of General de Gaulle. By 1941, they had become totally indifferent towards the Second Word War, fed up with the political football game being played by London and Paris in their country. 'Azm received the French and British newcomers with a brief solemn reception at the Grand Serail, saying that he hoped that the Free French would grant Syria its long-delayed independence. So unimportant was the speech that he didn't even feel it necessary to include it in his three-volume memoir.

The Allied war in Syria cost Dentz a total of 1,000 troops. They were killed in battle and laid to rest at the French cemetery, behind the Mezzeh orchards. Another five thousand were arrested and eventually shipped back to France. On 12 July, Dentz approached the British for an armistice, which was signed in Acre, Palestine on 14 July. Dentz returned to Paris and died a defeated soldier shortly afterwards in 1945. The Acre Agreement, to de Gaulle's horror, made no reference whatsoever to the Free French. To the grand dismay of Khaled al-'Azm, it also failed to mention Syrian independence.

De Gaulle was beyond mad, feeling betrayed by his British allies. He landed in Cairo on 20 July to negotiate amendments to the Acre Agreement. De Gaulle made such a fuss that the British went as far as to consider keeping him out of Syria altogether.[29] One suggestion was to stage a coup within the Free French forces and have him replaced him with General Catroux, who was far more cooperative. Fearing a crack in Allied ranks, however, Churchill eventually agreed to co-administer Syria with de Gaulle.[30] The British would control military affairs, while Free France would handle politics and government. Khaled al-'Azm would still report to the French, not to the British. He hated the new agreement. At Churchill's advice, de Gaulle agreed to abolish the title of 'High Commissioner' and replace it with that of 'Delegate General' in Syria. It was merely a cosmetic change; the French were still in control of Syria.

De Gaulle appointed Catroux as his man in Damascus, tasked with negotiating revival of the 1936 Treaty. To do that, he needed to change the prime minister of Syria, who the Free French considered a creation of Vichy. Khaled al-'Azm was formally asked to resign on 12 September 1941 and immediately replaced by Taj al-Din al-Hasani, an all-time friend of colonial administrators, who had stood with the Allies in their war on Hitler. Sixteen days later, French warplanes dropped leaflets on the Syrian and Lebanese capitals, dated 28 September 1941. Signed by General Catroux, they read:

> Syrians and Lebanese, I come to put an end to the Mandate and proclaim you free and independent. A treaty in which our mutual relations will be defined will guarantee your independent and sovereign status. This treaty will be negotiated as soon as possible between your representatives and myself. Meanwhile, our mutual situation will be that of close alliance united in the pursuit of common ideas and objectives.[31]

'Azm's first term in office had lasted no more than five months in total. He liked the job and set out on returning to the Grand Serail, harbouring a presidential ambition that would last until his was ultimately ejected from Syria in 1963.

'Azm returns with Shukri al-Quwatli

Despite the history of animosity between them, 'Azm returned to politics under the wing of Shukri al-Quwatli in 1943, running for parliament on a National Bloc-backed ticket. He forgave Quwatli for having tried to bring down his government in 1941 and in return, Quwatlli agreed to turn a page with 'Azm, seeing that someone with his calibre would be a plus for any government coalition. After winning the presidency that summer, Quwatli called on the Bloc leader Sa'adallah al-Jabiri to form a government, in which Khaled al-'Azm was named minister of finance. On 14 November 1944, he was given the same portfolio under Prime Minister Fares al-Khoury. Six months later, the Free French ordered an air raid on the Syrian capital, striking at its parliament building, and the vicinity of the Grand Serail. De Gaulle was fed up with the backchannel deals between Damascus and the British, which had led to inviting Syria, very much against his will, to the founding conference of the United Nations in San Francisco. On 29 May 1945, de Gaulle's troops were given orders to arrest Shukri al-Quwatli, Sa'adallah al-Jabiri and Jamil Mardam Bey, who was dubbing as acting prime minister during Fares al-Khoury's absence in the United States. 'Azm and Mardam Bey fled from the Grand Serail in the pitch of dark, running through the contorted streets of Damascus, dodging French bombs and bullets. 'Azm opened the doors of his family mansion in Souq Sarouja, welcoming a total of one hundred guests fleeing the shelling. When French intelligence reported that the government was hiding at the 'Azm residence, the French Army ordered the bombing of Sarouja.[32]

That was to prove the last battle, both for the French and for the people of Syria. On 1 June 1945, Churchill issued a famous ultimatum to the French, asking them to begin evacuating from Syria. It was the beginning of the end of the French Mandate. Twenty-six years of occupation were coming to an end, and 'Azm took part in the first Independence Day celebrations on 17 April 1946, standing side-by-side with President Quwatli. A new cabinet was formed by Prime Minister Jabiri, in which 'Azm was named minister of justice and economy.

The honeymoon with Quwatli snapped, however, when in 1947, a handful of Damascus MPs lobbied to amend Article 68 of the constitution, allowing him a second term at the presidency. Four years had passed very quickly, and the battle with France had consumed most of Quwatli's time and energy. In order to implement his roadmap for the future, he needed another round at the presidency, claimed his allies. According to the constitution, which the National Bloc had penned with prudence in 1928, a president could not seek two consecutive terms in office. Hashem al-Atasi, author of the 1928 charter, argued that a sitting president seeking re-election would spend the last months of his term year campaigning, rather than administering state affairs. By this logic, a president should therefore first leave his position and carry out his election campaign as a private citizen. Only then could he return to power, after a full four years had passed. An ambitious president, therefore, could indefinitely get re-elected, but never in one consecutive shot. Quwatli, however, was determined to serve as president for a full eight years in a row. Only kings spend eight years in office, said 'Azm.[33] He told the president exactly what he thought of the constitutional amendment, saying that it would create a precedent that future heads of state would surely repeat, thereby distorting the core values of Syrian democracy.[34] His objection was drowned by a majority vote in Parliament. Pro-Quwatli lawmakers argued that Syria was in transition and not ready for a sudden change of leadership.

'Azm returns with the Palestine War

To silence 'Azm and keep him away from the political stage in Damascus, Quwatli appointed him ambassador to France, right before the constitutional amendment was debated in parliament. 'Azm considered it a form of dignified banishment, but took up the job nevertheless. One year later, he was recalled in the midst of the Palestine War and appointed prime minister in December 1948. 'Azm called on two of his earlier ministers, Muhsen al-Barazi and Jean Sehnawi, appointing them to the portfolios of education and economy. An old notable from Deir ez-Zour, Mohammad al-Ayesh, was made minister of agriculture, while the prime minister himself took over the ministries of defence and foreign affairs. It was a non-partisan cabinet, made up entirely of independents.

Syria by then was reeling from the effects of a nationwide slump. The collective Arab defeat in Palestine had forced the officer class to drag their feet home with vengeance, blaming their defeat on President Quwatli and his associates. Martial law had been imposed, along with a 7.00 pm curfew. Police were granted permission to arrest suspects of political offences without a court warrant. The Syrian government postponed all high school and university exams for the academic year 1947–8. Ba'ath Party founder Michel Aflaq was arrested for anti-government demonstrations, and when Yusuf Faisal of the Communist Party came to his defence, he too was jailed. The country, which could barely provide for its own population, suddenly found itself flooded with anywhere between 85,000 to 90,000 Palestinian refugees. The majority of them came from northern Palestinian cities like Safad, Haifa, Acre, Tiberias and Nazareth. They were penniless, devastated and in desperate need of schools, hospitals and shelter.

We sup on him before he dines on us

'Azm came to blows with Army Commander Husni al-Za'im, a former protégé of the president who by early 1949 was planning a coup to bring down the Quwatli administration.[35] Za'im was furious with a fiery campaign launched against him by the Zabadani MP Faisal al-'Asali, a protégé of President Quwatli. He was a flamboyant parliamentarian who led the para-military Nazi-inspired Social Cooperative Party. 'Asali blamed the officers for defeat in Palestine. The officers, for their part, blamed Shukri al-Quwatli.

Za'im expected 'Azm, in his capacity as minister of defence, to stand up for the officer class and shelter them from criticism in parliament. To his utter dismay, 'Azm sat back in his seat in the front row of the chamber of deputies, listening attentively to 'Asali's tirade, without even interrupting him to defend the soldiers. Not only did he not mind 'Asali's words, he also seemed to agree with everything he said. Za'im drafted a petition asking for 'Asali's arrest, signed in al-Qunaytra by officers destined to become history-makers in future years, like Adib al-Shishakli and Sami al-Hinnawi.[36] 'The army is wrought with anxiety and anger because of what is happening and will increase in both if our demands are not met.'[37] Za'im presented the document to the president, who refused to read it: 'The official channel for such a petition is the Minister of Defense. You cannot give it directly to the Presidency.'[38] Bitter, Za'im headed back to the 'Azm residence in Souq Sarouja at midday. 'Azm was entertaining Fakhri al-Barudi over lunch, and kept Za'im waiting for thirty minutes. He eventually accepted the petition but refused to budge on any of its requests, telling Quwatli: 'This man is dangerous. We must sup on him before he dines on us.'[39] He even suggested transferring Za'im to the post of governor in any city but Damascus, in order to minimize his interaction with like-minded disgruntled officers.

Colonel Za'im ordered his troops to march on the Syrian capital shortly after midnight on 29 March 1949. Syria's borders were closed and all communication with the outside world suspended. One unit headed through the sleeping capital to the president's residence, and another was ordered to arrest Khaled al-'Azm. A third was despatched to the headquarters of Damascus Radio and a fourth to pick up other officials from the Quwatli administration. Not a single shot was fired on the night of 29 March, and no blood was spilt.

At Za'im's orders, however, the soldiers were exceptionally brutal with Khaled al-'Azm. 'Who are you and how dare you invade my home?' he shouted. The officer shoved him down the narrow staircase of his mansion and dragged him out to the street, barefoot, at gunpoint. 'We are the new government! Do not resist or we will kill you.' Surrendering to his fate, the premier groaned: 'How can I resist when you're carrying guns and I am unarmed!' He was bundled into a jeep and prevented from fetching his glasses and dentures.[40] Dressed in silk pajamas, 'Azm was hauled off to the Mezzeh dungeon. Blood was gushing from his right arm, due to the heavy thud caused by him being thrown down the staircase. The Damascus aristocrat was placed in a cell with drunks, thieves and drug addicts. One inmate, stretched on a flee-filled mattress, eyed him from top to bottom. 'You seem well off. What brings you to this rat hole?' The premier muttered: 'I am Khaled al-Azm!'

The scruffy man rolled over laughing: 'That's a good one! Khaled al-'Azm here in jail! If you are Khaled al-'Azm, then I am Shukri al-Quwatli!'[41]

From his prison cell 'Azm was forced to resign from the premiership on 7 April 1949. So was Quwatli, who had also been arrested on the night of 29 May. Za'im spent a total of 137 days in power, before he was toppled and shot by military coup on 14 August 1949. The coup mastermind, Sami al-Hinnawi, called for a meeting at army headquarters, attended by all politicians who had been sidelined by Husni al-Za'im. 'Azm was first to arrive, thrilled to see the end of Za'im. Former president Hashem al-Atasi was called out of retirement and appointed premier, and he asked Khaled al-'Azm to join him as minister of finance. He was also re-elected to the Syrian Chamber, leading a group of independents who identified themselves as the Democratic Bloc.

Detente with Shishakli

In December 1949, another coup rocked Syria, the third in less than a year, carried out by Adib al-Shishakli, who opposed Hinnawi's intention of merging Syria with Iraq. Shishakli kept Atasi at his post, but conditioned that he appoints an army officer as defence minister to make sure that the legislative branch never mentions unity with Iraq ever again. The coup leader's choice for the portfolio of defence would be his trusted friend, Fawzi Selu.

Under this détente with the officer class, 'Azm created two more governments in January 1950 and March 1951. Abiding by the dictates of Adib al-Shishakli, he made sure to appoint Fawzi Selu as minister of defence. Still bitter at how he had been treated by Husni al-Za'im, 'Azm was not ready to confront the officers once again, and end up in jail. All he wanted was for them to get off his back, so he could concentrate on economic reform, which, he believed, was the only path for progress in Syria. To relieve Syrians from relying on the port of Beirut, he began construction of a major port in the coastal city of Latakia, at a cost of 25 million SP. Syrian coffers were empty and 'Azm did not want to invite a foreign company to help build the port, hoping to keep the project a Syria-only enterprise.[42] He reached out to the private sector, promising businessmen a 5 per cent annual revenue on their investment in the Latakia Port. Eighty thousand shares would go to the Syrian government and 130,000 for private investors, at the price of 100 SP per share. A joint board from the private and public sectors was established, to be headed by 'Izzat Tarabulsi, an AUB-trained economist. 'Azm attended the port's inauguration on 12 February 1950, delivering a famous speech saying: 'Congratulations to he who owns an inch of land in Latakia.'[43]

'Azm visits France and the United States

In November 1951, the democratic government of Hashem al-Atasi was toppled by military coup, led for the second time by Adib al-Shishakli. He propped up Fawzi Selu as president, before assuming the presidency himself between July 1953 and February 1954. ʿAzm spent the Shishakli years in Lebanon, returning to Syria only after Shishakli's ouster with the restoration of civilian rule on 1 March 1954. The ageing Hashem al-Atasi was restored to the seat of power to complete what remained of his presidential term, and ʿAzm was appointed minister of foreign affairs. By then Syria had started inching towards the Eastern Bloc, taking sides in the Cold War against the United States.

On 18 April 1955, Foreign Minister ʿAzm attended the Bandung Conference in Indonesia, an event that brought Egyptian President Gamal ʿAbdul Nasser to the world's attention. An aristocrat to the bone, ʿAzm despised socialism but found himself suddenly on the same page with men like Nasser, Chinese Premier Zhou Enlai and Yugoslavia's president Josip Tito. Two months after Bandung, he was invited to the tenth anniversary of the United Nations in New York, on 22 June 1955. It was his first visit to the United States and the first by a Syrian cabinet minister since bilateral relations were established in 1944. Although opposed to American policies in the Middle East, he respected the American way of life, along with the country's capitalist system, its banking sector, infrastructure and universities. While travelling to New York, ʿAzm stopped in Paris for talks with President Rene Coty, asking for arms to defend Syria from Israeli aggression. He warned his French hosts that if French arms were not forthcoming, then he would have to look for other sources, hinting at the USSR. Coty expressed sympathy for France's former colony, adding that he wished to visit Damascus in the near future. 'I didn't invite him', noted ʿAzm in his memoirs, still bitter with what the French had done to his country.[44]

In the United States, ʿAzm was taken on a tour of the Empire State Building and lodged at the prestigious Waldorf Astoria Hotel, where he met with World Bank President John McCloy.[45] At a banquet held in honour of the international delegations, ʿAzm came face-to-face with President Dwight Eisenhower, an encounter that made him very uneasy. In his memoirs, ʿAzm wrote: 'He (Eisenhower) paced around his guests, shaking hands and conversing either at length or briefly, depending on the weight attached to any particular country. Naturally, my share was a slight bow, followed by a cordial "How do you do?"'[46] As the days passed, ʿAzm had started losing hope in reaching any compromise with the United States. His UN speech was riddled with criticism for American foreign policy. Halfway through, he was interrupted by chairman of the session, who reminded him that this gathering was aimed at finding common ground within the family of nations and not building on differences between member states. It was a polite way of asking him to stop trashing the United States. ʿAzm pointed to the Soviet Minister Vyacheslav Molotov, who had delivered a thundering anti-US speech the day before, asking why the UN tolerated such rhetoric by a powerful country like the USSR and deprived it to smaller states like Syria?[47]

ʿAzm was then invited to the University of California to attend a ceremony granting an honorary PhD to UN Secretary-General Dag Hammarskjold. He was taken on a tour of Hollywood Boulevard and Beverly Hills.[48] In his memoirs, he expressed admiration for American civilian aeroplanes, and the infrastructure of San Francisco, after learning that it had been rebuilt by its residents after a 1905 fire. He complained of US cuisine, however, 'which was not suitable for the United States as a world power', noting that when it comes to hospitality, Americans are no match for the Russians.

Hopes dashed at becoming president

In September 1955, Hashem al-Atasi's presidential term came to an end and he announced that due to his advanced age, he would not seek re-election. ʿAzm nominated himself for presidential office, running against Shukri al-Quwatli, who had just returned from exile in Egypt. Becoming president was a lifelong dream that he had harboured since 1941. Victory required a two-third majority of the 142-member parliament, which ʿAzm did not have. Despite support from the country's business community, he was nowhere as popular as Quwatli, who marketed himself as a man of the people, in contrast to ʿAzm, who was seen as a man of the educated urban elite. To widen his powerbase, ʿAzm had allied himself with Khaled Bakdash, president of the Communist Party, running a joint list for parliament, which was popularly called 'List of the two Khaleds'.[49] He had nothing in common with Bakdash, a Damascene Kurd and declared atheist, but hoped that, through him, he could win the vote of peasants and farmers from the Syrian countryside.

During the first round of voting on 18 August 1955, Quwatli got eighty-nine votes, ʿAzm got forty-two and six votes were invalidated, calling for a second round. At that point Quwatli got ninety-one votes, ʿAzm got forty-one, five were left blank and two were declared invalid. Quwatli was re-elected, much to ʿAzm's dismay, officially succeeding Hashem al-Atasi as president. ʿAzm was compensated with the powerful post of defence minister, despite the fact that he was a civilian with no military background. He was also not on good terms with the officers, former protégés of Husni al-Zaʾim whom he had crossed during the Palestine War. In fact, some were the very same men who had helped topple and arrest him during the Zaʾim coup of 1949.

The Red Millionaire

As defence minister, ʿAzm travelled to Moscow to sign a military agreement in August 1957, securing $570 million in Soviet credit for weapons, to be financed by Syrian grain production. It was to last for twelve years.[50] That same year, Syria also bought weapons from Czechoslovakia, paid for in cotton rather than cash.[51] The Soviets had already given Syria $60 million worth of military aide since 1955.[52] Young Syrian Navy officers were flown to Moscow for training on Soviet-built ships, while Russian technicians were sent to the military bases near Latakia, which became suddenly packed with MiG jets and Soviet technicians. ʿAzm warned Soviet Vice-Premiere Alexei Kosygin that economic hardships were preventing Syria from moving forward with its pro-Soviet 'progressive foreign policy'. The Soviets pledged to buy Syria's textile and agricultural surplus, and to develop hydraulic infrastructure, transportation and mechanized farming. Although a hard-core capitalist and wealthy landowner, 'Azm was nicknamed from hereafter 'The Red Millionaire'.[53] It was a name that stuck to him for many years, although it contradicted with everything he had stood for throughout his life.

The end of Syria as we knew it

On 11 January 1958, fourteen officers boarded a charter flight to Cairo, pleading for union with Gamal 'Abdul Nasser's Egypt. They made the trip without authorization from their boss, Defense Minister 'Azm, travelling in the pitch of dark with no passports. Nasser was leading a police state in Egypt, crushing any opposition to his rule. He had nationalized the old Egyptian elite, confiscating its land and presenting it to Egyptian farmers as a token of the 'socialist revolution.' Many of Cairo's old pashas were sent to jail or found themselves in financial ruin, thanks to the Free Officer Revolution. Those who complained were accused of being enemies of the people and agents of Zionism. 'Azm had first met him at Bandung back in 1955. All earlier admiration for Nasser was over by 1958. He was among the very few who lost faith in Nasser at such an early stage of the Egyptian leader's career. Others would continue to support him blindly until the Six Day War of 1967. 'Azm feared, very correctly, that if given control of Syria Nasser would impose hardline socialism on its liberal economy, nationalizing banks, factories, land and private enterprise. His prophesy would soon prove correct when in September 1958 the Egyptian president issued his famous Agricultural Reform Law, targeting Syria's landed notability. The beginning of Nasser's rule was also the end of the 'Azm family and that of Syria 'as we knew it,' 'Azm would often say.

'Azm was furious with the officers who travelled to Cairo without his permission or that of the president. He asked Quwatli to have them arrested once they set foot in Syria, describing them as 'gamblers and traitors'. Such an aggressive response, argued the president, would undoubtedly trigger a new coup, sending both him and Khaled al-'Azm- back to jail, exactly like what had happened in 1949. Instead of banishment or arrest, Quwatli went for legitimization of the officers, sending Foreign Minister Salah al-Bitar to help with their negotiations in Cairo.

At 6.40 am on 30 January, President Quwatli got on a plane with the entire Syrian government and flew off to Cairo. The director of Syrian intelligence Colonel 'Abdul Hamid Sarraj instructed the pilot to take a long route south, flying over Jordan and Saudi Arabia. Addressing the passengers, he explained: 'We need to avoid being spotted by Israeli radars, fearing that they will try downing the plane to prevent us from reaching Cairo alive.'[54] 'Azm summered: 'I wish! I wish that they do! Let them knock us down to stop us from committing such a crime against our country.'[55] Everyone on the plane pretended to have not heard him. The union was officially signed that February, and in all photos of its grand celebrations, he can be seen standing at a short distance behind Quwatli and Nasser, with a long face reeking of silent disapproval.

Six months after creation of the United Arab Republic (UAR), Nasser issued his Agricultural Reform Law in September 1958, targeting Syria's landed notability and triggering their collective demise. Khaled al-'Azm's prophesy had been fulfilled. The decree applied to the very same politicians and urban notables who had voted for union in February. Big families were on Nasser's hit list, like the Mardam Beys, the Yusufs, the 'Abeds and the 'Azms. They were now prohibited, by law, from owning more than 800 dunums of irrigated lands (80 hectares) and 800 dunums of dryland (3,000 dunums).[56] The socialist leader Akram al-Hawrani, serving as vice-president of the union republic, played a pivotal role in convincing Nasser to pass the law. He claimed that these landowning families were treating the peasants as slaves, subjugating them to long hours of hard labour, with mediocre compensation for their work. They owned far more land than what they deserved, he said, claiming that many of their plantations had been acquired either through thuggery or as gifts from the Ottoman sultan. 'Land should be owned by those who plough it', thundered Hawrani at his peasant rallies, popularizing a phrase that fit in nicely with Nasser's peasant background.[57]

Agriculture accounted for 50 per cent of Syria's GDP, and 75 per cent of the population lived off agricultural activity. A handful of big families like the 'Azms owned much of the irrigated land, estimated at 750,000 hectares in 1938.[58] By 1958 the families combined controlled no less than 1.3 million hectares.[59] According to government statistics, there were 292,000 people registered as landowners in Syria in 1958. Nasser's measures eliminated them as a social class, and all their fertile plantations were transferred to the farmers. When union collapsed three years later, serious consideration was given to revoking the Agricultural Reform Law. Lawmakers advised government officials to think twice, however, saying that this would enrage the peasants and workers, who remained staunchly pro-Nasser. After returning to the premiership in late 1962, 'Azm gave a speech from Aleppo, saying: 'We are determined to move ahead with agricultural reform and we will not meddle with the law's core objectives. I am one of those whose lands were seized during the union, and yet, I say: congratulations to my brother farmers, and blessed is your work.'[60] He then added a quick defence of the old landowning elite, reminding that they were also the ones who brought Syria its independence. 'All of them – with no exceptions – were the sons of respected families and owners of vast plantations, in addition to being capital investors in industry and real estate. To say that that they hoarded the country's riches is simply unacceptable.'[61] Before signing off he made sure to blame Nasser for every single one of Syria's problems.[62]

1961: 'Azm's last bid for president

The United Arab Republic was toppled by military coup on 28 September 1961, carried out by a thirty-five-year-old colonel named 'Abdul Karim al-Nehlawi. 'Azm attended a meeting of old school politicians, hosted at the residence of ex-Defense Minister Ahmad Sharabati, signing a declaration supporting Nehlawi's coup.[63] It described the coup as 'heroic' and criticized Nasser for having imposed a dictatorship in Syria. The army engineered nationwide parliamentary elections, followed by presidential ones that December. Running as an independent for Damascus, 'Azm won the highest number of votes throughout Syria, a total of 33,279. Coming in second was former prime minister Ma'moun al-Kuzbari with 31,835.[64] To put that in perspective, one must measure it to 'Azm's previous victory during the 1954 elections, where he had won 23,000 out of 42,000 votes.[65] Although still relatively young, at fifty-eight, 'Azm looked older than his years, suffering from major obesity that made it difficult for him to walk and remain seated for long hours of office work. He nevertheless decided to try his luck with the presidential elections – one last time – nominating himself to succeed Gamal 'Abdul Nasser.

Two other candidates were competing for the post of president: Nazem al-Qudsi of Aleppo and Ma'moun al-Kuzbari of Damascus. Qudsi was a former premier and parliament speaker and Kuzbari had led the chamber of deputies under Shishakli. The two rivals then struck a secret deal: Kuzbari would withdraw his candidacy in favour of Qudsi, who would appoint him speaker of parliament when and if he became president. 'Azm was left out of the deal, and saw it as joint effort to deprive him of the presidency, yet again. Unlike Qudsi, who headed the People's Party, he had no party behind him, and unlike Kuzbari, he was not backed by the armed forces. 'Azm felt that he was too old now, and too senior for another defeat. On 13 December 1961 he withdrew his candidacy, writing in his memoirs: 'The 1955 elections were a lesson for me, to know the manners of people and to what extent they abide by their promises. Victory was not guaranteed.'[66]

Back to jail then to the Grand Serail

Nazem al-Qudsi was elected president, only to be toppled by another military coup on 28 March 1962, led by none other than 'Abdul Karim Nehlawi, architect of the 1961 putsch against Nasser. Nehlawi accused the Qudsi government of trying to clip the wings of the very same officers who had brought it to power. Nehlawi claimed that had it not been for him and his comrades, then Qudsi would not be at the Presidential Palace. He ordered a mass arrest throughout Syria, jailing ministers, parliamentarians and party leaders. Although out of office, 'Azm was arrested and sent first to the premises of military police in al-Baramkeh, then driven in a military truck to a cavernous cell at Mezzeh Prison, a few metres from the one in which he had been incarnated by Husni al-Za'im back in 1949.[67]

The Nehlawi coup of March 1962 was short-lived. Army officers refused to abide by his orders, holding a conference in the city of Homs on 1 April. It was decided that Qudsi would be restored to office and all political prisoners would be set free. Ten days later, on 10 April, 'Azm was released from jail and Nehlawi was banished from Syria. On 17 September 1962, President Qudsi invited him to form his fifth, and soon to be last, government. 'Azm decided to go for a broad coalition of Islamists, socialists, capitalists and independent technocrats who had worked with him in previous governments. The Ba'ath Party was accommodated with the Ministry of Finance, while the Muslim Brotherhood was given the portfolios of health and supply. Army commander ʿAbdul Karim Zahr al-Din was made minister of defence, in reward for rebelling against Nehlawi's March coup. In early January 1963, the ʿAzm government lifted martial law which had been in place since the secession coup in September 1961.

Azm's health failed him as premier, however, and he was frequently checked into hospital for lengthy stays, appointing Justice Minister Asʿad Korani to deputize during his absence.[68] His legs were swollen and he could no longer climb the staircase of the Grand Serail, creating an alternative office for himself in on the ground floor of parliament to run state affairs, when his health permitted. He also suffered from family problems due to daily gatherings hosted at his home by his second wife, Layla al-Rifaii. They deprived him of comfort in his own residence, making life unbearable.[69] Layla was a common girl from Latakia, whom he had met through her brother, a policeman stationed at ʿAzm's doorsteps during his various stints as prime minister. She bore him no children (which forced him to adopt a baby girl) and greatly tarnished his reputation because of her gambling indulgences. Members of the ʿAzm family had asked him to divorce her ahead of the 1955 presidential elections, saying that she was unfit for the position of First Lady. His defence minister ʿAbdul Karim Zahr al-Din sums up ʿAzm's conditions in early 1963, saying:

> Khaled al-ʿAzm was left with nothing but his reputation. I watched him in all meetings that we attended together. He never gave a decisive opinion or took a firm decision. He would listen to us, keeping himself busy by sketching drawings and geometric shapes. I would ask myself: Is this the seasoned statesman? Is this the balanced economist? Khaled al-ʿAzm has changed and I can hardly believe that I am serving in a cabinet headed by someone who has been in the seat of power for so long, moving from one ministry to another and one premiership to the next.[70]

On 8 March 1963, a junta of Nasserist and Baʿathist officers staged a new coup in Damascus, pledging to restore the United Arab Republic, with Nasser as its president. ʿAzm was accused of 'usurping power' and forced into hiding at the Turkish Embassy in Damascus, located at the ground floor of his building in al-Rawda, making the asylum easy and swift.[71] Hoodlums rooted at his window, pelting it with stones and calling for his execution. One woman, a Nasserist schoolteacher named Thuraya al-Hafez, carried a thick rope, saying that she wanted to drag ʿAzm to death through the streets of Damascus, just like Iraqi rebels had done to their prime minister Nuri al-Saʿid in July 1958.[72] He was accused of legitimizing the 'secession regime', which the Baʿathists said was a criminal offence, publishable by death. An enemy of Nasser and Arab unity does not deserve to live, they said. ʿAzm's already failing health deteriorated further during his confinement at the Turkish embassy, and he asked for his doctor Madani al-Khiyami. As Khiyami walked through the corridor of soldiers guarding the premises, one grabbed his arm and whispered: 'Why don't you just give him an injection and kill him?'[73]

The final exile

The Revolutionary Command of the Ba'ath Party decided to keep 'Azm alive, however, eventually banishing him to Beirut, with orders never to return to Syria. All his remaining property was seized, including the great 'Azm family mansion in Souq Sarouja, where forty-seven years ago, Enver Pasha had prophetically said to him, 'Don't be in a hurry to get in politics'. The 'Azm residence was given to the Ministry of Culture, and now houses the Friends of Damascus Society and the Museum for Historical Documents. Parts of the mansion were destroyed by a terrible fire as this book was in its final stages, on 16 July 2023. His private office facing Sibki Garden was taken over by the Syrian presidency and was to become premises for future vice-presidents 'Abdul Halim Khaddam and Farouk al-Shara. His summer home in al-Ghouta was transformed into state-run medicine factory called Tameco. Khaled al-'Azm was unable to reclaim his property and never returned to Syria. He died at his Beirut exile at the relatively young age of sixty-two, on 18 February 1965. His three-volume memoirs, penned during his Lebanon exile, became a cornerstone for modern Syrian history. Officially, they remain banned in Syria as of 2023. There is not a single street, school or monument carrying Khaled al-'Azm's name in Syria.

Figure 9 Khaled al-'Azm (right) with ex-prime minister Husni al-Barazi (left) and Khaled al-'Asali, director of protocol at the Nazem Pasha Palace in the 1950s.

Chapter 10

TAJ AL-DIN AL-HASANI (1941–3)

In May 1942, British ambassador Sir Edward Spears walked the red carpet of the Syrian Presidential Palace to present his credentials to President Taj al-Din al-Hasani. He scribbled a note in his diary, describing the Syrian leader as 'an extraordinary little man, the shape of a child's toy balloon, stuffed into grey pinstripe trousers cut on the model of a lavatory basin, or a neckless violin'.[1] Few politicians in modern Arab history have been the subject of so much ridicule and strikingly un-diplomatic language. Beneath what seemed like a very burlesqued appearance to foreigners, however, stood a shrewd statesman who had dominated the Syrian political landscape from the mid-1920s until his untimely death at the age of fifty-two in January 1943. History books have been cruel to the man, often describing him as a pawn in the hands of French intelligence. Sheikh Taj's systematic character slaughter has stood the test of time and remains dominant in almost everything written or said about him as of 2023.

For two solid decades Sheikh Taj was the fulcrum of Syrian politics. He held the premiership twice, in 1928 and 1934, creating four cabinets before going on to become Syria's first appointed president in 1941. It was during his tenure that Syria got its independence from the mandate, although French troops did not evacuate until 1946, three years after his death. During an illustrious career that began in 1919, Sheikh Taj successfully managed to take down all of his many opponents, one after another, explaining why many hated him and strove to ruin his reputation. In the age of nascent Syrian democracy, he ruled with no parliament or constitution, which made it easy to disparage him as a French agent. While some of the stories attributed to Sheikh Taj were undoubtedly true, others were entirely false and fabricated. No serious attempt has been made at revisiting Sheikh Taj's life and career within the broader scope of Syrian politics during the inter-war period. His name has been systematically dropped from all Syrian schoolbooks. When he is mentioned, it's almost always in negative connotation, sometimes in no more than a passing footnote. It is time to challenge that image, and to give Sheikh Taj his due place in Middle East history.

Sheikh Badr al-Din, the scholar of Damascus

No study of Sheikh Taj would be complete without understanding the family into which he was born and from which he derived his political legitimacy. His father, Sheikh Badr al-Din al-Hasani, was a renowned Islamic scholar with disciples throughout the Arab world. In Damascus, his students often referred to him as *Al-Muhaddith al-Akbar,* which roughly translates as 'The Greatest Speaker', a title bestowed upon the most learned scholars of Islam. Born to a Moroccan family in 1850, Badr al-Din had received an Islamic education at al-Azhar in Cairo, returning to teach Islamic jurisprudence at the Umayyad Mosque of Damascus. Members of the Hasani family were a*shraf* like King Faisal, tracing their lineage to the Prophet Mohammad.[2] Sheikh Badr al-Din's reputation spread far and wide, and in 1913 he was invited to attend the 300th anniversary of Romanov rule in Russia, as a representative of Islam and the Muslim World. He declined the invitation, however, possibly, because it was held at the Greek Orthodox Church of St Petersburg.[3] One of his students, Sheikh 'Ali al-Tantawi, later senior Sharia judge in Damascus, affectionately described him saying: 'He was the secret of Damascus' strength.'[4]

Sheikh Taj was the second male child among eight children, born in 1890. His elder brother 'Issam had followed in their father's footsteps, pursuing a religious career. Their mother came from the Kuzbari family of Damascus, whose members had assumed the title of mufti during the second half of the nineteenth century.[5] Such lineage was crucial for members of the Syrian middle class, especially for someone like Sheikh Taj, who invested heavily in family relations to broaden his powerbase in Old Damascus. In addition to the Kuzbaris, he was related by marriage to the Madani family that hailed from Medina, the city to which the prophet had emigrated and from which he had cemented his authority across the deserts of Arabia. Sheikh Taj had married twelve-year-old Masara al-Madani, who gave birth to their first child at the age of fourteen. She was a student of his father and was soon to become his friend, confidant and sounding board. She lived for many years after her husband, until her passing in Beirut in 1977.[6] Marriage at such a tender age might seem outrageous to Western readers in 2023 but it was very common 100 years ago throughout the Muslim world.

Sheikh Taj's brother 'Issam died young during the First World War, leaving him as the only male heir to Bader al-Din al-Hasani, who died at the ripe age of eighty-seven in June 1935.[7] Syrian historians argue whether Badr al-Din approved of his son's political career, with many saying that he had disavowed him for being pro-French. That has never been confirmed, however, since Badr al-Din never criticized his son in public. He did skip his son's inauguration as premier in February 1928, and never visited him at the Grand Serail, which might explain why people thought that the two men did not get along. There is no sermon, essay or reliable quote from Sheikh Bader al-Din about his son; what we know for sure is that Sheikh Taj was extremely proud of his father and had commissioned Sheikh Mahmud al-'Attar to write a biography of him, at the urging of Egyptian historian

Ahmad Taymour Pasha.[8] It was only completed in 1944, however, one year after Sheikh Taj's death.[9]

Sheikh Taj was tutored by his father at the Umayyad Mosque and started his career at state-run schools, teaching Islamic Sharia and history. He was then appointed member of a special committee charged with reforming schools in Ottoman Damascus.[10] Unlike young men of his generation, Sheikh Taj stood at arms' length from politics, refusing to join any of the secret societies that mushroomed throughout Syria in the years prior to the First World War, all working secretly against the Ottoman Empire. He also refused to support the Great Arab Revolt of Sharif Hussein. Sheikh Taj's unwavering support for the Ottomans put him on good terms with Djemal Pasha, who chose him to edit an Arabic newspaper in Damascus, created to disseminate Ottoman propaganda during the Great War.

Al-Sharq newspaper

Sheikh Taj was a complete newcomer to the world of journalism. A large photo of Djemal Pasha was placed at the offices of *al-Sharq* (The East), next to a poetic verse comparing the Ottoman general to God, penned by the poet Khayr al-Din al-Zirikli: 'Bow your heads and look down, here is the reliever of anguish.'[11] Damascus had known only a handful of newspapers in its recent history, like the government gazette called *Souriyya*, and *Dimashq*, a private paper established by Ahmad 'Izzat al-'Abed. Third was *al-Qabas*, edited by the Damascus MP in the Ottoman Parliament, Shukri al-'Asali, who was executed by Djemal Pasha in 1916. All three were printed in Arabic and Ottoman Turkish. The 26-year-old Sheikh Taj appointed Emir Shakib Arslan, a respected Druze essayist and philosopher, twenty years his senior, as deputy editor of *al-Sharq*.[12] The first issue was published on 27 April 1916, nine days before Djemal Pasha ordered the execution of twenty-one Arab nationalists in Beirut and Damascus, accused of treason and conspiracy against the Ottoman Empire. The list included former parliamentarians like Shukri al-'Asali and his friends. Sheikh Badr al-Din called on Djemal Pasha, seeking a special pardon for the Syrian nationalists, but the stern Ottoman officer turned down his request, saying that it was unwise for a respected prelate of his standing to seek clemency for 'traitors'. Sheikh Taj did not object, however, and published news of the execution on the front page of *al-Sharq*, abiding by the official government line that those executed in Marjeh Square were 'traitors to the Sultan'.

The executions struck a particularly raw nerve in Ottoman Syria, prompting Shakib Arslan to resign from *al-Sharq*. Sheikh Taj swiftly had him replaced him with Mohammad Kurd 'Ali, a scholar and historian who was to serve as his education minister in the 1920s. Kurd 'Ali was already in his forties, having edited the Ottoman gazette in Damascus before moving to Egypt in 1906, where he founded the immensely popular monthly *al-Muqtabas*. Throughout the war, Kurd 'Ali and Sheikh Taj continued to print *al-Sharq*, adding photos to its front page to make it more attractive to readers. They didn't rely on advertisements, given that the paper's budget came straight from the Ottoman treasury in Istanbul. Towards the end of the war, that money became irregular and was often slashed due to budget constraints, and yet *al-Sharq* continued to print, against all odds, until the Ottomans left Damascus in September 1918. Throughout its existence, never did news of Sheikh Taj appear on the front pages of *al-Sharq*, despite his numerous sermons and speaking engagements. He preferred to remain in the shadows, a habit that was to change in future years, when his activities as premier became front page news in all Damascus dailies, at his request. Once Ottoman troops had fully evacuated Damascus, the offices of *al-Sharq* were seized by Emir Sa'id El Djezairi, who had it re-named *Al-Istiqlal al-Arabi*.[13]

Working with Faisal

On his first day in Damascus, Emir Faisal called on Sheikh Badr al-Din at his home, seeking his blessing to legitimize Hashemite rule in Syria. The elderly Sheikh delivered an oath of allegiance to Faisal, the famed *ba'ya* of Islam, placing himself and his family at the disposal of the Hashemites. Sheikh Taj stood by his father, seconding his allegiance to Faisal. They had first met during Sheikh Bader al-Din's pre-war pilgrimage to Mecca, where he had conferred with Faisal's father, Sharif Hussein. At his father's residence, Sheikh Taj delivered a lengthy speech before Faisal, addressing the needs of Islamic schools in Damascus. He had prepared his presentation with facts and figures, which Faisal found impressive.

In fact, so impressed was Faisal that one week later, he issued a *firman* appointing Sheikh Taj as director of the new royal palace.[14] Faisal also made him member of the Shura Council and the Court of Appeals. Many Syrians objected, claiming that Sheikh Taj was too young for the influential jobs that had just been bestowed upon him, arguing he had no credentials to his name, apart from being the son of Bader al-Din al-Hasani. For Emir Faisal, that was more than enough.

A seat in parliament

In 1919, Sheikh Taj made his political debut, running for a seat on the Syrian National Congress. Within parliament, Sheikh Taj joined a coalition of like-minded scholars that included Sheikh ʿAbdul Qader al-Khatib of the Umayyad Mosque, a relative of his father, and Sheikh Rashid Rida. Their first joint action was blocking an attempt to drop religious phraseology from parliament's official address to Faisal. Sheikh Taj opposed omitting what Muslims referred to as *al-basmala*, a Quranic phrase that reads: *Bismillah al-Rahman al-Raheem* (In the name of God, the Gracious and Merciful).[15] Seculars had suggested doing away with the phrase, arguing for a total separation between religion and politics. Sheikh Taj also spoke out against unveiling of women in Syrian society, describing it as un-Islamic.[16] When Sheikh Taj adopted a more secular approach to politics in future years, his critics would remind him of his early parliamentary speeches under Faisal, asking how a turbaned cleric like himself could change colours so swiftly and dramatically.

Apart from his limited interventions in the Syrian National Congress, which dealt mainly with social and Islamic issues, Sheikh Taj kept a low profile during the waning months of Faisal's rule, focusing on his work at the Shura Council while teaching Islamic jurisprudence at the Arab Faculty of Law. He was allowed to leave the royal palace unharmed after Faisal's exodus in July 1920, spending the next six months at his home in al-Qanawat within the Old City, before heading to Paris. He described it as a short mission to familiarizing himself with those in-charge of France's Middle East colonies.

Sheikh Taj and the French

Sheikh Taj's 'brief' mission in France would last for six long years. His main contact was ʿAbdul Qader Ben Ghabrit, an Algerian intellectual who headed the French Muslim community and worked as a translator at the French Foreign Ministry.[17] At the opening of the Grand Mosque of Paris in 1926, Ben Ghabrit introduced him to Philibert Collet, the head of French intelligence in Syria. The two men bonded well and a close friendship developed between them, which led to Collet adopting Sheikh Taj politically. He nominated him for the premiership in December 1925, in light of Subhi Barakat's resignation.[18] The French had just bombed the Syrian capital and needed a figure who could appease the angry street. Sheikh Badr al-Din was heading a relief committee to compensate the families of those killed during the French onslaught. Emir Saʾid El Djezairi had hurried to Beirut, pleading for a ceasefire with the French High Commissioner Maurice Sarrail.[19] With emotions souring, Sheikh Taj couldn't possibly accept the post of prime minister, seeing it as akin to political suicide. But he couldn't reject the offer without a proper excuse. Sheikh Taj outlined a series of conditions that were impossible to meet, like restoring the four *cazas* of Baalbak, Rashayya, Hasbayya and the Beqqa Valley, which had been annexed to Greater Lebanon since 1920, while demanding that a plebiscite is held in Tripoli, Sidon and Tyre, to see if residents wanted to unite with mother Syria. And finally, he asked for a general amnesty, a treaty to regulate Syria's future relations with France, and admittance to the League of Nations.[20] The French refused to meet any of his conditions, not before the rebels of al-Ghouta and the Druze Mountain lay down their arms and surrender.

Sheikh Taj clashed with the National Bloc when it was first established in October 1927, claiming that Hashem al-Atasi had purposely omitted him from its founding conference. In future years he would insist that the National Bloc was his idea, saying that it had been 'stolen' by Atasi and his colleagues. He would eventually set aside his differences with Atasi when forming his first government in 1928, hoping to create a cabinet of national unity, now that the Great Revolt was over. One of his father's students, Sheikh ʿAref Sawwaf al-Douaji, presented him with a list of mosque imams and religious scholars, expecting that the son of Badr al-Din would naturally rely on clerics to serve in his cabinet. Sheikh Taj read through the list and promised Douaji that he would carefully study all the names. No sooner had Douaji turned his back than he threw away the paper, forming a cabinet entirely from secular Muslims and Christians.[21] The first Sheikh Taj cabinet was announced on 10 February 1928, with six ministers. Four of them, like him, were natives of Damascus.[22] Two were members of the National Bloc: 'Abdul Qader al-Kaylani of Hama, who became minister of agriculture, and Tawfiq Shamiyya, a Christian, who was made minister of public works. Taj even tried convincing the Bloc's dean Fares al-Khoury, (another Christian) to join the government, but his efforts were unsuccessful.[23] His favourable view of Christianity was also reflected through the marriage of his son, Shams al-Din, to a Christian lady from the Touma family of Damascus.

In his carefully worded cabinet formation statement, the new premier promised to 'work with the France, within the framework of the mandate, to achieve Syrian national aspirations'.[24] Sheikh Taj was fully aware of his weaknesses, realizing that he had been brought to power by the mandate regime, with no constitutional legitimacy or parliament, just like his predecessor Ahmad Nami. These were two faults that continued to haunt him during all the offices that he assumed in his life. With the exception of the Constitutional Assembly of 1928, he had never been elected to a post, only appointed by the French. The National Bloc had agreed to join his government as representatives of the opposition, and there was no telling when they would withdraw their support. To ensure a bare minimum of political legitimacy, he conditioned that an amnesty is issued prior to his swearing-in ceremony, pardoning all those accused of having worked for the Great Revolt. He also demanded that press censorship be lifted, along with martial law that had been in-place since 1925.[25] The French agreed to the pardon but left out seventy names described as 'dangerous' like the two revolt leaders Sultan al-Atrash and 'Abdul Rahman Shahbandar.[26] Nationalist newspapers criticized the premier for accepting the omissions, describing his amnesty as 'crippled'.

A sour relationship with the Damascus press

During his first years in government, Sheikh Taj had a troubled relationship with Syrian journalists. Many had begun their careers as freelancers for *al-Sharq*, and they accused the premier of trying to bribe them into praising his government. Ragheb al-'Uthmani, publisher of al-*Istiqlal*, ran a story saying that Sheikh Taj's agriculture minister had used modern machinery to cultivate his farms, while other ministers were using chauffeur-driven automobiles to run errands for their families, at the state's expense. Sheikh Taj ordered his police chief, Bahij al-Khatib, to close *al-Istiqlal* and issued a warrant for 'Uthmani's arrest. The publisher, a turbaned cleric like Sheikh Taj, fled to Lebanon but was tried in *absentia* and sentenced to six months in jail.[27] Another article said that during a nationwide tour, Sheikh Taj had distributed state funds to the masses so they could greet him in large numbers at the gates of every city. On his return to Damascus, he was received with so much pomp and splendour that one foreign diplomat drew parallels with the lavish ceremony that had been organized to welcome Kaiser Wilhelm II to Damascus back in 1898.[28] Sheikh Taj was also accused of purging the civil service (8,000 employees in 1928) from all opponents and critics.[29] In September 1930, he passed a law making it illegal for any government official to join a political party, thus eroding the National Bloc's membership base, whose adherents were scattered across the Syrian bureaucracy.[30]

Sheikh Taj and the 1928 constitution

Shortly after coming to power, Sheikh Taj was tasked with supervising elections for Syria's Constitutional Assembly. The country had no constitution, with the last one having been penned under Faisal but abolished by the invading French Army in 1920. He ran for a seat for his native Damascus, offering cooperation with his rivals in the National Bloc. Sheikh Taj needed a nationalist blanket that only Hashem al-Atasi could provide, while the Bloc leadership reasoned that it was wiser to have the prime minister on their side, despite their political differences, given that he controlled the Ministry of Interior, which was supervising the elections. Atasi hoped that by creating a joint list with Sheikh Taj, he might even drive a wedge between him and the French, thus depriving the mandate of one of its most capable allies. A joint list was assembled, with four candidates from the National Bloc and six named by the prime minister. Sheikh Taj placed himself atop both lists, earning the title *Taj al-Qawa'im* (Crown of the Lists).

This alliance snapped on Election Day, however, after Sheikh Taj's Interior Minister Sa'id Mahasin was caught red-handed using the police to intimidate voters.[31] Fawzi al-Ghazzi led a big demonstration on 12 April 1928, accusing Sheikh Taj of deception and duplicity.[32] He also said that Sheikh Taj had sent government cars to al-Ghouta, with the aim of buying votes from its villages.[33] Bloc supporters then clashed with Sheikh Taj's men at the gates of government headquarters in Marjeh Square, leading to the death of five young men. Out of the nine MPs elected in the Syrian capital, seven were members of the Bloc. In total, they won seventeen out of seventy seats in the Constitutional Assembly, a little less than one-third, and Atasi was elected to draft the new constitution. Addressing the chamber, Sheikh Taj said: 'I would like to stress that there is no such thing as a constitution by force. The constitution will be free and reflective of the national will of the Syrian people.'[34]

Within two weeks, the new constitution was ready, inspired by principles of the French Revolution. Sheikh Taj played a significant role in penning the new charter, yet all credit went to the National Bloc. The French demanded the modification of six articles and adding a seventh that explicitly mentioned the mandate, which the Bloc had purposely left out. Hashem al-Atasi said no but Sheikh Taj nodded approvingly. He defended his position saying that the end objective must be a charter for Syria, regardless of how restricted it may seem. 'Take what you can now and ask for more later', he said to the Bloc MPs, quoting Otto Von Bismarck: 'Politics is the art of the possible.'³⁵ Quoting Bismarck was no accident; Sheikh Taj was appealing to young university students and the educated urban elite of Damascus. He wanted to be seen as worldly intellectual, with more substance than that of a mainstream turbaned cleric. The nationalists stood by their position, saying that a charter without the six articles was equal to no constitution at all.³⁶ Fakhri al-Barudi took to the podium, accusing Sheikh Taj of treason. Fuming, the prime minister walked out of the Assembly.³⁷

The next morning, a caricature appeared in the magazine *Al-Mudhiq al-Mubki*, owned by National Bloc member Habib Kahaleh. Raising eyebrows at the Grand Serail, it showed a caricature of Barudi asking Sheikh Taj: 'Isn't it time for you to fall?' To that, the premier replies: 'Never! Not one hair will fall from my head without permission of the High Commissioner.'³⁸ It had become customary for *Al-Mudhiq al-Mubki* to draw caricatures of Sheikh Taj on its covers, always as a fat and gullible French puppet. It once showed him singing the French National Anthem, which led to its closure for six months. The premier ordered Habib Kahaleh arrested, while Fakhri al-Barudi was attacked on the street and beaten by masked thugs, believed to be acting at Bahij al-Khatib's orders.³⁹ When the Damascus daily *al-Qabas* blamed him for the assault on Barudi, it was closed down for five months.⁴⁰ Sheikh Taj's disdain for the press was reflected by his clear distance from any journalist, even those who showed him absolute loyalty. He never gave an interview to any newspaper or magazine, neither during his two terms as premier nor after becoming president in 1941.

On 11 August 1928, the Syrian Chamber of Deputies ratified the constitution, overruling Sheikh Taj's objections. Ponsot retaliated by adjourning the chamber for three months, and on 5 February 1929, issued a decree dissolving the Constitutional Assembly.⁴¹ Rather than object, Sheikh Taj travelled to France to attend the funeral of First World War hero Ferdinand Foch, who died that March and was buried at the Les Invalides, next to Napoleon. It was a big event in Paris, and the Syrian premier knew that he would meet all kinds of senior French officials, able to advance his career in Damascus.

Great builder

The Syrian treasury in 1928 boasted of 6.5 million gold coins. By the time Sheikh Taj left office three years later, only 1.5 million remained in its coffers.⁴² Much of it was spent on construction projects across Syria, with the premier insisting to go down in history as a great builder. Three modern hospitals were opened under Sheikh Taj, one in Aleppo, one in Deir ez-Zour and one in al-Qusayr, south of Homs, reserved exclusively for the mentally ill.⁴³ He financed paving of the Damascus-Aleppo Highway, in addition to the construction of government headquarters in Aleppo, Idlib, Afrin, al-Bab, Manbij, Jarablus (all in the Syrian north), and Douma and Qatana in the Damascus countryside.⁴⁴ Those monuments remained standing until they were set ablaze by the Syrian civil war after the year 2011. He also ordered the building of Syria's current parliament on 'Abed Street in central Damascus, on the remains of old theatre.

Every single one of these edifices was inaugurated with festive ceremony, attended by Sheikh Taj and his entire cabinet. Photographers took pictures of the premier smiling next to large marble plaques carrying his name. They were then run on the front page of Syrian dailies, under bold headlines that referred to the premier as *Ra'is al-Mi'mar* (The Builder President). Sheikh Taj asked his Education Minister Mohammad Kurd ʿAli to author a book about his achievements, which he did, very unwillingly. The two men had originally worked together at *al-Sharq* during the First World War. Kurd ʿAli chose not to write his name on the book, and yet, Sheikh Taj offered him 1,000 pounds in reward (a handsome amount by standards of the 1930s), which Kurd ʿAli claimed to have turned down.[45] The book was published by the Government Press, using state funds. When he travelled to Aleppo in 1930, Sheikh Taj distributed 10,000 SP to make sure that flag-waving supporters awaited him at every street corner, calling for his long life and good health.[46] He then published a small book about his trip to the Syrian north, called *Al-Rihla al-Tajiyya ila Souriyya al-Shamaliyya* (The Tajian Journey to Northern Syria). It was printed in limited circulation and is currently one of the rarest books on twentieth-century Syria.

The Sheikh's cultural legacy

Despite his traditional upbringing, Sheikh Taj often tried coming across as a cultured and Westernized statesman, very different from his image as a young parliamentarian under King Faisal. He asked his ministers to purchase tuxedos and frac coats, saying that this is how European statesmen dressed at state functions, arguing that it would make them look dignified and sophisticated. 'It will make you look like Frenchmen', he would say. Kurd ʿAli objected: 'Fracs are worn by porters only!'[47] Sheikh Taj ignored him, insisting on wearing a black frac with his white turban, prompting Kurd ʿAli to remark in his memoirs: 'It just didn't fit him. He was short and fat, with a limp and turban.'[48]

Sheikh Taj would also invest greatly in the arts, inspired by the theatres and cinemas that he had visited in Paris.[49] When an amateur theatrical group from Damascus went bankrupt in 1929, he ordered that its actors and musicians are compensated from state funds. He then helped them set up a new acting troupe, not wanting history to say that art had suffered under Sheikh Taj.[50] He also supported Syria's first production house ahead of the screening of the country's first silent film, *Al-Mutaham al-Bare'e* (The Accused Innocent) in 1928. It was scheduled to premiere at the Cosmograph Cinema, amidst uproar from religious zealots who objected that a Syrian actress was billing in the lead role, unveiled. Sheikh Taj argued that cinemas were good for Syria, defending the young actress and saying that she was mature enough and had obtained permission of her parents. Still, they refused and demanded banning the film.[51] French censors stood by the clerics, however, not with Sheikh Taj. Fearing that the film controversy would reach Friday sermons and cause a headache for mandate authorities, the French banned it on a wobbly pretext, saying that its musical scores were copyrighted (although there was no copyright law in Syria). The movie was only shown after all the scenes of the Syrian woman were cut and re-shot with a German dancer from the Olympiad Cabaret in Damascus.[52] To show his support, Sheikh Taj attended the premier at the Cosmograph Cinema. He was obviously upset with the clerical establishment, claiming that the actions of its top ulema were making him look backward and weak in front of the French. That same year, he gave permission to the owners of Cinema Nasr in Marjeh Square to host a women's matinee, which, again, put him at daggers end with the religious establishments. They tried talking the prime minister into withdrawing his support, and when he failed to listen, they torched the cinema on 20 December 1928, killing ten of its workers.

Sheikh Taj and the veil

Unveiling in high society was starting to become popular throughout the Levant, influenced by anti-hijab legislation in Turkey that had been ordered by Kemal Ataturk, and by Iran's Westernized monarch, Reza Shah Pahlavi, who was starting to ban the chador in Tehran. In 1928, a young Druze woman named Nazira Zayn al-Din published a book in Beirut called *Al-Sufoor wa al-Hijab* (Unveiling and Veiling). Inspired by Ataturk and by Egyptian writer Qassem Amin, who had also lobbied against the hijab during the late nineteenth century, Zayn al-Din argued that she had read the Quran and given herself the authority of interpreting it, saying that none of its phrases explicitly called on women to cover their heads and faces. She described the practice as 'un-Islamic' and called for mixing of the sexes at school, and for the education of women, comparing 'veiled Arab societies' to unveiled Western ones.[53]

The book caused a storm in the Muslim world. Fakhri al-Barudi wrote a treatise on the hijab, backing Zayn al-Din's argument. Damascus clerics called on the prime minister, saying that the book should never be allowed in Syria. Far from banning it, Sheikh Taj approved its sale and circulation, writing a congratulatory letter to its author, praising her indefatigable dedication to the emancipation of women. He then sent a copy of the book to his education minister, Mohammad Kurd 'Ali, asking that he writes a review in the period journal of the Arab Language Assembly. Kurd 'Ali was founding president of the Assembly, considered since its establishment in 1919 as the highest international institution for the protection of the Arabic language. Its magazine was widely read by students and young academics. Kurd 'Ali wrote a favourable review, transforming the book into a bestseller in Syria.[54] A second edition was soon published by Zayn al-Din, with Sheikh Taj's blessing. When prelates asked how the son of Badr al-Din al-Hasani could sign off such a heretical book, he replied: 'The Muslim World has its own share of problems. You ought to be busy with your mosques, your sermons and authoring your own books.'[55]

Sheikh Taj then went a step further, allowing Syrian women to host a conference at the 'Azm Palace in 1930. They showed up unveiled, taking turns at calling for the emancipation of women. Delegations came from Iraq, Lebanon, Iran and Afghanistan, and were hosted by Safwat Mardam Bey, wife of Jamil Mardam Bey, and Asma Eid, wife of Fares al-Khoury. Sheikh Taj's wife did not attend, nor was she invited to the Grand Serail when he hosted a reception for the attending delegates. He posed for a souvenir photo with the ladies, further infuriating his critics. To get away with licensing the conference, meeting the women and allowing Nazira Zayn al-Din's book to sell in Syria, he decided to appease the clerics on other matters. Coinciding with the women's congress was a visit by Egyptian musician Mohammad ʿAbdul Wahab to Damascus, where he was billed to perform before two women matinees at the Abbasid Opera, near the Hejaz Station (now premises for the Semiramis Hotel). ʿAbdul Wahab was one of the giants of contemporary Arab music, with fans on all four corners of the Arab World. His first show went by with no disturbances, where he performed before a packed audience of 1,500 Syrian women. The second was banned by Sheikh Taj's government, ostensibly because the women in the audience had danced to ʿAbdul Wahab's music.[56] The Egyptian crooner gave an interview to an Egyptian magazine after leaving Damascus, angrily saying: 'If animals dance and sway their heads to music, then it is only natural for human beings to feel the same. Is my music more of a threat than the inflammatory speeches on women's rights, delivered at the women's congress in Damascus?'[57] Sheikh Taj was fine with the dancing. It didn't trouble him, yet he needed a pretext to call off the show, regardless of how flimsy it seemed, in order to please the clerics.

Sheikh Taj's first downfall

By the winter of 1931, Sheikh Taj had been in power for nearly four years, longer than any of his predecessors. Twice he had reshuffled his cabinet, in August and October 1930. As time passed, the list of his opponents became longer and longer, starting with the National Bloc, onto the clerics and a long list of politicians who were eager to replace him at the premiership. He had signed off a series of unpopular decrees that hastened his downfall, like raising taxes at a very untimely moment, as the Syrian currency was devaluating due to its peg to the French Franc.[58] This was in the midst of the Great Depression, which had hit the French economy hard, and by extension, its satellite colony in Syria. On 19 November 1931, Sheikh Taj resigned from office, at the request of the High Commission Henri Ponsot. He immediately headed to France to talk colonial administrators into supporting his next benchmark: Syria's upcoming parliamentary elections, scheduled in two stages for December 1931–January 1932.

Running for president in 1932

On Election Day, the police were anything but impartial, taking their cue from Police Chief Bahij al-Khatib and Damascus governor Wathiq Mou'ayyad al-ʿAzm, two Sheikh Taj protégés who intimidated people into voting for their former boss.

Sheikh Taj was no longer prime minister now but running as a private citizen, yet the civil service was still packed with his appointees, who all wanted to see him return to power. They were accused of rigging the elections in the neighbourhood of al-Qaymariya, within the Old City.[59] When the Bloc tried objecting, the governor of Damascus refused to register their complaint.[60] Bloc chief Zaki al-Khatib then attempted to break into the polling stations to monitor its ballots, but was denied entry by the police.[61]

Another anti-Sheikh Taj demonstration was staged at the gates of the Grand Serail, headed by Shukri al-Quwatli of the National Bloc, who was to succeed Sheikh Taj at the presidency in 1943. Senegalese troops from the French Army of the Levant were rushed to the scene, using water pumps and live ammunition to disperse the demonstrators. Five people were killed and fifty were injured.[62] Government meddling in the elections led to a stunning defeat for the National Bloc list in Aleppo. What horrified them more than the defeat was the notion of a possible victory for either Sheikh Taj or Subhi Barakat. The seventeen Bloc MPs decided to vote for Mohammad 'Ali al-'Abed, at Hashem al-Atasi's orders. Sheikh Taj stormed out of the chamber, skipping 'Abed's inauguration on 11 June 1932.

Comeback 1934–6

President 'Abed's first choice for premier was Haqqi al-'Azm, followed by Sheikh Taj in March 1934. He was nominated for the job by Henri De Martel, a former French ambassador to Japan who had replaced Henri Ponsot as French high commissioner in October 1933. When Sheikh Taj's new government was announced, all the markets of Damascus shut down at the orders of the National Bloc.[63] It was a five-man cabinet, in which he assumed the premiership and the Ministry of Interior. The premier's long-time friend and neighbour Jamil al-Ulshi was made minister of public works, which was the most important portfolio for Sheikh Taj due to his obsession with building roads, schools and hospitals. Once again, Sheikh Taj came to blows with the National Bloc, this time after they led a city-wide campaign targeting the French-owned tobacco manufacturing company: Regie de Tabac and the Belgian-registered Damascus Tram and Electricity Company. They accused both establishments of stealing the riches of Syria, demanding that Sheikh Taj do the impossible: nationalize the two companies and take action against European interests in Syria. They knew that he was both incapable and unwilling of taking such a confrontationist move. When he travelled to Aleppo to inaugurate a statue of the eighteenth-century Bishop Jermanos Farhat, the prime minister was welcomed with a massive demonstration, organized by the National Bloc, calling for his downfall.[64] Young people threw rotten tomatoes at Sheikh Taj and occupied his seats at the Umayyad Mosque of Aleppo, forcing him and President 'Abed to be evacuated by the police.[65]

Then came the death of Ibrahim Hananu in November 1935, eighteen months after Sheikh Taj's political comeback. The Bloc used his death to drum up both anti-French and anti-Sheikh Taj sentiment on the Syrian street, mobilizing 150,000 people to march at his funeral, chanting loud insults against the prime minister. Hundreds were arrested by Senegalese forces, and Hananu's home was raided at French orders. The Bloc leadership blamed Sheikh Taj for the crackdown. Those clashes accumulated with the General Strike of 1936. Henri de Martel appointed General Charles Huntiznger, commander of the Levant Army, as military governor of Syria.[66] He had Sheikh Taj dismissed and replaced with 'Ata al-Ayyubi as premier, who led marathon talks with the French in Beirut, aimed at ending the strike. Sheikh Taj took a backseat, disappearing for the next five years. He watched his enemies in the National Bloc sign the 1936 Treaty with France, which led to the election of Hashem al-Atasi as president.

No news could have been more painful for Sheikh Taj. He harshly criticized the 1936 Treaty, saying that it gave France too much and took little in return.[67] Throughout the years of the Atasi presidency (1936–9) Sheikh Taj decided to settle permanently in Paris. From that distance, he smiled as the National Bloc era began to fall apart, due to opposition from 'Abdul Rahman Shahbandar, who, like him, thought lightly of the 1936 Treaty. Then came the step-by-step annexation of the Sanjak of Alexandretta, which was finalized in 1939, sealing the fate of the National Bloc.

Preparing for the presidency

Sheikh Taj was still in Europe when the Second World War began in September 1939 and he only returned to Syria in June 1940, days before the Nazi occupation of Paris. He had developed a deep affection for the city of Paris and could not tolerate seeing it fall under the boots of the Nazis. He had greatly matured as a statesman, abandoning much of his earlier stiffness and grudges, but not his landmark turban. He also completely outgrew his father's patronage, and to a certain extent, even that of colonial France. By then Sheikh Taj had carefully re-branded himself, now standing as an independent Damascene statesman, rather than a Francophile. Many Syrians longed for the stability and economic prosperity of the Sheikh Taj years and were earning for his comeback. Although close to the French, he hadn't suffered any of the humiliating setbacks of the National Bloc, and his name was not associated with the failed 1936 Treaty or with the annexation of the Sanjak.

By the time of his return to Syria, all of his traditional opponents had been disarmed, exiled or were long dead. Subhi Barakat and Ahmad Nami were both retired, living between Antioch, Beirut and Paris. So was Hashem al-Atasi, living peacefully at his home in Homs. His comrades in the National Bloc were struggling to save their reputations after their failure to implement the 1936 Treaty and their collective resignation in 1939. Mohammad 'Ali al-'Abed died in self-imposed exile at the French Riviera in 1939. Sheikh Taj was the last man standing in Damascus.

From Paris he set sail for Lebanon, spending a few weeks in the summer resort of Brummana in the Metn District. He then headed to the ancient town of Byblos, where he was a house guest of his friend, Bishop Boulos 'Akel. From there, he travelled by car to Damascus.[68] His sudden show-up created a buzz in the Syrian capital. He first appeared in al-Midan, home to the city's conservative clergy, attracting a large crowd of 2,000 people. Sheikh Taj didn't recognize many of the young men shouting his praise, but he embraced them with the warmth of old familiarity. This was the very same man whom the Damascenes had pelted with rotten tomatoes just four years earlier, now being raised shoulder-high by young Damascenes. Standing on a pedestal he delivered an improvised speech, saying that had returned to 'right all the wrongs done to Syria during my absence', blaming the National Bloc for all of Syria's political and economic woes.[69]

Community leaders showed up at the Hasani mansion in the al-Halbouni neighbourhood, standing in line to be received by Sheikh Taj. They listened carefully to every word he had to say, taking mental notes. Given his well-known connection to French intelligence, it was generally assumed that his views reflected those of policymakers in Paris. France had fallen under the control of the Third Reich, and the Vichy governor of Syria, General Henri Dentz, was suspicious of Sheikh Taj. Rumour had it that his return was the doing of Winston Churchill.[70] Dentz stationed troops around Sheikh Taj's residence, where he was still allowed to receive visitors but not to venture beyond his doorstep. His house arrest was only lifted with the Allied invasion of Syria and the defeat of the Vichy regime in the summer of 1941.

That July, General de Gaulle came to Syria and met with Hashem al-Atasi, inviting him to return to the presidency.[71] When that didn't work, de Gaulle summoned Sheikh Taj for a meeting at the French premises in al-'Afif, not far from the vacant Presidential Palace.[72] For three hours they negotiated the future of Syria. No minutes were kept and no other Syrian was in the room. De Gaulle decided that Sheikh Taj would become Syria's new president, to rule with no constitution or parliament until the war in Europe came to an end. This was music to the ears of Sheikh Taj.[73] To de Gaulle's surprise, Sheikh Taj set forth a few conditions before accepting Syria's top job. For starters, he wanted the unification of Syrian lands, stressing that if he were to assume the presidency, it would have to be of a united Syria that included both the Alawite and Druze Mountains.[74] The two districts had been forcefully detached by the French in 1920 and temporarily reunited with Syria at Hashem al-Atasi's insistence in 1936, only to regain their former autonomy with the start of the Second World War. If Atasi had ruled over a unified Syria, then so would Sheikh Taj.

The president-designate then made a strange request. He asked de Gaulle to 'invite' him to become president, rather than parachute him into the palace. He took out a copy of the letter the British had sent to King Faisal back in 1921, where they had cordially invited him to assume the throne of Iraq, seeking something similar. 'I would highly appreciate it if such a request is made in the name of France. I cannot say yes to something unless I am officially asked.'[75] Such an invitation, he believed, would spare him the never-ending comparison with Mohammad 'Ali al-'Abed and Hashem al-Atasi, who had been both voted into office. De Gaulle played along, sending him an official letter on 12 September 1941, formally inviting him to assume the presidency. The letter started out with the words 'Your

Excellency', which is how all former and incumbent premiers are addressed, and ended with 'Respectfully yours, Mr. President'. Sheikh Taj responded with a letter of acceptance, and was sworn-in as president on 16 September 1941. It was the very same day that Mohammad Reza Pahlavi had assumed the throne in Tehran, replacing his deposed father, Reza Shah, who Sheikh Taj admired greatly. Reza Shah had been toppled for standing neutral towards the Germans since 1939, triggering an all-out Anglo-Soviet invasion of Iran in 1941. He was toppled and exiled to the island of Mauritius, a British colony. Sheikh Taj took note, going out of his way to show support for the Allied war effort, not wanting to end up like the ex-shah.

President Hasani (September 1941–January 1943)

Upon setting foot in the palace, the new president instructed his son-in-law and bureau chief Munir al-'Ajlani to communicate with all daily newspapers, asking that they should stop referring to him as 'Sheikh Taj'.[76] Although having stuck to him since early manhood, it was no way to address a president, certainly not by his first name. His new title ought to be 'His Excellency Taj al-Din Effendi al-Hasani, president of the Syrian Republic'. President Hasani then began shortlisting names for the premiership. He wanted a respected political figure by his side, preferably a nationalist who would give his era an honourable start. The new premier had to be well connected, clean, independent and anti-Nazi. A nationalist would give credibility to the un-constitutional era, and dilute opposition from the National Bloc, which had threatened revolution if Sheikh Taj is named president.[77] Since none of Hashem al-Atasi's colleagues were willing to work with him, Sheikh Taj turned to their opponents in Shahbandarist circles, inviting the admired technocrat Hasan al-Hakim, to create a government.[78] Like him, Hakim was a native of Damascus, with a long and diverse career in government administration, banking and politics. He was one of the co-founders of the Arab Bank in Palestine, a co-leader of the Great Syrian Revolt, and had briefly served as minister of education during the final months of Hashem al-Atasi's presidency, between April and July 1939. Sheikh Taj had first met him in 1919, when Hakim was director of posts & telegraphs under King Faisal. It was easy to accuse Sheikh Taj of all sorts of things but nobody could say a word about Hasan al-Hakim.

Long after retirement in the mid-1960s, Hakim published a two-volume memoir, where he gave a detailed explanation on why he had agreed to serve under somebody as controversial as Sheikh Taj. He said that he took up the job assuming that the French were about to leave the country, based on Charles de Gaulle's promises and a statement by Prime Minister Churchill on 9 September 1941, saying that it was time to grant Syria its full independence.[79] Hakim successfully talked three National Bloc leaders into joining his cabinet: Fayez al-Khoury, one of the chief authors of the 1928 constitution, Faydi al-Atasi, a nephew of former president Hashem al-Atasi, and Mohammad al-'Ayesh of Deir ez-Zour. They respectively assumed the portfolios of foreign affairs, education and national economy. A fourth nationalist, Zaki al-Khatib, was appointed minister of justice. He was a former Bloc member who had defected into 'Abdul Rahman Shahbandar's orbit in the mid-1930s. To prepare for the return of the Druze and Alawite Mountains to Syria, Hakim appointed a member of each community to his cabinet, making it the first time in the history of Syria that members of the two religious minorities are represented in government. The Alawite notable Munir al-'Abbas was appointed minister of public works and charged with building roads, digging aqueducts and improving irrigation and infrastructure of the Alawite villages. 'Abdul Ghaffar Pasha al-Atrash of the Druze became minister of defence. He was one of the leaders of the Great Revolt and a cousin of its commander, Sultan Pasha al-Atrash. There was only one Francophile on the Hakim cabinet: Bahij al-Khatib, who had been named minister of interior.

On 12 January 1942, the Alawite and Druze Mountains were formally and permanently reunited with Syria.[80] One week later, Sheikh Taj hosted a lavish reception at the Grand Serail, celebrating Syrian unity. Nationalist leaders, Alawite and Druze notables, and French officials mingled together in the main reception hall, showering the new president with praise. To commemorate the event in a manner typical to his style, Sheikh Taj issued a collection of postal stamps, carrying his picture next to the tricolours of the Syrian Flag.

On 27 April 1942, Sheikh Taj sent a cable to world capitals, declaring Syria officially independent from the French Mandate. Letters of recognition flooded the Presidential Palace, from the kings of Saudi Arabia, Egypt and Great Britain. Belgium, Yugoslavia and Czechoslovakia all followed suit.[81] This was Sheikh Taj's moment of glory – the apogee of his political career. At home, however, things were not well. He came to blows with Hasan al-Hakim when the premier tried to re-open the murder case of 'Abdul Rahman Shahbandar. Hakim said that he was never convinced of its original verdicts, claiming that it was the French and Jamil Mardam Bey, rather than Ahmad 'Assasa, who had killed Shahbandar. Sheikh Taj was not ready for a confrontation with the Bloc – nor with the French – dismissing Hakim's efforts as 'untimely'.

Hakim then accused the president of trespassing on his executive powers, meddling with cabinet affairs through his bureau chief Munir al-'Ajlani. Sheikh Taj was accused of secretly calling on Hakim's ministers and asking them to resign, hoping that this would weaken Hasan al-Hakim and bring him running to the president.[82] By mid-1942, Hakim realized that he could no longer work with Sheikh Taj, presenting his resignation on 17 April. He was swiftly replaced by Husni al-Barazi, the Hama notable who had served as education minister under Sheikh Taj's second cabinet in 1934. Barazi was an outspoken statesman who never minced his words. He cared little for age, history and seniority, trashing the most senior of figures if they dared to cross or defy him. His cabinet included all the previous nationalists who had served under his predecessor, in addition to Munir al-'Ajlani, the president's son-in-law, who was made minister of youth affairs, a portfolio tailor-made to his liking. The Druze leader 'Abdul Ghaffar al-Atrash died and was replaced by Emir Hasan al-Atrash at the Ministry of Defense. He too was a Druze notable and husband of the Syrian diva Asmahan. Despite the personal friendship between Barazi and Sheikh Taj, he was to become his worst and final nightmare.

Shortly after the new cabinet was formed, Sheikh Taj held a reception at the Presidential Palace. Premier Barazi skipped the event saying: 'If I show up, I will have to give a speech, and if I do, I cannot but say that the independence we have been given by France is nothing but an illusion.'[83] Sheikh Taj stared back at him, with eyebrows raised in shock. Barazi added: 'I am the prime minister here and yet I do not feel that I have any real authority. I don't control the police or the gendarmerie. Let us achieve real independence first, and then hold receptions, Mr. President.'[84]

Then came another incident, when Sheikh Taj asked Barazi to allocate 100,000 Syrian pounds from the state budget for families in need. Barazi secured the money from the Ministry of Finance, and sent 50,000 pounds to the president. Sheikh Taj got on the phone and asked about the remaining amount. Barazi replied: 'Your Excellency. You are president of the republic and I am president of the council of ministers. You are in need of money, and so am I. That is why I have divided the amount equally between us.' Husni al-Barazi abruptly ended the stormy conversation, slamming the phone in the president's face.[85] Days later, he was fired and was replaced with Jamil al-Ulshi, who was tasked with forming a new government in January 1943. Barazi was accused of pocketing funds allocated for the purchase of wheat, and of secretly meeting with European officials without consulting with the president.[86] He had in fact met secretly with Winston Churchill's son-in-law, British MP Duncan Sandys, and accompanied him on a trip to Lebanon, without informing the president. Policemen were stationed at Barazi's doorstep, at Sheikh Taj's orders, keeping tabs on his visitors.[87] He wanted him summoned to court on charges of corruption, but died before striking back at Husni al-Barazi.

Death of the Syrian president

Jamil al-Ulshi was of different creed than Husni al-Barazi. He had genuine respect for Sheikh Taj and would never cross him. The two men went a long way back, having worked together first under Faisal, when Sheikh Taj was secretary-general of the royal palace and Ulshi was private chamberlain to the king. They were lifelong friends, neighbours and political allies. The president did not live long enough to see Ulshi's government see the light. After a busy day at work with his prime minister-designate, Sheikh Taj asked to be excused, complaining from chest congestion, although he was not a smoker. He collapsed at his home, and his doctors were quickly summoned from Beirut. According to Nasuh Babil, the doyen of Syrian journalists, they diagnosed him with 3.5 centigrams of blood poisoning. They also told his family that it was too late to do anything to save his life.[88] Sheikh Taj died at 1.40 pm on 17 January 1943. He was fifty-two.

As mandated in Islam, the president was given a speedy burial the very next morning. No autopsy was performed, despite suspicion of murder. Babil is the only Syrian to mention blood poisoning as the source of Sheikh Taj's death. The official press statement by the Presidential Press Office said that he had died of 'natural causes'. In his memoirs, Husni al-Barazi takes credit for many events in Syrian history, including the death of Sheikh Taj, which he attributes to a heart attack caused by his numerous quarrels with the president.[89] Sheikh Taj was given a state funeral, attended by Ambassador Spears, Lebanese president Alfred Naccache and Sheikh Taj's long-time foe, Hashem al-Atasi. His familiar white turban was placed neatly atop his coffin, which was driven through the streets of Damascus on a cannon, shrouded with the Syrian Flag. Green-turbaned dervishes from the Sufi order danced before the mourners, swirling next to the guards of honour, marching solemnly in impeccable white uniforms. Thousands gathered on the streets and on rooftops to bid farewell to their president. Spears remembered the event, saying: 'The senior members of my staff and I rushed over from Beirut to attend the funeral, so pressed for time that we changed into our morning coats in the cars. The funeral I shall never forget, under a clear blue sky, very cold, as hundreds of wailing women screaming continuously the most doleful dirges under immense twirling of pigeons.'[90]

Sheikh Taj was the first president to die while in office and would remain the last until Hafez al-Assad's death in June 2000. To date, nobody knows for sure whether he was actually killed or died naturally. Speaking to the author in the late 1990s, one of his daughters hinted that he might have been eliminated by the French because he was starting to free himself from their tutelage.[91] His sudden demise, however, put everybody in a difficult position. Neither the French nor the British were prepared for the power vacuum, and nor was the National Bloc. Jamil al-Ulshi assumed the duties of acting president until March 1943 and was then replaced by 'Ata al-Ayyubi, who, like in 1936, was charged with supervising parliamentary and presidential elections, set for July.[92] Those elections led to the victory of Sheikh Taj's long-time opponent Shukri al-Quwatli, who assumed the presidency in August 1943. Syria's new leadership worked on erasing Sheikh Taj's name from collective memory of the Syrian nation. Quwatli's first act was moving the presidential premises back to the Nazem Pasha palace in al-Muhajireen, not wanting to take over the desk, furniture and belongings of a deceased president.[93] When independence was achieved in April 1946, Sheikh Taj's name was omitted from school textbooks or the Independence Day celebrations that were held throughout Syria. Not a single street, school or hospital was named in his honour, despite his reputation for having been a great builder. To deprive him the nationalist credit, consecutive Syrian governments have drawn a clear distinction between 'independence', which took place under Sheikh Taj in September 1941, and 'emancipation', which happened during the Quwatli presidency in April 1946. Nobody in Syria celebrates – let alone remembers – Sheikh Taj's Independence Day on 27 September 1941. The official holiday in Syria is 'Emancipation Day' on 17 April 1946.

Sheikh Taj was no villain and certainly not a saint. No politician is and nor is he expected to be one, certainly not in a complex world like the Middle East. A handful of Sheikh Taj's friends insist that he was a fine patriot who collaborated with the French with the sole purpose of securing Syria's independence. This view was defended by ʿAbdullah al-Khani, aide-de-camp to President Quwatli, who, speaking to the author many years later, said: 'Poor Sheikh Taj. He was both wronged during his lifetime and after his death. Nobody gave him his due place in history.'[94]

Figure 10 Taj al-Din al-Hasani.

Chapter 11

ʿATA AL-AYYUBI (MARCH–AUGUST 1943)

ʿAta al-Ayyubi sat glued to his train seat, holding the arm of Prime Minister Alaa al-Din Droubi, who was seated to his left. They were on a mission, travelling from Damascus to the village of Khirbet Ghazaleh, north of the city of Daraa, when heavy gunfire rippled through the sky. It lasted for around five minutes, what seemed like an eternity in the hot summer sun. The mandate was barely a month old, and Ayyubi was serving as minister of interior. Senegalese troops were accompanying the delegation, to protect its members. Colonial officers erroneously believed that as Muslims, these African foot-soldiers would know how to deal with the locals. Senegalese troops knew nothing about Syrian society, and they did not speak Arabic. They had been shipped to the Middle East from their faraway country, with no briefing about the ways of life in the Syria, where carrying arms was common in the countryside, especially in times of unrest and political instability. Armed men from Daraa had showed up at the station ahead of the train's arrival from Damascus. When seeing guns in the hands of the locals, one Senegalese soldier opened fire, triggering an immediate response from the Houranis. Chaos came next. Three Senegalese soldiers were killed.

Ayyubi turned to his colleagues, Prime Minister Droubi and President of the Shura Council ʿAbdul Rahman al-Yusuf. They too were shivering, looking downwards at their feet so as not to see the dead around them. The prime minister tried calling out the names of policemen accompanying the delegation from Damascus. None replied. They were either dead or had to run for their lives. Without warning, he dashed to the rear and tried escaping through the regular passengers exit. He was apprehended and shot, left to drown in a big pool of blood. Yusuf was screaming out the window: 'Send your sheikhs so we can talk to them.'[1] He then gathered the courage to leave the train to call Damascus for reinforcements. Ayyubi begged him to stay onboard, saying: 'If you get out, they will kill you.' The pasha put on a back *abaya* (traditional women's dresswear) and got off the train. As he walked up the stairs of the station, he was shot in the back with one bullet.[2] Ayyubi watched the scene in horror, thinking that his turn was next. The government delegation had come to Houran to talk residents into paying a tax imposed by the mandate regime, a staggering 15,000 dinars in punishment for having hosted ex-king Faisal in Daraa before his final expulsion from Syria, three weeks earlier. There was nothing Ayyubi could do and nowhere to hide.

He thought of grabbing a gun to defend himself, but there was one problem: he didn't know how to use it. Ayyubi had never carried a gun in his life. He suddenly heard a voice calling his name from the deck.

"Ata Bey ... you don't know me, but I know you. I am from Damascus ... from al-Midan. Come with me. Let's get out of here quickly."

The voice was completely unfamiliar. He didn't recognize the stranger but had no choice except to believe and follow him. He looked descent, wearing a striped silk *qumbaz*, while speaking in the local Damascene accent. Ayyubi finally got off the train, trampling on the dead bodies around him. The stranger from al-Midan asked him to take off his *tarboosh* and jacket, in order to blend with the angry crown. The minister unbuttoned his shirt and threw away his tie, walking calmly towards the station doors, towards safety. Reinforcements were sent to Damascus that evening, escorting him back home. His two colleagues, or what remained of them, followed one month later in wooden coffins, wrapped with the flag of the French Republic. Roads between the capital and Houran had been sealed off by the rebels, delaying their return until 20 September 1920. They were given an official funeral in Damascus, attended by a special envoy for Henri Gouraud. Ayyubi walked solemnly behind his colleague's coffins, glad to be alive. In future years, he was to become Syria's penultimate president under the mandate, holding office from March to August 1943.

A professional bureaucrat

'Ata al-Ayyubi was born in Damascus in 1874, hailing from a large and influential family that traced its roots back to the Ayyubi sultan Saladin. His father Mohammad 'Ali was a prominent notable during the era of Sultan 'Abdulhamid II, while his grandfather had been a judge in Ottoman courts.[3] Ayyubi studied public administration at Mektabi-Sultani in Istanbul, joining the Ottoman civil service upon graduation. He rose the hierarchical ladder, becoming *qa'im maqam* then *mutasarrif* of Latakia, Mersin and, finally, al-Karak in present-day Jordan. He stood at arm's length from Arab nationalist parties that emerged prior to the First World War, like al-'Ahd and al-Fatat, insisting that as a professional bureaucrat, politics was not his business.[4] That changed in 1912, when he ran for the Ottoman Parliament, winning a seat for al-Karak. He refused to support the Arab Revolt of Sharif Hussein, however, standing with the Ottomans until curtain fall. When they were defeated and forced out of Syria in September 1918, Ayyubi was invited to join the interim government of his in-law, Emir Sa'id El Djezairi. In the immediate aftermath of the Battle of Maysaloun, he was named minister of interior in the cabinet of 'Alaa al-Din Droubi on 26 July 1920. It lasted until Droub's assassination in Houran on 21 August 1920. Ten days later he was once again named minister under Droubi's successor, Jamil al-Ulshi. Everybody seemed to like the professional civil servant: the Ottomans, Faisal and the French.

On 23 December 1925, Ayyubi was approached by the French High Commission, days after the resignation of Subhi Barakat, and asked to assume the presidency of

Syria. The French were looking for a respected notable to lead the nation, with no record of animosity towards the mandate. He turned down the post, however, given that the Great Revolt was still raging in the Druze Mountain, and the French military had just bombed Damascus.[5] He also refused to join People's Party or the National Bloc, despite being good friends with both ʿAbdul Rahman al-Shahbandar and Hashem al-Atasi. He often described himself as a 'friend' of the Bloc, but never as an official member although he did serve as president of its economic enterprise, the National Cement Company.[6] Four years later, in 1934, he helped establish another project, the National Conserves Company, specialized in the processing of fruits and vegetables from al-Ghouta and selling them in Egypt, Palestine and Iraq.[7]

Ayyubi's first government in 1936

During the 60-Day Strike of 1936, the National Bloc demanded the dismissal of Sheikh Taj and his replacement with someone who wasn't as provocative or controversial. Young people were constantly on the streets, demanding his resignation. Alarm bells were ringing, as people went to bed hungry. Food prices had soared, hoarding was common and goods rotted in storehouses. After brutally suppressing the Bloc leadership and arresting its top command, the French sat down for talks with Hashem al-Atasi. He was asked to suggest a replacement to Sheikh Taj. Without hesitation, he replied: "ʿAta Bey al-Ayyubi. He is a moderate and we trust him.'[8] The high commissioner said that Ayyubi was indeed a fine choice but he had twice turned down the premiership during the Great Revolt. 'Don't worry', said Atasi, 'I will talk to him.'[9]

Ayyubi and Atasi were good friends, having worked together since Ottoman times. He couldn't say no to Atasi, and on 22 February 1936, he formed a small cabinet of independent technocrats. Its only job was to restore calm to Syria. Ayyubi and Atasi then travelled to Beirut for talks with High Commissioner Henri de Martel, convincing him to grant a general amnesty to set free all those arrested with no warrant for their role in the 60-Day Strike. Eight thousand young men had been hauled before the military courts since January 1936. On 1 March the French announced that after talks with Prime Minister Ayyubi, it had been decided to free them all. National Bloc offices would be reopened, and its two suspended newspapers, *al-Qabas* and *al-Ayyam,* would return to print. Ayyubi promised de Martel that they would refrain from publishing any article calling for civil strife or revolution. In exchange, the Bloc leaders would call off the strike and head to Paris for talks with the French government.[10] A delegation was drawn up, headed by Atasi, and attached to it were two of Ayyub's ministers, Edmond Homsi and Mustapha al-Shihabi. They sailed to France in March 1936 and only returned six months later after signing the 1936 Treaty. Ayyubi supervised nationwide elections that December, which led to the National Bloc victory. Atasi was elected president and chose Jamil Mardam Bey as his first prime minister. On 21 December, Ayyubi stepped down from the premiership, having completed his task with rare perfection.

Ayyubi as president (25 March–17 August 1943)

'Ata al-Ayyubi played no political role for the next seven years, watching as the Atasi administration collapsed in July 1939, two months before the outbreak of the Second World War. Sheikh Taj was subsequently called upon to assume the presidency in September 1941, and died while in office on 17 January 1943. His prime minister Jamil al-Ulshi assumed the job of acting president. On 25 March, General Charles de Gaulle's delegate George Catroux issued two decrees, one restoring the 1928 constitution, which had been aborted during the 'Abed presidency, and the second appointing 'Ata al-Ayyubi as both head of state and prime minister, charged with supervising upcoming parliamentary and presidential elections. He was the third politician to assume both the premiership and presidency under the mandate, after Subhi Barakat and Ahmad Nami. He returned to power seven years after having created his first cabinet in 1936, taking over the portfolios of interior and defence, in addition to the premiership. His former minister Mustapha al-Shihabi was brought onboard, this time as minister of economy and supply, while Hashem al-Atasi's nephew Faydi al-Atasi was made minister of justice and education. Another newcomer was the Aleppine lawyer Na'im Antaki, who, like Atasi, was a member of the National Bloc. The new president called for a press conference at the Grand Serail, outlining his government policy. 'I have one task, to restore democratic life and make sure that elections are carried out in a calm and civilized manner.' Ayyubi spoke slowly in flawless classical Arabic, saying: 'I respect integrity and am extremely bias when it comes to my neutrality. I don't belong to a single party, but to all parties. Names come and go, but the Syrian government will remain.'[11]

During presidential election later that summer, Shukri al-Quwatli emerged as the National Bloc candidate, running unopposed. Ayyubi's son tried talking his father into nominating himself for Syria's top job. When that failed, he began lobbying on his behalf, meeting with former MPs from the 1936–9 parliament, asking them to sign a petition calling on 'Ata al-Ayyubi to run for president. Seventy-two of them signed the document, which was brought to the attention of Shukri al-Quwatli. Upset, he asked Foreign Minister Na'im Antaki to approach President Ayyubi, saying that if he wanted the presidency for himself, then he would gladly withdraw his candidacy. Ayyubi summoned his son for a dressdown, saying: 'It is in the nation's best interest that Shukri al-Quwatli, and not anybody else, becomes president. I will not challenge him.'[12] On 17 August 1943, Ayyubi handed over power to Quwatli, officially announcing his retirement from politics.

From there Ayyubi took a back seat, appearing occasionally at charity events hosted by his daughter Saniyya, deputy president of the Gout de Lait Society. He used his connections to help her set up an orphanage for Palestinian children after the 1948 war with Israel. His last public appearance was in July 1949, when he showed up at the Grand Serail to congratulate his friend, Muhsen al-Barazi, on becoming prime minister.[13] This was right after Husni al-Za'im had staged his infamous coup, sending Shukri al-Quwatli to jail. A year and a half later,

'Ata al-Ayyubi died in Damascus on 21 December 1950. He was seventy-six. His long-time friend Hashem al-Atasi was in power at the time, and he ordered that a beautiful street in the Nuri Pasha neighbourhood of Damascus be named in his honour. It still stands today as 'Rue 'Ata al-Ayyubi'. The title 'president' has been dropped out of its name and the mansion premises were abandoned, its doors and windows shuttered and closed.

Figure 11 Ata al-Ayyubi.

Chapter 12

SHUKRI AL-QUWATLI (1943–9)

In the early morning hours of 29 March 1949, soldiers invaded the residence of President Shukri al-Quwatli located in an elegant street called Bustan al-Ra'is, not far from the Presidential Palace. Without much effort they managed to disarm the one guard on duty. The president was startled at the presence of strangers in his living room, armed to the teeth. One of the officers, Ibrahim al-Husseini, read out a warrant. 'You are under arrest, Mr. President.'[1] Quwatli froze. An entire political career flashed before his eyes. He had heard this exact same phrase often throughout his life, first from Turkish soldiers and then from French sergeants, but never from one of his own countrymen. Never from a Syrian. Quwatli got dressed at gunpoint, his wife slowly handing him items of clothing, whispering: 'Who is behind this Abu Hassan? Is it the Jews?'[2] Abu Hassan is how Shukri al-Quwatli was popularly called in Damascus, where all men are identified by the name of their eldest male offspring. He shook his head with a silent 'no' and she would ask again, 'Then is it King ʿAbdullah (of Jordan)?' Not for a moment did she imagine that ordinary Syrians would stage a coup against their own president, whom they had just hailed three years earlier as 'father' of independence.

Shukri al-Quwatli was not handcuffed but escorted out of his home with dignity. The entire neighbourhood was awake. Women and children were on balconies and young men had descended to the street and were now crowding the gates of the Quwatli residence, pushing their way through the tanks and armoured vehicles. Quwatli took a long hard look at them all. He smiled to familiar faces and said good morning to others, addressing them by their first names. He then slowly ascended into the military jeep, paternally patting the driver's shoulder, before he was driven to the notorious Mezzeh Prison. Two men carrying rifles sat on either side of him. Their eyes were trained on the rear-view mirror, on the driver, the street – anything but the president in their custody. They were carrying out orders and were not convinced that Shukri al-Quwatli deserved such a fate. The streets of Damascus were foggy and empty. A morning dew covered the trees and jasmine flowers that dotted balconies in Bustan al-Ra'is and the adjacent al-ʿAfif and Muhajireen neighbourhoods. It was chilly, predawn Damascus. A few people were already heading to work either on foot or by bicycle. Tanks and machine guns were placed at every strategic corner throughout the Syrian capital.

President Quwatli was taken to jail for the night, on a hilltop in western Damascus. Under the French it had been used to jail his friends in the National Bloc. By sunrise, Quwatli began complaining of a stomach cramp – a pain often afflicted while under stress and in anxiety. It was dark, cold and damp in Mezzeh. From neighbouring cells, he could hear inmates screaming under torture. Losing his nerve, Quwatli banged on his cell's metal door: 'Soldiers! Where is Husni al-Za'im! I am the president of the republic! Get me Husni al-Za'im!' The stomach pain eventually caused him to collapse, sending the prison guards running frantically into his cell. When they confirmed the gravity of his medical condition, Husni al-Za'im ordered that Quwatli be transferred to the nearby military hospital, also in Mezzeh. This time he was taken out of the car on a stretcher, groaning with pain. Quwatli noticed that the Syrian flag had not been raised on the hospital's rooftop, although it was way past 8.00 am when government buildings opened in Syria. He snapped at the doctor on duty: 'Where is the flag? Why haven't you hoisted the flag?'[3] This was a man who had just lost everything and, yet, still had the decency to look after the flag of Syria. This story seems up the career, and values, of Shukri al-Quwatli.

The Quwatli family

Shukri al-Quwatli was born in Damascus on Wednesday, 21 October 1891. Originally al-Nahhas, literally 'copper worker', the family name was changed to Quwatli, signifying strength or *quwwa* in Arabic, sometime during the 1300s.[4] Indeed, men of the Quwatli family were strong and muscular, with a solid build and broad shoulders. Shukri al-Quwatli himself was tall and moustached, with black hair and thick black eyebrows. His grandfather was an affluent merchant and community leader, while his great-uncle had served as president of the Ottoman Agricultural Bank of Damascus. A second uncle, Hasan Pasha al-Quwatli, served as president of the Damascus Chamber of Commerce and Industry. Another uncle, Mohammad Sa'id, was the only Syrian standing next to Khedive Ismail at the inauguration of the Suez Canal in 1869.[5]

Quwatli was very close to his mother, a saintly woman with whom he had an exceptionally close relationship. She was his mother, friend and guardian. Her father 'Ata al-Qudsi was a prominent member of the Damascus *ashraf*. Najiya al-Qudsi's family tree went all the way back to Imam Hussein, the son of the fourth Muslim caliph 'Ali Ibn Abi Talib from his first wife Fatima al-Zahra, daughter of the Prophet Mohammad.[6] The family had an ancient manuscript stored in its coffers, a written letter from the Prophet Mohammad to the Holy Roman emperor Heraclius, dated 628.[7] This was a constant source of pride for the young Quwatli – that his family was well rooted in Islamic history. His mother's black-and-white photo, frayed at the corners from the passage of time, travelled with him throughout his long exiles in Egypt, Switzerland and Lebanon. As a grown man he would cradle into her arms, bend over to kiss her hand, standing to full attention when she entered a room. He would often eek her blessing before taking a decision, be it as personal as naming a newborn or as public as signing a presidential decree.

Studying in Istanbul

Quwatli studied at Maktab ʿAnbar, the elite high school of Damascus, located in the Old City. The school was originally founded by his uncle in 1867, before it was sold to a Jewish notable named Yusuf ʿAnbar. It was among the earliest government-accredited high school in Ottoman Damascus. In 1908, Quwatli moved to Istanbul to study political science at the Mulkiyye School, another institution reserved for the Ottoman Empire's elite. Istanbul at the time was a densely populated metropolis of nearly 900,000 inhabitants. It had everything that Damascus lacked, from posh hotels, theatres and cinemas, to fashionable shops, photography studios and foreign embassies. The Pera Palace Hotel offered facilities comparable with the palatial hotels of major cities in Europe. It even looked different from Damascus, with architectural designs that varied from neoclassical to rococo and ultra-modern, whereas Quwatli's city had clustered houses packed side-by-side, all looking remarkably similar. Quwatli rented an apartment near Taksim Square, a wealthy cosmopolitan neighbourhood frequented by European diplomats and inhabited by an assortment of Arabs, Greeks and Jews. Quwatli would engage in lengthy talks with classmates during their leisurely walks along the Bosporus, debating the three prevailing currents of that era: Ottomanism, pan-Islamism and, of course, the highly attractive concept Arab nationalism.

Membership in al-Fatat

At university Quwatli joined the Arab underground through al-Fatat, a secret society established by young Arab students studying in Paris in 1911. Two years later, a Damascus branch was opened, headed by Quwatli and the Bakri brothers, Nasib and Fawzi. Al-Fatat managed to remain secret until 1916. Of its seventeen members in Damascus, Shukri al-Quwatli was the youngest. In 1916, one of al-Fatat's members was arrested, being Shukri Pasha al-Ayyubi. He sent word to Quwatli through his son, seeking his help to get out of jail. The young boy's footsteps were tracked and he too was arrested, and so was Quwatli.[8] Prison authorities were severely brutal, pulling out his nails and whipping him with a leather rod. Doubting that he would get out of jail alive, Quwatli bribed his prison guard to get him a razor concealed in a loaf of bread, using it to slit his wrist.[9] A guard noticed blood gushing out of his cell, and summoned another prisoner, the physician Ahmad Qadri to save him. In his memoirs, Qadri says that while treating Quwatli's wounds, he whispered into his ear: 'Play dead! This is the only way to get out of here alive.'¹⁰ For the rest of his life, a pulse could not be felt through Quwatli's left arm.¹¹

Shukri al-Quwatli spent four weeks in hospital and five more months in prison, before being released on 28 January 1917. By then the Arab Revolt had broken out in Mecca, and would continue to rage until September 1918. Under the Faisal government, Quwatli was appointed assistant governor of Damascus. He and his comrades in al-Fatat would eventually inherit their king's failed state, spending their entire lives trying to repair what Faisal and the Great Powers did to Syria between 1918–20.

The first exile

As French troops marched into the Syrian capital on 25 July 1920, Henri Gouraud published his list of WANTED individuals who had worked prolifically against the Ottomans and would likely do the same against the French. Shukri al-Quwatli was number five on the list. The easiest thing to do was to have them shot, one after another, to make certain they wouldn't become a headache for France. Quwatli got on a train along with seventy of his colleagues, heading to Haifa, Palestine. From there, the nationalists parted ways. Some chose exile in Europe or went to the Arabian Desert. Quwatli chose Egypt. Here he was, once a proud citizen and rising star in political circles, now exiled and homeless. He was unmarried and leaving behind his beloved mother in Damascus. At only twenty-nine, he found himself immersed in Cairo's influential surroundings, and electrified by Arab nationalists of all stripes and colours. The country was going through its own democratic transition, and Quwatli witnessed first-hand the opening of Egypt's first elected parliament in March 1924. He would continue to have a soft spot for Egypt until his death.

In Cairo, Quwatli got married to Bahira al-Dalati, a beautiful young girl from Damascus, seventeen years his junior. She was to become his lifelong companion until death separated them in 1967. Like his mother, she too came from Muslim royalty, tracing her family tree back to Abu Bakr al-Sadiq, companion of the Prophet Mohammad and father of his favourite wife, 'Aisha.¹² Quwatli had only seen his bride once, when as a child, she came to visit her father Sa'id Dalati, who as serving jail time with Quwatli for their role in the Arab underground. Bahira was sent to Cairo, arriving at the same station and on the very same day as King Fouad. Electric lights, red carpets and flags were everywhere. Quwatli stood there in a black evening suit with silver cufflinks, wearing his traditional fez, smiling down at the young girl. Trembling, she couldn't look him straight in the face. 'Don't be afraid,' he said, pulling her chin upwards. 'Look around Bahira; I decorated the train station especially for you!'¹³ The young girl was proud of her rebel husband. When friends asked about his job, she would reply: 'He works for the Syrian Revolution.'¹⁴

In 1921, Quwatli co-established the Syrian Palestinian-Congress in Geneva, along with a number of Arab exiles. From Syria, it included Sheikh Rashid

Rida, former president of the Syrian National Congress, and ʿAbdul Rahman Shahbandar. Quwatli took charge of raising funds for its activities across the Arab World, and for the Great Syrian Revolt after its launch in 1925. That took him to *Bayt al-Umma al-Masriyya*, or House of the Egyptian Nation: the home of Saʿad Pasha Zaghloul, leader of the Egyptian Revolt of 1919.[15] No name could have been more iconic than Zaghloul and no residence more symbolic for the people of Egypt. The meeting between Quwatli and Zaghloul was arranged by a young member of the pasha's Wafd Party, ʿAbdul Rahman ʿAzzam, who would later become the first secretary-general of the Arab League. The Wafd Party had just won the 1924 elections, making Zaghloul prime minister of Egypt. He was old and tough, approaching the age of seventy. Humbly, he called Quwatli 'my son', taking him by the arm to his private office. Seated among maps and tomes on Pharaonic Egypt, Zaghloul took out a paper he had prepared for the Syrian Revolt. He promised to publish in al-Wafd's official paper, *al-Balagh*. He cleared his throat and read:

> Syria, to which we are bond by deep ties of history, language, religion, customs, and proximity, has these days experienced shattering events that shake nations all around her. It has experienced the most abdominal evils that man can commit against man. The French have reduced a strong people to want and misfortune, telling the entire world that the mandate was established not for the interests of Syria, but rather, of who are occupying Syria. We, the people of Egypt, lament this tragedy and will help in any way we can.[16]

Quwatli politely asked to change one word, replacing 'strong people' with 'proud people'.[17] Saʿad Zaghloul signed off the text, which was published on 6 November 1926. He then took out his cheque-book and donated 100 Egyptian pounds to the Syrian Revolt, made in Quwatli's name.[18] On the very same day, a military court sentenced Quwatli to death in Damascus.[19] Quwatli's support for the Great Revolt had led to the torching of his family orchards in al-Ghouta, and shelling of his family mansion in Damascus.

Leading from below

Quwatli remained in Egypt until 1931, when he returned to join the National Bloc, at the invitation of its president Hashem al-Atasi. He and Atasi didn't realize, at that early point of their careers, that they would one day rotate at the presidency, three times each, becoming symbols of Syrian democracy, nationhood and independence from colonial rule. Atasi developed an instant liking of Shukri al-Quwatli, who was nearly twenty years his junior, treating him like family. They worked closely together, helping orchestrate the 60-Day Strike of 1936. During Atasi's absence in France from March to September 1936, Quwatli was appointed acting president of the National Bloc. When Atasi was elected president that

December, Quwatli was voted into parliament and appointed minister of defence and finance in the cabinet of Jamil Mardam Bey.

Damascus had changed, however, and Quwatli could almost no longer recognize his city. Its population had swollen from 169,000 in 1920 to 198,771 by 1936. Many newcomers from the countryside had come to live behind its high wall after the French onslaught of 1925. The old quarters had lost much of their intimacy. Leadership had become competitive, costly and complicated; Quwatli had to re-introduce himself to people, from scratch. In as much as he excelled when speaking with kings and pashas, he was seemingly more at ease with simple people: labourers, shopkeepers and ordinary folks of Damascus. He would show up at their weddings and funerals, settle their hospital bills and show genuine interest in the schooling of their children.

Quwatli set out on broadening his power base in Damascus, one neighbourhood at a time. He was already the uncontested leader of his native al-Shaghour, and began weaving a political network in al-Qanawat, another affluent neighbourhood coined 'Little Istanbul' because of the abundance of wealth and treasures within its homes. From al-Qanawat he expanded to al-'Amara, home of the old ulema families, al-Qaymariya and Salhieh on the foothills of Mount Qassioun. Al-'Amara alone housed 13,024 of the total 198,000 homes in Damascus. All of its residents were affluent scholars whose financial and political endorsement would be vital for his political career.[20] Al-Qaymariya was a mixed Muslim-Christian neighbourhood of the Damascus middle class, while Salhieh was an orphaned district, with nobody to turn to for leadership. Dotted with mosques and religious schools, it was a gateway to the modern quarters of al-Shuhada and 'Arnous (both created during the mandate), and to the future premises of the Syrian parliament building, erected in the early 1930s.

Quwatli began his network through influencing each quarter's neighbourhood council (*majlis al-hay*), made up of the local mukhtar, imam and notables. Quwatli offered them protection from excesses of the mandate regime, while making sure that garbage was collected, streets were swept and patrolled by night, and that young people found jobs, either in the public or private sectors. He protected the old quarters from heavy taxes, supervising the construction of schools, courts and medical clinics. The local quarter bosses, known as *qabadayat* in Arabic, were the backbone of Quwati's power base in Damascus.[21] They protected women on the streets, helped apprehend thieves and secure the safe passage of merchandize from one bazaar to another. They enjoyed unrestricted access to Shukri al-Quwatli, even after becoming president in 1943. The Qabadayat of Damascus, men like 'Abbud al-Kurdi, Abu 'Abdu al-'Ashi and Mohammad Khaddam Srijeh, became his eyes and ears on the streets of the city, reporting to him on everyone and everything.[22] They received monthly stipends from Quwatli, roaming the capital daily, often armed with a small pistol, drumming up street demonstrations when needed and closing bazaars for any strike, at Quwatli's direct orders. They were his access to the ordinary folks of Damascus, and the secret of his success during parliamentary and presidential elections. They were to prove fundamental during the General Strike of 1936, when, at Quwatli and Atasi's call, they brought Damascus and all of Syria into a crippling halt.

Quwatli the businessman

Quwatli spent a good deal of the 1930s trying to raise money for himself, having suffered greatly from the torching of his orchards and destruction of his family mansion in 1925. Exceptionally harsh winters, low revenue from his agricultural plantations and the Great Depression had forced him to sell significant amounts of land. To keep property within the Quwatli family, he sold the land to his brother 'Adel. Quwatli would eventually inherit these very same plantations from his brother, only to sell them once again in the 1950s. But upon returning from exile, he spent quality time at his family village in Hosh Bala, al-Ghouta, introducing modern mechanized farming techniques, which he had observed first hand on the Nine Delta.

Damascene produce, especially apricots, was in high demand throughout the Arab World. Syria ranked third in world apricot production, inspiring Quwatli to establish a factory for the manufacturing of dried fruits and vegetables.[23] He reasoned that Damascus produced an abundance of sweet and flavourful fruits that never reached other Arab markets as they would rot in transit. His company, the National Conserves, was established with the aim of bringing the produce of al-Ghouta to every corner of the Arab world. The company was capitalized at 30,000 gold coins, divided into 15,000 shares.[24] His partners in the project were Salim al-Shallah, a member of the Damascus Chamber of Commerce, and Sa'id Ghraoui, Jamil al-Bizreh and Tawfiq Qabbani, pioneers of the sweets and confectionary industries.[25] They were made shareholders and board members at the National Conserves Company.

Within five years, the company's capital was raised to 49,500 gold coins, with 22,000 shares.[26] To branch out, Quwatli sold shares to Bank Misr in Egypt and to the Arab Bank in Palestine, explaining that he wanted to keep the Conserves Company a pan-Arab enterprise.[27] Renowned Egyptian economist Talaat Pasha Harb, founder of Bank Misr, was hired as a consultant. By 1935, the company boasted a staff of 200 workers and was producing twenty-five tonnes of dried and processed fruits and vegetables, canned and shipped to Palestine, Iraq and Egypt.[28] Quwatli himself earned the title *Malek al-Mishmosh* (King of Apricots).[29] He would present newlyweds and friends on their firstborn with shares in the National Conserves Company, which continued to operate until it was nationalized by the Ba'ath Party in 1965, seven years after Quwatli's resignation from the presidency.[30]

Quwatli as minister 1936–8

Quwatli served as cabinet minister once in his life, for a total of fifteen months from December 1936 until March 1938. During Prime Minister Mardam Bey's frequent travels to France, Quwatli deputized on his behalf as acting prime minister, in addition to his duties at the ministries of finance and defence.[31] In February 1937, Mardam Bey raised two issues that put him at odds with Quwatli. One was the renewal of a French company's contract to dig for oil in Syria. The second was the French request to renew an agreement with Banque du Syrie et Liban, prolonging Syria's reliance on the French franc.[32] As finance minister, Quwatli objected to both. 'Our duty is to dismantle France's interests in Syria, one at-a-time', he told Mardam Bey, 'what you are doing is giving France more reason to stay in Syria.'[33] The premier believed that by conceding on both issues, he would appeal to pro-treaty MPs in the French Parliament, giving them ammunition to push for long-delayed ratification. Mardam Bey waited for Quwatli to travel to Mecca for his annual hajj pilgrimage, and then took the liberty of signing both agreements without informing his minister.[34] Upset, Quwatli resigned from the Mardam Bey government on 22 March 1938, citing medical reasons rather than disagreement with the premier. Although still in his forties and too young for failing health, he wrote to Mardam Bey that he was not feeling well and had to check into the American University Hospital in Beirut.[35]

The road to the Presidential Palace

During the Second World War, Shukri al-Quwatli attracted the attention of Great Britain's ambassador General Edward Spears. When he first arrived to the region in April 1941, Spears knew nothing about Syria. He was exceptionally smart, dashing and a close friend of Churchill. After the Nazi occupation of Paris, he had masterminded Charles de Gaulle's escape to London, making the French general forever indebted to him. Spears worked closely with Free France, his country's wartime allies, but was instrumental in orchestrating their downfall in both Syria and Lebanon. Instead of driving Syrian nationalists into the underground and sending them to jail or exile, Spears pushed for their empowerment, lobbying on their behalf at 10 Downing Street. He believed that they were men with whom he could do business, regardless of what the French thought of them. When the Free French exiled Quwatli to Iraq on dubious accusations of being pro-Hitler, it was Edward Spears who negotiated his comeback. Spears wrote to the Foreign Office, warning that the Free French 'will turn Quwatli back at the border if he attempts to cross from Baghdad'.[36] He wrote: 'Such action would do us great harm,' adding: 'My impression is that Shukri al-Quwatli is a sincere patriot who wishes to cooperate with us.'[37] De Gaulle's man in Syria, George Catroux, was unconvinced, telling the British ambassador:

> I still regard this person, Shukri al-Quwatli, as the most important of Syrian partisans of the Axis and as a man whose patriotism the Berlin wires paid tribute in August 1941. This man is not regarded in Cairo, Riyadh, or Baghdad as an outstanding political figure or as an intellectual enjoying widespread appeal. But rather, as a vigorous leader whose direct eloquence empowers him to work upon the poorer classes in Damascus. He is neither one of the heads of Syria nor one of the brains of Islam.[38]

At Spears' insistence, however, Catroux softened his stance, allowing Quwatli to return to Syria, on two conditions. One was to suspend his political activism and stop stirring anti-French sentiment. Second, he would have to reside in Beirut, not Damascus, in order to be detached from his powerbase. British foreign secretary Anthony Eden wrote back to the French: 'I cannot agree that such conditions should be imposed on Shukri al-Quwatli. I trust that Catroux will admit him into Syria unconditionally and consent himself with keeping a close eye on his movements.'[39]

Quwatli finally returned on 18 April 1942. Nine months later, President Taj al-Din al-Hasani died while in office, allowing for parliamentary and presidential elections. The National Bloc decided to contest the 1943 elections with full force, nominating Quwatli for the presidency. Atasi insisted that he did not want the post and Jamil Mardam Bey was still suffering from the loss of the Sanjak and failure to ratify the 1936 Treaty. His chances at victory were slim, leaving Quwatli as the only Bloc candidate. Before accepting the nomination, he needed to secure Atasi's blessing, travelling to Homs to meet him at his home.[40] 'I refuse to enter the palace without your blessing', he said to Atasi.[41] The ex-president gave him his approval, stressing that he would make a fine president. Quwatli then headed to Aleppo, where he received a mild, even icy reception from its traditional leaders. With the exception of Sa'adallah al-Jabiri, members of the Aleppine notability did not think highly of Quwatli. They often complained that since the beginning of French rule, three heads of state had been from Damascus ('Abed, Sheikh Taj, and Ayyubi), one from Homs (Atasi), one from Antioch (Barakat) and two from Lebanon (Ahmad Nami and Bahij al-Khatib). Aleppo was the only city that had not produced a single president. Former Aleppine members of the National Bloc, who had all resigned after the 1939 annexation of the Sanjak, argued that it was time to elect a present from their historic city, one who would cater to Aleppo's social, economic and political needs. They were led by Nazem al-Qudsi, a graduate of the University of Geneva, and Rushdi al-Kikhiya, a wealthy landowner. They demanded union with Hashemite Iraq and greater commercial ties with Baghdad – two things that Quwatli was unwilling to give due to his solid relations with Egypt and Saudi Arabia. For the next six years, Qudsi and Kikhiya created the crux of opposition to Quwatli's rule, which formalized into the People's Party in the summer of 1948. They would only get an Aleppine president when Qudsi was elected in December 1961.

After winning the lion's share of parliamentary seats, Quwatli ran for the presidency unopposed, despite a half-hearted attempt from former premier Haqqi al-'Azm at challenging him. Quwatli won 118 votes out of the total of 120 seats in Parliament, and was sworn-in as president on 17 August 1943. A gargantuan parade escorted him to the Bzurieh Market. Wearing a light summer suit and acting unusually swift and sporty, he dashed through the winding old alleys of Damascus, waving to onlookers. Quwatli was the son of Damascus and knew its people. He also knew its streets by heart. From the old spice market, he delivered his victory speech:

> The country has now passed one of the preparatory stages of its free constitutional life. Parliament is now about to convene. Our hearts are filled with tranquility

and joy. The nation, with all of its cities and towns, firmly stands today as one united body. It supports leaders that it knows too well; men whose nationalism and loyalty were put to the test, and who were found worthy of her trust.

To please Aleppo, he called on Sa'adallah al-Jabiri to form the first National Bloc government in four years. Jabiri was Quwatli's age, born in 1893, scion of one of the oldest landowning families in his city, reflecting Aleppine aristocracy at its best. Educated in Istanbul, he was conscripted into the Ottoman Army at the outbreak of the Great War. This is when he joined al-Fatat and established a close friendship with Quwatli, which would last a lifetime. He was soft spoken and calm, yet commanding and tough when needed. The Damascus press often remarked that he was the best-dressed politician in Syria, customizing all of his suits at Aleppo's finest tailors. A lifelong bachelor, Jabiri never married, but worked day and night as a full-time politician focused wholly on the independence of Syria. Politics was his obsession; he had no other life.

The palace under Quwatli

Quwatli's first decision was to move the presidential palace from Mustapha al-'Abed's mansion in al-Muhajireen to the old palace of Nazem Pasha. His life at the palace ran a fairly constant theme. He would wake early for morning prayer and be at his office by 9.00 am.[42] Friends and family were welcomed at his home for morning coffee before he headed to work, between 7.00–8.00 am. His day would then start with a stop at his mother's residence, located in a neighbourhood that would later be known as al-Malki.[43] Citizens wanting to meet their president had to fill out an application either in person or through post mail. He hardly ever turned down a request, unless it contained some legal violation.[44] For lunch Quwatli would take a two-hour break with his wife and children, before returning to the palace, where he usually stayed until past midnight. An observant Muslim, he made sure to pray five times a day, and never missed prayer time regardless of how busy he was.[45]

Quwatli chose an office for himself on the second floor of the Nazem Pasha Palace, next to that of his bureau chief, Najib al-Armanazi. A wide marble staircase, covered with a magnificent red carpet, took him from the second floor to the first foyer, which he would often walk down with his wife during official banquets. She was given the title of First Lady and played a very active role in society, unlike the wives of Sheikh Taj or Hashem al-Atasi, who were never seen in public. He introduced sweeping changes at the presidency, which until 1943 had housed only five employees: a secretary-general/bureau chief, a military assistant, a typist, an assistant and a cook. For starters, Quwatli hired three military escorts, all from prominent Damascus families: Suhayl al-'Ashi, Badih al-Ayyubi and Taleb al-Daghestani. He also liked to keep an eye on the children of martyrs, appointing Khaled al-'Asali as director of protocol. 'Asali was an accomplished artist whose father had been executed by the Ottomans in 1916. He was charged with designing the Syrian emblem and soon replaced at the protocol department 'Issam al-Inklizi, the son of another martyr also hanged in 1916. He had studied at AUB and was Syria's tennis champion.[46] In addition to the Libyan-Syrian Khalil al-Sa'adawi, who had been at the palace since the 1930s, Quwatli hired three additional staffers: 'Abdul Wahab Zein al'Abidin, Rafiq al-Ustwani and 'Abdul Hadi Diab. Sa'adawi was made deputy head of the Presidential Diwan.[47] Fouad al-Shayeb, a novelist, poet and journalist from the ancient Christian village of Maaloula, was made director of the newly founded Presidential Press Office. Muhsen al-Barazi, a former education minister, lawyer and professor at Damascus University, was soon appointed secretary-general of the palace, replacing Najib al-Armanazi, who was transferred to the Ministry of Foreign Affairs. At forty, Barazi was well travelled and well read, positioning himself as Quwatli's adviser, speechwriter and personal envoy to Arab kings and presidents. The president's bodyguard was Abu Mirii, a Circassian civilian who became his shadow. Abu Mirii dressed comically, always sporting high boots and a twisted moustache. Another loyal employee was Amin al-Kurdi, the president's driver, who was given strict instructions never to make a fuss over the presidential entourage. Quwatli took this matter very seriously. Motorcades, roadblocks and green lights were off-limits. One of the president's few indulgences was parading through Damascus in a convertible, especially on national holidays such as Martyrs Day, Independence Day and Army Day. Since neither he nor the palace owned such an automobile, he would rent one from a car dealer on Baghdad Street.[48] He also loved to walk, and would often stroll from his house or the palace to a nearby mosque for prayer, without any security. His military escort, Suhayl al-'Ashi, recalled how one day, the president glimpsed a security official among the mosque crowd, squatting behind him with a pistol hanging on his belt. He summoned 'Ashi for a dress-down, saying: 'Guns in the house of God are forbidden.'[49]

Reaching out to world leaders

President Quwatli spent the next two years focusing primarily on negotiations with the French. In October 1943, Prime Minister Jabiri was sent to Cairo for talks with King Farouk, aimed at securing Egyptian support for Syria's independence, and in January 1944, Foreign Minister Jamil Mardam Bey went to Baghdad, for the very same reason. Quwatli corresponded with Franklin Roosevelt, Joseph Stalin and Chiang kai-Shek of China, asking them to support Syria's national aspirations. He reminded the Allies of 'the high principles of freedom and liberty that are being put to the test. We trust that the world will not again be deceived by secret agreements made before the war (in reference to Sykes-Picot)'.[50] Similar letters were sent to King Ahmad Zahir Shah of Afghanistan, King Gustav V of Sweden and Mohammad Reza Pahlavi, the young king of Iran who had replaced his father as shah in 1941. By mid-1944, all of them had formally recognized Syria's independence, and so had all Arab states, with the exception of Jordan, due to King 'Abdullah's own ambitions of becoming king of Syria.

In the summer of 1944, Quwatli sent Aleppo MP Na'im Antaki to Cairo for talks with the Soviet Ambassador Nikolai Novikov, seeking Stalin's support for Syrian independence. Antaki had in-laws in Egypt, making his visit unsuspicious to French intelligence. On 11 July 1944, Soviet Foreign Minister Vyacheslav Molotov telephoned Quwatli, expressing Stalin's desire to open an embassy in Damascus. The Syrian scene, it appeared, was rapidly slipping out of French control. The Soviet leader sent a senior delegation to Damascus, charged with setting up the embassy. They stayed in the Syrian capital for fifteen days, and restricted their meetings to Quwatli, Jabiri and Mardam Bey, not calling upon any of France's men in Syria. One of de Gaulle's diplomats remarked, 'Novikov (who headed the delegation) showed disobliging reserve (towards the French). He passed two weeks in the Levant without contacting the Delegate General of France. This is clearly not agreeable for us. The misfortune of times, however, does not allow us to complain.'[51] The Kremlin was making a point: the only person they recognized in Damascus was Shukri al-Quwatli. They also skipped the annual French celebrations of Bastille Day, on 14 July 1944, arguing that in accordance with de Gaulle's 1941 promises, Syria should not be celebrating a French national day.

One month later George Catroux was replaced by a ruthless French officer named Etienne Beynet. Quwatli sent a letter to de Gaulle, co-signed with the new president of Lebanon Beshara al-Khoury, describing Beynet's appointment as 'bad humor'.[52] Beynet had nothing but distaste for Quwatli, and never missed an opportunity to show it. In August 1944 he wrote to de Gaulle, accusing Quwatli of scheming with Edward Spears to eject the French from Syria, based on an article that had recently been published in *The Palestine Post*.[53] In his despatch to de Gaulle, Beynet wrote:

> The interference of the British in all domains makes us believe, as indicated in the *Palestine Post*, that an accord has been made between the Syrian Government and the Spears Mission, at our expense. The President assured me that there was nothing of the sort. He added that the transfer of the (Levant) Army (from France to Syria) would give him the right and the means to defend the independence of his country. I told him that such a transfer would remove all possibility of defending this independence, and that he could not fail to realize that our situation in the world, which is improving daily, gives us more authority than the Syrian Government.[54]

Beynet's position was strengthened when Spears was recalled and replaced with Terence Shone in December 1944; a calm and serious diplomat who had all of his predecessor's shortcomings and none of his strengths. He would later become high commissioner of India and then permanent representative to the United Nations. After meeting Quwatli, Shone reported to London that the president's attitude 'is even harder than expected'. He added: 'If the Levant states feel that we are letting them down, they may well seek backing from some other power. The Soviet

Union would be a likely chance.'⁵⁵ Without a moment to lose, Quwatli turned to the United States, asking President Roosevelt to upgrade the status of his envoy, George Wadsworth, from 'political agent' to 'minister'. At Roosevelt's orders, Secretary of State Cordell Hull upgraded the status of his diplomat in Damascus. Quwatli automatically reciprocated, making Nazem al-Qudsi, his young opponent from Aleppo, Syria's first minister to Washington, DC.

The Quwatli-Churchill Summit

In February 1945, Quwatli boarded a plane to Saudi Arabia, where he dined with the kingdom's founder King ʿAbdul-ʿAziz, recalling a friendship that stretched back to the 1920s. Together they then headed to Egypt to meet with King Farouk, who was scheduled to receive both Churchill and Roosevelt as the two world leaders were returning from the Yalta Conference, held on 4–11 February 1945. Quwatli had tried inviting the 'Big Three' to Syria, reasoning that if they had come so close to region and met in Tehran in November 1943, then they might as well come to Damascus. It was a far stretch, but he actually sent an invitation letter to his American, British and Soviet counterparts through their delegates in Damascus. Roosevelt and Churchill didn't even bother to respond but Stalin did, politely saying that for security reasons, he could not come to Syria.⁵⁶

By then the Third Reich was beginning to collapse, and the 'Big Three' were certain that victory was just around the corner. Indeed, Hitler's suicide came only two months later, on 30 April. King Farouk and King ʿAbdul-ʿAziz arranged for a meeting in Cairo between Quwatli, Roosevelt and Churchill. No Syrian leader had ever met a US president before, with the exception of King Faisal, who had conferred with Woodrow Wilson in Paris back in 1919. He was not Syrian, however. Quwatli was very optimistic about the Syrian-British-American summit, hopeful that if the right buttons were pushed, Churchill and Roosevelt would apply enough pressure on the French to leave Syria. He also wanted Syria to be included on the list of invitations that were being made to the soon-to-be established United Nations, scheduled for San Francisco in April 1945. Syria needed to be there, at any cost, he ascertained, in order to present its claim to the international community. Countries that had contributed far less significantly to the Allied war effort had already been invited to the UN. Quwatli felt that it was unfair for Syria, which paid the price of Franco-British battles on its own territory, to be absent from the international convention. Only Roosevelt, he believed, could talk the French into lifting their veto over Syria's attendance, and only that would test how serious the Allies truly were about Syrian independence.⁵⁷ De Gaulle was insisting that before any of that happened, he needed a treaty with Damascus to guarantee French military, political and economic rights in post-mandate Syria.

The Syrian-British-American summit never happened because of Roosevelt's deteriorating health. After a historic meeting with the Saudi king, laying the foundations for future Saudi-American relations, Roosevelt was rushed back to Washington and died less than two months later on 12 April 1945, two weeks before Hitler. Quwatli did meet with Churchill on 17 February 1945, in a much-publicized Cairo summit attended by King Farouk, King ʿAbdul-ʿAziz and Haile Selassie, the emperor of Ethiopia. Churchill showed up in military fatigues with his landmark cigar and bulldog face, trying to talk the Syrian leader into signing a treaty with France before independence was put on the table. There are no minutes of the meeting in British and Syrian archives, and what was gathered about it comes from the recorded memoirs of the journalist Nasuh Babil, and then from Quwatli's bureau chief ʿAbdullah al-Khani, who heard it directly from the president in the late 1940s.

Quwatli started off saying: 'France is an alien within this region and a thorn in our backside. How do you expect us to side sign a treaty with the French?' Raising his voice, Churchill responded:

> You *must* reach a compromise with France at any cost; do *you* understand? I am warning Syria specifically that her negative and radical policies during these difficult times will not be tolerated. The entire world is threatened with destruction and entire populations are facing death and extinction. Many things have changed. What we could tolerate in the past, we will not tolerate today. We are facing a terrible world war and must do all that is possible to attain victory.[58]

Quwatli then pointed towards the Saudi king and said,

> This man ʿAbdul-ʿAziz is the dearest person to me on the face of this earth. I swear that if he were to force me to sign a treaty with France then I will fight him. Yes, I will fight him. If ʿAbdul-ʿAziz asked for my eyes I would offer them with no hesitation, yet if he were to ask what you are asking now, I will declare war and fight him.

Pointing a finger to the Nile, he added, 'We will not sign a treaty with France even if the waters of the Nile turn red! We are willing to spill enough blood to turn clear waters red Mr. Churchill.'[59]

Steaming at Quwatli's remark, the British prime minister stormed towards Quwatli and shouted: 'Are you threatening me? Don't you threaten me! Do you know who I am? I am Commander-in-Chief of the Allied forces. I will not let anyone in this world threaten or intimidate me.'[60] Churchill was amazed at Quwatli's audacity. Here was the strongest man in the world, on the verge of defeating Nazi Germany, coming to blows with the leader of a very small country, still occupied by France.

Quwatli tried calming him, saying,

> No Mr. Churchill, I am not threatening you. Trust me, I do know who you are, and this is why I am unable to challenge or threaten you. But if I should give what you ask of me, I would be signing my own execution warrant. My people will never forgive me. The Syrian people have sacrificed their youth, wealth, and property for the sake of freedom. They have fought France for a quarter of a

century. They never gave in - not for one single day. All they are asking the Allied powers to do is add them to the list of people who are privileged to live in this new world order that you are creating. Syria deserves the respect of all the world leaders, for she preaches the doctrines that this war was launched for in the first place.[61]

When the two men met the next day, Churchill was in a calmer mood and agreed that in return for supporting the Allied war effort, no treaty would be imposed on Syria.

Back in Damascus, Quwatli addressed the Syrian Parliament to brief its members on his meeting with Churchill. He spoke with a loud booming voice, projected powerfully like never before. From the speaker's pulpit, he declared war on Nazi Germany and Fascist Italy.[62] He was telling the world that Syria was fully and publicly now on the side of the Allies. Churchill had successfully swayed Syria from becoming a Nazi satellite. Quwatli's declaration was purely symbolic, however, since Syria had no army to fight with. It nevertheless helped advance Syria's application to join the UN, which is what mattered to the president. That evening US envoy George Wadsworth called on Quwatli at the Presidential Palace, carrying an official invitation to the UN conference in San Francisco.[63] On 12 April 1945, Fares al-Khoury headed to the United Nations.

Armageddon in Damascus

General de Gaulle was very mad at seeing Fares al-Khoury at the UN, speaking his mind, in impeccable English, on the French occupation of Syria. Re-enforcements were shipped to the Levant from North Africa, with the aim of muscling its leaders into signing a treaty with France, cementing the mandate and outdoing both London and Washington. Anthony Eden instructed his ambassador to Paris, Sir Duff Cooper, to ask de Gaulle for an explanation for the surge in troops. 'I don't understand why Great Britain should be concerned', replied the French leader. Anti-French demonstrations, particularly in Damascus, had become a daily routine. Young people filled the streets demanding evacuation of the French and the creation of a national army. French troops beat them with blackjacks and rifle butts. Warplanes were flying low over the city, hovering above mosques during prayer. Machine guns were permanently stationed on rooftops of French buildings. The US minister George Wadsworth wrote to the State Department: 'I am practically certain that there will be a showdown this weekend, unless some way or another, we are able to hold back the French.'[64]

At approximately 6.00 pm on 29 May 1945, French soldiers facing the Syrian Parliament on 'Abed Street lowered the Syrian flag and hoisted the French Flag instead. They then ordered the Syrian guards on duty to salute. The hot-tempered young Syrians, all in their twenties, refused to comply. The French responded with live ammunition, killing them all. Their blood gushed down the staircase of the parliament building and was splattered on the walls of its main entrance. Inside, civil servants tried sealing the main doors with couches, desks and chairs. Senegalese troops forced their way through, with orders to arrest acting premier Jamil Mardam Bey and Sa'adallah al-Jabiri, who had just been appointed speaker. Jabiri had already exited the building through its back door, driving towards the Orient Palace Hotel facing the Hejaz Station, where he usually resided when in Damascus. The French were bent on bringing down the Quwatli team by force. Once through with Jabiri and Mardam Bey, they were planning to arrest – or kill – the Syrian president.

When the Senegalese troops failed to find Jabiri, they set his office ablaze, confiscated documents and stole his parliamentary seal. The building was then bombed with cannon fire as soldiers smashed its mosaic walls and ripped open its furniture with their bayonets. They then headed for the Grand Serail, where Jamil Mardam Bey was speaking to reporters from VOA and BBC. French troops surrounded the building, cut off its electricity and shelled it from the skies. The city was left in complete blackout. Panicking, he tried telephoning President Quwatli, but the French had also cut telephone lines throughout the capital, and sealed Syria's borders with Jordan, Iraq and Lebanon. The entire cabinet was trapped until night crept upon the burning city. Like bandits, Mardam Bey and his ministers escaped through the fire exits of the Grand Serail, running down the narrow Rue Rami in Marjeh Square. Desperately, they began knocking on the doors of anyone brave enough to offer them sanctuary for the night. They eventually found their way to the home of former premier Khaled al-'Azm in Souq Sarouja. At midnight, Mardam Bey headed to the president's home in Bustan al-Ra'is, not far from Rue Nazem Pasha. Mardam Bey walked in to find a British diplomat by Quwatli's bedside. The president was surrounded by his mother, wife and children. Quwatli was in a nervous fit, screaming at the British official, 'Where is the big army that defeated Hitler?'[65] He was coughing heavily and gasping for breath. It was not a pleasant sight. The British visitor was shocked to see sight of Mardam Bey. 'We thought you were dead', he said to him.[66] He then offered Quwatli and Mardam Bey a safe exit from Damascus, until a ceasefire goes into effect. The offer was flatly rejected by the president, who rose from his bed and asked in bewilderment, extending his ear for emphasis: 'Did I hear correctly? Are you saying this to me? Shukri al-Quwatli is not one to leave Syria. The only place I am going is to the gates of Parliament, where I will die with the brave soldiers who were killed there today.'[67] From the window, he could see the flames eating large parts of his city. It was a soul-shaking moment for Shukri al-Quwatli. Damascus was on fire.[68]

Far from surrendering to the French, Quwatli pledged to arrest Oliva-Roget, de Gaulle's military commander in Damascus, and General Beynet. 'We will trial these monsters as war criminals', he promised.[69] Any Syrian on French payroll ought to resign immediately, ordered Quwatli, or stand trial for high treason.[70] Beynet had just remarked to foreign diplomats meeting him in Beirut: 'The situation in Damascus is not tragic. The abscess of Damascus has to be laced! Now that the barrel had been breached, wine must be drunk!'[71] Quwatli and Mardam

Bey spent the night writing letters of protest to US and British officials. They addressed every American listed in the directory of the Syrian presidential palace from White House officials to congressmen and State Department officials. At dawn they sent out foot messengers to Riyadh, Cairo and Amman to break news of the onslaught. The Damascus Post Office had been forcefully closed by the French, and telephones had been cut off.[72]

Seventy per cent of all officers and 40 per cent of soldiers in the French-created Levant Army deserted their posts and took up arms with the Syrian resistance.[73] Sultan al-Atrash called on his followers in the Druze Mountain to take up arms, promising another revolt like that of 1925. In Hama, two French warplanes were downed, and the commander of a French unit was ambushed and killed.[74] In Houran, French troops were rounded up and disarmed – their weapons distributed to young Syrian volunteers. British forces finally arrived in Damascus on 1 June 1945, immediately enforcing a ceasefire. Their commander cabled London saying: 'The city has been subjected to fire and much looting by the Senegalese during the morning. HM Minister has in no way exaggerated the damage done to the city. The scene is one of wanton destruction.'[75] The British advised that the two French generals, Beynet and Oliva-Roget, are evacuated immediately, stressing that in light of Quwatli's orders to have them arrested, nobody could guarantee their safety any longer. Under British pressure, French troops began their long journey back home, after an overstayed welcome that lasted for twenty-six long years. The French mandate was finished.

By the end of August, the Quwatli government had taken over military headquarters, all government buildings, military bases, the air force building, and also Arwad Island and the citadels of Damascus and Aleppo. President Quwatli declared 1 August as Army Day, registering it as an official holiday.[76] The armed forces were placed under the direct authority of the president of who would also serve as its commander-in-chief. The armed forces were placed under the direct authority of the president who would also serve as its commander-in-chief from hereon. The last French troops left Damascus on 7 April 1946. Over the next three days, the British handed over their barracks in Zabadani, al-Nabk, Dimas and Wadi al-Ajam to representatives of the Quwatli government. The French surrendered 10,000 rifles to the Syrians, with 100 bullets per rifle, along with 156 cannons, and 42 tanks.[77] By 15 April 1946, Syria was French-free. Two days later, on 17 April, the country celebrated its first Independence Day.

The day after the mandate was a new dawn for Syria. Quwatli realized that before embarking on any serious state-building, he needed a strong and stable Syrian currency. Before establishing a free press, he needed functioning state institutions and social welfare. He was also aware of the necessity of effective schools, free medication and a modern tax system. More than a balanced parliament, he needed fair and fearless judges in Syrian courts. Quwatli also had to forge a national identity, as most Syrians remained loyal to their sect, tribe, family and ethnicity, rather than to the young Republic. People would have a hard time adopting to a free Syria. They had little appreciation for the state institutions that the president wanted to introduce, or to the ones that he had inherited from the French. In order to centralize and empower different branches of government, Quwatli had to first penetrate and then dilute the authority of community leaders, tribal sheikhs and religious figures. Some of these men, however, were untouchable. They had fought both the Ottomans and the French, helping the National Bloc come to power twice, in 1936 and 1943. Limiting their influence would not be easy.

Quwatli's nationalist credentials were seemingly not enough to shield him from a small yet growing opposition that was beginning to take form in Aleppo. The fact that he had ejected the French without subjugating Syria to a colonial treaty meant little to his opponents, who criticized almost everything about his administration. Months into the independence era, Quwatli's supporters began toying with the idea of re-electing him president, in violation of the 1928 Constitution, which limited a presidential term to four years only. Hama MP Akram al-Hawrani, an exceptionally loud critic of the president, explained:

> Re-electing Quwatli would be catastrophic both for him and for Syria. If he showed no interest in re-election, I am sure the people will call on him again to become president. Shukri al-Quwatli outside the Presidential Palace would be much stronger than if he were at the presidency, with an embarrassing constitutional amendment to his record.[78]

During the parliamentary elections held in July 1947, Quwatli's allies in the National Party (successor of the National Bloc) won only 24 out of 127 seats. An impressive fifty seats went to the independents, while fifty-three went to a variety of opposition figures, led by the Democratic Bloc, a predecessor of the People's Party of Aleppo. The constitution was amended to allow for a second term, and when Quwatli marched up to the speaker's podium to deliver his inauguration address, a handful of MPs walked out, headed by Nazem al-Qudsi and Rushdi al-Kikhiya.

The road to Palestine

When attending Syria's first Independence Day celebrations in 1946, Palestinian nationalist Akram Zueiter warned the president of Syria: 'You don't have the right to consider yourself free from foreign control or independent and sovereign when southern Syria remains under a lurking occupation.'[79] Quwatli promised never to rest until 'southern Syria' is liberated, in reference to Palestine. This was not political jargon; Quwatli really meant it. Palestine, as far as he and his generation were concerned, was still a part of greater Syria, as were Jordan and Lebanon. Unlike future Arab leaders, who used and abused the Palestinian cause, Quwatli had a deep-rooted ideological commitment to the Palestinians. In May 1946, the president headed to Inshas, Egypt, for the first official Arab Summit. It was a significant photo-op for Arab leaders, dedicated entirely to the Palestinian Cause. The Arab leaders agreed that 'Palestine must remain Arab'.[80] Zionism, they added, was a threat not only to Palestine but to other Arab states as well, and to all the people of Islam.[81]

One month later, the Arab League held a meeting in the summer resort of Bloudan, near Damascus. It was co-chaired by Sa'adallah al-Jabiri and ʿAbdul Rahman Azzam Pasha, the secretary-general of the League, and an old friend of Quwatli, who, in 1925, had introduced him to Sa'ad Zaghloul. They pledged to support the Palestinian resistance with arms, money and political cover. Quwatli instructed the Syrian press to launch a massive campaign against the Zionists.[82] Hours of radio broadcasts were dedicated to shedding light on the confiscation of lands, and the exponential Jewish immigration from Europe. Quwatli even ordered military drills on the Syrian-Palestinian borders. He had them filmed by a young filmmaker named Ismail Anzour, who was hired to produce audio-visual material on the army's readiness for war.[83] Some of these films were shown at movie theatres across the country. Reporters and foreign correspondents were taken to the training camp in Qatana near Damascus to cover the military preparations, and even allowed to interview soldiers and field officers.

When the partition plan for Palestine was passed, known as General Assembly Resolution 181, Quwatli instructed Fares al-Khoury to walk out of the UN building in protest. The resolution included a non-binding recommendation for a three-way partition into an Arab state and a Jewish state, with special status given to the religiously significant cities of Jerusalem and Bethlehem. The Jewish state was to receive 55 per cent of Mandatory Palestine. The UN debate was broadcasted live on radio, and Shukri al-Quwatli stayed up until the early hours of the morning to hear its resolution.[84] As the votes were counted, his face turned red in fury. It was a fatal blow to the entire Arab world, and he was aghast. Quwatli wrote to Fares al-Khoury, suggesting they take the matter to the International Court of Justice, claiming that the General Assembly was unauthorized to partition a country against the wishes of its inhabitants. This was narrowly defeated at the UN.

Fighting in Palestine began shortly after the Partition Plan was approved. In Cairo, angry demonstrations broke out, setting the British Institute in Zaghazig ablaze. In Aden, Yemen, seventy-five Jews were killed and eight were wounded by an angry mob. As young men stormed Jewish homes in Aleppo, Prime Minister Jamil Mardam Bey openly called for jihad in Palestine. The town's synagogue was torched and hundreds of Jewish families fled for their lives.[85] In Damascus, the American and Russian embassies were pelted with stones then set on fire. The British government expressed deep concern over the fate of Jews in Damascus, Baghdad and Beirut. Arab leaders came up with the idea of creating a voluntary force of Arab recruits to fight the Zionist militias in Palestine. Quwatli said that he would provide the troops with logistic and military support. A veteran Syrian officer and ranking anti-imperialist named Fawzi al-Qawuqji was chosen to lead the Arab guerrillas. His appointment was endorsed by the Arab League during the second week of December. The Saudi king, ʿAbdul-ʿAziz, had suggested the name *Jayesh Nusrat al-Islam* for the volunteer army (Army of Supporting Islam).[86] King Farouk objected, saying that there were bound to be Christians in its ranks, suggesting *Jayesh Tahrir Filastine* (Army of Liberating Palestine). Quwatli made his recommendation, *Jayesh Inqath Filastine* (Army of Deliverance of Palestine). The name caught on and was approved by the Arab League.[87]

Many young men were eager to join the Army of Deliverance. Approximately 10,000 were recruited two weeks after the Partition Plan was announced in 1947.[88] They included Syrians, Palestinians, Iraqis, Jordanians, Circassians, Kurds, Turks, Nazi Germans, who still had an axe to grind with the Jews, and some Yugoslavs.[89] By September, one training camp in Syria boasted 2,242 volunteers.[90] Two parliamentarians even abandoned the chamber to join the Army of Deliverance. One was the al-Raqqi deputy 'Abdulsalam al-Ujayli, a medical doctor and celebrated novelist, and the other was Quwatli's foe, Hama MP Akram al-Hawrani. The Army of Deliverance headquarters were set up in Damascus. Aiding Qawuqji were General Taha al-Hashemi of Iraq, Colonel 'Abdul Qader al-Jundi of Jordan and Colonel Mohammad al-Hindi of Syria, who had helped set up the Iraqi Army back in the 1920s. Qawuqji's field commanders were Palestinian nationalists Hasan Salameh and 'Abdul Qader al-Husseini. Salameh commanded units in Lodd, while Husseini was put in charge of the strategic Jerusalem area. The Army of Deliverance would coordinate directly with the Arab League Military Committee, headed by General Ismail Safwat, an Iraqi officer who was described by one British diplomat in Baghdad as 'extremely brave yet unutterably stupid!'[91]

Egypt was to pay for 42 per cent of the costs of the Army of Deliverance, Syria and Lebanon 23 per cent, Saudi Arabia 20 per cent and Iraq the remaining 15 per cent.[92] The Army of Deliverance marched into Palestine in December 1947. They were armed with light weapons, machine mortars and small stocks of shells.[93] On paper, Qawuqji commanded eight battalions, along with 9,800 rifles, and four million rounds of ammunition.[94] In the first month of fighting, 208 Arabs were killed, and 204 Jews.[95] For better or for worse, Syria found itself one step closer to war.

None of the young Arab armies had ever fought a proper war, and none of their leaders had commanded a battlefield, except for King 'Abdullah, who was a veteran of the Arab Revolt of 1916. King Farouk had received military training in London, but never took part in any active warfare and restricted his military involvement to collecting old rifles and displaying them at his Cairo palaces. Quwatli had never shot a gun in his life. Lebanese president Beshara al-Khoury and his prime minister, Riad al-Solh, were equally illiterate in military affairs. Syrian troops had been trained to soldier the country under the mandate, but they had no battlefield experience. The Arab command decided that they would officially invade Palestine the minute the British Mandate expired.

A few hours before midnight on 14–15 May 1948, Shukri al-Quwatli toured the warfront with Prime Minister Jamil Mardam Bey and Army Commander 'Abdullah 'Atfeh. He chatted with troops, drank tea with officers and performed dusk prayers at the warfront, attempting to boost morale.[96] In all of his conversations, the Syrian president made reference to Prophet Mohammad and drew parallels to 'Omar Ibn al-Khattab, the second caliph of Islam, whose name was dear to the hearts of Sunni Muslims.[97] The Syrian leader was obviously exhausted, having barely slept in over seventy-two hours. He walked slowly through the frontlines, whispering orders to his two military escorts Taleb al-Daghestani and Suhayl al-'Ashi, who scribbled them on a piece of paper. At midnight, he addressed his troops with a commanding voice that they knew only too well: 'Palestine is in your hands, my children. Go now and destroy the Zionists! God bless you.'[98]

Al Nakba breaks Syria's back

The Syrian Army stood strong at 10,000 men.[99] 'Abdul Wahab al-Hakim, a strong-willed and decorated officer, headed the First Brigade, with 2,000 troops and two infantry battalions.[100] The Second Brigade was less capable, with only two infantry battalions and armoured cars. They were equipped with old rifles left behind by the French Army. The Syrian Air Force was equally unprepared for battle, but its pilots performed with miraculous courage. Carrying the Syrian Flag, the army marched towards Afula, linking with the Iraqi army that was headed for the Mediterranean at Haifa. This move would effectively cut the newly created Jewish State in two, completely isolating the north of Palestine. They intended to take Lake Tiberias and the whole of the Sea of Galilee. On 15 May the Syrian Army attacked Kibbutz Ein-Gev on the eastern shore of Galilee. A relatively new settlement, it had been established by the Zionists in 1937, with settlers from Czechoslovakia, Germany, Austria and the Baltic countries. In 1948, it had a population of just under 500 people. Bombs were dropped on the settlement's concrete buildings, which collapsed like a house of cards. Meanwhile, the First Brigade struck the southern end of the lake in the lower Jordan Valley. They came face-to-face with Israeli soldiers in brown berets, members of the Golani Brigade that had just been created on 1 June 1948.

On the first day of war, Syrian troops crossed at al-Hamma, twelve kilometres southeast of Tiberius, shelling Israeli settlements throughout the day.[101] Located on a narrow strip of land in the Yarmouk valley, it was one of the stations on the Jezreel Valley railway, linking the Hejaz Railway to Haifa. A Syrian battalion occupied Tal al-Qasir, belonging to the Palestinian village of Samakh. They then pushed westward towards the eastern edge of Samakh, overtaking the village and declaring it liberated on 16 May. Syrian and Palestinian Flags were raised over the municipality of Samakh, as ebullient soldiers fired triumphantly into the air.[102] Fire from their 76-mm cannons and 81-mm mortars had been accurate and devastating for the Zionists.[103] Three Israelis were captured and fifty-four were killed.[104] The fall of Samakh shook the confidence of the Jewish forces, and was welcomed with grand celebrations in Damascus. The first twenty-four hours of the war were seen as a stunning success. Shukri al-Quwatli spent the night at army headquarters, closely following the news from the battlefield. Victory, he thought, was within reach.

He was wrong.

On 11 June, the first ceasefire went into effect, brokered by UN mediator Conte Folk Bernadotte. Grandson of the king of Sweden, Bernadotte was tasked with the difficult job of protecting religious sights and making sure that the ceasefire was respected by belligerents. When it expired, Israeli forces re-grouped and launched a counter-attack, driving the Syrians out of most positions gained during the early stage of the war. On 16 June, they took Nazareth. Operation Dani, led by future Prime Minister Yitzhak Rabin, aimed at occupying and depopulating the Palestinian cities of al-Lodd and Ramla. Refugees were thrown out of their homes with nothing but the clothing on their backs. Some children died on the streets because of the hunger and thirst. On 17 September, Bernadotte was shot dead by Israeli militias, commanded by another future Israeli premiere, Yitzhak Shamir.

From this point on the Israelis began to aggressively claim what was left of Palestine. On 12 October they occupied Bir al-Sabe, capital of the Negev Desert, forcing approximately 200,000 Palestinians to flee to Gaza. The bad news reached the Syrian president on the very same day as his fifty-seventh birthday. By late October, the Israelis had seized all of Galilee, which had been allocated to the Arabs by the 1947 Partition Plan. The war ended with Syria holding a narrow strip of land running the length of the Palestinian border, as well as three enclaves in the northern, central and southern regions.[105] Following the 1949 armistice, they all became de-militarized zones. In total, 6,000 Jews were killed in 1948, along with nearly 5,000 Arabs. Of that number, Egypt and Syria lost 1,000 troops each.[106] Over 400 Palestinian villages were razed to the ground, and three quarters of one million people were ordered out of their homes, some at gunpoint, while others fled in panic ahead of the advancing Israelis. Palestine as a country was wiped off the world map.

The 1948 war destroyed Shukri al-Quwatli both psychologically and politically. The respect he had enjoyed from the Syrian street began to erode, as they blamed him for defeat. Iraqi officer Taha al-Hashemi says that Quwatli would get worked into a state of 'fanatic enthusiasm', but then sink into a disheartened state of 'despondency' and 'irresolution'.[107] The war left Quwatli obsessed with where he and his country were heading; here he was, the creator of victory and independence, now leading his country into military defeat.

The 1949 coup

On 29 March 1949, President Quwatli was toppled and sent to jail by commander of the Syrian Army Colonel Husni al-Za'im. Army communiques blamed him for the defeat in Palestine. Much has been said about the 1949 coup, including charges of it being engineered by the Americans as the first overseas operation for the CIA.[108] From his prison cell, Quwatli stepped down on 11 April 1949, seemingly at the urging of Parliament Speaker Fares al-Khoury. Written on a small piece of paper his resignation letter read: 'I present to the noble people of Syria my resignation from the presidency, wishing them everlasting glory.' Za'im had it zincographed and printed in a propaganda booklet distributed free of charge by the Media Department of the Syrian Army.[109] When the resignation became public, Za'im ordered Quwatli's release. He was placed under house arrest for a few days, and then exiled first to Geneva and then to Egypt, a country that he chose and which he knew well. The Egyptian periodical *Akher Sa'a* sent a paparazzi photographer to Switzerland to take the first photos of Quwatli and his family in exile. *TIME* magazine commented on 11 April 1949: 'Most Syrians, sipping coffee in the bazaars and smoking their hubble-bubble pipes, took hardly any notice of the change in government. In their 4,000-year history they had tasted the rule of Persians, Greek, Romans, Mongols, Turks, and French. They were prepared to get used to Husni al-Za'im too.' The article went on, saying: 'tall, dignified Shukri al-Quwatli has been called the George Washington of his country'.[110]

The post-Quwatli years (1949–54) were very turbulent for Syria, as the presidency collapsed into a twisted and convoluted game of musical chairs. Husni al-Za'im spent 137 days in power, before he was toppled and killed by Colonel Sami al-Hinnawi on 14 August 1949. A democratic government was re-installed, headed by Quwatli's old friend, Hashem al-Atasi. But it too was crippled with gross intervention from the armed forces, resulting in two coups between December 1949 and November 1951. They were engineered by military strongman Adib al-Shishakli. Unable to share power with the soldiers, Atasi resigned and was replaced by a military head of state, Fawzi Selu, before Shishakli assumed the presidency in July 1953. Seven months later, he too was toppled and exiled, only to be gunned down in Brazil in 1964. Atasi returned to the presidency to complete what remained of his presidential term, which ended in September 1955.

A hero's return

At 5.00 pm on 7 August 1954, Shukri al-Quwatli's aeroplane landed at Damascus Airport. After five years in exile, he was returning home to fix what the officers had destroyed. Despite the hot weather, 5,000 people were waiting at the runway, waving flags and pictures of their former president.[111] Quwatli's heart began to pound fast. It was a powerful and emotional moment. Although shorter than his 1920 exile, it felt as though an entire lifetime had passed since he was last in Syria. The sight of so many well-wishers brought a tear to his eye and an empty feeling in his stomach. 'Welcome back to Damascus', said the pilot, saluting the president. Khaled Shatila, secretary-general of the Presidential Palace, was the first to come onboard, introducing himself: 'In the name of His Excellency President Hashem al-Atasi I welcome you back to your country, Mr. President.'[112] The minute Quwatli appeared on the staircase, the crowd broke into a hysteric frenzy. With one thundering voice, they began to chant, 'Shukri Bey.' Some tried to kiss his hand. Others just tried touching him, like fans coming face-to-face with their favourite rock star. Quwatli had aged and looked much older than his years. The Turkish tarboosh had now become démodé, making it easier for the masses to see the whiteness of his hair, and how tired and wrinkled his face had become. Quwatli went straight to the grave of his mother, who had died days into the Za'im coup, on 13 April 1949. Za'im had refused to grant him permission to take part in her funeral.[113] Quwatli stood next to her tombstone, weeping. She would have been very happy – and proud – to see him back in Damascus.

One year later Quwatli ran for the presidential elections on 18 August 1955, competing with his former prime minister, Khaled al-'Azm. He received a total of ninety-one votes and was sworn in on 6 September, becoming the first Syrian president to serve a third term. The first had been in 1943–8, the second cut short between 1948 and 1949. 'Abdullah al-Khani, who Quwatli had hired back in 1948, was still working at the Presidential Palace, now serving as director of protocol. He laid out the details of the inauguration ceremony, an imitation of the formalities of the French Republic. Quwatli was chauffeured from a rented home to the Presidential Palace, where President Atasi was awaiting him. The Guard of Honor was there, along with a military band playing the National Anthem. Inside, Atasi decorated him with the Umayyad Order, the highest medal of the Syrian Republic. The two men then entered a convertible and were driven to parliament on 'Abed Street. Atasi sat to the right, with Quwatli at his side. A military escort accompanied them, perched next to the driver. The speaker, Nazem al-Qudsi, awaited them at the gates of Parliament. The two men sipped on cold lemonade in the reception hall, and then walked in to a standing ovation and thundering applause. Atasi gave his farewell speech, and Quwatli took his oath on the Holy Quran.

The Suez War of 1956

On 26 July 1956, President Gamal 'Abdul Nasser took the historic decision of nationalizing the Suez Canal Company, changing – forever after – the political landscape of the Arab world. Nasser's groundbreaking speech, delivered before an enthusiastic crowd in the port city of Alexandria, was music to the ears of Shukri al-Quwatli. He hailed it as a 'great day in the history of the Arabs'. Nasser had sent a direct and very public message to his fans in Syria, saying:

> Today, compatriots, I turn towards the brothers, to you in Syria, dear Syria, sister Syria, who decided to unite with us, a union free, dignified, and grand, in order that we may together consolidate the principles of freedom, dignity, and prestige that we may build Arab nationalism and Arab unity together ...

Pro-Nasser demonstrations broke out in every city across Syria. Commerce came to a halt, and schoolchildren flooded the streets of Damascus chanting the Egyptian president's name. Quwatli telephoned his Egyptian counterpart and placed 'all of Syria's resources, both governmental and public, at the disposal of sister Egypt!'[114] They set up military camps throughout the countryside, training men and women to carry arms in Egypt's defence. Quwatli became a regular visitor to these camps, raising the morale of young Syrians, who were volunteering for service in Suez. One of them, a young naval officer named Jules Jammal, was killed when he crashed into a French warship, for which he was forever immortalized in both Syria and Egypt. Months before the Suez War, Quwatli had chaired an arms week to raise money for the Syrian Army. In total, civil society raised twenty-five million SP for the armed forces. In October 1956, the army was called into full alert, ready to enter the Suez War on the president's orders. Meanwhile, British pipelines running through the Syrian dessert were sabotaged, and the ambassadors of London and Paris were asked to leave Damascus.

The Moscow visit 1956

On 30 October 1956, Shukri al-Quwatli landed in Moscow, the first ever visit by a Syrian president to the Soviet Union. At the Kremlin, Russian hospitality was gargantuan. Quwatli had seen plenty of splendour in his life, from the palaces of Egyptian royalty to the mansions of the Damascus aristocracy, but nothing quite like this. The magnificence of the meeting rooms, with golden domes and cut-glass chandeliers, along with the dazzling banquet halls, impressed him and his team, as did the power of a state that could afford such extravagance for its rulers. Quwatli frantically appealed to Soviet leaders, shouting: 'They want to destroy Egypt! It's a conspiracy!'[115] Soviet leader Nikita Khrushchev asked him what was expected of the Soviet Union. Seated across the roundtable were KGB strategists, army officers and top officials in the Communist Party. Leaning towards them, Quwatli commanded: 'Send in the mighty Red Army that defeated Hitler!'

Marshal Georgy Zhukov was called into the meeting. A legend in the Red Army, Zhukov had fought in the Second World War, and personally overseen the conquest of Berlin. He took out a map and placed it before the Syrian leader, explaining that for his army to move into Egypt, it had to pass through Iran, Iraq, Israel and Syria. 'This, Mr. President, will ignite World War III. What do you want us to do?' Quwatli replied in his hallmark Damascene accent, letting interpreters doing the translation. 'Marshal Zhukov, are you asking me to tell you what to do? You know what you have to do.'[116]

The Moscow trip failed to end the Suez War, but it did raise red flags in the United States. Here was a Syrian president not only cosying up to countries in the eastern bloc but being received at the Kremlin. Under his tenure, not only had Syria established full diplomatic ties with the USSR and China but similar exchanges were made with Czechoslovakia and Romania.[117] Something serious had to be done about Syria, the Eisenhower administration reasoned – and quickly – before the country morphed into a full-fledged Soviet satellite state.[118] In 1956, the Americans supported an ill-fated coup to topple Quwatli, funded by the Iraqi government. Among its architects were 'Adnan al-Atasi, the son of former President Hashem al-Atasi, and Munir al-'Ajlani, the son-in-law of the late president, Taj al-Din al-Hasani. When that failed, they tried again through their mission in Damascus, which led to the mutual expulsion of the US Ambassador James Moose from Syria and Syrian Ambassador Farid Zayn al-Din from Washington, DC.[119]

The United Arab Republic

On 11 January 1958 fourteen Syrian officers drove to Damascus Airport, boarding a charter flight headed for Cairo. Carrying no passports and dressed in full military uniform, they sneaked off without informing the Syrian leadership of their plans to unite their country with Egypt. The flamboyant Syrian officers were young, all in their mid-thirties. Leading them was Army Commander General 'Afif al-Bizri, a communist. All of them were veterans of the Palestine War, whose defeat had greatly awakened their political appetite, triggering Syria's first coup in 1949. Most had participated in the coups and countercoups that rocked Syria throughout the 1950s, putting them at daggers end with the country's civilian politicians. They were hot-tempered and restless and cared little for constitutionalism. They were willing to stage yet another coup if needed, should Quwatli stand in the way of their ambitions. When one officer commented that it would have been wiser to inform the president before leaving Damascus, Bizri snapped: 'No time for that. We must hurry!' He then looked at the young men and said: 'We cannot turn back now. There are two roads ahead of you. One leads to Cairo. The other leads to Mezzeh.'[120] Bizri was referring to an infamous prison situated on a hill overlooking the Syrian capital, used to jail dissidents and failed coup engineers. They knew Mezzeh only too well, having taken turns at jailing their opponents at the notorious prison. The thought of ending up in one of its horrible cells sent shivers down their spine. Either these officers carried out the job as planned or faced a lifetime in jail.

Bizri's deputy, Amin Nafuri, was left behind in Damascus to deliver a courtesy note to President Quwatli, explaining why the officers had travelled to Cairo. It was actually more of an ultimatum, leaving the Syrian leader speechless. Quwatli had tremendous respect for age and seniority, two redlines that the young officers had just trampled with their feet. Throughout his entire life, he had dreamt of Arab unity and worked towards its materialization during his active years in the Syrian underground, first against the Ottoman Turks and then under the French. In as much as he despised the officers for acting so carelessly and arrogantly, he was also convinced that only union with Egypt would save Syria from the non-stop saga of coup d'etats. A total of nine had rocked the nation in less a decade, but only five of them had succeeded. Two of Syria's coup leaders had ended up dead, shot by their enemies. Nasser was an authoritarian leader, no doubt, yet if he came to power, Quwatli reasoned, he would put an end to officer adventurism.

The Egyptian officer who accompanied the delegation, 'Abdul Muhsen Abu al-Nour, wrote in his memoirs that he disapproved the manner in which the Syrian officers had travelled to Egypt. 'I feared that it would be wrongly assumed that a pre-set deal had been arranged between them and President Nasser, from behind the back of President Quwatli.'[121] Before take-off, 'Abu al-Nour cabled authorities in Cairo to refrain from downing the unidentified aircraft coming from Damascus.[122] The plane flew with no headlights, to prevent tracking by Israeli radars, taking a long route that lasted for six hours (although the normal journey from Damascus to Cairo took only two). They reached Almaza Air Force Base, northeast of the capital, at 6.00 am. Greeting them was General Hafez Ismail, chief-of-staff of the Joint Army Command, and General Mohammad ʿAbdul Karim, the director of military intelligence. They were informed that Nasser was unavailable for a meeting, busy hosting Indonesian President Ahmed Sukarno at Aswan in the Egyptian south.[123] They waited for three days before finally being given an audience on the night of 14–15 January 1958. Very surprisingly, nobody in Damascus tried to communicate with the young officers throughout those three days, neither the president nor his prime minister, Sabri al-ʿAsali. Their families remained at their homes, untouched.

General Bizri spoke first, proposing a complete merger with Egypt, with one president, one army and one capital, in addition to united legislative, executive and judiciary branches. After listening attentively, Nasser asked: 'Do you have the approval of your President?' The officers just looked sideways at each other, taken aback by the unexpected question. Bizri broke the silence, saying: 'We represent public opinion. We represent the army. This is what matters. The President has no choice but to accept.'[124] Nasser briskly waved his right arm; 'I am sorry. I cannot accept this. You have an elected government that decides for Syria. As far as I am concerned, you represent nobody but yourselves.'[125] So enthusiastic were the young officers that one of them, Amin al-Hafez, blurted: 'We are your servants, Mr. President. If you order me, I will bomb Damascus without hesitation!'[126] Nasser shrugged at the ghastly thought of bombing the Syrian capital in his name, poetically telling Hafez that he would sacrifice his soul for Damascus. Five years later, Amin al-Hafez would become president of Syria during the early years of Baʿath rule, ruling the very same city he had suggested bombing in 1958.

No conditions

Shukri al-Quwatli took the historic decision of legitimizing the officers, instead of punishing them. Foreign Minister Salah al-Bitar was sent to Cairo to negotiate on his behalf as an official representative of the Syrian government. Despite having plenty of time to do so, Bitar had prepared nothing for the meeting: no written agenda and no notes, only verbal instructions from the president. He travelled alone with not a single staffer from the Foreign Ministry. Nasser pointed out that although he supports the principle of Arab unity, he was uncertain of how it would play out, citing geographical distance between the two countries and gross differences in their political systems. When Nasser asked for Syria's conditions for union, Salah al-Bitar replied: 'Nothing. We have no conditions, Mr. President.' With that single phrase, Bitar gave Nasser full authority to devour Syria, politically, economically and militarily.

Unlike Bitar, however, Nasser had plenty of conditions. He wanted to do away with political parties and impose a strictly censored press. He wanted to discharge politicized officers from the Syrian Army and suspend the Syrian constitution, while dissolving its current chamber of deputies. He also wanted the union charter to be signed in Egypt, only after the entire Syrian parliament was flown to Cairo for additional legitimacy. And finally, he wanted the capital to be Cairo, rather than Damascus, although the Syrian capital was far older than that of Egypt. Salah al-Bitar nodded, saying yes to every one of those conditions.

Quwatli had first met Nasser in Cairo just weeks after the Egyptian Revolution in 1952. Young, passionate and handsome, he seemed like a breath of fresh air in the Arab world. The two men were introduced through the king of Saudi Arabia, Saud Ibn ʿAbdul-ʿAziz. Nasser developed an immediate affection for Quwatli, who was seventeen years his senior. The unorthodox relationship between the two presidents was strange, because Quwatli had been a close friend of ex-king Farouk. Nasser and his Free Officers were inspired in their own revolution by the Husni al-Zaʾim coup of 1949, which put them at odds with Shukri al-Quwatli. While Quwatli had been raised in the splendour of Damascus, hailing from a highly cultured and influential family, they had grown up in poverty in the Egyptian countryside, developing a hatred for all notability. Despite their differences, however, Quwatli and Nasser developed a sound friendship, built on mutual trust and respect. Nasser admired Quwatli's lifelong struggle against the Ottomans, French and Israel. Quwatli was one of the few regulars at King Farouk's court who remained welcome at the offices of the Free Officers. They would debate world politics, Islamic history and Arab affairs. He would spend hours with Nasser sharing anecdotes, secrets and advice on how to run a country. Quwatli introduced Nasser to Syria, a country he had only read about in history books. These sessions, which were never recorded, taught Nasser all he knew about Arab politics and contemporary affairs. Quwatli was to him both a father figure and a mentor.

In today's world, it seems rather awkward for an Arab president to voluntarily step down and hand over power to another president from a faraway country. For Quwatli, not only was it logical but it was also a national obligation to save his country from chaos and embark on the ambitious project of Arab unity.

At 6.40 am on 30 January 1958, President Quwatli got on a plane with the entire Syrian government and flew off to Cairo. Before an army of journalists, the two presidents signed the union charter at the magnificent Qasr el-Qubba in Cairo on 22 February 1958. Jamil Mardam Bey, by now retired in Egypt, was invited to witness the ceremony. As Quwatli's signature graced the union document, elsewhere, Syrian politicians were signing off the official dissolve of their political parties, at Nasser's request. The next step was bringing the Egyptian leader to Syria. Hundreds of thousands awaited their hero, carrying his heavy bullet-proof automobile through the streets of Damascus. His photos were plastered on every wall across the city and songs were sung in his praise. Even soldiers were dancing in the streets. Everybody who was somebody in Syria came out to greet him at Qasr al-Diyafa, a two-floor villa at the tip of Abu Rummaneh Street in central Damascus. Crowds camped outside Qasr al-Diyafa for three days non-stop, waiting for Nasser to address the nation. Entire families filled Abu Rummaneh Street, from toddlers to ageing men. Loudspeakers were placed at the balcony of Qasr al-Diyafa to bring Nasser's voice ringing loud and strong throughout the Syrian capital. Syrian ministers and MPs stood like soldiers behind the Egyptian president, rather disgracefully. From that balcony, he announced birth of the United Arab Republic (UAR).

If ranked in today's world, the UAR would have been the twenty-fifth largest nation on the planet; comparable in size to South Africa and twice the size of France. The Syrian Parliament met at 11.00 am and voted unanimously in favour of union. The meeting was transformed into a circus festival, very unfit for seasoned politicians and congressmen, with Damascus MP Suhayl al-Khoury screaming: 'Long live President Gamal ʿAbdul Nasser!' Deputies took turns at the podium and obsessively ranted about how glorious of a leader Nasser was.

When Nasser and Quwatli appeared on the balcony of the Diyafa Palace, palm pressed into palm, the crowd broke into hysteric frenzy. Nasser smiled and waved to the masses. Quwatli took a step back. This was no longer his show and the crowds were there not for him but for Nasser. When it was time to vote for a new president, Quwatli cast his ballot at his native Shaghour in Old Damascus, voting for Nasser, who, of course, ran for president unopposed. Nasser won the presidency with 99.25 per cent in Syria and 99.8 per cent in Egypt.[127] Quwatli just bit his lips and said nothing. He hosted Nasser at his home, and so huge were the crowds that they almost strangled the Egyptian president to death as he entered. It took the entourage two hours to walk from Quwatli's residence in Abu Rummaneh to Qasr al-Diyafa, a mere five-minute walking distance. Nasser rewarded the Syrian president with the honorific title 'First Arab Citizen,' hailing Quwatli as 'the Arab face of Syria'. Addressing his fellow Egyptians, he said:

> Today, compatriots, I will tell you of the jihad of Shukri al-Quwatli, who fought for the freedom of his country. He fought the French, was arrested by them and sentenced to death. He also fought for Arab nationalism. I congratulate Shukri al-Quwatli, who has able to attain his dream of Arab unity. Based on his principles and role model, the United Arab Republic will move forward. In your name, I address my older brother Shukri al-Quwatli, and say, we all salute you. God bless you. Arabs all over the world will remember your sacrifice. We present you with a gift, being birth of the United Arab Republic. This union is a product of your lifelong jihad.[128]

Shukri al-Quwatli spent the union years dividing his time between Beirut, Cairo and Geneva. His home base, however, remained in his native Damascus. He was a relatively quiet ex-president, refusing to say much or appear too often in public, not wanting to trespass on Nasser's fiefdom. People were turning to Shukri al-Quwatli for advice, financial assistance and leadership. Some just came to pour out their hearts, complaining that life was becoming too expensive, and that the excesses of the intelligence services were too much to bear. They had legitimate concerns and questions. The wise old man of Damascus became a magnet for journalists, politicians and army officers who flocked to his home, seeking advice on how to handle Gamal ʿAbdul Nasser. In a rapidly changing world, Shukri al-Quwatli became the only constant in Syria. He was someone whom people trusted and had known for a long, long time.

Anyone with eyes could see that the United Arab Republic was a mess, from day one. Political dissent was ruthlessly suppressed by 'Abdul Hamid Sarraj, the merciless intelligence chief who was promoted UAR minister of interior. Telephone conversations were tapped and spies were placed on street corners and in cafes, trying to pick up the slightest criticism of Nasser. Those suspected of opposition views were arrested with no warrant and thrown into prison. Nasser gave junior officers in the *mukhabarat* a free hand to arrest and torture at will. Quwatli was particularly annoyed and personally insulted by Nasser's decision to cancel all celebrations on Syria's Independence Day. April 17 had been a national holiday since 1946 and all Syrians took great pride in it. 'People have memoires and history' he would say to Nasser, 'You cannot take it away from them.' The Egyptian leader insisted that there were only two holidays in the United Arab Republic. One was 23 July, the date of the Egyptian Revolution. The second was 22 February, when the Syrian-Egyptian Union was signed. He also banned playing the Syrian National Anthem *Humat al-Diyar*, replacing it with the Egyptian *Nashid al-Huriyya*.[129]

On 28 September 1961, a coup brought down the United Arab Republic. Quwatli waited for an entire month to express his support for the young Damascene officers who had toppled Gamal 'Abdul Nasser. On that day he was in Zurich, from where he called Syria's new prime minister, Ma'amoun al-Kuzbari, to congratulate him on ridding the country of the Egyptians.[130] From Switzerland, he gave a televised address on 23 October 1961, speaking slowly yet firmly, reading from a stack of paper. He sat behind a Louis Quinze desk, with golden fittings. It was a sober occasion that required high preparation and no improvisation. It was the first and last time Syrians were to see him on TV. 'My disappointment is great and my amazement greater', he said. He described Egyptian authorities who had administered the union as 'executioners of the people' presiding over a system of '1,001 spies'. Looking straight at the camera, Quwatli wrapped up: 'You the people are responsible for determining your own future. Ranks and titles come and go but you the people are immortal! I have known you for a long time and am certain that you cannot be wrong.'[131] Quwatli was confident and tough. He had made up his mind and broken completely with Nasser. They were never to meet again.

Hours into the coup, the rebel officers began discussing who their next president would be. Despite his age (now at seventy) Shukri al-Quwatli's name was put on the table, with a suggestion to restore him to power so that he completes what remained of his constitutional term.[132] When resigning in 1958, Quwatli still had almost two years left at the Presidential Palace. Syria's old parliament would be restored, and all decrees, especially land redistribution, would be revoked and the country would act as if the UAR regime never existed. It was Quwatli's signature after all that graced the union documents of 1958, and it seemed rather strange to restore him for a fourth round at the presidency. The idea was debated briefly, and then put down by one of the putsch leaders, Haydar al-Kuzbari.[133] In December 1961, Nazem al-Qudsi was elected president. Syria's new leaders invited Quwatli to attend the sixteenth anniversary of independence, on 17 April 1962. He declined, saying that his health did not permit.

Quwatli continued to live in Syria and then decided to quietly relocate to Switzerland two months after the 8 March 1963 coup that brought the Ba'ath Party to power. He returned briefly in October 1964, only to leave again to Beirut, this time for good.¹³⁴ When Syria and Egypt were defeated in the 1967 war with Israel, Quwatli was at his home, listening to the Lebanese diva Fairuz sing the glory of Jerusalem – a city that had just been occupied by the Israeli Army, along with the West Bank, the Sinai Peninsula and the Syrian Golan Heights. Quwatli was crying, like all Arabs of his generation, lamenting the disaster that had just befallen the Arab nation. It was extremely hard for a man of his creed to see the army that he had created being crushed, for the second time in his own lifetime. Quwatli looked at his wife and said: 'Jerusalem has become a song! We tried to protect it. We tried hard. But now, it is just a song!'¹³⁵ Two weeks later, he suffered a massive stroke, as a result of anger, pain and stress, and was rushed to the American University Hospital. Quwatli objected: 'Don't take me to hospital. Take me to my bed. I want to die in my bed.'¹³⁶ As doctors rushed him into the operating room, Quwatli began slipping away. One of his daughters held him gently saying: 'You used to say you could see the moon on my face. Look at my face now. Maybe God will look at ours.' Quwatli raised his right finger, as all Muslims do before death, trying to pronounce the *shahada*: that there is only one God and Mohammad is his prophet. He just moved his lips, unable to utter the words. He died a few minutes later on 30 June 1967. Sorrow, rather than old age, had killed him.

The news of Quwatli's death ripped through the Arab world like fire. News agencies ran stories about his life and career. One British newspaper commented: 'Syria Dies.' In Damascus, a scary silence overcame the city as news of the passing of the 'First Arab Citizen'. The people of Damascus feared what the future had in store for them. Quwatli's death was a sudden reminder of how terrible their current state of affairs in the aftermath of the Six Day War. People made automatic comparisons between him and the ruling junta that had been in power since 1963. The last thing the Ba'athists needed was to have to deal with Shukri al-Quwatli during this critical juncture of their regime. Official mourning was not announced and flags were not flown at half-mast.¹³⁷ On the contrary, government officials went to work the next morning, as if nothing had happened. Quwatli's death received no more than passing mention in the two state-run Syrian dailies, *al-Ba'ath* and *al-Thawra*. When the Quwatli family asked to bury him in Damascus, according to his will, President Nur al-Din al-Atasi refused. Quwatli's funeral was bound to attract a very large crowd, and Syrian security feared it would snowball into an anti-regime demonstration. Even in death, the officers feared Quwatli.

The veto was dropped at the urging of Saudi king Faisal, an old friend of the late president. For two hours, the funeral procession was held up at the Syrian-Lebanese borders, as its route coincided with the passing of Soviet president Nikolai Podgorny, who was travelling from Syria to Lebanon.¹³⁸ The road to Damascus was lined with thousands of people with their hands open, reading *al-Fatiha*, the first sura of the Quran.¹³⁹ Grown men wept like little children. Formally representing the government of President Nur al-Din al-Atasi was his economy minister, Zuheir al-Khani, who had been head of the customs department in Homs under Quwatli.¹⁴⁰ Atasi could attend in person, but he chose not to. As thousands walked behind Quwatli's coffin, people gathered on balconies and climbed trees to watch the procession. 'Shukri Bey, we miss you', they shouted. Others were chanting: 'Welcome back Shukri Bey!¹⁴¹' Never before in living memory had Damascus seen such a funeral. More than 100,000 were attending.¹⁴²

At the Hejaz Station, Quwatli's mourners broke open the doors of the ambulance and pulled out the coffin, wrapped with the Syrian Flag. Shining with the tri-colours, it glided over a sea of hands, floating on fingertips. Most of the young men were too young to remember Quwatli's struggle against the French. Some were born during his first presidency. All of them, however, knew what he represented. He was taken to the Umayyad Mosque, where people prayed three times for Quwatli, and then was laid to rest at the Bab al-Saghir cemetery in Old Damascus. He was buried near the neighbourhood into which he was born seventy-five years ago.

Figure 12 Shukri al-Quwatli.

NOTES

Chapter 1

1. These palaces are: The Nazem Pasha and Mustapha Pasha al-ʿAbed palaces in al-al-Muhajireen (founded in 1905 and 1910 respectively), the Diyafa Palace in Abu Rummaneh (founded by President Adib al-Shishakli in 1953), the al-Rawda Palace in the al-Rawda neighbourhood (founded by President Hafez al-Assad in 1978), the People's Palace on Jabal ʿAntar (1991) and Tishreen Palace, which were also established by Assad as a presidential guesthouse in the late 1980s.
2. For further reading, see Shimon Shamir, 'Asʾad Pasha al-ʿAzm and Ottoman Rule in Damascus 1743–58,' *Bulletin of the School of Oriental Studies*, University of London 1963, volume 26: 1, 1–28, and Michel Ecochard, 'Le Palais Azem de Damas,' *Gazette des Beaux-Arts* (Paris 1935), 1–14.
3. Sami Moubayed *Khidewi Souriyya: Dirasa ʿan Marhalet Midhat Pasha fi Dimashq* (Damascus: Bustan Hisham 2022), 15–21.
4. In August 1831, Ottoman governor Salim Pasha had triggered an uprising in Damascus by trying to force a tax on Muslim real estate. He retaliated by bombing the city, before surrendering to the rebels after running out of ammunition. He was taken to a home in al-ʿAsrunieh, near the Grand Umayyad, where he was summarily executed by the locals. For more see, Mohammad Kheir Safi, *Thawrat al-Dimashqiyyen ʿam 1831*, Al-Azhar Magazine (Gaza), volume 14, issue #2, 78–9. Three decades later a third Ottoman governor Ahmad ʿIzzat Pasha was relieved of his duties by the sultan for encouraging, or failing to end sectarian strife in Damascus, in reference to the bloody events of July 1860 when a Muslim mob ransacked the Christian neighbourhood of Bab Touma, massacring 5,000 Christians. He was fired, court martialled and executed by an Ottoman firing squad. See Sami Moubayed, *Nakbat Nasara al-Sham: Ahl Dhimmet al-Saltana wa Intifadat 1860* (Beirut: Riad El Rayyes 2020).
5. Qutayba al-Shihabi, *Dimashq: Tareekh wa Souuwar* (Damascus: Al-Nouri, 1990), 398.
6. ʿAzza Aqbiq, *Aʾlam fi Dhakirat al-Sham* (Damascus 2020), 17–19.
7. Ahmad al-Ibish and Qutayba al-Shihabi, *Maʿalim Dimashq al-Tarikhiyya* (Damascus: Ministry of Culture 1996), 504.
8. Ibid.
9. Author interview with ʿAbdullah al-Khani, secretary-general of the Syrian Presidency (Damascus, 19–22 November 2019).
10. ʿAli al-Tantawi, *Qisas min al-Hayat* (Jeddah: Dar al-Manara 1990), 103.
11. Ibid.
12. ʿAli al-Tantawi, *Dimashq; Souwar min Jamaluha wa ʿIbar min Nidaluha* (Damascus 1959), 157.
13. Yusuf al-Hakim, *Souriyya wa al-ʿAhd al-ʿOthmani* (Beirut: Dar Annahar 1966), 56.
14. Bader al-Din al-Shallah, *Al-Masira al-Tijariyya* (Damascus 1992) 342.
15. Ibid.

16 Ibid.
17 Ibid.
18 Ibish and Shihabi, *Ma'alim Dimashq*, 525–6.
19 Khani (19–22 November 2019).
20 For more on Nazem Pasha's three tenures, see 'Amr al-Mallah, *Nazem Pasha: Al-Wali al-Othmani al-Akthar Shuhra fi Dimashq* (*Al-Quds Al-Arabi*, 21 May 2022).
21 Khani (19–22 November 2019).
22 Ibid.
23 Ibid.
24 Ibid.
25 Ibid.
26 Ibid.
27 Ibid.
28 Shallah, *Al-Masira al-Tijariyya*, 342–3.
29 Khani (19–22 November 2019).
30 Shihabi, *Dimashq*, 397.
31 Colette Khoury, *Awraq Fares al-Khoury*, volume I (Damascus 1989) 152.
32 Khani (19–22 November 2019).
33 Ibid.
34 Leila Hudson, *Transforming Damascus: Space and Modernity in an Islamic City* (London: IB Tauris 2008), 111.
35 Author interview with Syrian novelist Colette Khoury, granddaughter of Prime Minister Fares al-Khoury (Damascus, 1 August 2022).
36 Shihabi, *Dimashq*, 403.

Chapter 2

1 Salim Hatum (1928–1967) was a Syrian Army officer who helped the Ba'ath Party seize power in 1963. He played an important role in the second Ba'ath coup of 23 February 1966 and tried to launch a third coup in September 1966, which was foiled by Defense Minister Hafez al-Assad. He fled to Jordan, returning in the aftermath of the 1967 war with Israel, where he was arrested and shot.
2 Interview with Emir Fateh El Djezairi, son of Emir Sa'id (Damascus, 11 March 2015).
3 Thomas Edward Lawrence (1888–1935), a British army general who helped defeat the Ottoman Empire in the First World War, fighting alongside Sharif Hussein and his sons. A 1962 film was made about his wartime activities called *Lawrence of Arabia*, starring Peter O'Toole and Omar Sharif.
4 T.E. Lawrence, *Seven Pillars of Wisdom: A Triumph* (London: Jonathan Cape 1935), 573.
5 Malcolm B. Russell, *The First Modern Arab State: Syria under Faisal I* (Minneapolis: Bibliotheca Islamica 1985), 212.
6 Emir Fateh El Djezairi (11 March 2015).
7 Ibid.
8 Nasuh Babil, *Sahafa wa Siyasa: Souriyya fi al-Qarn al-'Ishreen* (London: Riad El Rayyes 1987), 16.
9 Lawrence, *Seven Pillars of Wisdom*, 684.

10 For more on Emir ʾAbdelkader El Djezairi's pre-Damascus career, see Charles Henry Churchill, *The Life of Abdel Kader: Ex-Sultan of the Arabs of Algeria* (London: Chapman & Hall 1867) and a more contemporary biography by John W. Kiser, *Commander of the Faithful: The Life and Times of Emir Abd al-Kader* (Rhinebeck NY: Monkfish Book Publishing 2010).
11 Emir Mohammad Pasha El Djezairi, *Tihfet al-Zaʾir fi Maʾather al-Emir ʾAbdelkader wa Akhbar al-Jazaʾir* (Cairo 1903), 618.
12 Brigide Keenan, *Damascus: Hidden Treasures of the Old City* (London: Thames & Hudson 2000), 162.
13 Ibid.
14 For further reading on the 1860 events in Damascus, see Sami Moubayed, *Nakbet Nasara al-Sham: Ahl Dhimmet al-Saltana wa Intifadet 1860* (Beirut: Riad El Rayyes 2020) and Leila Tarazi Fawaz, *An Occasion for War: Civil Conflict in Lebanon and Damascus in 1860* (California: University of California Press 1994).
15 Keenan, *Damascus*, 162.
16 Interview with Emir Jaʾafar El Djezairi, great-grandson of Emir ʾAbdelkader (Damascus, 5 May 2015).
17 Lawrence, *Seven Pillars of Wisdom*, 676.
18 Ibid., 677.
19 Fakhri al-Barudi, *Mudhakarat*, volume I (Beirut: Dar al-Hayat 1951), 112–13.
20 Qadri al-Qalaji, *Al-Thawra al-ʾArabiyya al-Kubra* (Beirut: Shariket al-Matbuʾat 1998), 256.
21 Elizabeth Thompson, *Colonial Citizens: Republican Rights, Paternal Privilege and Gender in French Syria and Lebanon* (New York: Columbia University Press 2000), 22.
22 Ibid.
23 Ibid.
24 TNA, 371/3384 (Gilbert Clayton to FO, #127, 15 October 1918).
25 Subhi al-ʾOmari, *Lawrence: Al-Haqiqa wa al-Ukdhuba* (London: Riad El-Rayyes 1991), 188–190.
26 Thompson, *Colonial Citizens*, 22.
27 Ibid.
28 Ibid.
29 Sharif Hussein (1854–1931), the thirty-seventh descendant of the Prophet Mohammad, he served as emir of Mecca from 1908 until launching the Great Revolt in 1916. He led an armed insurgency against the Ottomans, declaring himself king of the Hejaz until 1924, when he was forced to abdicate in favour of his eldest son, Emir ʾAli. Sharif Hussein's kingdom was toppled by the House of Saud and he was exiled to British-controlled Cyprus, moving to Amman after suffering a stroke in 1930. He died one year later and was buried in Jerusalem.
30 Khaled al-ʾAzm, *Mudhakarat*, volume I (Beirut: Al-Dar al-Mutahida 1972), 1–2.
31 Emir Saʾid El Djezairi, *Mudhakarati an al-Qadaya al-Arabiyya wa al-ʾAlam al-Islami* (Algiers: Dar al-Yakza al-ʾArabiyya 1968), 128.
32 Emir Fateh El Djezairi (Damascus, 11 March 2015).
33 Djezairi, *Mudhakarati*, 128.
34 Ibid., 129.
35 Ibid.
36 Ibid.
37 Emir Fateh El Djezairi (Damascus, 11 March 2015).

38 Ibid.
39 Ibid.
40 Ibid.
41 Djezairi, *Mudhakarati*, 100–3.
42 Russell, *The First Modern Arab State*, 10.
43 Yusuf al-Hakim, *Souriyya wa al-Hukum al-Faisali* (Beirut: Dar Annahar 1966), 38.
44 Ahmad Qadri, *Mudhakarati an al-Thawra al-ʿArabiyya al-Kubra* (Damascus: Ibn Zaydun 1956), 73.
45 Ibid.
46 Ahmad Qodama, *Maʿalim wa Aʿlam fi Bilad al-ʿArab* (Damascus 1965), 243.
47 For more on Rida al-Rikabi, see Sami Moubayed, *Steel & Silk: Men and Women Who Shaped Syria* (Seattle: Cune Press 2005), 319–20, and Ibrahim al-Kaylani's *ʿAbqariyyat Shamiyya fi al-Hukum wa al-Siyasa wa al-Idara* (Damascus 1946), 40–8.
48 Qodama, *Maʿalim wa Aʿlam*, 93.
49 Khoury, *Awraq Fares al-Khoury*, volume I, 215.
50 ʿAli Sultan, *Tareekh Souriyya: Hukum Faisal Ibn al-Hussein* (Damascus: Dar Tlass 1996), 21.
51 Djezairi, *Mudhakarati*, 130.
52 Khayriyah Qasmiyyah, *Al-Hukuma al-ʿArabiyya fi Dimashq* (Beirut: Al-Mouassa al-ʿArabiyya lil Dirasat 1982), 48.
53 Ibid.
54 Emir Fateh El Djezairi (11 March 2015).
55 *al-Muqtabas* (27 September 1918).
56 Khoury, *Awraq Fares al-Khoury*, volume I, 19.
57 *al-Muqtabas* (27 September 1918).
58 Lawrence, *Seven Pillars of Wisdom*, 675.
59 Ibid.
60 Emir Fateh El Djezairi (11 March 2015).
61 Ibid.
62 Djezairi, *Mudhakarati*, 134.
63 Ibid.
64 Qutayba al-Shihabi, *Sahet al-Marjeh wa Mujawaratuha fi Dimashq: Bayn al-Ams wa al-Yawm* (Damascus: Secretariat of the Damascus Capital of Arab Culture 2008 Celebrations 2008), 123.
65 Author interview with George Lathqani, Syrian physician and officer in the Ottoman Army during the First World War (Damascus, 1 June 1996).
66 Djezairi, *Mudhakarati*, 188.
67 Khayriyah Qasmiyyah, *Al-Raʿel al-ʿArabi al-Awwal: Hayat wa Awraq Nabih wa ʿAdel al-ʿAzma* (London: Riad El Rayyes 1991), 21.
68 The Museum of Historical Archives, 'The Arab Government 1918' (Damascus).
69 Author interview with Munir al-ʿAjlani (Beirut, 12–15 September 1999).
70 ʿAbdul Ghani al-ʿOtari, *Hadeeth al-ʿAbqariyyat* (Damascus: Dar al-Bashair 2000), 86.
71 Qodama, *Maʿalim wa Aʿlam*, 200.
72 George Fares, *Man Hum fi al-Alam al-ʿArabi* (Damascus 1957), 609–610.
73 Elie Kedourie. 'The Capture of Damascus, 1 October 1918,' *Middle Eastern Studies*, volume 1:1 (October 1964), 69.
74 Lawrence, *Seven Pillars of Wisdom*, 665.
75 Djezairi, *Mudhakarati*, 137.
76 Ibid.

77   Ibid.
78   Ibid.
79   Emir Fateh El Djezairi (11 March 2015).
80   Ibid.
81   Mohammad Jamil Bayhum, *Souriyya wa Lubnan 1918–1922* (Beirut: Dar al-Tali'a 1968), 52.
82   Ibid.
83   Djezairi, *Mudhakarati*, 139.
84   Adham al-Jundi, *Tareekh al-Thawrat al-Souriyya fi 'Ahd al-Intidab al-Faransi* (Damascus 1960), 191.
85   Djezairi, *Mudhakarati*, 139.
86   Lawrence, *Seven Pillars of Wisdom*, 675.
87   Djezairi, *Mudhakarati*, 140.
88   Bayhum, *Souriyya wa Lubnan*, 54.
89   Ibid.
90   Djezairi, *Mudhakarati*, 140.
91   Ibid.
92   Ibid.
93   Ibid.
94   Ibid.
95   Djezairi, *Mudhakarati*, 155.
96   Bayhum, *Souriyya wa Lubnan*, 57–62.
97   Ibid., 94.
98   Ibid., 62.
99   Emir Fateh El Djezairi (11 March 2015).
100 Ibid.
101 Djezairi, *Mudhakarati*, 233–9.
102 Ibid.
103 Philip S. Khoury, *Syria and the French Mandate: The Politics of Arab Nationalism 1920–1945* (New Jersey: Princeton University Press 1987), 338.
104 Ibid., 337.
105 Yusuf al-Hakim, *Souriyya wa al-Intidab al-Faransi* (Beirut: Dar Annahar, 1982), 202.
106 Khoury, *Syria and the French Mandate*, 338.
107 For more on the throne issue, see A.M. Gomaa, 'The Syrian Throne: Hashemite Ambitions and Anglo-French Rivalry 1930–1935', in Uriel Dann (ed), *The Great Powers in the Middle East 1919–1939* (Colorado: Lynne Rienner Publishers 1988), 183–97.
108 Emir Fateh El Djezairi (11 March 2015).
109 Ibid.
110 Ibid.
111 Emir Ja'afar El Djezairi (Damascus, 5 May 2015).
112 Mohammad Radwan al-Atasi, *Hashem al-Atasi: Hayatuhu wa 'Asruh* (Damascus 2005), 148.
113 Emir Ja'afar El Djezairi (5 May 2015).
114 Ibid.
115 Ibid.
116 Ibid.
117 Sami Moubayed, *Tareekh Dimashq al-Mansi: Arba' Hikayat 1916–1936* (Beirut: Riad El Rayyes 2015), 60.

Chapter 3

1 ʿAzm, *Mudhakarat*, volume I, 107.
2 Ibid.
3 Ibid.
4 Rustom Haydar, *Mudhakarat Rustom Haydar* (Beirut: Al-Dar al-ʿArabiyya Lil Mawsu'at 1988), 187.
5 ʿAbdul Ghani al-ʿOtari, *A'lam wa Mubdi'oun* (Damascus: Dar al-Bashair 1999), 26.
6 ʿOtari, *Hadeeth al-ʿAbqariyat*, 257.
7 ʿAli ʿAllawi, *Faisal I of Iraq* (New Heaven: Yale University Press 2014), 15.
8 Queen Huzaima Bint Nasser (1884–1935), an Arabian princess from Mecca, she married Emir Faisal in 1904 and bore his only son and heir, Ghazi, who became king of Iraq upon his father's death in 1933.
9 Alec Kirkibride, *A Crackle of Thorns: Experiences in the Middle East* (London: John Murray 1956), 18.
10 ʿAli al-Tantawi, *Dhikrayat*, volume I (Riyadh: Dar al-Manara 1985), 80.
11 ʿAllawi, *Faisal I*, 175.
12 Ibid., 20.
13 Yusuf al-ʿAzma (1884–1920), a native of al-Shaghour in Old Damascus, he studied at the military schools of Istanbul and Berlin before he was appointed first military attaché to Cairo, then as division commander in the Balkans, and finally as military escort to Ottoman war minister Enver Pasha.
14 ʿAbdul Latif Tibawi, *A Modern History of Syria, Including Lebanon and Palestine* (London: Palgrave Macmillan 1970), 77.
15 Ibid.
16 Mohammad ʿAbidin Hamada and Tayseer Dhubian, *Faisal Ibn al-Hussein* (Damascus 1933), 23.
17 Saqr Abu Fakhr, *A'yan al-Sham wa I'aqat al-ʿIlmaniyya fi Souriyya* (Beirut: Al-Mou'assa al-ʿArabiyya lil Dirasat wa al-Nashr 2013), 57.
18 Fayez al-Ghusayn, *Mudhakarati ʿan al-Thawra al-ʿArabiyya*, volume I (Damascus 1956), 250.
19 Elizabeth Thompson, *How the West Stole Democracy from the Arabs: The Syrian Arab Congress of 1920 and the Destruction of Its Historic Liberal-Islamic Alliance* (New York: Atlantic Monthly Press 2020), 23.
20 Yaron Harel, *Zionism in Damascus: Ideology and Activity in the Jewish Community at the Beginning of the Twentieth Century* (London: IB Tauris 2015), 186.
21 Atasi, *Hashem al-Atasi*, 69–74.
22 Shihabi, *Dimashq*, 398.
23 Khani (19–22 November 2019).
24 Suhayl al-ʿAshi, *Fajr al-Istiqlal fi Souriyya* (Beirut: Dar al-Nafa'is 1999), 65.
25 Thompson, *How the West Stole Democracy from the Arabs*, 172.
26 Mary Shahrestan, *Al-Mo'utamar al-Souri al-ʿAam* (Beirut: Dar Amwaj 2000), 105.
27 Ibid., 175.
28 Khani (19–22 November 2019).
29 Shahrestan, *Al-Mo'utamar al-Souri al-ʿAam*, 121–32.
30 Ibid.
31 Nizar Kayyali, *Dirasa fi Tareekh Souriyya al-Siyasi al-Mouassir 1920–1950* (Damascus: Dar Tlass 1997), 38–40.

32 Munir al-Malki, *Min Maysaloun ila al-Jalaa* (Damascus: Ministry of Culture 1991), 86–7.
33 Hasan al-Hakim, *Mudhakarati: Safahat min Tareekh Souriyya al-Hadeeth 1920–1958*, volume I (Beirut: Dar al-Kitab 1965), 21.
34 Malki, *Min Maysaloun ila al-Jalaa*, 86–7.
35 Ghaleb al-ʿAyyashi. *Al-Idahat al-Siyasiyya wa Asrar al-Intidab al-Faransi fi Souriyya* (Beirut: Ashqar Ikhwan 1955), 108.
36 Malki, *Min Maysaloun ila al-Jalaa*, 21–3.
37 James Gelvin, *Divided Loyalties: Nationalism and Mass Politics in Syria at the Close of Empire* (Berkley: University of California Press 1999), 174.
38 Emir Zayd (1898–1970), the youngest son of Sharif Hussein, fought with the Hashemites during the Great Arab Revolt, becoming deputy to King Faisal in Syria. Then in Iraq, he served as envoy to Ankara and Cairo before he was appointed ambassador to London from 1946 to 1958.
39 Sa'ad Abu Diyah, *Al-Masʾa al-Nabeel: Al-Ameer Zayd wa al-Hukuma al-Wataniyya fi Dimashq* (Amman 2016), 208.
40 As'ad Dagher, *Mudhakarati ala Hamesh al-Qadiyya al-ʿArabiyya* (Doha: Arab Center for Research and Policy Studies 2020), 232.
41 Ibid., 255–6.
42 ʿAbdul Ghani al-Ustwani, *Al-ʿArab min Waraʾa al-Lahab: Mudhakarat al-Mujahid ʿAbdul Ghani al-Ustwani* (Damascus: Dar Qutayba 1986), 36.
43 Kamel al-Qassab (1860–1954), a Salafi cleric from Damascus, was exiled to the Hejaz after the downfall of King Faisal's government, working briefly with King ʿAbdul-ʿAziz as director of education in the newly formed kingdom of Saudi Arabia. He then moved to Haifa in Palestine, where he took up arms against the British in 1935, fighting alongside another Syrian resistance leader named ʿIzz al-Din al-Qassam.
44 See Sami Moubayed *Siket al-Tramway: Tareekhu al-Hadatha Mara Bi Dimashq* (Beirut: Riad El Rayyes 2022), 121, and Thompson, *How the West Stole Democracy from the Arabs*, 283.
45 Abu Diyah, *Al-Masʾa al-Nabeel*, 292.
46 Dagher, *Mudhakarati*, 210.
47 Ibid.
48 Gelvin, *Divided Loyalties*, 99.
49 Ustwani, *Al-ʿArab min Waraʾa al-Lahab*, 36.
50 Suhayla al-Rimawi *al-Hukum al-Hizbi fi Souriyya ayyam al-ʿAhd al-Faisali 1918–1920* (Amman: Dar al-Majdalawi 1997), 57.
51 Ibid.
52 Russell, *The First Modern Arab State*, 114.
53 Rashid Rida (1865–1935), a Salafi theologian and revivalist, left Syria to work with Egyptian scholar Mohammad ʿAbdo in Cairo in 1897. One year later, he founded *al-Manar*, first as a weekly then monthly publication, dedicated to Islamic discourse.
54 Qasmiyyah, *Al-Hukuma al-Arabiyya*, 202.
55 Sati al-Husari, *Yawm Maysaloun* (Beirut: Maktabat al-Kashaf 1948), 121–32.
56 Hasan Tahseen Pasha al-Faqir, *Al-Intidab al-Faransi al-Ghashem ʿala Souriyya* (Damascus 2004), 53 and ʿAyyashi, *Al-Idahat al-Siyasiyya*, 95.
57 Ihsan al-Hindi, *Maʾaraket Maysaloun* (Damascus: Ministry of Culture 1967), 143–4.
58 Mustapha Tlass *Tareekh al-Jaysh al-ʿArabi al-Souri 1901–1948*, volume I (Damascus: Ministry of Defense 2000), 362.

59 Hindi, *Ma'araket Maysaloun*, 186.
60 Babil, *Sahafa wa Siyasa*, 20.
61 Subhi al-'Omari, *Maysaloun: Nihayet 'Ahd* (London: Riad El-Rayyes 1991), 194.
62 Hakim, *Souriyya wa al-Intidab al-Faransi*, 25–6.
63 Sultan, *Tareekh Souriyya*, 329.
64 'Omari, *Maysaloun*, 194.
65 Sami Moubayed, *Bayn al-Qasrayn: Faisal al-Awal ma bayn Tammuz 1920 wa Nisan 1921* (Al-Mustaqbal al-Arabi Magazine, Issue 507, May 2021).
66 Allawi, *Faisal I*, 297.
67 Yaacoub Yusuf Koriya, *Malek Souriyya Faisal Ibn al-Hussein* (Baghdad 2001), 107.
68 Allawi, *Faisal I*, 298.
69 Ronald Storrs, *The Memoirs of Sir Ronald Storrs* (New York 1937), 456.
70 Allawi, *Faisal I*, 303.
71 Haydar, *Mudhakarat Rustom Haydar*, 715–16.
72 Ibid.
73 'Awni 'Abdul Hadi, *Mudhakarat 'Awni 'Abdul Hadi* (Beirut: Center for Arab Unity Studies 2002), 127.
74 Fayek al-Sheikh 'Ali, *Mudhakarat warithat al-'Urush* (London: Dar al-Hikma 2002), 221.
75 Itamar Rabinovich, *The View from Damascus: State, Political Community and Foreign Relations in Twentieth-Century Syria* (England: Valentine Mitchell 2008), 56.
76 TNA, 371/5485, volume 15364 (3 November 1931).
77 Ajlani (12–15 September 1999).
78 Ibid.
79 Khoury, *Syria and the French Mandate*, 338.
80 Khani (19–22 November 2019).
81 Stephan Longrigg, *Syria and Lebanon under the French Mandate* (Oxford: Oxford University Press 1953), 196.

Chapter 4

1 Quincy Wright. 'The Bombardment of Damascus', *The American Journal of International Law*, 20:2 (April 1926), 264.
2 Hakim, *Mudhakarati*, volume I, 283–4.
3 Ibid.
4 Khoury, *Syria and the French Mandate*, 498.
5 Jundi, *Tareekh al-thawrat al-Souriyya*, 70–1.
6 Kayyali, *Dirasa fi Tareekh Souriyya al-Siyasi*, 47–50.
7 Archives of the French Foreign Ministry (La Courneuve, Paris), Millerand to Gouraud, (12 June 1920), N 613–18, Série E-Levant (Syrie-Liban 1918–1940), volume 30, 67–9.
8 Hasan al-Hakim, *Al-Watha'iq al-Tarikhiyya al-Muta'liqa bil Qadiyya al-Souriyya fi al-Ahdayn al-Faisali al-'Arabi wa al-Intidab al-Faransi* (Beirut: Dar Sader 1974), 250.
9 Khoury, *Awraq Fares al-Khoury*, volume II (Damascus 1997), 235.
10 Babil, *Sahafa wa Siyasa*, 27.
11 Hakim, *Al-Watha'iq al-Tarikhiyya*, 256.
12 Fares, *Man Hum fi al-'Alam al-'Arabi*, 302.
13 Khoury, *Syria and the French Mandate*, 116.

14 E.J. Brill's, *First Encyclopedia of Islam, 1913–1936*, volume II (Leiden: Brill Press 1987), 301.
15 Hakim, *Al-Watha'iq al-Tarikhiyya,* 253.
16 *Al-Taqaddum* newspaper (11 August 1926).
17 Khoury, *Syria and the French Mandate*, 144.
18 Mohammad Fouad Al-Entabi & Najwa Othman, *Halab Fi Mi'at 'Aam min 'aam 1850 hata 1950*, volume II, (Aleppo: Ma'had al-Turath al-'Ilmi al-'Arabi 1992), 232.
19 Kamel al-Ghazzi, *Nahr al-Dahab fi Tareekh Halab*, volume III (Aleppo: Al-Matba'a al-Maroniyya 1923–1926), 747.
20 Babil, *Sahafa wa Siyasa*, 28.
21 *Al-'Asima* newspaper (20 September 1920).
22 *First Encyclopedia of Islam*, volume II, 301.
23 As'ad Korani, *Dhikrayat wa Khawater mimma Ra'yet wa Sam'et wa Fa'let* (Beirut: Riad El Rayyes 2000), 54.
24 Entabi & Othman, *Halab fi Mi'at 'Aam,* volume III, 3.
25 Korani, *Dhikrayat wa Khawater*, 55.
26 For more on minorities, see Itamar Rabinovich, 'The Compact Minorities and the Syrian State 1918–1945,' *Journal of Contemporary History*, 14:4 (1979), 693–712.
27 *First Encyclopedia of Islam*, volume II, 301.
28 See Stefan Winter, *A History of the 'Alawis: From Medieval Aleppo to the Turkish Republic* (New Jersey: Princeton University Press 2016).
29 Khani (19–22 November 2019).
30 Longrigg, *Syria and Lebanon,* 8.
31 Ibid., 125.
32 French National Archives, Official Bulletin, Arrête 319, 1 September 1920.
33 Hashem Uthman, *Tareekh al-'Alawiyeen: Waka'i wa Ahdath* (Beirut: Al-'Alami Press 1987), 61.
34 Longrigg, *Syria and Lebanon*, 125.
35 Ibid.
36 Patrick Seale, *Asad: Struggle for the Middle East* (Berkley: University of California Press 1989), 17.
37 Khoury, *Syria and the French Mandate,* 73.
38 Longrigg, *Syria and Lebanon*, 20.
39 Hakim, *Souriyya wa al-Intidab al-Faransi*, 65.
40 Khoury, *Awraq Fares al-Khoury*, volume II, 215.
41 Ibid.
42 TNA, 371/530/531, volume 9053, Damascus Consul to FO (12 January 1923).
43 Khoury, *Syria and the French Mandate*, 136.
44 Hakim, *Souriyya wa al-Intidab al-Faransi*, 56.
45 TNA, 371/6856, vol 7847, Damascus Consul to FO (26 June 1922).
46 Hakim, *Al-Watha'iq al-Tarikhiyya, 261.*
47 Jundi, *Tareekh al-Thawrat al-Souriyya,* 70–1.
48 'Adel al-Solh, *Al-Ab'ad al-Taharuriyya lada al-Nukhab al-Lubnaniyya* (Jdeidet al-Metn: Dar Sa'ir al-Mashriq 2013), 277.
49 Babil, *Sahafa wa Siyasa*, 29.
50 Solh, *Al-Ab'ad al-Taharuriyya lada al-Nukhab al-Lubnaniyya*, 277.
51 Babil, *Sahafa wa Siyasa*, 29.
52 Akram al-Hawrani, *Mudhakarat Akram al-Hawrani*, volume I (Cairo: Madbouli 2000), 109.

53 Khoury, *Awraq Fares al-Khoury*, volume II, 232.
54 Khoury, *Syria and the French Mandate*, 127.
55 TNA, 317/895, volume 10159, Aleppo Consul to FO (27 December 1923).
56 TNA, 371/6416, volume 10160, Aleppo Consul to FO (15 June 1924).
57 TNA, 371/3500, volume 9053, Smart to FO (5 April 1923).
58 Khoury, *Syria and the French Mandate*, 128.
59 TNA, 371/6416, volume 10160, Aleppo Consul to FO (15 June 1924).
60 Longrigg, *Syria and Lebanon*, 130.
61 Ni'mah Zeidan, *'Alamuna al-'Arabi: Souriyya wa Lubnan* (Beirut 1956), 596–7.
62 Korani, *Dhikrayat wa Khawater*, 92.
63 Khoury, *Awraq Fares al-Khoury*, volume II, 230.
64 Ibid.
65 Ibid., 212.
66 Ibid.
67 Anthony Clayton, *General Maxime Weygand 1867–1965* (Bloomington: Indiana University Press 2015), 43–4.
68 Mohammad Hawwash. *An al-'Alawiyeen wa Dawlatuhum al-Mustaqilla* (Casablanca: Al-Sharika al-Jadida lil Tiba'a al-Mutahida 1997), 207.
69 TNA, 371109, volume 9053, Palmer (Damascus) to FO (29 October 1923).
70 TNA, 371/2142/630, volume 20849 (6 May 1937).
71 TNA, 371/393, volume 9054, Damascus Consul to FO (2 April 1923).
72 TNA, 371/11009, volume 9053, Palmer (Damascus) to FO (29 October 1923).
73 Khoury, *Syria and the French Mandate*, 132.
74 TNA, 371/10159 (1924), Smart to Curzon (15 December 1923).
75 TNA, 371/1109, volume 9053, Palmer (Damascus) to FO (29 October 1923).
76 TNA, 371/11020, volume 9053, Damascus Consul to FO (3 November 1923).
77 TNA, 371/11020, volume 9053, Damascus Consul to FO (3 November 1923).
78 Khoury, *Syria and the French Mandate*, 133.
79 TNA, 371/11243, volume 9053 (6 November 1923).
80 TNA, 371/11014, volume 9053, Damascus Consul to FO (31 October 1923).
81 Hakim, *Souriyya wa al-Intidab al-Faransi*, 90.
82 TNA, 371/11014, volume 9053, Damascus Consul to FO (31 October 1923).
83 Maxime Weygand. *Les Mémoires du général Weygand*, volume II (Paris: Flammarion 1957), 253.
84 TNA, 371/10160, Palmer to Curzon (21 January 1924).
85 TNA, 371/10165, Satow to Chamberlain (8 December 1924).
86 Babil, *Sahafa wa Siyasa*, 61.
87 Salma al-Haffar al-Kuzbari, *Lutfi al-Haffar 1885–1965: Mudhakaratuh, Hayatuh, wa 'Asruh* (London: Riad El Rayyes 1997), 110–22.
88 Khoury, *Awraq Fares al-Khoury*, volume II, 217.
89 Hakim, *Souriyya wa al-Intidab al-Faransi*, 56.
90 Solh, *Al-Ab'ad al-Taharuriyya lada al-Nukhab al-Lubnaniyya*, 254.
91 Ibid.
92 Khoury, *Syria and the French Mandate*, 441.
93 Farid Shora, *Al-Kitab al-Ahmar: Souriyya al-Mujahida fi Sabeel al-Istiqlal* (Damascus 1936), 35.
94 Solh, *Al-Ab'ad al-Taharuriyya lada al-Nukhab al-Lubnaniyya*, 278.
95 Ibid.
96 'Ayyashi, *Al-Idahat al-Siyasiyya*, 386.

97 Shora, *Al-Kitab al-Ahmar*, 35–48.
98 Author interview with Seniyeh Barakat, daughter of President Subhi Barakat (Istanbul, April 2021).
99 Ibid.

Chapter 5

1   Edmond Rabbat, *Tatawwur Souriyya al-Siyasi fi Dhil al-Intidab* (Doha: The Arab Center for Research and Policy Studies 2020), 208.
2   Jens-Peter Hanssen, *The Effect of Ottoman Rule on Fin de Siècle Beirut* (Oxford: The University of Oxford 2001), 330.
3   Jamil Adra, *Dâmad Ahmed Nami Bey: Une chronologie biographique* (France 2019), 19.
4   Edouard Blondel, *Deux ans en Syrie et en Palestine 1838–1839* (Paris: Chez P. Dufart 1840), 52–3.
5   Adra, *Dâmad Ahmed Nami Bey*, 14.
6   ʿAyyashi, *Al-Idahat al-Siyasiyya*, 319.
7   Hakim, *Souriyya wa al-Intidab al-Faransi*, 146.
8   Adra, *Dâmad Ahmed Nami Bey*, 53.
9   Ibid., 148.
10 Babil, *Sahafa wa Siyasa*, 64.
11 ʿAdel Arslan, *Mudhakarat al-Emir ʿAdel Arslan*, volume I (Beirut: Dar al-Thaqafa 1973), 108.
12 Haffar al-Kuzbari, *Lutfi al-Haffar*, 142–5.
13 Ibid., 142.
14 TNA, 371/4684, volume 11507, Air Minister to FO (26 July 1926).
15 Hakim, *Souriyya wa al-Intidab al-Faransi*, 174.
16 Wathiq Mouʾayyad al-ʿAzm (1890–1941) studied at the Mulkiyye school in Istanbul, becoming Ottoman ambassador to Spain in 1914. After serving as interior minister under Ahmad Nami, he became the director of police and governor of Damascus during the premiership of Sheikh Taj al-Din al-Hasani (1928–31). He was then appointed director of posts and telegraphs until 1936.
17 Hakim, *Souriyya wa al-Intidab al-Faransi*, 179.
18 Ibid., 185.
19 Ibid., 187.
20 Hakim, *Souriyya wa al-Intidab al-Faransi*, 194.
21 Adra, *Dâmad Ahmed Nami Bey*, 82.
22 Ibid.
23 Ibid., 84.
24 ʿAzm, *Mudhakarat*, volume I, 200.

Chapter 6

1   TNA, 684/4/529 Hole to Simon, June 16, 1932.
2   The new flag was a remake of the 1916 flag of the Arab Revolt, adopted by King Faisal in 1920. For further information, see Qasmiya, *Al-Raʾel al-ʿArabi al-Awwal*, 48.

3 Author interview with Burhan al-ʿAbed, nephew of President Mohammad ʿAli al-ʿAbed (Damascus, 10 September 2012).
4 Author interview with Ayman Hawlu al-ʿAbed, niece of President Mohammad ʿAli al-ʿAbed (Cairo, 29 November 2021).
5 *Al-Shaab* (Issue 2161, 30 May 1935).
6 Ibid.
7 Burhan al-ʿAbed (10 September 2012).
8 ʿAjlani (12–15 September 1999).
9 Khani (19–22 November 2019).
10 ʿAshi, *Fajr al-Istiqlal fi Souriyya*, 65.
11 Burhan al-ʿAbed (10 September 2012).
12 ʿAjlani (12–15 September 1999).
13 *Al-Mudhik al-Mubki* (2 April 1930).
14 Linda Schilcher, *Families in Politics: Damascene Families and Estates in the 18th and 19th Centuries* (Stuttgart: Franz Steiner 1985), 199.
15 Mohammad Saʾid al-Ustwani, *Mashahed wa Ahdath Dimashqiyya fi Muntasaf al-Qarn al-Tase' 'Ashar* (Damascus 1994), 180.
16 Ibid.
17 ʿAbdulrazzaq al-Bitar, *Huliyyat al-Bashar fi Tareekh al-Qarn al-Tase' 'Ashar*, volume I (Damascus 1993), 269.
18 Schilcher, *Families in Politics*, 199.
19 Philip S. Khoury, *Urban Notables and Arab Nationalism: The Politics of Damascus 1860–1920* (Cambridge: Cambridge University Press 2009), 378.
20 Moubayed, *Nakbet Nasara al-Sham*, 145.
21 Ibid.
22 Kaylani, *ʿAbqariyyat Shamiyya*, 27.
23 Schilcher, *Families in Politics*, 155–6.
24 Kaylani, *ʿAbqariyyat Shamiyya*, 28.
25 ʿAdnan Mihyar al-Malouhi, *Muʾjam al-Jaraʾid al-Souriyya 1865–1965* (Damascus: Dar al-Oula 2002), 12–13.
26 Ibid.
27 al-ʿOtari, *Aʾlam wa Mubdiʿoun*, 11.
28 Kaylani, *ʿAbqariyyat Shamiyya*, 36–9.
29 *Al-Nasr* (2 February 1961).
30 Shihabi, *Dimashq*, 60.
31 Ibid.
32 Burhan al-ʿAbed (10 September 2012).
33 Ibid.
34 Ibid.
35 Ibid.
36 Khayr al-Din al-Zirikli, *Al-Aʾlam*, volume 7 (Cairo 1954–1957), 197.
37 Amin Saʾid, *Sirati wa Mudhakarati al-Siyasiyya*, volume I (Damascus 2004), 431.
38 Burhan al-ʿAbed (10 September 2012).
39 Yusuf al-Hakim, *Souriyya wa al-Hukum al-ʿUthmani* (Beirut: Dar Annahar 1980), 58–9.
40 Arslan, *Mudhakarat*, volume I, 291.
41 Moubayed, *Tareekh Dimashq al-Mansi*, 224–5.
42 Ibid.
43 Ibid., 227–8.

44 Kaylani, ʾAbqariyyat Shamiyya, 29.
45 Ibid., 28–9.
46 Arslan, Mudhakarat, volume I, 291.
47 Buhran al-ʾAbed (10 September 2012).
48 Kaylani, ʾAbqariyyat Shamiyya, 26.
49 Ibid.
50 Ibid., 31.
51 Khoury, Syria and the French Mandate, 379.
52 Al-Ahram (16 October 1924).
53 Hani al-Khayyer, Tara'if wa Souwar min Tareekh Dimashq (Damascus: Al-Nouri 1989), 104–05.
54 Zeidan, ʾAlamuna al-Arabi, 596–7.
55 Burhan al-ʾAbed (10 September 2012).
56 Najib al-Armanazi, Souriyya min al-Ihtilal hata al-Jalaa (Beirut: Dar al-Kitab al-Jadid 1973), 88.
57 Hakim, Souriyya wa al-Intidab al-Faransi, 227.
58 Centre des Archives Diplomatiques de Nantes (CADN), ʾAbed to Ponsot, Damascus, 30 May 1932), volume 469.
59 Al-Mudhik al-Mubki (19 July 1930).
60 Hakim, Souriyya wa al-Intidab al-Faransi, 228.
61 Sa'id, Sirati wa Mudhakarati, volume I, 430.
62 al-Ahram (12 June 1932).
63 ʾAbdul Rahman al-Kayyali, Al-Marahel fi al-Intidab al-Faransi wa Nidaluna al-Watani min ʾAam 1926 hata Nihayet 1936, volume I (Aleppo: Matba'at al-Dad 1958), 173.
64 Ibid., 174.
65 Mohammad Kurd ʾAli, Mudhakarat, volume I (Damascus: Matba'et al-Taraqi 1948), 269.
66 Ibid.
67 Al-Qabas (3 July 1933).
68 TNA, 317/683, volume 7847, Palmer (Damascus) to FO, 21 July 1922).
69 TNA, 371/2142, volume 20849 (6 May 1937).
70 Sai'd, Sirati wa Mudhakarati, volume I, 433.
71 Khoury, Syria and the French Mandate, 447.
72 TNA, 684/7/25. MacKereth to Simon.
73 Ibid.
74 Les Echoes (21 April 1934).
75 TNA, 371/2398, volume 17946, MacKereth to Simon (24 March 1934).
76 Khoury, Syria and the French Mandate, 447.
77 Armanazi, Souriyya min al-Ihtilal hata al-Jalaa, 91.
78 Hakim, Souriyya wa al-Intidab al-Faransi, 237.
79 Ibid., 238–9.
80 Armanazi, Souriyya min al-Ihtilal hata al-Jalaa, 91.
81 Sa'id, Sirati wa Mudhakarati, volume I, 432.
82 Armanazi, Souriyya min al-Ihtilal hata al-Jalaa, 97.
83 Ibrahim Hananu (1869–1935) was born in the village of Kafar Takharim in the Idlib province and raised in Aleppo. He studied law in Istanbul and taught briefly at the military college, joining the Committee of Union and Progress in 1908. He then served as MP in the Syrian National Congress of 1919, after which he took up arms to fight the French, leading the Aleppo Revolt until 1922. He fled to Transjordan but

was extradited by the British, standing trial in Aleppo. In October 1927, he helped co-found the National Bloc with Hashem al-Atasi.
84 Zuhayr al-Shuluq, *Min Awraq al-Intidab: Tareekh ma Ahmaluhu al-Tareekh* (Beirut: Dar al-Nafa'is 1989), 125.
85 Ibid., 125.
86 Kurd ʿAli, *Mudhakarat*, volume I, 270.
87 ʿAyyashi, *Al-Idahat al-Siyasiyya*, 397.
88 Armanazi, *Souriyya min al-Ihtilal hata al-Jalaa*, 98.
89 Ibid., 99.
90 Anwar al-ʿUsh, *Fi Tareek al-Huriyya* (Damascus: Maktab al-Kutla al-Wataniyya 1937), 17.
91 Hakim, *Souriyya wa al-Intidab al-Faransi*, 263.
92 Armanazi, *Souriyya min al-Ihtilal hata al-Jalaa*, 103.
93 Shuluq, *Min Awraq al-Intidab*, 121.
94 Ayman Hawlu al-ʿAbed (29 November 2021).
95 Ibid.

Chapter 7

1 Atasi, *Hashem al-Atasi*, 486.
2 Joel Parker. 'The Atassis of Homs: The Rise and Decline of One of Syria's Founding Families', *The Journal of the Middle East and Africa*, 7:4 (2016), 373.
3 Atasi, *Hashem al-Atasi*, 20.
4 Ibid., 31.
5 Najat Qassab Hasan, *Saniou al-Jalaa Fi Souriyya* (Beirut: Shariket al-Matbu'at 1999), 101.
6 Atasi, *Hashem al-Atasi*, 32–5.
7 Thompson, *How the West Stole Democracy from the Arabs*, 176.
8 ʿAjlani (12–15 September 1999).
9 Mohammad ʿIzzat Darwaza, *Mudhakarat wa Tasjeelat*, volume II (Damascus: Manshurat al-Jam'iyya al-Filastiniyya Lil Tareekh 1984), 106.
10 Qassab Hasan, *Saniou al-Jalaa Fi Souriyya*, 103.
11 Ibrahim Daraji, *Al-Abaa al-Dustouriyyoun: Hikayat Siyasiyya wa Dustoriyya min ʿAmal Al-Jam'iyya al-Ta'sisiyya li Dustoor Souriyya al-Awal ba'ad al-Istiqlal* (Damascus: Bustan Hisham 2021), 286.
12 Mohammad Harb Farzat, *Al-Hayat al-Hizbiyya fi Souriyya 1908–1955* (Damascus: Dar al-Ruwwad 1955), 103.
13 Ibid.
14 ʿAjlani (12–15 September 1999).
15 Qassab Hasan, *Saniou al-Jalaa fi Souriyya*, 107.
16 Khani (19–22 November 2019).
17 Ibid.
18 Ibid.
19 Ibid.
20 ʿAjlani (12–15 September 1999).
21 Khoury, *Syria and the French Mandate*, 250–1.
22 Ibid., 252.

23 Ibid.
24 Ibid.
25 Ibid.
26 Patrick Seale, *The Struggle for Arab Independence: Riad el-Solh and the Makers of the Modern Middle East* (Cambridge: Cambridge University Press 2010), 718.
27 Khoury, *Syria and the French Mandate*, 531–5.
28 Atasi, *Hashem al-Atasi*, 127.
29 Author interview with 'Abdul Wahab Homad of the People's Party (Damascus, 6 February 1998).
30 Ibid.
31 Thompson, *Colonial Citizens*, 51–2.
32 TNA, 371/4390, volume 13074, Hole to Lord Cushenden (9 August, 1928).
33 TNA, 371/4429, volume 13037 (25 August 1928).
34 TNA, 371/4488, volume 13074 (15 August 1928).
35 Homad (6 February 1998).
36 'Ajlani (12–15 September 1999).
37 Quai d'Orsay Archives – The Franco-Syrian Treaty of Friendship and Alliance (10 September 1936).
38 Khoury, *Syria and the French Mandate*, 468.
39 TNA, 371/20066, Ogden to FO (3 October 1936).
40 TNA, 371/6716, volume 20066, Ogden to Eden (3 October 1936).
41 TNA, 371/20848, Damascus Consul to FO (28 December 1936).
42 Jamil Mardam Bey (1895–1960) studied politics in France and was one of the original founders of al-Fatat in 19111. He served as interpreter to King Faisal during the Paris Peace Conference and was an early member of the National Bloc. Mardam Bey was the principal negotiator of the 1936 Treaty and created five governments during his career, the first being in December 1936 and the last in August 1948. He then retired from politics and settled permanently in Egypt until his death in March 1960.
43 TNA, 371/6968, volume 20066, MacKareth to Eden (27 October 1936).
44 For more, see George Lathqani, *Limatha dufinat fi Baris al-Mou'ahada al-Faransiyya al-Souriyya wa al-Mou'ahada al-Faransiyya al-Lubnaniyya 'am 1936* (Damascus, 2003).
45 Seale, *The Struggle for Arab Independence*, 348.
46 'Ajlani (12–15 September 1999).
47 Khoury, *Syria and the French Mandate*, 486.
48 Ibid.
49 Ibid.
50 TNA, 371/7773, volume 20068, Parr to FO (14 February 1936).
51 TNA, 371/196, volume 20845, Ward to FO (11 January 1932).
52 *Al-Qabas* (10 February 1937).
53 TNA, 371/106, volume 13072, Satow to FO (2 December 1927).
54 Khoury, *Syria and the French Mandate*, 498.
55 TNA, 371/7357, volume 20067, Fox to FO (25 November 1936).
56 Khoury, *Syria and the French Mandate*, 499.
57 *Al-Ayyam* (30 November 1936).
58 TNA, 371/413, volume 20845, Catoni (Aleppo) to Eden (24 November 1936).
59 TNA, 371/7759, volume 20068, Parr (Aleppo) to FO (13 December 1936).
60 Ibid.
61 TNA, 371/881, volume 20845, MacKareth to Eden (31 December 1936).

62 TNA, 371/3008, volume 2191, Lorraine to FO (22 May 1938).
63 Khoury, *Syria and the French Mandate*, 513.
64 'Ajlani (12–15 September 1999).
65 Ibid.
66 Ibid.
67 *Al-Mudhik al-Mubki* (10 December 1938).
68 'Ajlani (12–15 September 1999).
69 Ibid.
70 Ibid.
71 Author interview Radwan al-Atasi, grandson of President Hashem al-Atasi (Damascus, 6 December 2010).
72 'Ajlani (12–15 September 1999).
73 Nazih Mou'ayyad al-'Azm Papers (16 October 1938) at the Historical Documents Museum in Damascus and *al-Ayyam* (18 March 1938).
74 Babil, *Sahafa wa Siyasa*, 111.
75 Hasan al-Hakim, *?Abdul Rahman al-Shahbandar: Hayatuh wa 'Asruh* (Beirut: Al-Dar al-Mutahida 1985), 197–206.
76 Homad (6 February 1998).
77 Khoury, *Syria and the French Mandate*, 577.
78 'Ajlani (12–15 September 1999).
79 TNA, 371/3199, volume 23276 (31 March 1939).
80 Seale, *The Struggle for Arab Independence*, 352.
81 Atasi (6 December 2010).
82 TNA 371/27308, E 5638, Spears to Spears Mission (12 September 1941).
83 Atasi, *Hashem al-Atasi*, 263–4.
84 Ibid.
85 Patrick Seale, *The Struggle for Syria: A Study in Post-War Arab Politics 1945–1958* (London: IB Tauris 1987), 34.
86 Sami al-Hinnawi (1897–1950), an army officer from Aleppo, served with the Ottomans in the Balkans, before defecting to join the Arab Revolt in 1916. He was subsequently enlisted into the French-led Army of the Levant and in 1946, was one of the founders of the Syrian Army. He fought during the Palestine War of 1948 and helped Husni al-Za'im stage his coup on 29 March 1949.
87 'Ajlani (12–15 September 1999).
88 Adib al-Shishakli (1909–64) was an army officer from Hama who served in the French-created Army of the Levant, until defecting in 1945. He was one of the co-founders of the Syrian Army, fighting with the Army of Deliverance in Palestine. He then joined official combatants in May 1948 and rose to nationwide fame for his battlefield performance. Shishakli helped topple Shukri al-Quwatli in March 1949 and led two coups, one that December and another in November 1951. He was elected president from July 1953 to February 1954. He then fled to Lebanon, and then to Saudi Arabia, finally setting up base in Brazil, where he was killed in September 1964.
89 Bashir Fansa. *Al-Naqbat al-Mughamarat: Tareekth ma Ahmaluhi al-Tareekh fi Asrar al-Inqilabat al-'Askariyya 1949–1958* (Damascus: Dar Yaarob 1996), 228.
90 Khani (19–22 November 2019).
91 Abdul Qaddus Abu Saleh, *Mudhakarat Ma'arouf al-Dawalibi* (Riyadh: Dar Obeikan 2005), 147.
92 Bassam Barazi and Sa'ad Fansa, *Adib al-Shishakli 1909–1964: Al-Hakika al-Mughayyaba* (Beirut: Riad El Rayyes 2022), 193.

93   Andrew Rathmell. *Secret War in the Middle East: The Covert Struggle for Syria 1949–1961* (London: IB Tauris 2013), 76.
94   Ibid., 83–4.
95   Khani (19–22 November 2019).
96   Ibid.
97   Ibid.
98   Ibid.
99   Seale, *The Struggle for Syria*, 196.
100 *The New York Times* (5 March 1954).
101 Seale, *The Struggle for Syria*, 171.
102 Khani (19–22 November 2019).
103 Rathmell, *Secret War in the Middle East*, 96.
104 Seale, *The Struggle for Syria*, 169.
105 Rathmell, *Secret War in the Middle East*, 105.
106 ʿAbdullah al-Khani *Souriyya bayn al-Dimocratiyya wa al-Hukum al-Fardi: Ashr Sanawat fi al-Amana al-ʿfi a li Riʾasat al-Jumhuriyya 1948–1958* (Beirut: Dar al-Nafaʾes 2004), 140–143.
107 ʿAjlani (12–15 September 1999).
108 Ibid.
109 Ibid.
110 Atasi (10 March 2010).

Chapter 8

1   Ibrahim Ghazi, *Nashʾat al-Shurta wa Tareekhuha fi Souriyya* (Damascus 1999), 179.
2   *Al-Jarida al-Rasmiyya*, al-Qararat al-Idariya, volume I (Damascus 1940–41), 103–5.
3   Parliamentary Minutes, special session dedicated to negotiating the annual budget (5 January 1939).
4   Ghazi, *Nashʾat al-Shurta,* 177.
5   Fares, *Man Hum,* 139–40.
6   *Al-Jarida al-Rasmiyya* (29 February 1941).
7   Hakim, *Souriyya wa al-Intidab al-Faransi*, 219.
8   Ibid., 37.
9   Ibid., 15.
10 TNA, 371/2683, volume 13074. Hole to Chamberlain (25 April 1928).
11 Ibid.
12 Souʾad Jarrous, *Min al-Intidab ila al-Inqilab: Souriyya fi Zaman Najib El Rayyes 1898–1952* (Beirut: Riad El-Rayyes 2015), 123 and ʿAzm, *Mudhakarat*, volume I, 242.
13 Ibid., 125.
14 Ibid.
15 TNA, 371/2740, volume 13037, British Liaison Officer (25 April 1928).
16 Ibid.
17 Jartous, *Min al-Intidab ila al-Inqilab,* 124.
18 Ibid.
19 al-ʿOtari, *Abqariyat*, 75.
20 Hashem ʿUthmam, *Al-Muhakamat al-Siyasiyya fi Souriyya* (Beirut: Riad El Rayyes 2004), 58.

21 Ibid., 63.
22 al-Jundi, *Tareekh al-Thawrat al-Souriyya*, 235.
23 Ibid.
24 Fares, *Man Hum*, 429.
25 Mohammad Jamil al-Chatti, *Ay'an Dimashq fi al-Qarn al-Thaleth 'Ashar wa Nusf al-Qarn al-Rabe' 'Ashar* (Damascus: Dar al-Bashair 1994), 200.
26 Hakim, *Mudhakarati*, volume II, 179.
27 Babil, *Sahafa wa Siyasa*, 114.
28 TNA, 371 Secret political report from the British Consul in Damascus, no 22, (22 July 1939).
29 Ibid.
30 Sa'id, *Sirati wa Mudhakarati*, volume I, 522.
31 TNA, 371/2092, volume 16974 (31 March 1933).
32 TNA, 371/4055, volume 16974 (8 March 1933).
33 Ibid.
34 Fares, *Man Hum*, 138.
35 Khoury, *Syria and the French Mandate*, 585.
36 Hakim, *Souriyya wa al-Intidab al-Faransi*, 304.
37 Shuluq, *Min Awraq al-Intidab*, 191.
38 Gotz Nordbruch, *Nazism in Syria and Lebanon: The Ambivalence of the German option 1933–1945* (London: Routledge 2009), 122.
39 TNA, 371/1895, volume 23276. MacKereth to Baxter (3 March 1939).
40 Peter Shambrook, *French Imperialism in Syria 1927–1936* (Reading: Ithaca Press 1998), 258.
41 TNA, 371. Secret political report from British Consul (Damascus) to FO (London), no. 23 (4 September 1939).
42 Ibid.
43 TNA, 371. Secret political report from British Council (Damascus) to FO (London), no. 25 (7 October 1939).
44 TNA, 371/2837/2837, volume 27291. Gardner (Damascus) to FO (9 April 1941).
45 Ibid., no. 26 (17 October 1939).
46 TNA, 371/1778, volume 24591 (26 April 1940).
47 al-'Otari, *A'lam wa Mubdi'oun*, 217–22.
48 'Uthman, *Al-Muhakamat al-Siyasiya*, 87.
49 TNA, Secret political report from British Consul (Damascus) to FO (London), number 9 with appendix (26 April 1940).
50 Hawrani, *Mudhakarat*, volume I, 211–14.
51 Ibid.
52 Jarrous, *Min al-Intidab ila al-Inqilab*, 71.
53 TNA, 371/24591, Political Report (28 May 1940).
54 Ibid.
55 TNA, 371/23276, Political Report (28 January 1940).
56 TNA, Secret political report from the British Consul (Damascus) to FO (London), no. 30, 28 November 1941.
57 'Ajlani (12–15 September 1999).
58 Ibid.
59 TNA, Secret political report from British Consul in Damascus, no. 23 (3 September 1939).

60 TNA Report from Aleppo to His Majesty's Principal Secretary of State for Foreign Affairs, no. 67, 5/3/3, 5 September 1939).
61 TNA, Secret political report from British Consul (Damascus) to FO (London), no. 11 (28 May 1940).
62 TNA, 371/24594. Telegram # 48. Damascus to FO (26 October 1940).
63 TNA, Annual Economic Report (B) 15762/347/89. From Consul General G.T. Havard to Viscount Halifax (20 November 1939).
64 Ibid.
65 TNA, British Consul in Damascus to FO, no. 8 (10 April 1940).
66 Ibid., no. 30 (28 November 1941).
67 TNA 624/19, Gardner (Damascus) to Baghdad (6 July 1940).
68 TNA, Gardner to FO, no. 26 (6 July 1940).
69 Sa'id, *Sirati wa Mudhakarati*, volume I, 528.
70 Ibid., 529.
71 Babil, *Sahafa wa Siyasa*, 129.
72 Salma Mardam Bey, *Awraq Jamil Mardam Bey* (Beirut: Sharikat al-Matbu'at 1994), 147.
73 Ibid., 104.
74 Babil, *Sahafa wa Siyasa*, 146.
75 Mardam Bey, *Awraq Jamil Mardam Bey*, 106.
76 'Ajlani (12–15 September 1999).
77 Ibid.
78 Munzer Mousilli, *Mudhakarat al-Mujahid al-Sheikh Mohammad al-Hersh* (Damascus: Dar al-Marwa 2006), 144.
79 Ibid.
80 Arslan, *Mudhakarat*, volume I, 281.
81 'Abdul Rahman Shahbandar, *Mudhakarat wa Khutab* (Damascus: Ministry of Culture 1993), 154.
82 Ibid., 110.
83 'Ajlani (12–15 September 1999).
84 Ibid.
85 TNA 371/1778, volume 24591, Odgen to FO (26 April 1940).
86 'Ajlani (12–15 September 1999).
87 Arslan, *Mudhakarat*, volume I, 319.
88 'Ajlani (12–15 September 1999). At the time of the interview in 1999, Munir al-'Ajlani was the last surviving lawyer of the murder case, who had served on the legal defence of the Shahbandar family.
89 Ibid.
90 Ibid.
91 Ibid.
92 Ibid.
93 TNA, 371/24594. Telegram number 633 from Badgert to FO (21 October 1941).
94 TNA, 371/655, vol. 27330, RA Beaumont Memorandum (11 June 1941).
95 TNA, 371, Gardner (Damascus) to FO, no 48 (26 October 1940).
96 Mardam Bey, *Awraq Jamil Mardam Bey*, 19.
97 Babil, *Sahafa wa Siyasa*, 154–5.
98 Ibid.
99 Mardam Bey, *Awraq Jamil Mardam Bey*, 118.

100 Haffar al-Kuzbari, *Lutfi al-Haffar*, 302.
101 Ibid.
102 TNA, 371/3082, vol. 24595, Gardener to FO (11 January 1941).
103 'Ajlani (12–15 September 1999).
104 *Al-Inshaa* (20 July 1941).
105 *Al-Jarida al-Rasmiyah* (29 February 1941).
106 'Azm, *Mudhakarat*, volume I, 200.
107 Ibid.
108 Hakim, *Souriyya wa al-Intidab al-Faransi*, 302.
109 Hakim, *Mudhakarati*, volume II, 16.
110 Babil, *Sahafa wa Siyasa*, 157–8.
111 Sa'id, *Sirati wa Mudhakarati*, volume I, 599.
112 Babil, *Sahafa wa Siyasa*, 193.
113 Ibid.
114 Khani (19–22 November 2019).
115 *Al-Jarida al-Rasmiya* (13 October 1943 and 16 October 1943).
116 Sa'id, *Sirati wa Mudhakarati*, 599.
117 Ibid., 600.
118 Ibid., 601.

Chapter 9

1 'Azm, *Mudkhakarat*, volume I, 73.
2 Ibid.
3 Akram Hasan al-Olabi, *Khaled al-'Azm: Akher Hukkam Dimashq min Al al-'Azm* (Damascus: Shahrazad Press 2005), 43.
4 'Azm, *Mudhakarat*, volume I, 3.
5 Ibid., 10.
6 Ibid., 73.
7 Ibid., 61.
8 Ibid., 121.
9 Ibid.
10 Author interview with 'Abdul Ghani Hammour, last director of the National Cement Company before it was nationalized in 1965 (Beirut, 23 October 2017).
11 Said Himadeh, *Economic Organization of Syria* (Beirut: The American University of Beirut 1936), 157.
12 Philip S. Khoury, 'The Syrian Independence Movement and the Growth of Economic Nationalism in Damascus,' *British Society for Middle Eastern Studies*, 14:1 (1988) 29–30.
13 Khoury, *Syria and the French Mandate*, 281.
14 Khani, *Souriyya bayn al-Dimocratiyya wa al-Hukum al-Fardi*, 224.
15 Hammour (Beirut, 23 October 2017).
16 For more on Azm's work in sports, see Samuel Dolbee, *Mandatory Bodybuilding: Nationalism, Masculinity, Class, and Physical Culture in 1930s Syria* (Georgetown University Thesis 2010).
17 TNA, 371/23277 Consul General Harvard to FO (13 September 1940).
18 Seale, *The Struggle for Arab Nationalism*, 117.

19 Salma Mardam Bey, *Syria's Quest for Independence 1939–1945* (Reading: Ithaca Press 1997), 30. For more, see Henri Dentz's memoir *Affaires de Syria* (Hoover Institution Library and Archive 2008).
20 Ibid., 207.
21 Ibid., 208.
22 Ibid.
23 *Al-Qabas* (1 June 1941).
24 A.B. Gaunson, *The Anglo-French Clash in Syria and Lebanon 1940–45* (Macmillan Press 1987), 41.
25 Khani (19–22 November 2019).
26 Ibid.
27 For more, see Henri De Wailly, *Invasion Syria 1941: Churchill and De Gaulle's Forgotten War* (London: IB Tauris 2006).
28 Seale, *The Struggle for Arab Nationalism*, 429.
29 Ibid., 431.
30 François Kersaudy, *Churchill and De Gaulle* (New York: HarperCollins Publishers 1990), 192–210.
31 Albert Hourani, *Syria and Lebanon* (Massachusetts: Harvard University Press 1991), 241.
32 'Azm, *Mudkhakarat*, volume I, 295–6.
33 Khani (3 October 2019).
34 Ibid.
35 Husni al-Za'im (1897–1949), an army officer from Aleppo, served under the French-led Army of the Levant but was discharged and arrested in 1941 on charges of corruption. Quwatli returned him to service in 1946, making him chief of military police and, then, chief of staff of the Syrian Army during the Palestine War.
36 Nazir Fansa, *Ayyam Husni al-Za'im: 137 Hazzat Souriyya* (Damascus: Al Nouri 1993), 21–2.
37 Khani, *Souriyya bayn al-Dimocratiya wa al-Hukum al-Fardi*, 73.
38 Ibid., 75.
39 'Azm, *Mudhakarat*, volume II, 191.
40 Fansa, *Ayyam Husni al-Za'im*, 30.
41 Author interview with Haitham Kaylani, military escort to Husni al-Za'im (Damascus, 10 August 2002).
42 'Azm, *Mudhakarat*, volume II, 120.
43 Sami Moubayed, *'Abdul Nasser wa al-Ta'meem: Waqai al-Inqilab al-Iqtisadi fi Souriyya* (Beirut: Riad El Rayyes 2019), 319.
44 'Azm, *Mudhakarat*, volume II, 414.
45 Ibid., 422–37.
46 Ibid.
47 Ibid., 466.
48 Ibid., 432.
49 Seale, *The Struggle for Syria*, 184.
50 'Azm, *Mudhakarat*, volume III, 5.
51 Parker, *The Atassis of Homs*, 380.
52 Bonnie F. Saunders, *The United States and Arab Nationalism: The Syria Case 1953–1960* (Praeger Press 1996), 61.
53 'Azm, *Mudhakarat*, volume III, 49.
54 Ibid., 143.

55 Ibid.
56 Moubayed, *'Abdul Nasser wa al-Ta'meem,* 153–4.
57 Hani al-Khayyer, *Akram al-Hawrani bayn al-Tanaqullat al-Siyasiyya wa al-Inqilabat al-Askariyya* (Damascus 1996), 61.
58 Moubayed, *'Abdul Nasser wa al-Ta'meem,* 154.
59 International Monetary Fund Report (Syria 1956), 18.
60 Khaled al-'Azm speech at the Economic Conference in Aleppo (2 November 1962).
61 Ibid.
62 'Azm, *Mudhakarat,* volume III, 426.
63 Mutih Al-samman, *Watan wa 'Askar: Mudhakarat 28 September 1961–8 March 1963* (Beirut: Bisan Bookstore 1995), 64–5.
64 'Azm, *Mudhakarat,* volume III, 220.
65 Ibid.
66 Ibid., 223.
67 Samman, *Watan wa 'Askar,* 137.
68 Ibid., 415.
69 Ibid., 64–6.
70 'Abdul Karim Zahr Al-din, *Mudhakarati an Fatrat al-Infisal fi Souriyya* (Beirut: Dar al-Itihad 1968), 331.
71 Ibid., 249.
72 'Azm, *Mudhakarat,* volume III, 438.
73 Author interview with Ambassador Sami al-Khiyami (Beirut, 3 October 2013).

Chapter 10

1 Edward Spears, *Fulfillment of a Mission: The Spears Mission to Syria and Lebanon 1941–1944* (Connecticut: Archon Books 1977), 162.
2 Schilcher, *Families in Politics,* 125.
3 Mohammad Sharif al-Sawwaf, *Al-Muhaddeth al-Akbar al-Sheikh Badr al-Din al-Hasani wa Atharuhu fi al-Nahda al-'Ilmiyya* (Damascus: Dar Tiba 2015), 50.
4 Tantawi, *Dikrayat,* volume III, 215.
5 Ibid., 15.
6 'Ajlani (12–15 September 1999).
7 'Otari, *'Abqariyat wa Mobdi'oun,* 142.
8 Mahmud al-'Attar, *Al-Sheikh Badr al-Din al-Hasani* (Damascus: Dar al-Bashair 2008), 13.
9 Ibid.
10 'Otari, *'Abqariyyat,* 26.
11 'Azm, *Mudhakarat,* volume I, 73.
12 Malouhi, *Mu'jam al-Jara'id al-Souriyya,* 45–6.
13 Russell, *The First Modern Arab State,* 10.
14 'Otari, *'Abqariyyat,* 26.
15 Hakim, *Souriyya wa al-'Ahd al-Faisali,* 95.
16 Shahrestan, *Al-Mo'utamar al-Souri al-'Aam,* 195.
17 TNA, 371/2395, volume 17944. MacKereth to Simon (19 March 1934).
18 Hakim, *Souriyya wa al-Intidab al-Faransi,* 209.
19 Seale, *The Struggle for Arab Nationalism,* 201.

20 Khoury, *Syria and the French Mandate*, 189.
21 Author interview with Sheikh Sharif al-Sawwaf (Damascus, 8 December 2022).
22 Hakim, *Souriyya wa al-Intidab al-Faransi*, 206.
23 Khoury, *Awraq Fares al-Khoury*, volume III (Damascus 2015) 177.
24 *Alef Bae* (11 February 1928).
25 Ibid., 13.
26 Hakim, *Souriyya wa al-Intidab al-Faransi*, 206.
27 Ibid., 219.
28 Khoury, *Syria and the French Mandate*, 331.
29 Kayyali, *Al-Marahel*, volume I, 239–40.
30 Jarrous, *Min al-Intidab ila al-Inqilab*, 91.
31 Shambrook, *French Imperialism in Syria*, 37.
32 Ibid., 15.
33 TNA, 371/2683, volume 13074. Hole to Chamberlain (25 April 1928).
34 Babil, *Sahafa wa Siyasa*, 68.
35 ʿAjlani (12–15 September 1999).
36 Khoury, *Syria and the French Mandate*, 341.
37 TNA, 371/4390, volume 13074. Hole to Lord Cushendun (9 August 1928).
38 Shambrook, *French Imperialism in Syria*, 43.
39 Jarrous, *Min al-Intidab ila al-Inqilab*, 92.
40 Ibid.
41 TNA, 371/4488 vol. 13074 (15 August 1928).
42 Badr al-Din al-Shallah, *Lil Tareekh wa al-Dhikra* (Damascus 1990), 225.
43 Al-Matbaʿa al-Hukumiyya, *Al-Hukuma al-Souriyya fi Thalal Sanawat min 15 Shubat 1928 ila 18 Shubat 1931* (Damascus 1931), 12–13.
44 Ibid., 37–9.
45 Kurd ʿAli, *Mudhakarat*, volume II, 335.
46 Kayyali, *Al-Marahel*, volume II, 200.
47 Kurd ʿAli, *Mudhakarat*, volume II, 326.
48 Ibid.
49 Jarrous, *Min al-Intidab ila al-Inqilab*, 545.
50 Wasfi al-Maleh, *Tareekh al-Masrah al-Souri* (Damascus 1984), 100.
51 Jean Alexan. *Tareekh al-Cinema al-Souriyya 1928–1988* (Damascus 2012), 23–29.
52 Ibid., 23–9.
53 For more on Nazira Zayn al-Din, see Thompson, *Colonial Citizens*, 127–40.
54 *Majalet Majmaʿa al-Lugha al-ʿArabiyya bi Dimashq* (July–August 1928), 501–8.
55 ʿAjlani (12–15 September 1999).
56 *Masr wa al-Dunya* Magazine (July 1930).
57 Ibid.
58 Jarrous, *Min al-Intidab ila al-Inqilab*, 91.
59 TNA, 371/171, volume 16085, Hole to Simon (22 December 1931).
60 *Al-Shaab* (24 December 1931).
61 ʿAjlani (12–15 September 1999).
62 TNA, 371/172, volume 16085, Hole to Simon (23 December 1931).
63 TNA, 871/2395, volume 17944. MacKereth to Simon (19 March 1934).
64 Korani, *Dikrayat wa Khawater*, 121.
65 ʿAjlani (12–15 September 1999).
66 *Al-Shaab* (11 February 1936).
67 ʿAzm, *Mudhakarat*, volume I, 197.

68 Babil, *Sahafa wa Siyasa*, 175.
69 TNA, 371/27327. Consulate General in Aley, 13–24 April 1941.
70 Babil, *Sahafa wa Siyasa*, 174–5.
71 Atasi, *Hashem al-Atasi*, 262–5.
72 'Azm, *Mudhakarat*, volume I, 236–7.
73 TNA, 371/31471. Spears to FO (Beirut, 21 February 1942).
74 Author interview with Inaam al-Hasani, daughter of President Taj al-Din al-Hasani (Beirut, 12 September 1999).
75 Ibid.
76 'Ajlani (12–15 September 1999).
77 Yossi Olmert, 'A False Dilemma? Syria and Lebanon's Independence during the Mandatory Period,' *Middle Eastern Studies*, 32:3 (July 1996), 48.
78 Hasan al-Hakim (1886–1982), a statesman from Damascus, debuted in the Ottoman civil service, becoming director of posts & telegraphs under King Faisal. He was one of the co-founders of the People's Party with 'Abdul Rahman Shahbandar in 1925, and took part in the Great Syrian Revolt. In addition to helping set up the Arab Bank in Palestine, he was also made director of the Agricultural Bank in Damascus, before serving briefly as minister of education under President Hashem al-Atasi in 1939.
79 Hakim, *Mudakarati*, volume I, 7.
80 Kayyali, *Dirasa fi Tareekh Souriyya*, 125.
81 TNA 684/14, Gardner's Diary (23 November 1941).
82 Hakim, *Souriyya wa al-Intidab al-Faransi*, 324.
83 Memoirs of Husni al-Barazi at the American University of Beirut Oral History Project (Lebanon 1969).
84 Ibid.
85 Sa'id, *Sirati wa Mudhakarati*, volume I, 556.
86 Husni al-Barazi Memoirs.
87 Ibid.
88 Babil, *Sahafa wa Siyasa*, 182.
89 Barazi Memoirs.
90 Spears, *Fulfillment of a Mission*, 162.
91 Hasani (12 September 1999).
92 *Hakim, Souriyya wa al-Intidab al-Faransi*, 326.
93 Khani (19–22 November 2019).
94 Ibid.

Chapter 11

1 Hakim, *Souriyya wa al-Intidab al-Faransi*, 35–6.
2 Ibid.
3 Qodama, *Ma'alim wa A'lam*, 93.
4 TNA, 226/240/9/3/119, Gardner to Chancery (17 March 1943).
5 Khoury, *Awraq Fares al-Khoury*, volume III, 169.
6 Emir Fateh El Djezairi (11 March 2015).
7 Nadim Demashkiyyeh, *Mahatat fi Hayati al-Diblomasiyya* (Beirut: Dar Annahar 1995), 36.
8 Khani (19–22 November 2019).

9   Ibid.
10 TNA, 371/1744, volume 20065, MacKereth to Eden (31 March 1936).
11 'Otari, *Hadeeth al-Abqariyyat*, 87.
12 Ibid.
13 Korani, *Dhirayat wa Khawater*, 206.

Chapter 12

1   Khani (19–22 November 2019).
2   Ibid.
3   Fansa, *Ayyam Husni al-Za'im*, 31–2.
4   'Abdullah al-Khani, *Jihad Shukri al-Quwatli fi Sabeel al-Istiqlal wa al-Wehda* (Beirut: Dar al-Nafa'es 2003), 20–22.
5   'Abdul Latif Yunis, *Shukri al-Quwatli: Tareekh Umma fi Hayat Rajul* (Cairo: Dar al-Ma'arif 1959), 23.
6   Khani, *Jihad Shukri al-Quwatli*, 19.
7   Ibid.
8   Khoury, *Awraq Fares al-Khoury*, volume I, 110–12.
9   Khani, *Jihad Shukri al-Quwatli*, 24.
10 Qadri, *Mudhakarati*, 60–1.
11 Khoury, *Awraq Fares al-Khoury*, volume I, 110–12.
12 Nabil Quwatli, *Bahth Mukhtasar fi Shajaret Ailat al-Quwatli* (Damascus: Dar al-Bashari 2018), 112.
13 Khani (19–22 November 2019).
14 Ibid.
15 Ralph Coury, *The Making of an Egyptian Arab Nationalist: The Early Years of Azzam Pasha 1893–1936* (Reading: Ithaca Press 1998), 289.
16 *Al-Balagh* (9 November 1925).
17 Khani (19–22 November 2019).
18 Ibid.
19 Mohammad Usama al-Quwatli, *Qira'a fi Hayat Shukri al-Quwatli* (Damascus 1992), 3.
20 Author interview with Raja Shurbaji, a former member of the Steel Shirts and National Youth (Damascus, 18 October 2010).
21 Ibid.
22 Ibid.
23 Shallah, *Al-Masira al-Tijariyya*, 307.
24 Khoury, 'The Syrian independence movement and the growth of economic nationalism in Damascus', 29–30.
25 Ibid.
26 Khoury, *Syria and the French Mandate*, 282.
27 Author interview with Uthman al-'Aidi, a banker from the late 1950s whose father, Ahmad Munif, served on the board of the Syrian Conserves Company in the 1930s (Damascus, 18 September 2017).
28 Moubayed, *'Abdul Nasser wa al-Ta'meem*, 179–82.
29 'Aidi (18 September 2017).
30 Moubayed, *'Abdul Nasser wa al-Ta'meem*, 179–82.
31 Qassab Hasan, *Saniou al-Jalaa fi Souriyya*, 112.

32 'Ajlani (12–15 September 1999).
33 Ibid.
34 Ibid.
35 Shukri al-Quwatli, *Shukri al-Quwatli Yukhatib Ummatuh* (Beirut: Markaz al-Watha'iq al-Mu'asira 1970), 13–16.
36 TNA, 371, volume 31481, Catroux to FO (9 March 1942).
37 TNA, 371/31481, British Consul to FO (4 March 1942).
38 TNA, 371, Cromwallis (Baghdad) to FO (9 March 1942).
39 TNA, 371, Anthony Eden (London) to Catroux (Damascus, 10 March 1942).
40 Hakim, *Souriyya wa al-Intidab al-Faransi*, 330–1.
41 Atasi, *Hashem al-Atasi*, 291.
42 Author interview with Suhayl al-'Ashi, military escort to President Quwatli (Damascus, 6 June 2001).
43 Ibid.
44 Ibid.
45 Khani, *Jihad Shukri al-Quwatli*, 22.
46 Khani, *Souriyya bayn al-Dimocratiya wa al-Hukum al-Fardi*, 63.
47 'Ashi (6 June 2001).
48 Ibid.
49 Ibid.
50 Ibid.
51 Mardam Bey, *Syria's Quest for Independence*, 127.
52 Ibid., 120.
53 *Palestine Post* (3 July 1944).
54 Mardam Bey, *Syria's Quest for Independence*, 134.
55 Ibid., 169.
56 Sai'd, *Sirati wa Mudhakarati*, volume I, 622.
57 Mardam Bey, *Syria's Quest for Independence*, 88–9.
58 Babil, *Sahafa wa Siyasa*, 194–9.
59 Khani (19–22 November 2019).
60 Babil, *Sahafa wa Siyasa*, 194–9.
61 Khani (19–22 November 2019).
62 Ibid., 182–3.
63 Ibid., 190.
64 TNA, 371/45565, Political Report (23 May 1945).
65 Khani, *Jihad Shukri al-Quwatli*, 54.
66 Khani (19–22 November 2019).
67 Ibid.
68 Khani, *Jihad Shukri al-Quwatli*, 54.
69 Mardam Bey, *Syria's Quest for Independence*, 217.
70 Khani (19–22 November 2019).
71 Ibid.
72 Ibid.
73 Ibid.
74 Ibid.
75 Mardam Bey, *Syria's Quest for Independence*, 217.
76 Moubayed, *Politics of Damascus*, 212.
77 Sami Jumaa, *Awraq min Daftar al-Watan 1946–1961* (Damascus: Dar Tlass 2000), 18.
78 Hawrani, *Mudhakarat*, volume I, 634.

79 'Ashi (6 June 2001).
80 Ibid.
81 Ibid.
82 Khani (19–22 November 2019).
83 Ibid.
84 Ibid.
85 TNA, 371/62184, 'What happened in Aleppo on 30.11.1947' Report.
86 Author interview with General Wadih Muqabari, former commander of the Syrian Air Force and veteran of the 1948 war in Palestine (Damascus, 16 December 2016).
87 Ibid.
88 Ibid.
89 Benny Morris, *1948 and After* (Oxford: Clarendon Press 1990), 85.
90 Author interview with Syrian novelist 'Abdulsalam al-Ujayli, veteran of the Army of Deliverance (Beirut, 10 June 1998).
91 TNA, 371/68364, Bush to FO (31 December 1947).
92 Ujayli (Beirut, 10 June 1998).
93 For more on the Army of Deliverance see Fauzi al-Qawuqji, 'Memoirs I', *Journal of Palestine Studies*, 1:4 (Summer 1972), 27–58, and 'Memoirs II', *Journal of Palestine Studies*, 2:1 (1973), 3–33.
94 Morris, *1948 and After*, 91–2.
95 Ibid., 632.
96 Muqabari (16 December 2016).
97 Ibid.
98 'Ashi (6 June 2001).
99 Muqabari (16 December 2016).
100 Author interview with 'Abdul Rahman Mardini, veteran of the 1948 Palestine War (Damascus, 23 January 2005).
101 Muqabari (16 December 2016).
102 Ibid.
103 Morris, *1948 and After*, 254.
104 Muqabari (16 December 2016).
105 Ibid., 652.
106 Henry Laurens, *La Question de Palestine: L'accomplissement des Propheties*, volume III (Paris: Fayard 2007), 175–94.
107 Taha al-Hashemi, *Mudhakarat Taha al-Hashemi 1942–1955,* volume II (Beirut 1968–1978), 189–90.
108 See Miles Copeland, *The Game of Nations: The Amorality of Power Politics* (Simon & Schuster 1970) and Andrew Rathmell, 'Copeland and Za'im: Re-evaluating the Evidence', *Intelligence and National Security,* 11:1 (January 1996), 89–105.
109 Bashir al-'Awf, *Al-Inqilab al-Souri: 30 Athar 1949* (Damascus: Al Nouri 1949), 149–50.
110 TIME magazine (11 April 1949).
111 Khani, *Jihad Shukri al-Quwatli*, 86.
112 Quwatli, *Qira'a fi Hayat Shukri al-Quwatli*, 4.
113 Ibid.
114 Mohamad H. Haikal. *Cutting the Lion's Tail: Suez Through Egyptian Eyes* (London: Deutsch 1986), 187.
115 Ibid., 192.
116 *Al-Ahram* (7 December 1958).

117 *Al-Ahram* (19 February 1956).
118 TNA, 371/121867 – British Embassy in Moscow (5 November 1956).
119 Rathmell, *Secret War in the Middle East*, 136–40.
120 Author interview with Ahmad ʿAbdul Karim of the Higher Military Council (Damascus, 4 May 2010).
121 ʿAbdul Muhsen Abu al-Nour, *Al-Haqiqa an Thawret 23 Yuniou* (Cairo 2001), 111.
122 Ibid., 112.
123 Khani, *Jihad Shukri al-Quwatli*, 114.
124 Ibid., 115.
125 Ibid.
126 Abu al-Nour, *Al-Haqiqa*, 77.
127 Ibid., 164–5.
128 Khani, *Jihad Shukri al-Quwatli*, 15.
129 Ibid., 200.
130 Zahr al-Din, *Mudhakarati*, 91.
131 Quwatli, *Shukri al-Quwatli Yukhatib Ummatuh*, 451–66.
132 Samman, *Watan wa ʿAskar*, 70.
133 Ibid., 71.
134 Quwatli, *Qiraʾa fi Hayat Shukri al-Quwatli*, 6.
135 Khani (19–22 November 2019).
136 Ibid.
137 Ibid.
138 Ibid.
139 Quwatli, *Qiraʾa fi Hayat Shukri al-Quwatli*, 7–8.
140 Khani (19–22 November 2019).
141 Ibid.
142 Ibid.

BIBLIOGRAPHY

Interviews

ʿAbdul Ghani Hammour, last director of the National Cement Company and former manager of the Damascus Chamber of Commerce (Beirut 23 October 2017).
ʿAbdullah al-Khani, former secretary-general of the Syrian Presidency (Damascus, 19–22 November 2019).
ʿAbdul Rahman Mardini, former governor of Damascus and veteran of the 1948 Palestine War (Damascus 23 January 2005).
ʿAbdulsalam al-Ujayli, novelist, cabinet minister and veteran of the Army of Deliverance (Beirut, 10 June 1998).
ʿAbdul Wahab Homad, minister, MP, and co-founder of the People's Party (6 February 1998).
Ahmad ʿAbdul Karim of the Higher Military Council, former minister in the United Arab Republic (Damascus, 4 May 2010).
Ayman Hawlu al-ʿAbed, niece of President Mohammad ʿAli al-ʿAbed (Cairo, 29 November 2021).
Burhan al-ʿAbed, nephew of President Mohammad ʿAli al-ʿAbed (Damascus, 10 September 2012).
Colette Khoury, novelist and granddaughter of Prime Minister Fares al-Khoury (Damascus, 1 August 2022).
Emir Fateh El Djezairi, son of Emir Saʿid El Djezairi (Damascus, 11 March 2015).
Emir Jaʿafar El Djezairi, great-grandson of Emir ʿAbdelkader El Djezairi (Damascus, 5 May 2015).
George Lathqani, Syrian physician and officer in the Ottoman Army (Damascus, 1 June 1996).
Haitham Kaylani, military escort to President Husni al-Zaʾim (Damascus 10 August 2002).
Inaam al-Hasani, daughter of President Taj al-Din al-Hasani (Beirut 12 September 1999).
Munir al-ʿAjlani, MP, cabinet minister and son-in-law of President Taj al-Din al-Hasani (Beirut, 12–16 September 1999).
Radwan al-Atasi, grandson of President Hashem al-Atasi (Damascus, 6 December 2010).
Raja Shurbaji, member of the National Bloc (Damascus, 18 October 2010).
Sami al-Khiyami, former Syrian ambassador to London (Beirut, 3 October 2013).
Seniyeh Barakat, daughter of President Subhi Barakat (Istanbul, April 2021).
Sharif al-Sawwaf, director of the Ahmad Kaftaro Complex and rotating speaker at the Umayyad Mosque (Damascus, 8 December 2022).
Suhayl al-ʿAshi, military escort to President Shukri al-Quwatli (Damascus, 6 June 2001).
Uthman al-ʿAidi, banker, investor, founder of Cham Hotels (Damascus, 18 September 2017).
Wadih al-Muqabari, army general, veteran of the 1948 Palestine War and air force commander in 1957–63 (Damascus, 16 December 2016).

Newspapers and magazines

Al-'Asima (Damascus), al-Jarida al-Rasmiyya (Damascus), al-Muqtabas (Damascus), al-Nasr (Damascus), al-Ayyam (Damascus), al-Qabas (Damascus), al-Inshaa (Damascus), Alef Bae (Damascus), Majalet Majma'a al-Lugha al-'Arabiyya fi Dimashq (Damascus), Al-Mudhik al-Mubki (Damascus), al-Shaab (Damascus), Palestine Post (Jerusalem), al-Ahram (Cairo), al-Balagh (Cairo), Misr wa al-Dunya (Cairo), Al-Taqaddum (Beirut), Annahar (Beirut), Les Echoes (Beirut), New York Times (New York), Time Magazine (New York), Al-Sharq Al-Awsat (London), Al-Hayat (London).

Unpublished papers

Dentz, Henri. *Affaires de Syria* (Hoover Institution Library and Archive 2008).
Dolbee, Samuel. *Mandatory Bodybuilding: Nationalism, Masculinity, Class, and Physical Culture in 1930s Syria* (Georgetown University Thesis 2010).
Husni al-Barazi Memoirs (American University of Beirut Oral History Project 1969).
Landis, Joshua. '*Politics of the Zu'ama*' (PhD Dissertation, Princeton University 1998).
Mohammad Usama al-Quwatli. *Qira'a fi Hayat Shukri al-Quwatli* (Damascus 1992).
Nazih Mouayyad al-'Azm Papers (Historical Documents Museum Damascus).
Parliamentary Minutes (Syrian People's Assembly 1939–1949).
Yusuf Gibran Gaith. *Fakhamet al-Ra'is Shukri al-Quwatli* (University of Baghdad MA Dissertation 1998).

Academic articles

Caplan, Neil. 'Faisal Ibn Husain and the Zionists: A Re-examination with documents', *The International History Review*, 5:4 (November 1983), 561–614.
Çiçek, Talha. 'Visions of Islamic Unity: A Comparison of Djemal Pasha's al-Sharq and Sharif Husayn's al-Qibla Periodicals', *Die Welt des Islams*, 54:3/4, 460–82.
Ecochard, Michel. 'Le Palais Azem de Damas', *Gazette des Beaux-Arts* (Paris 1935), 1–14.
Eppel, Michael. 'Syrian-Iraqi Relations during the 1948 Palestine War', *Middle Eastern Studies*, 32:3 (July 1996), 74–91.
Eppel, Michael. 'The Arab States and the 1948 War in Palestine: The Socio-political Struggles, the Compelling Nationalist Discourse and the Regional Context of Involvement', *Middle Eastern Studies*, 48:1 (January 2012), 1–31.
Husri, Khaldun S. 'King Faysal I and Arab Unity 1930–1933', *Journal of Contemporary History*, 10 (1975), 323–40.
Kedourie, Elie. 'The Capture of Damascus, 1 October 1918', *Middle Eastern Studies*, 1:1 (October 1964), 66–83.
Khoury, Philip S. 'Factionalism among Syrian Nationalists during the French Mandate', *International Journal of Middle Eastern Studies*, 13:4 (November 1981), 441–69.
Khoury, Philip S. 'Syrian Urban Politics in Transition: The Quarters of Damascus during the French Mandate', *International Journal of Middle East Studies*, 16:4 (November 1984), 507–40.
Khoury, Philip S. 'Divided Loyalties? Syria and the Question of Palestine 1919–39', *Middle Eastern Studies*, 21:3 (July 1985), 324–48.

Khoury, Philip S. 'The Syrian Independence Movement and the Growth of Economic Nationalism in Damascus', *British Society for Middle Eastern Studies*, 14:1 (1988), 25–36).
Khoury, Philip S. 'Continuity and Change in Syrian Political Life: The Nineteenth and Twentieth Centuries', *The American Historical Review*, 96:5 (December 1991), 1374–1395.
Melki, James A. 'Syria and State Department 1937–47', *Middle Eastern Studies*, 33:1 (January 1997), 92–106.
Moubayed, Sami. 'Syria's Forgotten President Mohammad Ali al-Abed', *British Journal of Middle Eastern Studies*, 41:4 (October 2014), 419–41.
Moubayed, Sami. 'Two September Weeks That Saved Damascus', *Arab Studies Quarterly*, 37:4 (Fall 2015), 367–87.
Newman, Elias. 'The Bombardment of Damascus', *Current History*, 23:4 (January 1926), 490–1941.
Olmert, Yossi. 'A False Dilemma? Syria and Lebanon's Independence during the Mandatory Period', *Middle Eastern Studies*, 32:3 (July 1996), 41–73.
Parker, Joel. 'The Atassis of Homs: The Rise and Decline of One of Syria's Founding Families', *The Journal of the Middle East and Africa*, 7:4 (2016), 369–85.
Porath, Yehoshua. 'Abdallah's Greater Syria Programme', *Middle Eastern Studies*, 20:2 (April 1984), 172–89.
Porath, Yehoshua. 'Nuri al-Sa'id's Arab Unity Programme', *Middle Eastern Studies*, 20:4 (October 1984), 76–98.
Provence, Michael. 'Ottoman and French Mandate Land Registers for the Region of Damascus', *Middle East Studies Association Bulletin*, 39:1 (June 2005), 32–43.
Qattan, Najwa. 'Litigants and Neighbors: The Communal Topography of Ottoman Damascus', *Comparative Studies in Society and History*, 44:3 (July 2002), 511–33.
Qawuqji, Fauzi. 'Memoirs I', *Journal of Palestine Studies*, 1:4 (Summer 1972), 27–58.
Qawuqji, Fauzi. 'Memoirs II', *Journal of Palestine Studies*, 2:1 (1973), 3–33.
Rabinovich, Itamar. 'The Compact Minorities and the Syrian State 1918–1945', *Journal of Contemporary History*, 14:4 (1979), 693–712.
Rafeq, Abdul-Karim. 'Sources of Wealth and Its Social and Political Implications in Nineteenth-Century Damascus', *Oriens*, 37 (2009), 253–69.
Rathmell, Andrew. 'Copeland and Za'im: Re-evaluating the Evidence', *Intelligence and National Security*, 11:1 (January 1996), 89–105.
Rathmell, Andrew. 'Brotherly Enemies: The Rise and Fall of the Syrian-Egyptian Intelligence Axis, 1954–1967', *Intelligence and National Security*, 13:1 (Spring 1998), 230–53.
Reilly, James. 'Properties around Damascus in the Nineteenth Century', *Arabica*, 37 (1990), 91–114.
Reilly, James. 'Property, Status, and Class in Ottoman Damascus: Case Studies from the Nineteenth Century', *Journal of the American Oriental Society*, 112:1 (January–March 1992), 9–21.
Reilly, James. 'Damascus Merchants and Trade in the Transition to Capitalism', *Canadian Journal of History*, 27:1 (Spring 1992), 1–27.
Reilly, James. *The ʿAzms of Hama: Patricians in an Ottoman TownQasr al-iʿAzm: Ein osmanischer Gouverneurspalast in Hama/Westsyrien*, 15–22. Edited by Karin Bartl and ʿAbdelqader Farzat. (Darmstadt: Verlag Philipp von Zabern, 2013).
Salem, Elie. 'Syrian Aspirations and Realities', *International Journal*, 11:4 (Autumn 1956), 261–69.

Shamir, Shimon. 'As'ad Pasha al-'Azm and Ottoman Rule in Damascus 1743–58', *Bulletin of the School of Oriental Studies*, 26:1 (1963), 1–28.
Simon, Reeva. 'The Hashemite "Conspiracy:" Hashemite Unity Attempts 1921–1958', *International Journal of Middle East Studies*, 5:3 (June 1974), 314–27.
Sorby Jr., Karol. 'The Last Days of King Faysal I (1930–1933)', *Asian and African Studies*, 19:2 (2010), 255–74.
Tauber, Eliezer. 'Rashid Rida and Faysal's Kingdom in Syria', *The Muslim World*, 85:3–4 (July–October 1995), 235–45.
Winder, Bayly. 'Syrian Deputies and Cabinet Ministers 1919–1959', *Middle East Journal*, 16:4 (1962), 407–29.
Wright, Quincy. 'The Bombardment of Damascus', *The American Journal of International Law*, 20:2 (April 1926), 263–80.
Zamir, Meir. 'An Intimate Alliance: The Joint Struggle of General Edward Spears and Riad al-Sulh to Oust France from Lebanon 1942–1944', *Middle Eastern Studies*, 41:6 (November 2005), 811–32.
Zamir, Meir. 'The "Missing Dimension:" Britain's Secret War against France in Syria and Lebanon 1942–45, Part II', *Middle Eastern Studies*, 46:6 (November 2010).

Books in Arabic

'Abdul Hadi, 'Abbas. *Al-Arad wa al-Islah al-Zira'I fi Souriyya* (Damascus: Dar al-Yaqtha al-'Arabiyya 1962).
'Abdul Hadi, 'Awni. *Mudhakarat 'Awni 'Abdul Hadi* (Beirut: Center for Arab Unity Studies 2002).
'Abdul Karim, Ahmad. *Adwa ala Tajrubat al-Wihda* (Damascus: Dar al-Ahali 1991).
'Abdul Karim, Ahmad. *Hasad: Sineen Khusba wa Thimar Murra* (Beirut: Bisan Bookstore 1994).
'Abdul Karim, Nahed. *Al-Qadaya al-Iqtisadiyya wa al-Ijtima'iyya fi Souriyya 1946–1958* (Damascus: Dar Tlass 1996).
'Abdullah, King of Jordan. *Mudhakarati* (Amman 1951).
Abu Diyah, Sa'ad. *Al-Mas'a al-Nabeel: Al-Ameer Zayd wa al-Hukuma al-Wataniyya fi Dimashq* (Amman 2016).
Abu Fakhr, Saqr. *A'yan al-Sham wa I'aqat al-'Ilmaniyya fi Souriyya* (Beirut: Al-Mou'assa al-'Arabiyya lil Dirasat wa al-Nashr 2013).
Abu al-Nour, 'Abdul Muhsen. *Al-Haqiqa an Thawret 23 Yuniou* (Cairo 2001).
Abu Saleh, 'Abdul Qadoos. *Mudhakarat Ma'arouf al-Dawalibi* (Riyadh: Dar Obeikan 2005).
'Adel, Fouad. *Qissat Souriyya bayn al-Intikhab wa al-Inqilab 1943–1963* (Damascus: Dar al-Yanabee 2001).
Adhami, Mohammad Mazhar al-. *Al-Malik Faisal al-Awwal: Dirasat fi Hayatih al-Siyasiyya* (Baghdad: Dar al-Shu'oun al-Thaqafiyya al-Amma 1988).
Adra, Jamil. *Dâmad Ahmed Nami Bey: Une chronologie biographique* (France 2019).
'Ajlani, Shams al-Din al-. *Wujooh wa Kalam min Bilad al-Sham* (Damascus 2010).
'Allaf, Ahmad Hilmi al-. *Dimashq fi Matla'a al-Qarn al-'Ishreen* (Damascus: Dar Dimashq 1983).
Alexan, Jean. *Tareekh al-Cinema al-Souriyya 1928–1988* (Damascus 2012).
Aqbiq, 'Azza. *A'lam fi Dhakirat al-Cham* (Damascus 2020).

Armanazi, Najib al-. *Souriyya min al-Ihtilal hata al-Jalaa* (Beirut: Dar al-Kitab al-Jadid 1973).
Arslan, Emir ʿAdel. *Mudhakarat al-Emir ʿAdel Arslan*, 3-volumes, (Beirut: Dar al-Thaqafa 1973).
Ashrafi, Munir al- & Ashrafi, Nazir al-. *Istiqlal Souriyya* (Aleppo 1936).
Atrash, Mansur al-. *Al-Jeel al-Mudan: Sira Dhatiyya min Awraq Mansur al-Atrash* (Beirut: Riad El Rayyes 2008).
Atrash, Sultan Pasha al-. *Ahdath al-Thawra al-Souriyya al-Kubra kama Saradaha Qa'iduha al-ʿAam* (Damascus: Dar Tlass 2007).
ʿAttar, Mahmud al-. *Al-Sheikh Badr al-Din al-Hasani* (Damascus: Dar al-Bashair 2008).
Atasi, ʿAdnan al-. *Azmat al-Hukum fi Souriyya* (Damascus, 1954).
Atasi, Mohammad Radwan al-. *Hashem al-Atasi: Hayatuhu wa ʿAsruh* (Damascus 2005).
ʿAwf, Bashir al-. *Al-Inqilab al-Souri: 30 Athar 1949* (Damascus: Al Nouri 1949).
ʿAyyashi, Ghaleb al-. *Al-Idahat al-Siyasiyya wa Asrar al-Intidab al-Faransi fi Souriyya* (Beirut: Ashqar Ikhwan 1955).
ʿAzma, ʿAbdul-ʿAziz al-. *Mir'at al-Sham: Tareekth Dimashq wa Ahluha* (London: Riad El Rayyes 1987).
ʿAzma, Bashir al-. *Jeel al-Hazima bayn al-Wihda wa al-Infisal* (London: Riad El Rayyes 1991).
ʿAzm, ʿAbdul Qadir al-. *Al-Usra al-ʿAzmiyya* (Damascus: Matbaʿet al-Inshaa 1960).
ʿAzm, Khaled al-. *Mudhakarat*, 3-volumes (Beirut: Al-Dar al-Mutahida 1972).
Babil, Nasuh. *Sahafa wa Siyasa: Souriyya fi al-Qarn al-ʿIshreen* (London: Riad El Rayyes, 1987).
Bahra, Nasr al-Din al-. *Dimashq fi al-Arba'iniyat wa ʿAabr al-ʿUsour* (Damascus: Dar al-Bashair 2002).
Bakdash, Khaled. *Mulahathat wa Araa fi Ba'ad Qadaya al-Fikr wa al-Falsafa wa al-Adab* (Damascus 1976).
Bakdash, Khaled. *Khaled Bakdash Yatahadath* (Beirut: Dar al-Taliʿa 1993).
Barazi, Bassam al- & Fansa, Sa'ad. *Adib al-Shishakli 1909–1964: Al-Hakika al-Mughayyaba* (Beirut: Riad El Rayyes 2022).
Barout, Mohammad Jamal. 'Al-Mout'amar al-Souri al-ʿAam 1919–1920', Tabayun Magazine, Issue 3 (Doha: Arab Center for Research and Policy Studies 2013).
Barout, Mohammad Jamal (ed). *Al-Hukuma al-ʿArabiyya fi Dimashq: Al-Tajruba al-Mubakira lil Dawla al-ʿArabiyya al-Haditha 1918–1920* (Doha: Arab Center for Research and Policy Studies 2020).
Barudi, Fakhri al-. *Fasl al-Khitab Bayn al-Sufour wa al-Hijab* (Damascus: Taraqi Press 1934).
Barudi, Fakhri al-. *Mudhakarat*, 2-volumes (Beirut: Dar al-Hayat, 1951).
Bayhum, Mohammad Jamil. *Souriyya wa Lubnan 1918–1922* (Beirut: Dar al-Taliʿa 1968).
Bitar, ʿAbdulrazzaq al-. *Huliyyat al-Bashar fi Tareekh al-Qarn al-Tase' ʿAshar*, 3-volumes (Damascus 1993).
Bizri, ʿAfif al-. *Al-Nasriyya fi Jumlat al-Isti'mar al-Hadeeth* (Beirut: Dar al-Sharq lil Nashr 1962).
Chatti, Mohammad Jamil al-. *Rawd al-Bashar fi A'yan Dimashq fi al-Qarn al-Thaleth ʿAshar 1201–1300 Hijri* (Damascus: Dar al-Yaqtha al-ʿArabiyya 1946).
Chatti, Mohammad Jamil al-. *Ay'an Dimashq fi al-Qarn al-Thaleth ʿAshar wa Nusf al-Qarn al-Rabe' ʿAshar* (Damascus: Dar al-Bashair 1994).
Dagher, As'ad. *Mudhakarati ʿala Hamesh al-Qadiyya al-ʿArabiyya* (Doha: Arab Center for Research and Policy Studies 2020).
Daraji, Ibrahim al-. *Al-Abaa al-Dustouriyyoun: Hikayat Siyasiyya wa Dustoriyya min ʿA'mal Al-Jam'iyya al-Ta'sisiyya li Dustoor Souriyya al-Awal ba'ad al-Istiqlal* (Damascus: Bustan Hisham 2021).

Darwaza, Mohammad ʿIzzat. *Mudhakarat*, 2-volumes (Damascus: Manshurat al-Jam'iyya al-Filastiniyya Lil Tareekh 1984), 106.
Demashkiyyeh, Nadim. *Mahatat fi Hayati al-Diblomasiyya* (Beirut: Dar Annahar 1995).
Djemal, Pasha, *Kayfa Jalat al-Quwwat al- al-ʿUthmaniyya ʿan Bilad al-ʿArab* (Beirut, 1932).
Djemal, Pasha. *Mudhakarat Djemal Pasha* (Beirut: Al-Farabi 2003).
Djezairi, Emir Mohammad Pasha El. *Tihfet al-Za'ir fi Ma'ather al-Emir ʿAbdelkader wa Akhbar al-Jaza'ir* (Cairo 1903).
Djezairi, Emir Sa'id El. *Mudhakarati ʿan al-Qadaya al-Arabiyya wa al-ʿAlam al-Islami* (Algiers: Dar al-Yakza al-ʿArabiyya, 1968).
Entabi Mohammad, Fouad el- & Othman, Najwa. *Halab Fi Mi'at ʿAam min ʿaam 1850 hata 1950*, 3-volumes, (Aleppo: Ma'had Al-turath Al-ʿilmi Al-ʿarabi 1992).
Fansa, Bashir. *Al-Naqbat al-Mughamarat: Tareekth ma Ahmaluhi al-Tareekh fi Asrar al-Inqilabat al-ʿAskariyya 1949–1958* (Damascus: Dar Yaarob 1996).
Fansa, Nazir. *Ayyam Husni al-Za'im: 137 Hazzat Souriyya* (Damascus: Al Nouri 1993).
Faqir, Hasan Tahseen Pasha al-. *Al-Intidab al-Faransi al-Ghashem ʿala Souriyya* (Damascus 2004).
Fares, George. *Man Hum fi al-ʿAlam al-ʿArabi* (Damascus 1957).
Farhany, Mohammad al-. *Fares al-Khoury wa Ayyam la Tunsa* (Beirut: Dar al-Ghad 1965).
Farzat, Mohammad Harb. *Al-Hayat al-Hizbiyya fi Souriyya 1908–1955* (Damascus: Dar al-Ruwwad 1955).
Ghazi, Ibrahim. *Nash'at al-Shurta wa Tareekhuha fi Souriyya* (Damascus, 1999).
Ghazzi, Kamel al-. *Nahr al-Dahab fi Tareekh Halab*, 3-volumes (Aleppo: Al-Matba'a al-Maroniyya 1923–1926).
Ghusayn, Fayez al-. *Mudhakarati ʿan al-Thawra al-ʿArabiyya*, 2-volumes (Damascus 1956).
Haffar Kuzbari al-, Salma. *Lutfi al-Haffar 1885–1965: Mudhakaratuh, Hayatuh, wa ʿAsruh* (London: Riad El Rayyes 1997).
Haffar, Lutfi al-. *Dhikrayat*, 2-volumes (Damascus: Ibn Zaydun Press 1954).
Hakim, Da'ad al-. *Safahat min Hayat Nazih Mou'ayyad al-ʿAzm* (Damascus: Ministry of Culture 2006).
al-Hakim, Hasan. *Mudhakarati: Safahat min Tareekh Souriyya al-Hadeeth 1920–1958*, 2-volumes (Beirut: Dar al-Kitab 1965).
Al-Watha'iq al-Tarikhiyya al-Muta'liqa bil Qadiyya al-Souriyya fi al-Ahdayn al-Faisali al-ʿArabi wa al-Intidab al-Faransi (Beirut: Dar Sader 1974).
al-Hakim, Hasan. *ʿAbdul Rahman al-Shahbandar: Hayatuh wa ʿAsruh* (Beirut: Al-Dar al-Mutahida 1985).
Hakim, Yusuf al-. *Souriyya wa al-Hukum al-Faisali* (Beirut: Dar Annahar 1966).
Hakim, Yusuf al-, *Souriyya wa al-Hukum al-ʿUthmani* (Beirut: Dar Annahar 1980).
Hakim, Yusuf al-. *Souriyya wa al-Intidab al-Faransi* (Beirut: Dar Annahar 1982).
Hamada, Mohammad ʿAbidin and Dhubian, Tayseer al-. *Faisal Ibn al-Hussein* (Damascus 1933).
Hamdan, Hamdan. *Akram al-Hawrani: Rajul lil Tareekh* (Beirut: Bisan Bookstore 1996).
Hanna, ʿAbdullah. *Al-Itijahat al-Fikriyya fi Souriyya wa Lubnan 1920–1945* (Damascus: Dar al-Taqaddum al-Arabi 1973).
Hanna, ʿAbdullah. *Al-Haraka al-Munahida lil Fashiyya fi Souriyya wa Lubnan 1933–1945* (Beirut: Al-Farabi 1975).
Hanna, ʿAbdullah. *ʿAbdul Rahman Shahbandar 1879–1940: ʿAlam Nahdawi wa Rajul al-Wataniyya wa al-Taharur al-Fikri* (Damascus: Dar al-Ahali 1992).
Haroun, Nizar As'ad. *Souriyya alati ʿArift* (Beirut: Al-Farabi 2017).

Hashemi, Taha al-. *Mudhakarat Taha al-Hashemi*, 2-volumes (Beirut 1968–1978).
Hawrani, Akram al-. *Mudhakarat Akram al-Hawrani*, 4-volumes (Cairo: Madbouli 2000).
Hawwash, Mohammad. *'An al-'Alawiyeen wa Dawlatuhum al-Mustaqilla* (Casablanca: Al-Sharika al-Jadida lil Tiba'a al-Mutahida 1997).
Haydar, Rustom. *Mudhakarat Rustom Haydar* (Beirut: Al-Dar al-'Arabiyya Lil Mawsu'at 1988).
Haykal, Mohammad Hasanein. *Ma Aladhi Jara fi Souriyya* (Cairo 1962).
Hindi, Ihsan al-. *Ma'araket Maysaloun* (Damascus: Ministry of Culture 1967).
Homsi, Naziha al-. *Al-Janna al-Da'ia: Mudhakarat Naziha al-Homsi haram Akram al-Hawrani* (2003).
Husri, Sati al-. *Yawm Maysaloun* (Beirut: Maktabat al-Kashaf 1948).
Husseini, Wael al- & 'Adnan, Mohammad. *Khaled al-'Azm 1903–1965: Siratuhu wa Dawruhu fi Siyasat Souriyya* (Damascus: Dar Amal Al-Jadida 2015).
Ibish, Ahmad al & Shihabi, Qutayba al-. *Ma'alim Dimashq al-Tarikhiyya* (Damascus: Ministry of Culture, 1996).
Ismail, Hikmat 'Ali. *Nitham al-Intidab al-Faransi 'ala Souriyya 1920–1928* (Damascus: Dar Tlass 1998).
Jabiri, Riad al-. *Sa'adallah al-Jabiri wa Hiwar Ma'a al-Tareekth* (Damascus: Itihad al-Kuttab al-'Arab 2006).
Jamil, Sayyar al-. *Mudhakarat Tahseen Qadri 1892–1986: Al-Murafeq al-'Askari al-Aqdam lil Malik Faisal al-Awwal* (Amman: Dar al-Ahali 2018).
Jamil, Sayyar al-. *Al-Malik Faisal al-Awwal 1883–1933* (Beirut: Arab Center for Unity Studies 2021).
Jumaa, Sami. *Awraq min Daftar al-Watan 1946–1961* (Damascus: Dar Tlass 2000).
Jundi, Adham al-. *Tareekh al-Thawrat al-Souriyya fi 'Ahd al-Intidab al-Faransi* (Damascus 1960).
Jarrous, Sou'ad. *Min al-Intidab ila al-Inqilab: Souriyya fi Zaman Najib El Rayyes 1898–1952* (Beirut: Riad El-Rayyes 2015).
Jassem, Mohammad Alaa. *Al-Malik Faisal al-Awwal 1833–1933: Hahatuh wa Dawruh al-Siyasi fi al-Thawra al-'Arabiyya wa Souriyya wa al-Iraq* (Baghdad).
Kahaleh, Habib. *Dhikrayat Na'ib* (Damascus).
Kaylani, Ibrahim al-. *'Abqariyyat Shamiyya fi al-Hukum wa al-Siyasa wa al-Idara* (Damascus 1946).
Kayyali, 'Abdul Rahman al-. *Al-Jihad al-Siyasi* (Aleppo 1946).
Kayyali, 'Abdul Rahman al-. *Rad al-Kutla al-Wataniyya ala Bayan al-Mufawwad al-Sami lil Jumhuriyya al-Ifaransiyya fi Souriyya wa Lubnan* (Aleppo 1933).
Kayyali, 'Abdul Rahman al-. *Al-Marahel fi al-Intidab al-Faransi wa Nidaluna al-Watani min 'Aam 1926 hata Nihayet 1936*, 4-volumes (Aleppo 1958).
Kayyali, Nizar al-. *Dirasa fi Tareekh Souriyya al-Siyasi al-Mouassir 1920–1950* (Damascus: Dar Tlass 1997).
Khani, 'Abdullah al-. *Jihad Shukri al-Quwatli fi Sabeel al-Istiqlal wa al-Wehda* (Beirut: Dar al-Nafa'es 2003).
Khani, 'Abdullah al-. *Souriyya bayn al-Dimocratiyya wa al-Hukum al-Fardi: Ashr Sanawat fi al-Amana al-'Amma li Ri'asat al-Jumhuriyya 1948–1958* (Beirut: Dar al-Nafa'es 2004).
Khayyer, Hani al-. *Tara'if wa Souwar min Tareekh Dimashq* (Damascus: Al-Nouri 1989).
Khayyer, Hani al-. *Adib al-Shishakli: Al-Bidaya wa al-Nihaya* (Damascus: Maktabet al-Sharq al-Jadid 1994).
Khayyer, Hani al-. *Akram al-Hawrani Bayn al-Tanaqullat al-Siyasiyya wa al-Inqilabat al-'Askariyya* (Damascus 1996).

Khoury, Beshar al-. *Haqa'iq Lubnaniyya*, 4-volumes (Beirut: Al-Dar al-Lubnaniyya lil Nashr 1973).
Khoury, Colette. *Awraq Fares al-Khoury*, 3-volumes (Damascus 1989–2015).
Khoury, Colette. *Al-'Eid al-Dhahabi lil-Jalaa* (Damascus: Dar Tlass 1996).
Koriya, Yaacoub Yusuf. *Malek Souriyya Faisal Ibn al-Hussein* (Baghdad 2001).
Kurd 'Ali, Mohammad. *Mudhakarat*, 4-volumes (Damascus 1948).
Kurd 'Ali, Mohammad. *Khuttat al-Sham*, 6-volumes (Damascus: Al-Nouri 2008).
Lathqani, George. *Limatha dufinat fi Baris Al-mou'ahada Al-faransiyya Al-souriyya Wa Al-mou'ahada Al-faransiyya Al-lubnaniyya 'am 1936* (Damascus, 2003).
Maarouf, Mohammad. *Ayyam 'Ishtuha 1949–1969* (Beirut: Riad El Rayyes 2003).
Maleh, Wasfi al-. *Tareekh al-Masrah al-Souri* (Damascus 1984).
Malki, Munir al-. *Min Maysaloun ila al-Jalaa* (Damascus: Ministry of Culture 1991).
Malouhi, 'Adnan Mihyar al-. *Mu'jam al-Jara'id al-Souriyya 1865–1965* (Damascus: Dar al-Oula 2002).
Mardam Bey, Salma. *Awraq Jamil Mardam Bey* (Beirut: Sharikat al-Matbu'at, 1994).
Mardam Bey, Tamim. *Safahat min Hayat 'Amid al-Kutla al-Wataniyya Jamil Mardam Bey 1893–1960* (Damascus: Dar Tlass 2010).
Matba'a al-Hukumiyya. *Al-Hukuma al-Souriyya fi Thalal Sanawat min 15 Shubat 1928 ila 18 Shubat 1931* (Damascus, 1931).
Motadel, David. *Fi Sabeel Allah wa al-Fuhrer: Al-Naziyyoun wa al-Islam fi al-Harb al-'Alamiyya al-Thaniyya* (Cairo: Dar Madarat 2019).
Moubayed, Sami. *Al-Rasa'el al-Mafquda bayn al-Doctor 'Abdul Rahman Shahbandar wa al-Ra'is Hasan al-Hakim* (Damascus: Dar al-Bashair 2015).
Moubayed, Sami. *Tareekh Dimashq al-Mansi: Arba' Hikayat 1916–1936* (Beirut: Riad El Rayyes 2015).
Moubayed, Sami. *'Abdul Nasser wa al-Ta'meem: Waqai al-Inqilab al-Iqtisadi fi Souriyya* (Beirut: Riad El Rayyes 2019).
Moubayed, Sami. *Nakbet Nasara al-Sham: Ahl Dhimmet al-Saltana wa Intifadet 1860* (Beirut: Riad El Rayyes 2020).
Moubayed, Sami. *Bayn al-Qasrayn: Faisal al-Awal ma bayn Tammuz 1920 wa Nisan 1921* (Al-Mustaqbal al-'Arabi Magazine, Issue 507, May 2021).
Moubayed, Sami. *Khidewi Souriyya: Dirasa 'an Marhalet Midhat Pasha fi Dimashq* (Damascus: Bustan Hisham 2022).
Mousilli, Munzer. *Mudhakarat al-Mujahid al-Sheikh Mohammad al-Hersh* (Damascus: Dar al-Marwa 2006).
Nasr, Salah. *'Abdul Nasser wa Tajrubat al-Wihda* (Beirut: Al-Watan al-Arabi lil Nashr 1986).
Olabi, Akram Hasan al-. *Khaled al-'Azm: Akher Hukkam Dimashq min Al al-'Azm* (Damascus: Shahrazad Press 2005).
'Omari, Subhi al-. *Lawrence Kama 'Ariftuhu: Al-Haqiqa wa al-Ukdhuba* (London: Riad El-Rayyes 1991).
'Omari, Subhi al-. *Al-Ma'arek al-Oula: Al-Tarek ila Dimashq* (London: Riad El Rayyes 1991).
'Omari, Subhi al-. *Maysaloun: Nihayet 'Ahd* (London: Riad El-Rayyes 1991).
'Otari, 'Abdul Ghani al-. *'Abqariyyat* (Damascus: Dar al-Bashair 1997).
'Otari, 'Abdul Ghani al-. *A'lam wa Mubdi'oun* (Damascus: Dar al-Bashair 1999).
'Otari, 'Abdul Ghani al-. *Hadeeth al-'Abqariyyat* (Damascus: Dar al-Bashair, 2000).
Owen, Jonathan. *Akram al-Hawrani: Dirasa Hawl al-Siyasa al-Souriyya ma Bayn 1943–1954* (Homs: Dar al-Ma'arif 1997).
Polulleau, Alice. *Dimashq that al-Qanabil* (Damascus 1967).

Qadri, Ahmad. *Mudhakarati 'an al-Thawra al-'Arabiyya al-Kubra* (Damascus: Ibn Zaydun 1956).
Qalaji, Qadri al-. *Al-Thawra al-'Arabiyya al-Kubra 1916–1925* (Beirut: Sharikat al-Matbou'at 1998).
Qasmiyyah, Khayriyah. *Al-Hukuma al-'Arabiyya fi Dimashq* (Beirut: Al-Mouassa al-'Arabiyya lil Dirasat 1982).
Al-Ra'el al-Al-Ra'el al-'Arabi al-Awwal: Hayat wa Awraq Nabih wa 'Adel al-'Azma (London: Riad El Rayyes, 1991).
Qasmiyyah, Khayriyah. *Mudhakarat Muhsen al-Barazi 1947–1949* (Beirut: Dar al-Ruwwad 1994).
Qassab Hasan, Najat. *Hadeeth Dimashqi* (Damascus 1998).
Qassab Hasan, Najat. *Jeel al-Shaja'a hata 'am 1945* (Damascus 1994).
Qassab Hasan, Najat. *Saniou al-Jalaa fi Souriyya* (Beirut: Shariket al-Matbu'at 1999).
Qodama, Ahmad. *Ma'alim wa A'lam fi Bilad al-'Arab* (Damascus 1965).
Quwatli, Mohammad Nabil al-. *Bahth Mukhtasar fi Shajarat 'Ailat Aal al-Quwatli* (Damascus 2008).
Quwatli, Shukri al-. *Majmou'at Khutab* (Damascus 1956).
Quwatli, Shukri al-. *Shukri al-Quwatli Yukhatib Ummatuh* (Beirut: Markaz al-Watha'iq al-Mu'asira 1970).
Rabbat, Edmond. *Tatawwur Souriyya al-Siyasi fi Dhil al-Intidab* (Doha: Arab Center for Research and Policy Studies 2020).
Rafeq, 'Abdul-Karim. *Al-'Arab wa al-'Uthmaniyyoun 1516–1916* (Damascus: Dar Atlas 1974).
Ram Hamadani, Mustapha. *Shahed ala Ahdath Souriyya wa 'Arabiyya wa Asrar al-Infisal* (Damascus: Dar Tlass 1999).
Riad, Mahmud. *Mudhakarat Mahmud Riad*, 3-volumes (Beirut: Mansourat al-Mustaqbal al-Arabi 1986).
Rimawi, Suhayla al-. *al-Hukum al-Hizbi fi Souriyya ayyam al-'Ahd al-Faisali 1918–1920* (Amman: Dar al-Majdalawi 1997).
Saadeh, Khalil. *Souriyya wa al-Intidab al-Faransi 1920–1932* (Beirut: Saadeh Foundation 2014).
Safarjalani, Muhiddine al-. *Tareekth al-Thawra al-Souriyya*, with a forward by 'Abdul Rahman Shahbandar (Damascus: Dar al-Yaqtha al-Arabiyya 1961).
Faji'at Maysaloun wa al-Batal al-Azim Yusuf al-Azim Yusuf al-'Azma, with a forward by 'Abdul Rahman Shahbandar (Damascus: Al-Taraqi 1937).
Sai'd, Amin. *Al-Thawra al-'Arabiyya al-Kubra: Tareekh Mufassal Jame'e lil Qadiyya al-'Arabiyya fi Rubu' Qarn* (Cairo 1934).
Sa'id, Amin. *Sirati wa Mudhakarati al-Siyasiyya*, 2-volumes (Damascus 2004).
Sa'id, Nuri Pasha al. *Mudhakarat Nuri al-Sa'id an al-Harakat al-'Askariyya lil Jaysh al-'Arabi fi al-Hejaz wa Souriyya 1916–1918* (Beirut: Al-Dar al-'Arabiyya lil Mawsou'at 1987).
Samman, Mutih al-. *Watan wa 'Askar: Mudhakarat 28 September 1961–8 March 1963* (Beirut: Bisan Bookstore 1995).
Samman, Wasfi al-. *Awraq min al-Aywmiyyat al-Thawra al-Souriyya 1926–1927* (Damascus: Dar Tlass 2004).
Sawwaf, Mohammad Sharif al-. *Mawsou'at al-Usar al-Dimashqiyya: Tareekhuha wa Ansabuha wa A'lamuha*, 3-volumes (Damascus: Beit al-Hikma 2010).
Sawwaf, Mohammad Sharif al-. *Al-Muhaddeth al-Akbar al-Sheikh Badr al-Din al-Hasani wa Atharuhu fi al-Nahda al-'Ilmiyya* (Damascus: Dar Tiba, 2015).

Shahbandar, 'Abdul Rahman. *Haflat Iftitah Hizb al-Shaab* (Damascus: Dar al-Mufid 1925).
Shahbandar, 'Abdul Rahman. *Thawra Souriyya Kubra: Asraruha wa 'Awamiluha wa Nata'ijuha* (Amman 1940).
Shahbandar, 'Abdul Rahman. *Mudhakarat wa Khutab* (Damascus: Ministry of Culture 1993).
Shahbandar, 'Abdul Rahman. *Al-Maqalat* (Damascus: Ministry of Culture 1993).
Shahrestan, Mary. *Al-Mo'utamar al-Souri al-'Aam* (Beirut: Dar Amwaj 2000).
Shallah, Bader al-Din al-. *Lil Tareekh wa al-Dhikra* (Damascus 1990).
Shallah, Bader al-Din al-. *Al-Masira al-Tijariyya* (Damascus 1992).
Sheikh 'Ali, Fayeq al-. *Mudhakarat Warithat al-'Urush* (London: Dar al-Hikma 2002).
Shihabi, Qutayba al-. *Dimashq Tareekh wa Souwar* (Damascus: Al-Nouri 1990).
Shihabi, Qutayba al-. *Sahet al-Marjeh wa Mujawaratuha fi Dimashq: Bayn al-Ams wa al-Yawm* (Damascus: Secretariat of the Damascus Capital of Arab Culture 2008 Celebrations 2008).
Shora, Farid. *Al-Kitab al-Ahmar: Souriyya al-Mujahida fi Sabeel al-Istiqlal* (Damascus 1936).
Shuluq, Zuhayr al-. *Min Awraq al-Intidab: Tareekh ma Ahmaluhu al-Tareekh* (Beirut: Dar al-Nafa'is 1989).
Sibaii, Badr al-Din al-. *Adwa' 'ala al-Ra'esmal al-Ajnabi fi Souriyya 1850–1958* (Damascus: Dar al-Jamaheer 1967).
Solh, 'Adel al-. *Al-Ab'ad al-Taharuriyya lada al-Nukhab al-Lubnaniyya* (Jdeidet al-Metn: Dar Sa'ir al-Mashriq 2013).
Spears, Lady. *Qadiyet al-Istiqlal fi Souriyya wa Lubnan* (Beirut: Dar al-'Ilm lil Malayeen 1947).
Sultan, 'Ali. *Tareekh Souriyya: Hukum Faisal Ibn al-Hussein* (Damascus: Dar Tlass 1996).
Tantawi, 'Ali al-. *Dimashq; Souwar min Jamaluha wa 'Ibar min Nidaluha* (Damascus 1959).
Tantawi, 'Ali al-. *Dhikrayat*, 8-volumes (Riyadh: Dar al-Manara 1985).
Tantawi, 'Ali al-. *Qisas min al-Hayat* (Jeddah: Dar al-Manara 1990).
Tillawi, Sa'id. *Kayf Istaqallat Souriyya*, with a forward by President Shukri al-Quwatli, Damascus: Al-Dunia, 1950).
Tlass, Mustapha (ed.). *Tareekh al-Jaysh al-'Arabi al-Souri 1901–1948*, 3-volumes (Damascus 2000).
Ujayli, 'Abdulsalam al-. *Dhikrayat Ayyam Siyassa*, 2-volumes (Beirut: Riad El Rayyes, 2000–2004).
'Ush, Anwar al-. *Fi Tareek al-Huriyya* (Damascus 1937).
Ustwani, 'Abdul Ghani al-. *Al-'Arab min Wara'a al-Lahab: Mudhakarat al-Mujahid 'Abdul Ghani al-Ustwani* (Damascus: Dar Qutayba 1986).
Ustwani, Mohammad Sa'id al-. *Mashahed wa Ahdath Dimashqiyya fi Muntasaf al-Qarn al-Tase' 'Ashar* (Damascus 1994).
'Uthman, Hashem. *Tareekh al-'Alawiyeen: Waka'i wa Ahdath* (Beirut: Al-'Alami Press 1987).
'Uthman, Hashem. *Al-Ahzab al-Siyasiyya fi Souriyya: Al-Siriyya wa al-'Alaniyya* (Beirut: Riad El Rayyes 2001).
'Uthman, Hashem. *Al-Muhakamat al-Siyasiyya fi Souriyya* (Beirut: Riad El Rayyes 2004).
Yunis, 'Abdul Latif. *Shukri al-Quwatli: Tareekh Umma fi Hayat Rajul* (Cairo: Dar al-Ma'arif 1959).
Yunis, 'Abdul Latif. *Mudhakarat al-Doctor 'Abdul Latif Yunis* (Damascus 1992).
Zahr al-Din, 'Abdul Karim. *Mudhakarati an Fatrat al-Infisal fi Souriyya* (Beirut: Dar al-Itihad 1968).

Zeidan, Ne'mah. *'Alamuna al-'Arabi: Souriyya wa Lubnan* (Beirut 1956).
Zeine, Zeine. *Al-Sira'a al-Duwali ala al-Sharq al-Awsat wa Wiladat Dawlatayy Souriyya wa Lubnan* (Beirut: Annahar 1977).
Zirikli, Zhayr al-Din al-. *Al-A'lam*, 9-volumes (Cairo 1954–1957).

Books in English and French

'Allawi, 'Ali. *Faisal I of Iraq* (Yale University Press 2014).
Barr, James. *A Line in the Sand: Britain, France, and the Struggle for Mastery of the Middle East* (UK: Simon & Schuster 2011).
Batatu, Hanna. *Syria's Peasantry: The Descendants of Its Lesser Rural Notables and Their Politics* (New Jersey: Princeton University Press 1999).
Blondel, Edouard. *Deux ans en Syrie et en Palestine 1838–1839* (Paris 1840).
Buheiry, Marwan (ed.). *Intellectual Life in the Arab East 1890–1939* (American University of Beirut 1981).
Catroux, George. *Deux Missions Au Moyen Orient 1918–1922* (Paris 1958).
Chaitani, Yousef. *Post-Colonial Syria and Lebanon* (London: IB Tauris 2007).
Churchill, Charles Henry. *The Life of Abdel Kader: Ex-Sultan of the Arabs of Algeria* (London: Chapman & Hall 1867).
Clayton, Anthony. *General Maxime Weygand 1867–1965* (Bloomington: Indiana University Press 2015).
Copeland, Miles. *The Game of Nations: The Amorality of Power Politics* (Simon & Schuster 1970).
Coury, Ralph. *The Making of an Egyptian Arab Nationalist: The Early Years of Azzam Pasha 1893–1936* (Reading: Ithaca Press 1998).
Dann, Uriel (ed.). *The Great Powers in the Middle East 1919–1939* (New York 1988).
De Novo, John. *American Interests and policies in the Middle East 1900–1939* (Minneapolis: University of Minnesota Press 1963).
De Wailly, Henri De. *Invasion Syria 1941: Churchill and De Gaulle's Forgotten War* (London: IB Tauris 2006).
Gaunson, A.B. *The Anglo-French Clash in Syria and Lebanon 1940–45* (London: Macmillan Press 1987).
Gelvin, James. *Divided Loyalties: Nationalism and Mass Politics in Syria at the Close of Empire* (California: University of California Press 1999).
Haikal, Mohamed H. *Cutting the Lion's Tail: Suez through Egyptian Eyes* (London: Deutsch 1986).
Hanssen, Jens-Peter. *The Effect of Ottoman Rule on Fin de Siècle Beirut* (Oxford: The University of Oxford 2001).
Harel, Yaron. *Zionism in Damascus: Ideology and Activity in the Jewish Community at the Beginning of the Twentieth Century* (London: IB Tauris 2015).
Himadeh, Said. *Economic Organization of Syria* (Beirut: The American University of Beirut 1936).
Hitti, Philip. *History of Syria, Including Lebanon and Palestine* (London: Macmillan Press 1951).
Hourani, Albert. *Arabic Thought in the Liberal Age 1798–1939* (Oxford University Press 1962).
Hourani, Albert. *Syria and Lebanon* (Massachusetts: Harvard University Press 1991).
Hudson, Leila. *Transforming Damascus: Space and Modernity in an Islamic City* (London: IB Tauris 2008).

Husri, Sati. *The Day of Maysaloun: A Page from the Modern History of the Arabs* (Washington DC: Middle East Institute 1966).
Karsh, Efraim and Karsh, Inari. *Empires of Sand: The Struggle for Mastery in the Middle East 1789-1923* (Massachusetts: Harvard University Press 2001).
Keenan, Brigide. *Damascus: Hidden Treasures of the Old City* (London: Thames & Hudson, 2000).
Kersaudy, François. *Churchill and De Gaulle* (New York: HarperCollins Publishers 1990).
Khoury, Philip S. *Syria and the French Mandate: The Politics of Arab Nationalism 1920-1945* (Princeton, NJ: Princeton University Press 1987).
Khoury, Philip S. *Urban Notables and Arab Nationalism: The Politics of Damascus 1860-1920* (Cambridge: Cambridge University Press 2009).
Khuri, Fouad (ed.). *Leadership and Developments in Arab Society* (American University of Beirut 1981).
Kirkibride, Alec. *A Crackle of Thorns: Experiences in the Middle East* (London: John Murray, 1956).
Kiser, John W. *Commander of the Faithful: The Life and Times of Emir Abd al-Kader* (Rhinebeck NY: Monkfish Book Publishing 2010).
Laurens, Henry. *La Question de Palestine*, 5-volumes (Paris: Fayard 2007).
Lawrence, T.E. *Seven Pillars of Wisdom: A Triumph* (London: Jonathan Cape 1935).
Longrigg, Stephan. *Syria and Lebanon under the French Mandate* (Oxford: Oxford University Press 1953).
Mardam Bey, Salma. *Syria's Quest for Independence 1939-1945* (Reading: Ithaca Press 1997).
Martin, Kevin W. *Syria's Democratic Years: Citizens, Experts, and Media in the 1950s* (Indiana University Press 2015).
Morris, Benny. *1948 and After* (Oxford: Clarendon Press 1990).
Moubayed, Sami. *The Politics of Damascus 1920-1946* (Damascus: Dar Tlass 1998).
Moubayed, Sami. *Damascus between Democracy and Dictatorship 1948-1958* (Maryland: University Press of America 2000).
Moubayed, Sami. *Steel & Silk: Men and Women Who Shaped Syria* (Seattle: Cune Press 2005).
Moubayed, Sami. *Syria and the USA: Washington's Relations with Damascus from Wilson to Eisenhower* (London: IB Tauris 2012).
Moubayed, Sami. *The Makers of Modern Syria: The Rise and Fall of Syrian Democracy 1918-1958* (London: IB Tauris 2018).
Neep, Daniel. *Occupying Syria under the French Mandate: Insurgency, Space, and State Formation* (Cambridge: Cambridge University Press 2014).
Nordbruch, Gotz. *Nazism in Syria and Lebanon: The Ambivalence of the German Option 1933-1945* (London: Routledge 2009).
Ouahes, Idir. *Syria and Lebanon under the French Mandate: Cultural Imperialism and the Workings of Empire* (London: IB Tauris 2018).
Polk, William R. and Chambers, Richard L. (ed.). *Beginnings of Modernization in the Middle East: The Nineteenth Century* (Chicago: University of Chicago Press 1968).
Provence, Michael. *The Great Syrian Revolt and the Rise of Arab Nationalism* (Texas: University of Texas Press 2005).
Provence, Michael. 'Liberal Colonialism and Marshall Law in French Mandate Syria', in *Liberal Thought in the Eastern Mediterranean: Late 19th Century until the 1960s*, edited by Christoph Schumann (Leiden: Brill 2008), 51-74.

Rabinovich, Itamar. *The View from Damascus: State, Political Community and Foreign Relations in Twentieth-Century Syria* (England: Valentine Mitchell, 2008).
Ramet, Sabrina P. *The Soviet-Syrian Relationship since 1955: A Troubled Alliance* (Boulder: Westview Press 1990).
Rathmell, Andrew. *Secret War in the Middle East: The Covert Struggle for Syria 1949–1961* (London: IB Tauris 2013).
Russell, Malcolm B. *The First Modern Arab State: Syria under Faisal I* (Minneapolis: Bibliotheca Islamica, 1985).
Saunders, Bonnie F. *The United States and Arab Nationalism: The Syria Case 1953–1960* (Praeger Press 1996).
Schilcher, Linda. *Families in Politics: Damascene Families and Estates in the 18th and 19th Centuries* (Stuttgart: Franz Steiner 1985).
Seale, Patrick. *The Struggle for Syria: A Study in Post-War Arab Politics 1945–1958* (London: IB Tauris 1987).
Seale, Patrick. *Asad: Struggle for the Middle East* (Berkley: University of California Press 1989).
Seale, Patrick. *The Struggle for Arab Independence: Riad el-Solh and the Makers of the Modern Middle East* (Cambridge: Cambridge University Press 2010).
Shambrook, Peter. *French Imperialism in Syria 1927–1936* (Reading: Ithaca Press 1998).
Shikara, A. 'Faisal's Ambitions of Leadership in the Fertile Crescent: Aspirations and Constraints', in Abbas Kelidar (ed.). *The Integration of Modern Iraq* (London: Croom Helm 1979), 32–46.
Sluglett, Peter and Weber, Stefan (ed.). *Syria and Bilad al-Sham under Ottoman Rule: Essays in Honour of Abdul-Karim Rafeq* (Leiden: Brill 2010).
Spears, Edward. *Fulfillment of a Mission: The Spears Mission to Syria and Lebanon 1941–1944* (Connecticut: Archon Books 1977).
Storrs, Ronald Sir. *The Memoirs of Sir Ronald Storrs* (New York 1937).
Tarazi Fawaz, Leila. *An Occasion for War: Civil Conflict in Lebanon and Damascus in 1860* (University of California Press, 1994).
Thompson, Elizabeth. *Colonial Citizens: Republican Rights, Paternal Privilege and Gender in French Syria and Lebanon* (New York: Columbia University Press, 2000).
Thompson, Elizabeth. *Justice Interrupted: The Struggle for Constitutional Government in the Middle East* (Massachusetts: Harvard University Press 2013).
Thompson, Elizabeth. *How the West Stole Democracy from the Arabs: The Syrian Arab Congress of 1920 and the Destruction of Its Historic liberal-Islamic Alliance* (New York: Atlantic Monthly Press 2020).
Tibawi, Abdul Latif. *A Modern History of Syria, Including Lebanon and Palestine* (Palgrave Macmillan 1970).
Torrey, Gordon. *Syrian Politics and the Military 1945–1958* (Ohio: Ohio State University Press, 1964).
Weygand, Maxime. *Les Mémoires du général Weygand*, volume II (Paris: Flammarion 1957).
White, Benjamin Thomas. *The Emergence of Minorities in the Middle East: The Politics of Community in French Mandate Syria* (Scotland: Edinburgh University Press 2012).
Winter, Stefan. *A History of the 'Alawis: From Medieval Aleppo to the Turkish Republic* (New Jersey: Princeton University Press 2016).

INDEX

'Abbas Hilmi I 66
'Abbas Hilmi II, khedive of Egypt 26, 80
al-'Abbas, Jaber 55, 59
al-'Abbas, Munir 166
'Abdo, Mohammad 79, 215
'Abdul Wahab, Mohammad 161
'Abdul-'Aziz al-Saud, king of Saudi Arabia 87, 189, 190, 195, 215
'Abdulmejid II, Caliph 25, 90
'Abdul Nasser, Gamal 6, 26, 74, 91, 93, 107–111, 133, 144, 146–149, 200, 202–206
'Abdulhamid II, Sultan 2, 4, 20, 26, 30, 48, 50, 65, 67, 73, 77, 80–82, 84, 87, 94, 172
'Abdullah I, king of Jordan 30, 31, 32, 48, 177, 188, 196
al-'Abed, Ahmad 'Izzat Pasha 4, 76–83, 91, 134
al-'Abed, Burhan 80
al-'Abed, Hawlu Pasha 77–78
al-'Abed, Layla 54, 62, 83
al-'Abed, Mamduh 20
al-'Abed, Mohammad 'Ali 6, 54, 59, 61, 73, 75–78, 81, 82, 83–86, 90, 98, 100, 113, 116, 122, 162–164, early life 79–80, marriage 80, ambassador to the US 80–81, relation with Subhi Barakat 83, land sale in Palestine 86–87, and the Sixty-Day Strike 88–89, death of 90, mansion of 91–92
al-'Abed, Mustapha Pasha 4, 6, 76, 209
al-'Abed, Omar Agha 77
'Abed Palace 6, 76, 209
'Abidin, Abu al-Kheir 30
Abou Shahla, Habib 126
Abu al-Chamat, Mahmud 119
Abu al-Fateh, Mahmud 109
Abu al-Nour, 'Abdul Muhsen 202
Abu Saud, Fahmi 120
Aflaq, Michel 106, 141
Ahmad Mukhtar Pasha 134

'Aisha, Princess 65
al-'Ajlani, Munir 1, 96, 103, 165–166, 201
'Akel, Boulos 163
Albright, Madelene 7
'Ali, king of the Hejaz 30
Allenby, Edmund 21, 22, 40
Alype, Pierre 69–72
American University of Beirut (AUB) 4, 19, 21, 53, 57, 67, 72, 97, 113, 116, 122, 124, 143, 187
Amin, Qassem 160
'Ammoun, Iskandar 33
'Anbar, Yusuf 179
Antaki, Na'im 99, 174, 188
Antaki, Theodore 94
Anzour, Ismail 195
Arab Language Assembly 33, 85, 160
al-Armanazi, Najib 76, 86, 88, 130, 186–187
Army of Deliverance 195–196, 224
Arna'out, Ma'rouf 18, 20
Arslan, Emir 'Adel 33, 42, 82, 124
Arslan, Emir Shakib 153
al-'Asali, Faisal 142
al-'Asali, Khaled 186
al-'Asali, Sabri 105, 108, 203
al-'Asali, Shukri 153
al-Asfar, Beshara 4, 19
al-'Ashi, Abu 'Abdu 182
al-'Ashi, Suhayl 1, 186, 187, 196
al-'Askari, Ja'far 17
Asmahan 167
al-Assad, Asma 7
al-Assad, Hafez 6, 7, 209, 210
'Assasa, Ahmad 123–129
'Atallah, Yusuf 118–119
al-Atasi, 'Adnan 105, 110, 111, 135, 201
al-Atasi, Faydi 105, 108, 128, 165, 174
al-Atasi, Hashem 38–39, 48, 59, 71, 73, 84–87, 93, 101, 102, 107, 108, 109, 111, 115, 117, 118, 120, 122, 128, 135, 137,

141, 143, 144, 145, 155, 157, 162–165, 168, 173–175, 181–182, 185–186, 199–201, 222, early life 94–95, and Syrian National Congress 35–36, Elections (1932) 61, Sixty-Day Strike 89–90, and National Bloc 96–98, Paris talks 99–100, and Charles de Gaulle 105, relationship with Gamal Abdul Nasser 108–111
al-Atasi, Khaled 94
al-Atasi, Nur al-Din 6
al-Atasi, Taher 55
Atatürk, Mustafa 25, 48, 160
'Atfeh, 'Abdullah 196
al-Atrash, 'Abdul Ghaffar Pasha 117, 166
al-Atrash, Emir Hasan 117–118, 166
al-Atrash, Mansour 107
al-Atrash, Sultan Pasha 19, 33, 47, 69, 95–96, 107, 117, 156, 166, 193
al-Atrash, Tawfiq 117
al-'Attar, 'Abdulhamid 58
al-'Attar, Mahmud 152
Auriol, Vincent 61
al-'Awwa, Safwat 30
al-Ayesh, Mohammad 141, 165
al-Ayyubi, 'Ata 21, 26, 54–55, 71, 99, 135, 163, 168, early life 172, government of 36, as president 174–175
al-Ayyubi, Badih 186
al-Ayyubi, Mohammad 'Ali 172
al-Ayyubi, Raouf 71
al-Ayyubi, Saniyya 174
al-Ayyubi, Shukri Pasha 18, 23, 24, 179
al-'Azma, 'Adel 120–121
al-'Azma, Nabih 104
al-'Azma, Yusuf 32, 36, 37, 39, 95, 116, 214
al-'Azma, Zaki 21
al-'Azm, 'Abdul Qader 72
al-'Azm, 'Aliyya 135
al-'Azm, As'ad Pasha 2, 27, 91, 207
'Azm family 2, 73, 86, 97, 149, 150
al-'Azm, Haqqi 6, 49, 50, 53, 56, 57, 58, 61, 72, 84, 85–88, 113, 162, 185
al-'Azm, Khaled 73, 106, 127, 133, 134, 139, 140, 144–149, 192, 200, early life 135–136, and Shukri al-Quwatli 137–138, 140–141, and Husni al-Za'im 142–143, death of 1950

al-'Azm, Mohammad Fawzi Pasha 14, 72, 82, 133, 134
'Azm Palace 2, 47, 160
al-'Azm, Badi Mou'ayyad 21, 28, 58
al-'Azm, Nazih Mou'ayyad 103, 123, 127
al-'Azm, Safouh Mou'ayyad 116, 125
al-'Azm, Shafiq Mou'ayyad 3, 4, 71
al-'Azm, Wathiq Mou'ayyad 66, 70–72, 161, 219
'Azzam Pasha, 'Abdul Rahman 181, 195

Ba'ath Party 6, 11, 27, 43, 53, 91, 106–109, 141, 148, 150, 183
Bab al-Faradis 13
Bab al-Jabieh 16, 47
Bab Sharqi 16, 22, 114
Bab Touma 14, 16, 25, 77
Babil, Nasuh 12, 73, 103, 118, 167, 168, 190
Baghdad Pact 108
Bakdash, Khaled 99, 110, 145
Bakhash, Nasri 54
al-Bakri, Fawzi 31, 179
al-Bakri, Nasib 31, 73, 85, 89, 96, 97, 102, 117, 136, 179
Balfour Declaration 60
Balfour, Lord James 60
Bandung Conference 144
Barada River 2, 3, 7, 13, 14, 16, 19, 79
Barakat, Khaled 66
Barakat, Rifaat 48
Barakat, Subhi 6, 155, 162, 163, 172, 174, 185, death of King Faisal 43, early life, 47–48, as president of the Syrian Union 53–55, 58, elections (1923) 55–57, resignation of 47, 59, achievements 60, as speaker of parliament 61–62, death of 63
Barakat, Suhayla 66
Barakat, Zahra 66
al-Baramkeh 15
al-Barazi, Husni 67, 69, 70, 71, 129, 130, 166–168, 187
al-Barazi, Muhsen 136, 141, 174, 187
al-Barazi, Rashed 55
al-Barudi, Fakhri 55, 62, 85, 87, 88, 89, 96, 97, 116, 120, 121, 142, 158
al-Barudi, Mahmud 2
Battle of Maysaloun 37, 39, 87, 95, 98, 116, 135, 172

Bayhum, Ahmad Mukhtar 20
Beck, Walter 120
Bell, Gertrude 35
Ben Ghabrit, ʿAbdul Qader 155
Bernadotte, Folk 197–198
Beynet, Etienne 188
Billotte, Gaston 52
Bismarck, Otto Von 157–158
al-Bitar, Husni 118
al-Bitar, Salah al-Din 146, 203–204
al-Bizreh, Jamil 183
al-Bizri, ʿAfif 110, 202, 203
Blum, Leon 90, 99, 100, 101
al-Boukhari, Nasuhi 71, 104, 135
Boumédiène, Houari 26
al-Bunni, ʿAbdul Basit 53
al-Bzurieh Market 2, 37, 47, 58, 185

Caliphate Society 25–26
Catroux, George 139–140, 174, 184, 185, 188
Chahine, Nicolas 71
Chatti, ʿAbdul Latif 118
Chirac, Jacques 7
Churchill, Winston 138–140, 164–165, 167, 184, 189–191
Clemenceau, George 56
Clinton, Bill 7
Collet, Philibert 155
Coolidge, Calvin 57
Cooper, Duff 191
Coty, Rene 144
Curzon, Lord 41

Dagher, Asʿad 37
al-Daghestani, Taleb 186, 196
Daladier, Edouard 99
al-Dannoun, Yaacoub 33, 35
al-Daʿouk, Bahij 67
al-Daʿouk, Omar 20
al-Dalati, Bahira 97, 180
al-Dalati, Saʾid 97
Damascus University 72, 73, 89, 96, 110, 119, 120, 134, 135, 187
Darwaza, ʿIzzat 35, 120
al-Dawalibi, Maʿarouf 106–107
De Aranda, Fernando 79
De Caix, Robert 48, 52, 55, 59

De Gaulle, Charles 104, 105, 128, 137–140, 164, 174, 184, 188–191, 193
De Jouvenel, Henri 59, 66–69, 72
De Martel, Henri 62, 87, 88, 89, 162, 163, 173
Delbos, Yvon 90
Dentz, Henri 73, 127, 128, 136–139, 164
Diab, ʿAbdul Hadi 187
Diyafa Palace 6, 204, 205, 209
Djemal Pasha 4–6, 17, 31, 71, 133–134, 153
Djemal al-Saghir 5, 12, 15, 16

El Djezairi, Emir ʿAbdelkader 16, 22–23, 25, 77, 120, 211, Damascus events (1860) 13–14
El Djezairi, Emir ʿAbdelkader Jr 16, 23, 25–26, 56
El Djezairi, Emir Fateh 11, 12, 16
El Djezairi, Husniyya 26
El Djezairi, Emir Jaʾfar 27
El Djezairi, Emir Kazem 76, 119, 123
El Djezairi, Emir Omar 17
El Djezairi, Emir Saiʿd 11, 12, 13, 17, 18, 19, 20, 29, 55–56, 67, 73, 76, 119, 154–155, 172, with Djemal al-Saghir 16, cabinet of (1918) 21–22, confrontation with Lawrence 23–24, Caliphate Society 25–26, assassination attempt 26, death of 27
El Djezairi family 11, 13, 16–17, 19, 23, 25–26
al-Droubi, ʿAlaa al-Din 39–40, 48, 83, 95, 171, 172
Eden, Anthony 138, 185, 191
Edward VII, king of England 35
Eid, Asma 161
Eisenhower, Dwight 108, 144, 201
Elysée Palace 1
Enlai, Zhou 144
Enver Pasha 133, 134, 150, 214

Fairuz 109, 207
Faisal, Gamal 93
Faisal I, king of Syria 5, 6, 20–25, 29, 82, 83, 93, 94, 95, 97, 106, 108, 113, 118, 119, 134, 152, 154, 155, 157, 159, 164, 165, 167, 171, 172, 180, 189, 214, 215, 219, 223, 232, early life 30–31,

liberation of Damascus (1918) 31, coronation (1920) 34–35, relations with clergy 29, 32, and Paris Peace Conference 32–33, and minorities 33, and women's rights 35, confrontation with France 36–40, exile 40–41, death of 42–43
Faisal II, king of Iraq 42, 119
Faisal, Yusuf 141
Faqfaq, Hussein 32
al-Faqir, Tahseen Pasha 39
Farhat, Jermanos 162
Farouk, King of Egypt 1, 187, 189, 190, 196
Flandin, Etienne 90
Foch, Ferdinand 55–56, 158
Fouad, king of Egypt 32, 40

Galata Seray (Istanbul) 2, 134
Gemayel, Joseph 123
George II, king of Greece 128
George V, king of England 30, 41
George, Lloyd 32, 40, 41
Ghandour, Khalil 125–126
Ghazi I, king of Iraq 34, 41, 214
al-Ghazzi, Fawzi 56, 57, 67, 69, 98, 114, 115, 116, 157
Ghraoui, Sa'id 183
al-Ghusayn, Fayez 31
Gouraud, Henri 5, 6
Great Arab Revolt 15, 18, 19, 21, 30, 31, 34, 37, 39, 40, 82, 153, 172, 180, 196, 219, 224
Great Syrian Revolt 47, 59, 60, 65, 67, 95, 114, 117, 120, 121, 129, 155, 156, 165, 166, 173, 181, 232
Gustav V, king of Sweden 187

Haddad, Gregarious IV 35
al-Hafez, Amin 6, 203
al-Hafez, Thuraya 149
al-Hafi, Sa'id 19
al-Haffar, Lutfi 60, 70, 71, 89, 96, 97, 102, 138, in Damad government (1926) 67–69, cabinet of (1939) 104, Shahbandar murder 123–126
al-Haffar, Salma 97
al-Hakim, Hasan 35, 128–129, 165–166, 232
al-Hakim, Yusuf 17, 33, 67, 71, 84
Halefoglu, Vahit Melih 62

Hamdi Pasha 134
Hamidian Hospital (Damascus) 5, 134
Hamidieh Market 2, 16, 39, 47, 89
Hammarskjold, Dag 144
al-Hamzawi, 'Aref 130
al-Hanbali, Shaker 21, 71, 72
Hananu, Ibrahim 48, 61, 86, 88, 97, 162, 163, 221
Harb, Talaat Pasha 183
Haroun, 'Abdul Wahab 55, 59
Haroun, Asa'ad 135
al-Hasani, Badr al-Din 152–156, 160
al-Hasani, Taj al-Din 6, 30, 34, 65, 72, 84, 88, 97, 113, 114–117, 127, 128, 129, 139, 151, 155, 156, 159, 162–164, 173, 174, 185, 201, 219, early life 152–155, and veil 160–161, as president 165–167, death of 168–169
al-Hashemi, Taha 196
al-Hashemi, Yassin Pasha 32
Hatum, Salim 11, 210
al-Hawrani, Akram 53, 106, 110, 120, 121, 147, 194, 196
Hawwash, Ismail 55
Haydar, Rustom 33
Hejaz Station 23, 78, 100, 134, 197, 161, 192, 208
Heraclius, Roman Emperor 178
al-Hinnawi, Sami 105, 106, 142, 143, 199, 224
Hitler, Adolph 101, 120, 121, 136, 138, 140, 184, 189, 190, 192, 201
Homad, 'Abdul Wahab 98
Homsi, Edmond 89, 173
Hugo, Victor 80
Huntiznger, Charles 163
Hussein, Saddam 1
al-Husseini, 'Abdul Qader 196
al-Husseini, Ibrahim 177
al-Husseini, Sa'id 32
al-Husri, Sati 38, 41
Huzaima Bint Nasser 30, 214

Ibish, Hussein 87
'Ibn Abi Talib, 'Ali 178
Ibn al-Khattab, 'Omar 196
Ibn Khaldun 34
Ibrahim Pasha, viceroy of Egypt 66
Ibrahim Pasha, Ghaleb, 55

al-Idlibi, 'Aref Pasha 42
al-Idilbi, Hamdi 4, 6
al-Idilbi, Ulfat 4
al-Inklizi, 'Issam 187
Ismail, khedive of Egypt 78, 178
Ismail, Hafez 202
'Issa, 'Issa 33
al-Istanbuli, Efakat 134
'Izzat Pasha, Hasan 54

al-Jabiri, Ihsan 39, 42
al-Jabiri, Sa'adallah 67, 69, 88, 94, 104, 126, 130, 140, 185, 188, 192, 195, Paris talks 99–100, rivalry with Shahbandar 103, Shahbandar murder 123–125, cabinet of 186–187
Jabri, Shafiq 102
Jadid, Salah 27
al-Jallad, Hamdi 114
al-Jallad, 'Urfan 121
Jambart, Saleem 88
Jessup, Henry 13
al-Joukhadar, Suleiman 87
Junaid, Ismail 55
al-Jundi, 'Abdul Qader 196

Kahaleh, Habib 97, 158
Kahaleh, Nur al-Din 93
Kahaleh, Sa'adi 20
Kai-shek, Chiang 187
Karami, 'Abdul Hamid 97
al-Kasm, 'Atallah 25, 30, 35
Kaylani, Abdul 'Qader 94
Kayyali, 'Abdul Rahman 85, 100, 126
Khaddam, 'Abdul Halim 150
Khaled Ibn al-Walid 48, 134
Khalifat Movement 25
al-Khani, 'Abdullah 1, 3, 110, 169, 190, 200
al-Khani, Zuheir 207
Khanjar, Adham 49
al-Khatib, 'Abdul Qader 34
al-Khatib, Bahij 67, 90, 115–117, 122, 128–131, 136–137, 156, 158, 161, 166, 185, early life 113–114, cabinet of 118–122, Shahbandar murder 123–127
al-Khatib, Fouad 67, 119
al-Khatib, Mohammad Hasan 125
al-Khatib, Muhib al-Din 30

al-Khatib, Zaki 103, 162, 166
Khattabi, 'Abdul Karim 69
al-Khayyat, Abu Suleiman 34
Kheir, Adib 120, 130
al-Khiyami, Madani 149
al-Khoury, Beshara 188, 196
al-Khoury, Fares 6, 19, 33, 48, 52, 53, 55, 67, 69–71, 89–91, 96–97, 128, 140, interim government (1918) 21, Treat talks (1936) 99–100, cabinet (1955) 108–109, at the United Nations, 191–195
al-Khoury, Fayez 128, 165
al-Khoury, Suhayl 97, 205
Khrushchev, Nikita 201
Kikhiya, Rushdi 103, 105, 106, 185, 194
King-Crane Commission 24
Kissinger, Henry 6
Kiwan, 'Abdul Qader 39
Koraltan, Oguz 62
Koraltan, Refik 62
Kosygin, Alexei 145
Kurd 'Ali, Mohammad 85, 153, 159–160
Al-Kurdi, 'Abbud 182
al-Kurdi, Amin 76, 187
al-Kuttani, Mekki 126–127
al-Kuzbari, Haydar 206
al-Kuzbari, Ma'moun 148, 206

Lahhoud, Emille 126
Lawrence, T.E. (Lawrence of Arabia) 12, 19, 21–25, 31, 41, 210
Lincoln, Abraham 14

al-Madani, Masra 152
Madwar, Taha 70
Mahasin, Sa'id 115, 157
al-Malki, 'Adnan 109–110
al-Malki, Riad 109
al-Mallah, Mirii Pasha 34
Marjeh Square (Damascus) 5, 6, 13
Mardam Bey, Jamil 61, 85, 86, 89, 97, 104–105, 120, 129, 135, 138, 140, 161, 166, 173, 182–185, 187–188, 192, 195–196, 204, 223, Paris talks 99–100, assassination attempt 103, Shahbandar murder 123–126
Mardam Bey, Rashed Pasha 161
Mardam Bey, Safwat 161

Mardam Bey, Salma 97
Mardam Bey, Sami Pasha 38, 53
Mardam Bey, Seniyeh 134
Mardam Bey, Tamima 97
al-Masri, Khorshid 3, 4
McCloy, John 144
McMahon, Henry 30
Mehmed VI, Ottoman sultan 67
Menderes, 'Adnan 108
Midhat Pasha 2, 17, 78
Midhat Pasha Market 16, 47
Millerand, Alexander 48
Mohammad 'Ali Pasha 66
Molotov, Vyacheslav 144, 188
Moose, James 201
Muawiya 17
al-Mudarres, Nuri 118
al-Mudarres, Rashid 55
al-Muhajireen 1–7, 34, 75, 76, 168, 177, 186, 209
al-Mukhtar, 'Omar 39
al-Muradi, Bahiyya 78
Museum of Historical Documents (Damascus) 11
Muslim Brotherhood 7, 108, 149

Naccache, Alfred 168
Nafuri, Amin 202
Nahhas Pasha, Mustapha 87
Na'ili, 'Assem 127
Nami, Ahmad (Damad) 6, 25, 59, 75, 84, 114, 119, 129, 136, 163, 174, 185, 219, early life 65–66, first government (1926), 67–72, comeback during the Second World War 73, 136, death of 74
Nami, Emir Mahmud 66–67
Nami, Emir 'Omar 66
Nami, Emir 'Osman 66
Nammour, Yusuf 33
Napoleon III 13–14
Nasri, Ishak 55
National Bloc 26, 61–62, 67, 73, 84–88, 98–104, 113–118, 120–121, 130, 135–137, 140–141, 155–158, 161–168, 173–174, 181, 185, 194, 222, 223, founding of 95–97, Sixty-Day Strike 89, Shahbandar murder 123–125
National Party 105, 194
Nazem Pasha 2–6, 186

Nazli, queen of Egypt 32
Neguib, Mohammad 107
Al-Nehlawi, 'Abdul Karim 73, 147–149
Niéger, Emile 52
Nixon, Richard 6
Novikov, Nikolai 188
Nseiri, Maurice 7
Nubar Pasha 66

Olden, Arthur 21–22
al-'Omari, Subhi 39, 41
Orfali, Hussein 55
O'Toole, Peter 210

Pahlavi, Reza Shah 160, 165
Pahlavi, Mohammad Reza 165, 187
Paris Peace Conference (1919) 32–33, 56, 57
People's Party (Aleppo) 105–108, 148, 183, 194
People's Party (Damascus) 60, 103
Petain, Eugenie 83
Petain, Philip 83, 136–137
Pichon, Stephen 12
Podgorny, Nikolai 207
Poincare, Raymond 67
Ponsot, Henri 25, 72, 84, 85, 87, 98, 113, 158, 161, 162
Pope Pius IX 14
Putin, Vladimir 7

Qabbani, Tawfiq 183
Qadri, Ahmad 17, 23, 24, 31, 39, 41, 179
Qadri, Tahseen 31, 41
al-Qanawat 2, 115, 119, 155, 182
Qasr al-Diyafa (Damascus) 6
Qasr al-Shaab (Damascus) 7
Qasr al-Sonobar (Beirut) 52, 68
al-Qassab, Kamel 37–39, 215
al-Qassam, 'Izz al-Din 215
Qater Aghasi, Safwat 136
al-Qawuqji, Fawzi 195–196
al-Qaymariya 77, 162
al-Qodmani, Fouad 73
al-Qudsi, Ata 178
al-Qudsi, Kamel Pasha 50
al-Qudsi, Najiya 178
al-Qudsi, Nazem 6, 103, 105, 106, 109, 148, 185, 189, 194, 200, 206

al-Quwatli, 'Adel 183
al-Quwatli, Hasan Pasha 178
al-Quwatli, Mohammad Sa'id 178
al-Quwatli, Shukri, 1, 6, 42, 74, 87, 89, 96, 97, 99, 100, 105, 109–111, 115, 120, 123, 125, 126, 129, 130, 131, 137, 138, 140, 142, 145, 162, 168, 169, 174, 183–186, 192–196, early life 178–181, and Damascus 180–181, and world leaders 187–188, and Winston Churchill 189–191, and re-election (1947) 194, and Palestine War 196–197, and coup (1949) 142, 177, 198–199, and third term 200–201, and United Arab Republic 202–206, death of 207–208

Rabbat, Edmond 99
Rabin, Yitzhak 198
al-Rabweh 12
Raslan, Mazhar 86, 120
al-Rayyes, Najib 104, 115, 121
al-Rayyes, Munir 121
Rida, Rashid 30, 34, 38, 154, 180
Rifaat, Khalil 71, 118, 123–124
al-Rifaii, Layla 149
al-Rikabi, Rida Pasha 17–18, 23–25, 32, 42, 56–57, 84, 97
Roosevelt, Franklin D 187, 189
Roosevelt, Theodore 80–81
Root, Elihu 80

al-Sa'adawi, Khalil 76, 187
Sabe, Vladimir 123
al-Sadat, Anwar 111
al-Sadr, Sayyid Mohammad 33
Safwat, Ismail 196
Sa'id, Amin 123, 130, 131
al-Sa'id, Nuri 39
Saladin 123, 172
Salam, Saeb 97
Salameh, Hasan 196
Salem, Iskandar 55
Salengro, Roger 101
al-Salhieh 4, 16, 182
Sandys, Duncan 167
San Remo Conference 5
Sarrail, Maurice 25, 67, 155
al-Sarraj, 'Abdul Hamid 93, 109–111, 146, 206

Saud, king of Saudi Arabia 204
Sawwaf al-Douaji, 'Aref 155–156
Seale, Patrick 104
Sehnawi, Jean 136, 141
Selassie, Haile 190
Selu, Fawzi 106, 107, 143, 199
Shabat, Fouad 119
al-Shaghour 16, 47, 114, 182, 205, 214
Shahbandar, 'Abdul Rahman 57, 58, 60, 69, 95, 96, 99, 103, 128–130, 137, 156, 163, 166, 173, 181, 232, assassination and trial 122–127
al-Shallah, Salim 183
Shamdin Agha, 'Omar 130
Shamiyya, Tawfiq 38, 115, 156
al-Shara, Farouk 150
Sharabati, Ahmad 147
Sharabati, 'Uthman 123
Sharif Hussein, king of the Hejaz 17–21, 32, 37, 40–41, 94, 153, 172, 210, 215, background 30, 211, correspondences with the British 31
Sharif, Omar 210
Shatila, Khaled 199
Shawqi, Ahmad 79
al-Shayeb, Fouad 187
Shehadeh, Father Mikhail 38
al-Sheikh, 'Abdulhamid 20
al-Shihabi, Emir Mustapha 89, 173
al-Shishakli, Adib 6, 106–110, 142–144, 148, 199, 209, 224
Shuqayr, Sa'id 33
Shuqayr, Shawkat 107
Social Cooperative Party 142
al-Solh, 'Adel 53, 61
al-Solh, 'Afif 85
al-Solh, 'Alia 97
al-Solh, Mona 97
al-Solh, Riad 34, 97, 196
al-Solh, Rida 95, 113
Souq Sarouja 4, 80, 82, 86, 91, 133, 134, 137, 140, 142, 150, 192
Spears, Edward 151, 168, 184–185, 188
Stalin, Joseph 187, 188, 189
Stirling, Colonel 22
Sukarno, Ahmed 203
Sukkar, Shukri 125
al-Sukkari, Rushdi 58
Sultan, 'Abdul Raouf 123

Sultan, 'Ali 94
Sykes, Mark 18
Syrian Communist Party 99, 110, 145
Syrian National Congress 34, 35, 48, 82, 134, 155, 181, 221
Syrian-Palestinian Congress 180
Syrian Social Nationalist Party (SSNP) 109

al-Taji, Shukri 20
al-Tamimi, Amin 20
Tange, Kenzo 7
al-Tantawi, 'Ali 152
al-Tarabulsi, 'Izzat 143
Tawfiq Pasha, Khedive of Egypt 3
Taymour Pasha, Ahmad 153
al-Tirjiman, Bahiyya 26
Tishreen Palace 209
Tito, Josip 144
Trudeau, Arthur 108

al-'Ujayli, 'Abdulsalam 196
al-Ulshi, Jamil 21, 29, 32, 33, 34, 39, 58, 162, 172, 174, (government of 1943) 167–168
Um Kalthoum 109
Umayyad Mosque (Aleppo) 162
Umayyad Mosque (Damascus) 2, 4, 17, 13, 19, 123, 126, 152, 153, 208, 209
'Usseh, Ahmad 70
al-Ustwani, Rafiq 187
al-'Uthmani, Ragheb 156

Victoria Hotel (Damascus) 5, 13, 20, 22–23, 79
Victoria, Queen 14
Vienot, Pierre 99–100

Voltaire 80
Von Schirach, Baldur 120

Wadsworth, George 189, 191
Weizmann, Chaim 86–87
Weygand, Maxime 55, 56, 58, 59, 61, 67, 121
White House 1
Wilhelm II, Kaiser 157
Wilson, Andrew 40
Wilson, Woodrow 25, 33, 57, 189
Winter, Stefan 51

al-Yafi, 'Abdullah 97
Yazegi, Saleem 91
al-Yusuf, 'Abdul Rahman Pasha 4, 15, 34, 80, 82, 171
al-Yusuf family 86–87, 91
al-Yusuf, Sa'id 86
al-Yusuf, Zahra 80, 91

Zaghloul, Sa'ad Pasha 181, 195
Zahir Shah, Ahmad 187
Zahr al-Din, 'Abdul Karim 149
al-Zahraa, Fatima 29, 178
Zahra, 'Abdul Qader 73
al-Za'im, Husni 37, 63, 74, 105, 108, 133, 142–145, 148, 174, 178, early life 229, coup of 198–199
Zayd, Emir 37, 215
Zayn al-Din, Farid 201
Zayn al-Din, Nazira 160–161
Zein al-'Abidin, 'Abdul Wahab 187
Zeiter, Akram 194
Zhukov, Gregory 201
al-Zirikli, Khayr al-Din 152

www.ingramcontent.com/pod-product-compliance
Lightning Source LLC
Chambersburg PA
CBHW071817300426
44116CB00009B/1348